Germany and the Middle East

GERMANY AND THE MIDDLE EAST
PATTERNS AND PROSPECTS

Edited by Shahram Chubin

Pinter Publishers
London

© Shahram Chubin and contributors, 1992
First published in Great Britain in 1992 by
Pinter Publishers Limited
25 Floral Street, London WC2E 9DS

British Library Cataloguing in Publication Data
A CIP catalogue record for this book is available from the British Library

ISBN 1 85567 040 2

Typeset by Florencetype, Kewstoke, Avon
Printed and bound in Great Britain by
Biddles Ltd, Guildford and King's Lynn

Contents

This book is dedicated to the memory of Jonathan Alford and Avi Plascov, colleagues and friends.

List of contributors

Shahram Chubin is a freelance consultant based in Geneva. Formerly an Assistant Director of the International Institute for Strategic Studies (London) and the Program on Strategic Studies at the Geneva Graduate Institute for International Studies, he has been a consultant to various agencies and governments including the United Nations and the US Defense department. He is a specialist on the international politics of the developing countries, with particular interest in the Middle East and has published widely on the subject. His last book (written with Charles Tripp) was *Iran and Iraq at War*.

Gregory Treverton is a Senior Fellow at the Council on Foreign Relations (NY). He is the author of the forthcoming *America, Germany and Europe*. He has been an Assistant Director of the International Institute for Strategic Studies, served on the White House NSC staff of the Carter Administration and taught at the Kennedy School of Government, Harvard University.

Efraim Karsh is a Lecturer at the Department of War Studies, Kings College, University of London. His most recent books are: *Soviet Policy toward Syria since 1970* (1990) and *Saddam Hussein: A Political Biography* (1990).

David Witzthum is currently Chief Foreign Editor, Israel Television. He is also a part-time newspaper columnist. His academic background, besides Israel's Hebrew University, includes stints at the College d'Europe in Bruges and Wolfson College, Oxford.

Udo Steinbach is director of the German Orient Institute in Hamburg and a well-known commentator and scholar on Middle Eastern Affairs. He is the author of several books and a frequent contributor to journals on the subjects of Islam, current developments in the Middle East and the policies of European states and especially Germany towards that region.

Harald Müller is Director of International Programs at the Frankfurt Peace Research Institute. Previously he was Director of Studies at the European Centre for Policy Studies in Brussels. He is an expert on the Non-Proliferation of Nuclear Weapons and has written extensively on that and related subjects.

Richard Burt is at present a Special Consultant for McKinsey & Company, Inc. From 1989–91 he was Head of the US Delegation on Nuclear and Space Talks in Geneva and was Chief Negotiator on Strategic Arms Reduction Talks (START). Before that he was US Ambassador to Germany (1985–9) and Assistant Secretary of State for European and Canadian Affairs at the State Department (1983–5).

Hanns W. Maull is Professor of International Relations at the University of Trier, Germany, a Director of Studies at the German Foreign Policy Institute in Bonn, and Co-Director of the German Society for Foreign Policy (DGAP) in Bonn. He has written extensively on the Middle East and on German Foreign

Policy. His last books were *The Gulf War* (1989) and *Energy, Minerals and Western Security* (1985).

Josef Joffe is foreign editor and columnist at the *Süddeutsche Zeitung* in Munich. He is author of *The Limited Partnership: Europe, the United States and the Burdens of Alliance* (1987), and has published widely on German foreign policy, international relations and international security. A member of the International Institute of Strategic Studies, he has taught at the University of Munich and Johns Hopkins. He has been a Fellow of the Woodrow Wilson Center and a Senior Associate of the Carnegie Endowment, both in Washington, D.C.

Thomas Risse-Kappen, a former research associate of the Peace Research Institute, Frankfurt, West Germany, is now Assistant Professor of Government, Cornell University, Ithaca, New York. He was a Visiting Fellow at the International Security Program of Yale University in 1990-91. He has written extensively on West German foreign and security policy as well as on arms control issues in general.

Helmut Hubel is a Senior Research Fellow at the Research Institute of the Deutsche Gesellschaft für Auswärtige Politik, Bonn, and a lecturer at Rheinische-Friedrich-Wilhelms University of Bonn. He has carried out research projects and written publications on the Soviet Union in the Third World, the Middle East and East-West conflict, European Security and the Middle East, and Crises in the Arab World.

Stephen F. Szabo is Associate Dean for Academic Affairs at the Paul H. Nitze School of Advanced International Studies, The Johns Hopkins University. He is the author of numerous publications on German politics and public opinion, including *The Changing Politics of German Security* (1990).

Preface

Amid the rapid and major transformations in contemporary international relations no country has been as affected, nor is placed in so critical a position to influence the course of future events, as Germany. In the future evolution of Europe, in both the EC and the parts formerly known as the Eastern bloc, as well as in relations with the replacement to the former Soviet Union, Germany occupies literally and figuratively a central role. In the future development of Europe – East and West – Germany, now united, will play the part of an economic superpower. In whatever fashion the former Soviet republics are reconstituted, Germany's policies toward those states has influenced if not led Europe. Germany's role will also often be decisive and pivotal as Europe's economic and security relations with the United States in NATO, the WEU and the EC evolve.

Perhaps of less immediacy is the broader question of Germany and Europe's future relationship with the developing world and especially with the Middle East. A widened Community is bound to be more active and influential globally and within it Germany will doubtless play an enhanced role. The Middle East, for geographic and economic reasons, is an area where Europe and Germany may reasonably be expected to take on greater diplomatic responsibilities and engage in greater exchanges.

This volume was conceived in April 1990 before the crisis and subsequent conflict in the Gulf, and also before the formal unification of Germany. It seemed of particular importance then to look at Germany's past policy or approach to questions in the Middle East in order to have a better appreciation of the direction of future policies and constraints. The editor would like to thank the contributors for their careful and swift responses to his requests and ask in turn for their indulgence – together with that of the reader – for any egregious errors which may have crept inadvertently into this volume and for which the editor alone is responsible.

The editor is pleased to acknowledge the financial assistance of the M-Group in the publication of this book. He would like also to express his thanks for the editorial assistance and diligence of Jane Evans and the production staff of Pinter Publishers in the preparation of the book and to Nicola Viinikka for her encouragement and suggestions about it.

1 Introduction

Shahram Chubin

Germany has been at the centre of international politics and European security for well over a century. With the dismantling of the Soviet Eastern bloc, the disintegration and dissolution of the Soviet Union and the end of the confrontation of the Cold War symbolised by the Berlin Wall, Germany has emerged again, newly reunified, as the state of central importance for the security of Eurasia. Reflecting its economic power and political weight, Germany has taken on major responsibility in EC relations with the East European states, while providing economic assistance to Moscow to ease the transition from a unitary to a confederal system.

After some forty-five years as a passive (some would say too passive) partner, Germany has slipped into the role of key player in the dramas unfolding in the former Soviet Union and Eastern Europe, with many demands made on its resources. Not the least of these demands is the onerous but not altogether unpleasant prospect of committing resources for a sustained period for the revival and transformation of the economy of the former East Germany (DDR). With these new demands and commitments, it may appear that Germany's capacity or will to be involved in other areas will be limited.

This would be a reasonable prediction. However it is worth noting that foreign and security policies are to a greater degree than in the past enmeshed with domestic issues. An obvious example is immigration into Germany and Europe which has domestic political and economic implications. Acceleration of immigration from the Near East or Eastern Europe has increased an existing immigrant community. Such waves of immigration occur as much as a result of crises such as wars and revolutions as from economic motivation. The link between stability in the Middle East or Eastern Europe – a foreign policy issue – and the domestic impact on Germany needs little further elaboration.

A second reason for greater and, specifically, wider involvement by Germany in foreign affairs is that the distinctions between intra- and extra-European matters are increasingly artificial. In a Europe which *de facto* is daily being 'widened' as well as 'deepened' and where there are many different aspirants for entry into a successful club, the distinguishing criteria for priority will surely become the salience of the issue for German–European interests, whether internal to geographic Europe or just beyond it.

Germany's new responsibilities in easing reunification, within the the EC, *vis-à-vis* East and Central Europe and the New Commonwealth of former Soviet republics, and as the strongest economic power in Europe, are bound to fall short of some expectations. In the years of upheaval, 1989–91, Germany was criticised for moving too slowly or evading her responsibilities. Where her critics saw this as an extension of the commerce-as-foreign-policy syndrome, others saw it differently. After all it could be argued, in relation to the crisis of the Gulf War, that Bonn was trying purposefully to build a consensus to obtain a

1

majority in favour of assuming new responsibilities. This could not be done overnight and time was needed to get the German people to shed their inhibitions about such engagements.

The Middle East is not the most important area of German interests; East–West and NATO concerns take priority. In each, Germany has a pivotal role to play. But because of Germany's size and weight, it is bound to be a newly important and growing element in the post-cold war world beyond Europe. If this world is characterised by more centres of decision-making and greater emphasis on the economic dimensions of security, Germany will, because of its own economic importance, be a central actor in this drama, independently or as a leading player within the European Community. Germany will thus for good or ill, or both, influence and shape the course of the EC's relations with the outside world.

Approached from a different perspective, Germany's future role in the Middle East is of especial interest to local states. In a more decentralised world of multiple security concerns, the involvement of a state with the weight of an economic superpower, and with a record of political disinterest, will be welcomed and sought. Staggering under the costs of reunification and the burdens of emancipating itself from the past, Germany may be unable to respond. Yet the Middle East will remain an area of primary concern to Europe, whether for reasons of proximity, demography, energy, or trade and markets.

The contributions in this volume consider (West) Germany's past 'policy' or interaction with the region stretching from the Arab–Israel zone to the Gulf. The emphasis is not historical although the region resonates with romantic echoes, world wars and the receptivity of those in several countries of the region (Persia and Turkey among others) to close relations with pre-war Berlin. Today, if Germany is more passive, it is not because it is any less welcome by the regional states but owing to a double constraint. The regional inhibition stems from the horror of the Nazi past and holocaust and Germany's need for maintaining a special relationship with Israel. The other more broad constraint is the reluctance to take a high profile on any political issue, especially one so politically and emotionally charged as the Arab–Israel dispute.

As editor, it has been my assumption that Germany's 'policy' and interaction with the region in the recent past can be a guide to future behaviour and that constraints on a more active or decisive policy are unlikely to change radically in the near future. Whether this proves to be the case or whether Germany, in fact, is able to move to a more activist and decisive policy, Germany's encounter with the Middle East remains of more than passing interest. Chapters have thus been chosen to deal with the primary issues affecting German–Middle East relations: the international context; the historical relationship; domestic foreign-policy structure; public opinion; legislation and foreign policy and specific dimensions of foreign policy including arms sales and relations with Israel.

It might have been useful to have had a detailed chapter on Germany and Islam – perhaps with some concentration on the role of the Muslim community and immigrants in German society. Another chapter might have concentrated on the role of Germany in the EC's various Middle Eastern policies. The volume is thus far from being comprehensive or definitive. I have sought the best authors for the chapters that I have chosen, and these in turn reflect my own interest in the more traditional dimensions of security.

The Gulf crisis of 1990–1 has been called a watershed in that it represents the first global crisis after the cold war era. Whether it represented the last gasp of the previous order or the looming shape of the coming order, is still uncertain. Similarly, whether it will act as a catalyst to shape a more active German role in this new order is still unclear. Certainly the crisis did stimulate a new debate within Germany. And certainly the debate was unwelcome both in its timing – when Germany was preoccupied with its reunification – and in its content and implications – namely that Germany may soon have to confront anew the question of a more active and possibly military role in some situations outside Europe.

Germany's contribution to the allied war effort against Iraq was not insignificant; it included a pledge of some $5.5 billion to the military effort, aid to the states economically damaged by the crisis, logistical assistance, the deployment of Patriot missiles to Israel and the deployment of a minesweeper squadron to the Gulf's waters.

It was not so much what was given and as how it was given. The impression left was that the crisis did not really concern Germany, who was responding only to keep its allies sweet. The allies understood Germany's desire to steer clear of a military entanglement and avoid the political and constitutional hassle that would go with it. They understood, too, for the most part, that German policy could only evolve slowly in this respect as a result of such crises and as a domestic debate was launched and consensus was fashioned. The debate between the government of Herr Kohl and the Social Democrats as to whether Germany could participate in future European or alliance operations, or, as the opposition argued, only in the peacekeeping operations of the blue-helmeted UN forces, was one such movement in a process of evolution. What grated on Germany's European allies was the tone of moral equivalence emanating from Germany, as if the use of force was under all circumstances immoral. This seemed conveniently to forget the risks the allies had run in undertaking to defend Germany during the cold war. It smacked of a single-minded introversion that seemed incapable of reciprocity, underlined by Germany's slow and grudging response to a request for assistance by Turkey. In the circumstances Turgut Ozal, Turkey's President's comment: 'I think Germany has become so rich that it has completely lost its fighting spirit' was an understatement.[1]

The issue was not primarily one of tone, however ludicrous German *angst* might have looked to unsympathetic observers; it was more serious. If Germany could not undertake to fulfil its commitments to Turkey on the flanks of the alliance, it must mean that Germany considered itself merely a consumer in the alliance, with no reciprocal responsibilities at all. Yet it was clear as one journal subsequently observed: 'The threat to Europe has shifted from the centre to the flanks and threats there will still be. Because of its weight and where it stands, Germany cannot be a Switzerland – an introverted hedgehog in a turbulent world, quietly getting fatter.'[2]

Yet the evidence demonstrates that is just what Germans wanted to be. In the early stages of the crisis an Allensbach poll showed that 53 per cent opposed constitutional change that would allow German troops to take part in UN operations.[3] If owing to history there was a desire to avoid a military role in the Middle East, it was unclear under what circumstances such a role might be acceptable. After all, the Gulf crisis was a relatively easy one where the moral choices were as clear as they can be. The problem is a more general one unrelated to the region itself; it stems from serious doubts about the nature of security and the appropriate role for Germany in the modern world.

Another poll in early 1990 (also by the Allensbach Institute) found that the most important questions for most Germans were the environment, followed by economic issues and reunification – military security came last with a mere 3 per cent concerned about it.[4] Married to this detachment from the world of international politics has been a deeper flight from responsibility: '. . . national anonymity has been very comforting to the Germans,' observed William Pfaff, 'and they are not anxious at all for it to end'.[5] The passion for anonymity, the desire to be left cultivating their own garden, the emphasis on Green issues and on business sounds reminiscent of Switzerland, the country with which many Germans increasingly identify as a model: 40 per cent of Germans see Switzerland as a paradigm of 'wealth and independence'. Sweden was the runner-up as role model.[6] The aspiration is not so strange. In many ways Germans had already come to resemble the Swiss. It should be noted that Switzerland, like Germany, has been very slow to restrict arms and technology supplies however dubious the intended recipient.[7]

Germany's approach to the Middle East has been conditioned by its primary concerns with East–West and NATO issues. Necessarily, policy has reflected what Steve Szabo calls 'this Central European preoccupation and the double dependency' (see Chapter 6). At the same time as Udo Steinbach has argued that the Middle East 'in the overall context of German international policy turns out to be subordinate to deliberations and concerns which have nothing to do with the Middle East', Risse-Kappen in his clear and detailed analysis sees the Middle East (that is Arab–Israel issues) as the second most salient foreign policy issue for Germany 'next to East–West and transatlantic relations' (see Chapter 10).

Joe Joffe does not disagree. In Chapter 11 he argues that there has been 'no Middle East policy', as such and 'no autonomous German policy in the Middle East'. He sees the nature of the interaction as a product of three sets of considerations – the cold war, oil and the special relationship with Israel necessitating a balancing act. He also sees 'no real incentive to tread the minefield' of regional politics by taking a defined position or a particular side. Certainly regional politics rarely provides outsiders with easy choices.

No regional issue is more sensitive than the question of Germany's relations with Israel. David Witzthum in his sensitive discussion of this issue in Chapter 5 denies that the trauma of the past is the basis of the relationship: the mutual trauma 'enhanced the unique nature of each of the two states but not the link between them'. Witzthum is therefore sceptical about a 'special relationship'. He attributes the uniqueness of each state to the context of relations: the uniqueness in each state 'came into existence as a result of a global crisis and the old order it entailed'. Witzthum thus sees the development of German–Israeli relations as owing as much to domestic political considerations in Israel (including political expediency) and historical and practical pressures in Germany as to any superior or transcendent moral motive. The development of these ties was in some senses accidental, with Germany's implementation of the Hallstein Doctrine against Egypt (for recognising the German Democratic Republic) resulting in increased economic cooperation with Israel.

Witzthum sees the Gulf War of 1991 and the upheavals in Europe as having subjected the Israeli–German relationship to greater change than anything else in the past forty years. While the author admits that the psychological bases of the relationship cannot be separated from the practical one – for example the common Israeli view that sees Germany as 'stronger and more menacing than other countries' (and the German mirror-image of Jews as stronger than they are) – he none the less sees their future relationship, despite the unusual and special features, as likely to be forged on a pragmatic basis.

The Gulf War caught the German–Israeli relationship in flux. For two states created by the old order, the passing of the old order was especially meaningful: 'the war ended their era of uniqueness'. Witzthum argues that domestic pressures and politics in each state will determine the nature of future relations, which in any case will be markedly different. He expects future German policies filtered through the EC mechanism to be 'cushioned' from the kind of contention that might characterise bilateral ties.

Alan Sked's blistering criticism of German foreign policy in the Gulf War points in undiplomatic language and often harshly to some of the problems with Germany's policy. Above all as Sked correctly argues: 'The fate of Europe hinges more than ever before on the decisions of the German government'.[8] It is for this reason that Sked and others became so exercised by Germany's policy in the Gulf, for they saw its reaction to this crisis as reflecting 'Germany's attitude toward the Middle East and Germany's attitude toward the world in general'.[9]

The broader issue, raised earlier, of German identity and self-image which conditions the approach to the rest of the world, will remain uncertain for some time. One scholar, who has studied the German search for self-understanding since the eighteenth century, argues that failing to find a sense of national identity in political institutions, 'the Germans in the middle of the nineteenth century discovered that the performance of their economy was the most satisfactory measure of national integrity and the most crucial to their self-esteem', and this has continued to be true.[10]

Extreme competitiveness in business and exports interpreted as a sublimation of a competitive nationalist drive does not appear far-fetched in the case of Germany or indeed of Japan. In sketching the similarities between the two states one observer has noted:

Both countries have had a single-minded preoccupation with international competitiveness [and in both] the distinction between economics and foreign policy is far more blurred than it is in America. Partly because they are smaller nations and more dependent on the world economy, and partly because of constraints on their ability and willingness to have independent military capabilities, [they] have learned to make economics an extension of politics by other means.

But that is not all. Garten suggests that in both countries one result of an emphasis on exports has been the strong role played by the state in the economy. Furthermore they not only have closed economies, but also 'financial-industrial conglomerates that are extremely difficult for outsiders to penetrate' with government playing a 'heavy role in the private sector by way of regulations and subsidies. Corporate practice, so often a good reflection of society priorities, favors management and institutional owners rather than individual shareholders'.[11]

The upshot is that Germany as the world's largest exporter has defined its 'foreign policy', at least outside Europe, as virtually synonymous with its economic interests in exports and markets. At the same time, as we shall see, this 'policy' is undirected and until recently unregulated by government which, in any case, sees its interests as the same as the large corporations with which it enjoys an all too cosy relationship. The result, frequently, has been a clash between German economic interests and the broader considerations of global security usually championed by the United States. One has only to think of the dispute between Washington and Bonn in 1976–7 over Germany's provision of nuclear material and technology to Brazil which the United States considered insufficiently safeguarded (to take but one non-Middle Eastern example). German responses, then as now, have been unsatisfactory with an emphasis on American economic jealousy or complaints about Washington's bullying followed by denials of evidence of the need for technology controls or leakage and ending with promises of more attention to the issue in future.

As Harald Müller observes in Chapter 9, 'an all too parochial perspective seduced the Germans into ignoring the massive consequences of their world-wide economic activities'. In so far as there were 'controls' they were pro-industry and pro-exports; the 'liberal corporatist system' saw relations between government and industry as being close and government having a 'benevolent philosophy' on exports. Put differently, as Thomas Risse-Kappen formulates it: 'In the absence of public scrutiny, the free-trade orientation of the Federal bureaucracies and the business community prevails over broader considerations of foreign and security policy'. As Gregory Treverton suggests (see Chapter 3), there was, and is, a 'disturbing element' in the proposition that even where poison-gas technology was concerned (in the case of the Rabta plant in Libya) 'business was business' and it seemed 'none of the government's business'. From the record one might conclude that the 'business of government' was in fact business.

In Chapter 8 Efraim Karsh writes that controls in the Foreign Trade Act of 1961 were conceived 'in reflection of the deeply rooted German commitment to the notion of free trade . . . so that there is as little limitation of economic activity as possible'. In the mid-1960s 'the government virtually surrendered the country's arms exports to the commercial sector, remaining only as a watchdog'. By 1971 the 'link between arms sales and foreign policy was more tenuous than in the preceding period . . . and this in a phase of growth'. As Karsh notes, while the government allegedly put a 'restrictive' policy on arms exports, this was being violated 'incessantly'.

More recent attempts to put greater controls in place have similarly foundered. Legislation passed in mid-1990 was intended to end the problems in this sphere. Instead, during the Gulf crisis, the evidence suggests a less than perfect result. On the one hand Germany rebuffed Saudi Arabia's attempts to buy tanks on the grounds that they would be destined for an 'area of tension'. Yet at the same time it was revealed that German industry had, between 1982 and 1989 delivered weapons and related technology worth $700 million to Iraq with government permission.[12]

Edward Reuter, the Head of Daimler Benz, was quoted as saying: 'Nowhere in Germany is there an economic theme about which there is so much hypocrisy, cowardice and opportunism as arms exports'. He might have added deceit and fraud as well.[13]

The incongruity of Germany's position was nicely if inadvertently captured by Oscar Lafontaine who, on the campaign trail in the autumn of 1990, during the Gulf crisis but before the commencement of hostilities, observed: 'First we send our poison gas and rockets to Iraq. Then we're supposed to send our young men there? That we will never do.'[14]

Even before the crisis American specialists had been referring to 'West Germany's leading role in the spread of nuclear weapons, chemical weapons and long-range missiles'. The Carnegie Endowment for International Peace in its survey of nuclear proliferation called Germany the 'weak link' in the world's nuclear export control system. And, despite the passage of allegedly restrictive export control legislation in June 1990, reports of the continuing flow of technology to suspect destinations continued. Indeed, Germany was believed to have been, after Jordan, the most prominent country in the non-observance of the United Nations' embargo on Iraq.[15]

Israeli Prime Minister Shamir criticised 'the industrial establishment' in Germany which he characterised as very powerful and as having influence on the government and the entire political sphere. Moreover, he suggested the industrialists are heavily export-orientated. 'Exporting is, so to speak, the sacred principle. When they are tempted, they cannot resist. In fulfilment of Saddam Hussein's wishes they saw an outstanding opportunity to earn a lot of money, to sell technology and also to further develop technologies.'[16] The number of companies and individuals involved was significant; more than one hundred companies in Germany were investigated on suspicion of violating the embargo, and numerous individuals decided to stay behind in Baghdad and offer their services in the repair and maintenance of Iraqi equipment.

Reports in the *Wall Street Journal*, the *International Herald Tribune*, the *Financial Times* and others, between the autumn of 1990 and the spring of 1991, provided strong evidence that German companies had been heavily responsible for the transfer of technology. This enabled Iraq to build an extensive chemical weapons programme, upgrade its Scud surface-to-surface missiles by increasing their range and build a sophisticated and elaborate bunker system for the protection of its leadership and its command and control. The customary arguments were that much of the technology was dual use, or got through before controls were in place, or that there was a 'grey market' for many of the materials, or that they were third-party transfers (meaning that Germany had exported them in good faith to one destination only to see them re-exported to another) – all of these were old and rather tired arguments which no longer held water. As Alexander Batschari, an official at the German Machinery Industry Association, was quoted as saying: these constant revelations were 'more than an image loss. It casts doubt on Germany and how things are done here'.[17]

Illustrative of the kind of mentality that appears to have been typical, was the involvement of a Thyssen subsidiary, Thyssen Rheinstahl Technik, in both the building of Salman Park, the Iraqi chemical weapons complex, and in the provision of turbo-pumps to a project that turned out to be related to the Iraqi missile enhancement programme (as reported in *Stern* in February 1991). Thyssen threatened to sue *Stern*. Thyssen did not deny the substance of the reports but denied wilfully or knowingly contributing to these programmes and insisted that all its actions had been within the law. Thyssen agreed that its subsidiary Thyssen Industrie had won a contract to supply 305 pumps for the petrochemical industry. Only thirty-five had been delivered by 25 June 1990 with official certificates of approval. This approval was then withdrawn on suspicion that the equipment was being used to help modify Scud missiles.[18]

The subject became even more contentious when UN inspection teams in

Iraq to enforce Security Council Resolution 587 found parts of Iraq's missile launchers came from specific European countries, Germany prominently among them.[19]

Thyssen does not appear to have been the only offender using the letter of the law to defend questionable business practices, but it was certainly one of the most egregious – reports of a so-called "Israel exclusion clause" doing nothing to improve this reputation. In the past the company had also been accused of doctoring and inflating fictitious invoices and making huge pay-offs in its questionable business practices in the third world.[20] These allegations of cloudy morality and dubious business ethics are not unique to Thyssen, although they seem to have been fostered by the size and clout of the enterprise and the perception of invulnerability which has grown from the chummy relationship between business and government.

The record in this instance speaks rather revealingly for itself. A team of *Financial Times* writers examined the issue of German arms and technology transfers. They reported that many investigations had been conducted by the German government into the export of dual-use equipment. Herbert Brenke, chairman of Thyssen Rheinstahl Technik, was the head of one of the companies which worked on the Ferrostaat project which involved 'the apparently conscious supply of technology for the production of gun barrels'. Brenke 'uses logic typical of many German managements: "You can redirect each and everything. Suppose I sell you a knife to peel potatoes and 10 years later you kill your husband with it?"'

Another case examined by the *Financial Times* was based in Bochum and 'involved the delivery by Thyssen of turbo-pumps said to be destined for the oil industry but which investigators suspect were being used for Scud motors'. Thyssen's defence? 'We couldn't have known that.' Yet Hans Dieter Corvins, director of the Export Control division of the Federal Office of Economics in Eschborn had a different explanation: 'A lot of firms did not tell the truth. We had turbo-pumps going to petrochemical plants and parts for the milk industry that we know were going to improve Scud missiles.' The report concluded a shade melodramatically 'that the shadow of its close relationship with Iraq's military industries is likely to hang over Bonn for a very long time'.[21]

This appears unlikely. As long as Bonn and the major industrial conglomerates remain on the kind of intimate terms that appear to make the latter invulnerable to serious regulation, it is unlikely that these industries will define German national interests very differently from that of their own companies. Despite all the *angst*, public embarrassment, excuse-making and rationalisation; and despite a third attempt to tighten regulations governing arms and technology transfers, 'what the government has not done then or now is to remove the (oversight) office from under the wing of the Economics Ministry. Critics claim this is a serious flaw. The ministry, packed with enthusiastic free-traders, is likely to shy away from the tough rules that might block the odd illegal delivery but generally hamper above-board exporters'.[22]

Much of the concern about Germany in the past has been its reluctance to participate in, or contribute towards, measures aimed at securing Europe or stabilising its frontiers if this meant involvement beyond Europe. There was a tendency to define Europe's interests narrowly and to focus on immediate and even parochial concerns, often at the expense of broader considerations. While conscious of Germany's constitutional constraints on deploying forces beyond

NATO territory and of the need for domestic consensus within the country, outsiders were cognisant of German efforts to use these as alibis to shift responsibility to others.

As long as the American security umbrella was in place, Germany went along, however unhappily. This security connection also insulated American–German differences on economic issues from undue estrangement. With a much reduced need for this connection (as Ambassador Rick Burt points out in Chapter 2), there will also be less of a cushion in relations – with the implication that future differences cannot be subsumed as easily into a broader relationship of give and take, win and lose. In future, *quid pro quos* may have to be more explicit and balanced, that is a two-way street.

If in the past there was the feeling that Germany used the problems of 'domestic consensus' as an excuse to shirk responsibility and avoid exercising leadership domestically, since 1991 anxieties have shifted – as they tend to – to the other extreme, German overactivism. Now the concern is not too little but rather, too much; not that Germany will avoid decisions but that she will ram unilaterally made decisions down the throats of her European and transatlantic partners. This anxiety is barely formed as there is so far only one case of such behaviour and that is over the recognition of Croatia, where Germany arguably had good strategic and domestic political reasons for her position. Still this case, where Germany took the lead over the objections of allies and opposed by the EC and the United Nations but propelled by domestic opinion, showed outsiders that public opinion hitherto used as an excuse for inactivity need not always tend toward passivity.

Both criticisms of Germany – the inactive, passive, parochial partner and the newer, more independent activist state – share common characteristics. Each sees Germany as strong and its potential role as pivotal within the EC and beyond. Equally each sees Germany's future role as uncertain or unformed. This is in part due to the fluidity of current international politics, including those within Europe; but it also has its roots in the still uncertain response of Germany to the new situation.[23]

There is no question, as the chapters in this book make unmistakably clear, that German policy towards the Middle East has been defined in economic rather than political terms and has generally been characterised by the kind of commercialistic opportunism most evident in the area of arms and technology transfers. Germany's encounter with the Middle East has been neither intense nor sustained, and there are reasons some suggest for believing that they will not be so in the future either. Stephen Szabo and Hanns Maull (in Chapters 6 and 7) both see the area south of Europe, that is the Mediterranean/North Africa, assuming greater importance and the Middle East less. Thomas Risse-Kappen (in Chapter 10) is also sceptical of Germany's domestic political and institutional ability to take a more activist role in the Middle East.

Germany, however, is the pre-eminent state in Europe and a united Europe is likely to become a leading power internationally with an important role to play in the Middle East – all the more in light of the collapse of the other superpower. Also Germany and Japan, the two economic giants, can be expected to play more important roles internationally in general and both enjoy considerable credibility in the Middle East. There is little doubt that there is much respect for and goodwill towards Germany in the region. It would be a pity if it is not built upon by more conscientious policies even if they are not ideally suited to all the parties in the region or to the taste of all industrialists at home. For this to happen the German government may have to emancipate itself first from the embrace of 'big business' and then start on the road to educating the public on what constitutes German interests other than those narrowly defined as economic, or those that only affect the homeland directly and tangibly.

Notes

1. *Sunday Times*, 27 January 1991.
2. *The Economist*, 6 April 1991, p.11.
3. *International Herald Tribune*, 3 October 1990.
4. *International Herald Tribune*, 2 April 1990.
5. *International Herald Tribune*, 3 October 1990.
6. *The Financial Times*, 7 January 1991.
7. 'Arms Technology: Inside the Chocolate Box', *The Economist*, 7 September 1991, p.741.
8. Alan Sked, 'Cheap Excuses: Germany and the Gulf Crisis', *National Interest*, Summer 1991, p.59.
9. Ibid. p.54.
10. See Harold James, *A German Identity 1770–19?0*, London, Weidenfeld and Nicolson, 1989; and Gordon Craig's comments 'A new New Reich' in *New York Review of Books*, 18 January 1990, p.33.
11. Jeffrey Garten, 'Japan and Germany: American Concerns', *Foreign Affairs*, Winter 1989–90, **68**, No. 5, pp.87, 89–90.
12. See *Middle East Economic Digest*, 5 April 1991, p.24.
13. *Middle East Economic Digest*, 15 February 1991, p.14.
14. See Marc Fisher's report in the *International Herald Tribune* 22 November 1990.
15. See Lucas Delattre, *Journal de Genève*, 25 January 1991.
16. Interview in *Die Welt*, 31 January 1991.
17. *Wall Street Journal*, 11 February 1991.
18. See David Marsh, *Financial Times*, 21 February 1991; *Middle East Economic Digest*, 15 February 1991, p.14.
19. *International Herald Tribune*, 9 December 1991.
20. *Der Spiegel*, 6 October 1986, pp.69 *et seq*.
21. *The Financial Times*, 25 March 1991.
22. *The Economist*, 16 February 1991, p.23.
23. See David Marsh, 'Illusion Makes Way for Reality', 28 August 1991, *Financial Times*.

2 Germany and world politics

Richard Burt

Probably no single feature of the international landscape so typified postwar global politics as the division of Germany. Thus, it follows that German unification is part and parcel of a more sweeping transformation of the international system. In this chapter, the changes in postwar global politics will be examined through the German prism: in particular, the evolution of the Federal Republic of Germany from a client state in the 1950s to a newly unified, near-great power in the 1990s.

In part, this evolution reflects a remarkable political and economic success story for both the Federal Republic and its partners in the West, especially the United States. The imposition of democratic institutions in the Federal Republic by the American and British occupation authorities resulted in a now firmly established pluralistic political system. Germany, a nation with few liberal traditions, has come firmly to embrace democracy and a liberal civic culture. Meanwhile, the postwar regeneration of the country's economic order – the famous *wirtshaftswunder* – has become the model for every nation aspiring to achieve both economic growth and social equity. The Federal Republic, with one-quarter the population of the United States and one-half that of Japan, exported more (in dollar terms) than either in 1990. Indeed, despite concerns in some quarters about the costs and the social dislocations involved, the Germans are well on their way to launching a second economic miracle in what was East Germany.

As impressive as German performance in the postwar period has been, Germany's potential emergence as a major international player is due in equal part to the profound changes occurring in the international system. First and foremost, of course, is the 'implosion' of the Soviet empire. The decline of the Soviet military threat to Germany, together with the collapse of Soviet political control in Eastern Europe, not only paved the way for unification, it has also given Germany new room for diplomatic manoeuvre in Eastern Europe.

Second, the democratic and free-market-orientated revolutions in Eastern Europe have given Germany real opportunities for exploiting that diplomatic manoeuvring. Eastern Europeans, including even the Poles, are looking to Germany as their most valuable source of investment capital and management expertise.[1] For historical reasons, the new Germany will want to avoid assuming a profile in the East that is too visible, but it will inevitably play a dominant role in the reconstruction of Eastern Europe.

Third, the economic and political integration of Western Europe will also lead to new influence for Germany. In the past, the process of European integration offered the Federal Republic a means of avoiding undue prominence on the European or world stages: Bonn was able to assert itself as part of the broader European Community. The Community still serves this important function for Germany, but increasingly, Bonn is not afraid to take the lead in Community

11

affairs nor does it worry when it is seen to do so. As a result European integration – particularly the creation of a single market in 1992 and a European central bank – will not dilute German influence but amplify it. (This is a point that has not been missed by those, like some in Britain, who worry about German ascendency in European politics.)[2]

Finally, potential changes in the American role in Europe also herald increased German influence. As we will discuss in greater detail below, the postwar 'special relationship' between Germany and the United States which included, among other things, an American nuclear guarantee and the presence of hundreds of thousands of American troops on German soil inevitably produced a kind of love–hate reaction in German politics, particularly on the Left. From the 1960s onwards, anti-Americanism became a means of expressing, for some German politicians and groups, the desire to play a more active and autonomous role in world politics. It was also an expression of the frustrating fact that Germany, and the international system, was not yet ready for such a role. In the 1990s, however, a declining American security guarantee will enhance German confidence and allow Germany to play a major part in reshaping the existing security architecture for Europe. While it will remain necessary, as Joseph Nye has pointed out in his book, *Bound to Lead*, for the United States to continue to head any restructured Western security system, American–German relations will be characterised by greater equality, maturity and sensitivity. This prospect was underscored by the behaviour of the Bush administration's approach, during 1990, to the 'Two-plus-Four' diplomacy of German reunification: after obtaining assurances from Bonn on the need to consult closely on each step of the process, Washington was prepared to let Helmut Kohl set the pace.

Do all four of these developments mean that Germany will emerge in the 1990s as a first-rank power? And if so, what will this entail for Germany's role outside Europe, especially in volatile regions such as the Middle East? The answers to these questions will, in part, depend on the changing character of the international system. Germany's emergence is only one facet of a more general development – the passing of bipolarity in international relations and the emergence of multiple power centres within a more open, pluralistic international framework. Thus, with the end of the cold war, the absolute decline of the former Soviet Union and what some also argue is the relative decline of the United States, there seems to be both room and a role for a Germany possessing the traditional attributes of a great power. Indeed, some observers have gone beyond this, to suggest that in the future, the industrialised world could be organised into three economic coalitions or camps; one in a dollar zone led by the United States, the second in a Japanese-dominated yen zone and the third in a German Deutschmark zone.

Of course, this is a highly simplistic model that rests on a number of assumptions. Perhaps the most important is the idea that with the cold war over, we are entering an era of economic primacy. Accordingly, it is commonly suggested that Germany and Japan, with heavily commercial perspectives toward foreign policy, are strongly positioned to dominate an international system in which economic strength and technological prowess are the most important measures of influence. But the now fashionable view of economic primacy in international relations assumes politico-military stability, within and outside Europe.

Within the former Eastern bloc, the transition from Communist control to various forms and stages of democracy has been remarkably tranquil. But as the euphoria of 1989 wears off, the possibility of instability grows. In parts of Eastern Europe, the democratic revolution has yet to be completed. Meanwhile, the retreat of Soviet power has fed nationalist tendencies and thus rekindled territorial and ethnic differences. Finally, the growth of separatist tensions within the former Soviet Union has itself a very real potential for igniting wider conflict.

Outside of Europe, the picture is the same. Despite the tendency of many countries to argue that conflicts in the Third World stemmed from the tendency of the two superpowers to drag their differences into various regional conflicts, the reality was very different. More often than not, the threat of American–Soviet confrontation, including the threat of nuclear escalation, acted as a deterrent to regional conflicts. If this is the case, the end of bipolarity in international politics could mean greater – not less – instability and further conflicts in volatile regions like the Middle East. Unfortunately, Iraq's invasion of Kuwait, now commonly referred to as the world's first post-cold war conflict, seems to bear this out.

In the 1990s and beyond, the challenge facing a newly ascendant Germany could well become formidable. Working with its European partners, the United States and Japan, Germany may have to protect its global economic interests against a proliferating number of political and military threats in the Third World. Whether it likes it or not, Germany – as it has already done in Europe – may find it necessary to develop in other regions a political and even military influence commensurate with its economic presence.

Germany and the postwar world

Whether Germany will carve out a new international role for itself in the less-structured, more open international system of the 1990s is, of course, the critical question. In attempting to formulate an answer, it is important to note that the role of the Federal Republic evolved in a dramatic fashion during the postwar era. In fact, it is not an exaggeration to argue that from a small, militarily occupied rump state in 1945, the Federal Republic became, even prior to unification, perhaps the fourth or fifth most influential country in the world.

In retrospect this achievement, which all three of the major German parties share, seems to follow a pattern in which West German international horizons expanded through a series of phases. The first phase, that of building trust and credibility, roughly coincided with the Adenauer–Erhard period of the 1950s and early 1960s. Confronted with the consequences of failure and defeat – a divided nation, a shattered economy, and few, if any, friends and allies – the postwar leadership subordinated German foreign policy to the overriding requirements of political rehabilitation and economic recovery. Adenauer correctly understood that the long-term re-establishment of Germany's role in world politics depended on the successful completion of two tasks: the integration of the Federal Republic into an American-led, Western security framework abroad; and the creation of a successful 'social market' economy at home.

The first of these tasks effectively meant that the Federal Republic was prepared to accept constraints on its freedom of action in order to deter Soviet aggression and to demonstrate its solidarity with its new allies in the West. The task of rebuilding the German economy, meanwhile, was a necessary precondition to establishing respect and support for the Federal Republic's new democratic institutions. The result was that in its first decade, the Federal Republic's preoccupations were either domestic or focused on cementing ties with allied capitals whose support was essential for building security and legitimacy. In fact, the only real incentive that the Federal Republic had to take a broader view of international politics was Bonn's drive, in the mid-1950s, to keep open the short-term option of reunification by resisting East Germany's efforts to gain formal recognition. Under the so-called Halstein Doctrine, Bonn announced that it was only prepared to establish diplomatic relations with those governments that declined to recognise the German Democratic Republic (GDR). Thus, Bonn and East Berlin quickly found themselves in a world-wide contest for political legitimacy, a contest that Bonn won but at the cost of stunted relationships with those regimes, in Eastern Europe and elsewhere, that did recognise the GDR. An exception to this unidimensional approach to foreign policy beyond Europe was the Middle East. Here, early support by the Federal Republic for the new state of Israel was an important element of German rehabilitation. Nevertheless, in this first postwar phase of foreign policy, Bonn pursued the same low-profile course in the Middle East that it followed elsewhere.

A second phase of postwar policy began in the late 1960s, with Bonn's opening to the East. In part, Willy Brandt's *Ostpolitik* reflected the success of German policy: both in politico-military and economic terms, the Federal Republic was strong and confident enough to seek *détente* with the Soviet Union and its neighbours. Yet it also reflected a certain failure in the Adenauer position. The division of Germany had seemingly become a fixed part of the international landscape, and attempts to isolate the GDR, while partially successful, also had the effect of isolating the Federal Republic from the East. Thus, in a burst of diplomatic activism which was for the most part coordinated with the United States, the Brandt government negotiated a series of agreements with Eastern European regimes that essentially traded recognition and economic ties for a de-escalation of the cold war. Although Brandt's Eastern treaties were attacked from the right by Franz Joseph Strauss and others, they were well received by the West German public which had grown weary of the psychological wear-and-tear of the cold war. Moreover, in exploring an opening with the East, the Germans were not alone. Richard Nixon and Henry Kissinger's *détente* policy provided Bonn with valuable political cover. For the Germans, the high point of this period was the 1971 Quadrapartite Agreement in which the allies and the Soviet Union effectively agreed to settle (or at least moderate) their differences over Berlin. In taking this step, the allies, together with the two Germanies, appeared to take German reunification off the East–West political agenda. Thus, added to Adenauer's plank of Western solidarity came an additional element of postwar policy – political and economic normalisation with the East.

Helmut Schmidt's tenure as chancellor in the 1970s coincided with the next phase of West German foreign policy, the 'renegotiation' of the Federal Republic's role in the West by virtue of its growing economic clout and political confidence. Schmidt, with a quick mind and a quick tongue, represented in every way the new confidence of the Germans in the seventies; America, undergoing the traumas of Vietnam and Watergate as well as the *malaise* of the Carter era, no longer served as a model for German society. And while the Federal Republic continued to require an American nuclear guarantee and the presence of American troops on its soil, Schmidt did succeed in changing the character of the American–German security dialogue. In winning Washington's agreement to end West German 'off-set' payments for American troops stationed in the FRG, Schmidt was able to argue that Bonn was becoming less of a client and more of a partner for Washington.

Schmidt was correct. In the Nixon and Kissinger period, Bonn, for the first time in the postwar era, displaced London as America's special interlocuter in Europe. Indeed, in the aftermath of the 1973 Middle East war, there were complaints from London and Paris of an American–German bi-hegemony on global economic and even security questions. While this partnership fell on hard times during the Carter period, the very fact that Schmidt was prepared to disagree openly with American policy – and even let the press know that he had little respect for Jimmy Carter – was in itself an indication of a new German assertiveness in world affairs.

Two developments, in particular, underscored Bonn's new influence. The first was the introduction of the economic summits – the annual meetings of the Group of Seven industrialised countries – recognising the growing multipolarity of international economic power. The economic summits gave Germany and Japan seats at the top table for the first time in the postwar period. Although the meetings were originally organised by the French, Schmidt, with his close ties to Giscard d'Estaing, was able to emerge as a central player at the summits and the diplomacy that proceeded them.

The second development was Schmidt's concern that American–Soviet arms control might somehow undermine FRG security. Rather than merely relying on Washington's judgement, Schmidt in 1977 in a now-famous speech in London outlined his concerns. This led to the so-called NATO 'double-track' decision in 1979 in which the Alliance committed itself both to deploying intermediate-range nuclear forces (INF) in Europe and to seeking an arms control deal with Moscow to limit or even eliminate these systems. The decision turned out to be a momentous one, both for domestic politics in Germany and for East–West relations more generally. The key point, however, is that it signalled the emergence of a Germany that was no longer prepared to play second fiddle on security decisions.

Schmidt's successor, Helmut Kohl, continued the process of expanding the Federal Republic's international horizons while increasing Bonn's influence in core East–West security matters. In fact, it was during the 1980s that the Federal Republic's international influence began to rival that of Britain and France. The West German economy's continuing strength made Bonn the key European player in the G-7 while in the political realm, Foreign Minister Hans Dietrich Genscher's forward-leaning posture toward the Soviet Union represented new German influence and assertiveness in NATO. Most important, however, was Kohl's careful management of the German–American relationship. Just as Adenauer years before had recognised that American support was vital for Germany's political rehabilitation, Kohl appeared to understand that winning Washington's confidence was a necessary part of Bonn's new maturity. There were set-backs, of course, most notably with Kohl's botched effort to commemorate a new postwar relationship at the cemetery at Bitburg, but by and large Kohl succeeded in achieving a new level of respect and sensitivity in the United States towards the Federal Republic. An important factor in this regard was his willingness to run grave political risks in order to implement successfully the INF missile-deployment decision.

While Kohl and Genscher enhanced German leverage in the traditional East–West sphere, Bonn's influence also grew in other areas. Relying on economic aid and the activities of the political-party *stiftungen*, Bonn sought to help find a political settlement to the various conflicts in Central America. Bonn had little impact on the outcome there; what is interesting is that the Federal Republic even defined a role for itself in the region. In Asia, economic diplomacy was paramount. The Federal Republic's economic ties with China grew rapidly, and Bonn became the leading European supporter of ASEAN in South-east Asia. In the Middle East, meanwhile, Bonn sought to complement its careful cultivation of Israel with closer links with Arab regimes. In the main, this balancing act was successful. However, some delicate problems were raised by the transfer of sensitive technologies to the Middle East and beyond. While Kohl and Genscher were able to win domestic political support for transferring conventional arms to ASEAN countries, a proposal for selling Leopard II tanks to Saudi Arabia became too controversial at home and was dropped. Meanwhile, the Kohl–Genscher government found itself embroiled in controversies with Washington over allegations – most of them correct – that West German firms had provided radical Arab States, including Iraq and Libya, with materials and technologies to build chemical and even nuclear arms. Signalling a new maturity, the Bonn government in 1989 and 1990 finally enacted legislation to tighten German export rules, perhaps a symbol that Germany was in the process of broadening its economic diplomacy in the Third World to include regional security concerns.[3]

Thus, in forty years of postwar history, the Federal Republic's international role had grown in steady but still remarkable ways: Bonn had established a leadership position within Western Europe, a more co-equal relationship with Washington, an active posture in Eastern Europe, a much less dangerous relationship with Moscow and finally, a global export capability matched by an increasingly global foreign policy. In short, the Federal Republic was a success story. Perhaps this was one reason that when change accelerated in Eastern Europe, public support for the East German regime quickly collapsed and unification proceeded as quickly as it did.

The impact of unification

The key question stemming from German unification is one of change versus continuity. Will Germany's unification introduce important discontinuities into what had been a steady process of growing influence and expanding horizons?

Any attempt to answer this question must first deal with two ironies. The first is that while a united Germany, in theory, should be able to play a bigger role on the world stage, the actual political and economic process of absorbing the GDR into the Federal Republic could lead to a more parochial, introspective Germany. Inevitably, the huge effort and expense of democratising and developing the GDR's political and economic institutions will divert the Federal

Republic from assuming a more active international posture. Already, concerns have been voiced in Western Europe that reunification has led to a diminished interest in Bonn in constructing a single market for the European Community by 1992.[4] In Washington, meanwhile, there are similar fears that in a period in which the United States will be unable, by itself, to protect Western interests worldwide, a newly-unified Germany will be too preoccupied with the task of political and economic integration to take on new responsibilities for maintaining international order.[5]

The second irony flows directly from the first: while the United States will be seeking in a newly unified Germany a stronger partner on the global stage, this idea will surely be resisted by Germany's closest neighbours in Europe. Polish nervousness about a stronger Germany was noticeable throughout the unification process, while to the west, Dutch, Italian and Belgian concerns were openly expressed. Even Britain and France, who in the 'Two-plus-Four' process supported Bonn's drive for rapid unification, entertained more private concerns – as the Nicholas Ridley affair in London all too publicly demonstrated. For a new, potentially stronger Germany the challenge was clear: how to take on new global responsibilities without setting off alarm bells closer to home.

Germany's ability to master this challenge will depend on how it manages its key international relationships. In the case of the United States, Washington's strong and unqualified support for unification has produced the best atmosphere in German–American relations since the early 1960s. But it is not clear that this new atmosphere can be translated into a stronger relationship over the longer term. There are a number of points of potential friction that could test the relationship in the 1990s. One is the future security architecture for Europe. The United States will continue to view NATO as the primary institution for maintaining order in Europe, but American politicians will also push for a substantial reduction of the American military presence. Indeed, support in Congress for a significant withdrawal is likely to grow. A unified Germany will certainly preserve its membership in NATO, but stronger German emphasis on subordinating the Alliance to a more political, pan-European security structure like the CSCE is almost certain. At the same time, Germany will want to keep a much reduced but still sizable number of American troops on its soil – at least for an interim period – as an insurance policy in the event that the pan-European option fails.

Thus, a German–American debate over the focus and the organisation of European security seems difficult to avoid. So, too, does a debate over the presence and modernisation of nuclear weapons in Germany.[6] The debate is likely to be conducted on two levels. The first and more abstract level concerns the contribution of nuclear weapons to deterrence. Despite the decline of the Soviet military threat, Washington, together with London and Paris, is very likely to view nuclear weapons as a necessary component of Western security policy in the 1990s, if only because of their inherent quality of inducing prudence and caution. This argument will be reinforced by the turbulence in Eastern Europe and the political fragmentation in the former Soviet Union.

A unified Germany, however, is unlikely to be moved by these arguments. With the Red Army leaving the East and with a new appreciation of its own sovereignty, the idea of stationing foreign nuclear weapons on German soil will be questioned by elements at both ends of the political spectrum. This will especially be the case if the new Commonwealth complains about measures to modernise remaining American nuclear weapons in Germany. Severe instability in Eastern Europe could, of course, dampen anti-nuclear sentiment in Germany. Over time, however, the emergence of new threats to Germany could also lead to sentiment for the acquisition of a German nuclear option rather than continuing dependence on the American nuclear umbrella.

But a German nuclear option is not a problem for the immediate future. Instead, on the political level, it is the relationship between nuclear weapons and the presence of American troops. While, as explained above, there are strong reasons for Germany (and its neighbours) to welcome the presence of American forces, if the United States is unable to protect these through the deployment of a minimum number of nuclear weapons, it is unlikely that political support in the Congress will be found for keeping troops in Germany. To put it in bumper-sticker terms: 'no nukes, no troops'. For American policymakers the adoption by a new Germany of denuclearisation would constitute a violation of the important NATO principle of 'risk-sharing'. By prohibiting the deployment of nuclear weapons on its soil, Germany would be saying in effect that while it continued to depend on the American nuclear umbrella (and the risk this entails for the United States), it was unwilling to bear its fair share of the nuclear burden.

The United States, of course, can help lessen Germany's nuclear *angst* by pursuing nuclear deployment and arms control policies that recognise the changing requirements of deterrence. For a start, the withdrawal of systems no longer relevant to current circumstances namely nuclear artillery and short-range missiles could be accelerated. The deployment of new systems, such as new longer range land-based and air-to-surface missiles, could be put on the back burner, pending the outcome of the reform process in the former Soviet Union. And on the arms control front, the United States must make a convincing effort to reduce short-range nuclear forces (SNF). U.S. reassurance that does not instigate interest in German nuclearisation will be important. However, arms control, including the size of the residual U.S. presence in Europe, is unlikely to be a major issue in American–German relations. More important in the coming decade will be the coordination of policies towards other areas – the Commonwealth of Independent States and any possible successor, Eastern Europe and the Balkans. This in turn will depend on a clarification of the respective roles of America and the E.C.

American–German differences could emerge over so-called 'out-of-area' issues: the question of whether Germany will play a larger role in responding to security threats to Western interests in the Third World. While over the last decade the Federal Republic has expanded its economic and even political role outside of Europe, the German role has grown only gradually. American proposals, in 1986, to establish an embargo against Libya for its role in sponsoring terrorism were politely ignored by the Bonn government as were warnings, two years later, about the participation of German firms in the construction and operation of the Libyan chemical weapons facility at Rabta. To be sure, the Germans did respond to threats to close off all shipping in the Gulf in the last phases of the Iran–Iraq conflict. For the first time since World War II, German naval units were dispatched to the Mediterranean to permit American combatants to steam to the Gulf to participate in convoy and mine-sweeping operations. Nevertheless, as Iraq's invasion of Kuwait seems to have demonstrated, there are not only potential legal limits on the deployment of

German military forces abroad but also strong domestic political resistance. Thus, if as seems likely, Germany is seen as both preoccupied with the task of unification and unwilling to contribute to out-of-area contingencies, this too will contribute to growing strains with Washington. The political leadership in both American political parties will increasingly want a newly influential Germany – along with Japan – to become a producer, rather than a consumer, of stability in volatile regions.[7]

Economic differences, meanwhile, could exacerbate differences over East–West and out-of-area issues between Germany and the United States. During the 1980s the two generally pursued similar strategies on trade and economic growth: fighting inflation and resisting protectionism. A conspicuous exception was in agriculture, where American concerns over the European Community's subsidies to its farmers delayed completion of the GATT Uruguay Round. But the 1980s was an extended period of economic growth for both the United States and Europe, particularly the Federal Republic. If, as seems likely, the 1990s are a period of lower growth, then disagreements over monetary and trade policy could emerge as the most serious challenge to keeping the German–American relationship on an even keel.

Somewhat surprisingly, the outlook for Germany's relations with its European neighbours is brighter. Despite forebodings in both Eastern and Western Europe when the Wall came down, the pace of unification has not led to an outpouring of public concern. Indeed, as one observer has written, European governments and their publics appear more worried about the risks of instability in the East, including chaos in the former Soviet Union, 'In the face of such dangers, European attitudes toward Germany are precisely the opposite of what they were more than half a century ago – the old fears of strife, instability, and economic uncertainty have been replaced by hopes that Germany will help lead Europe into a new era of unity, stability, and prosperity.'[8]

In part, Europe's optimism about Germany's future role is based on the Federal Republic's overall successful effort to overcome its totalitarian history. For example, Professor Stanley Hoffman has written that 'it would take an extraordinary amount of mischief to turn the new German state into a modern version of the dangerous and unsettling Germany of the past. Neither Germany's partners, nor even its former adversaries in the East are in any way eager to antagonize or provoke it; and German elites have no desire to return to the past.'[9]

That said, Germany and its neighbours will have to be prepared to manage several potential problems. In the West, a unified Germany could upset the complicated 'triangular' balance with Britain and France. In Paris, there are concerns that a unified Germany will lose interest in a further deepening of the EC. In London, there are worries about German economic dominance and a German drift toward *Mitteleuropa*. So far, however, both capitals have been reassured by Germany's continued willingness to move ahead with the Single Market and other projects designed to enmesh Germany in a myriad of European arrangements. The movement toward a European central bank and then perhaps a single currency are prime examples. Germany will nevertheless have to make some important choices about the kind of Europe it wants to assist in building a 'deepened' Europe along the lines of what the French would prefer or a 'broadened' Europe of the sort that had been favoured by Mrs. Thatcher.

So far, the Germans have tried to support both, with Genscher maintaining that a more integrated community will contribute to the ultimate goal of a unified Europe. But if 'push comes to shove', one suspects that a unified Germany, rediscovering its central European roots, will opt for a broadened conception of European integration, a development that would generate fears in Paris and other capitals in the West.

Such a development might also cause jitters in the East. The Eastern Europeans are clearly ambivalent about a larger, more influential Germany. As Soviet military predominance fades, there are concerns about a new German economic predominance. At the same time, there is a recognition that without German participation, the economic development of Eastern Europe will not be possible. This ambivalence is strongest in the case of Poland where there are understandable fears about German revanchism concerning the movement west of their mutual border in 1945. After some hesitation, Helmut Kohl made it clear in 1990 that the existing border would be respected by a unified Germany.[10] This dampened fears in Warsaw somewhat, but Poland, together with Hungary and Czechoslovakia, are still concerned about the long-run implications of a newly influential Germany.

Eastern Europeans appear worried, in particular, about the prospect of a fundamental change in their relationship with the new Commonwealth. In years past, of course, the Eastern Europeans were most concerned about a conflict between the Soviet Union and the West, including the Federal Republic: their territory would have served as a theatre for any NATO–Warsaw Pact war. Now, however, the East Europeans have an entirely different worry – the possibility that a new, cooperative relationship between Bonn and Moscow could lead to a German–Russian 'condominium' over Eastern Europe. This fear is probably exaggerated, but it is nevertheless true that prospects for German–Russian relations are quite bright. Simply put, the new Germany and the new Commonwealth of Independent States need one another. The Germans have long understood the centrality of the relationship with the former Soviet Union. The FRG's conduct of *Ostpolitik* twenty years ago was designed, in part, to promote unification. More recently, German willingness to provide substantial financial aid to the Soviet Union was meant to offer Moscow incentives to permit, in the context of the Two-plus-Four process, unification. Germany has invested heavily in the reform process taking place in the Commonwealth – more heavily than any other state – and has done so when its own resources were constrained by the high cost of reunification.

Germany recognises more directly than the more distant allies the detente nature of the post-Soviet transition and would be most directly and adversely affected by any breakdown or regression from the move towards democracy and the market system.

For their part, the former Soviets seem receptive to these blandishments. Like the Germans, who must turn to the task of integrating its five new eastern states into the Federal Republic, the Commonwealth leaders find themselves similarly preoccupied with the task of politico-economic renewal. And Germany, for centuries a strategic rival to the west, now looms as a principal source of aid and investment capital for Commonwealth reform programmes. While the prospects appear good for a stronger, more cooperative relationship, there seems little reason to fear a new 'Rapollo', that is, the creation of a Bonn–Moscow axis arrayed against the Western democracies. Indeed, closer ties between Moscow and Bonn would have the effect of hastening the reform process in the new Commonwealth.

Germany and the Third World

Germany's potential new role outside of Europe is perhaps the most difficult to project. As we have seen, the Federal Republic developed a global foreign policy in the 1970s and 1980s, exercising what Genscher has called a policy of 'example' meant to help find peaceful solutions to volatile situations in the Middle East or Central America. Looking ahead, it is clear that many nations in the Third World will want Germany to play a more activist role on the global stage. However, unlike the United States, which is mainly interested in Germany's contribution to security, the less-developed countries will look to Germany for help in solving their pressing economic problems. Clearly, it will be impossible for Germany to be all things to all nations. Germany will be under pressure to keep a low military profile by its close neighbours east and west. At the same time, the United States and perhaps others will expect it to play a larger global security role. At home, German voters and politicians will be uninterested (at least for a time) in the world stage and instead will be preoccupied with the domestic mechanics of unification. But Germany's chief trading partners as well as the Third World will place more, rather than fewer, demands on its economic resources. The new Germany, in other words, will find itself tugged in all directions.

That this is so was amply demonstrated by the international crisis that flowed from Iraq's invasion of Kuwait. The crisis very clearly underscored the conflicting pressures at home and abroad that a new Germany will confront in the face of Third World conflicts in the 1990s.

The first thing to note is that the Iraqi crisis did not seize the attention of the German political elite as it did elsewhere in the world: unification dominated the front pages of the German press, not the Iraqi invasion. Second, while some leading Germans, most notably Helmut Kohl, wanted to play a more assertive role in this out-of area crisis, there seems to have been a general consensus that Germany needed to proceed with caution.[11]

The issue focused on the Federal Republic's constitution, the so-called Basic Law, which was said to forbid the deployment of German troops to the Gulf. However, this was more a political issue than a legal one. Article 87a of the Basic Law states that the German armed forces may only be used 'for defence purposes'. The question, of course, is how 'defence purposes' is defined, particularly for an oil-importing nation like Germany which is heavily dependent on shipments from the Gulf. Kohl, responding in part to strong American support for unification, sought approval for sending German forces to the Gulf, but was rebuffed by his own party as well as by the Free Democrats and the Social Democrats. The decision, instead, was to consider a constitutional amendment that would permit German participation in UN-sanctioned and supervised military operations.

The outcome of this important debate was thus ambiguous. Although all-party support for constitutional changes reflected tacit agreement with Kohl's view that the new Germany needed to take a more active international role,

Genscher and the Social Democrats would clearly rather concentrate on unification than the emotional issue of out-of-area deployment. Ironically, in apparently agreeing that a constitutional amendment is necessary for the deployment of troops outside of Europe, Kohl has opened the door to an amendment that could actually restrict German options by limiting the Bundeswehr only to UN operations. To make matters worse, there was also the perception – in the United States and elsewhere – that Germany was slow to respond to American appeals for financial help to sustain its forces in the Gulf as well as aid for regional states, most notably Turkey and Egypt, that participated in the embargo against Iraq. After a visit to Bonn by Secretary of State James Baker and sustained pressure from Washington, Bonn agreed to add some $5 billion to its initial sum of $1.8 billion towards the cost of the war. Yet as with Japan the actual contributions which were reasonable were perceived as niggardly and inadequate because of the manner in which they were dispensed. In the end, probably the most important contribution that Germany made to the Western response to the crisis was that Bonn permitted Washington to use its major bases at Rhein-Main and Ramstein for ferrying troops and supplies to the Gulf. In this way, Germany acted as a critical staging area for the projection of American power into the Middle East. Looking to the future, the ability of the United States to continue to use these bases could be of major importance.

Back to the future?

Of course, Germany's reaction to the crisis in the Gulf must be seen as a special case because it coincided with the last phases of the unification process. Nevertheless, the episode does underscore an important point about the new Germany's role in a new period of international politics: if the transition from a bipolar international system to something more fluid and pluralistic is an orderly one and if, as some suggest, indices of state power move away from military force towards economic and technological capability, then Fritz Stern will have been vindicated – Germany will become one of the world power centres.[12] But as others have noted, Germany's position is perhaps as fragile as Japan's: both have aging populations and some of the most rigidly-structured labour environments in the industrialised world. Like Japan, Germany is highly dependent for its economic well-being on the stability and prosperity of the international system.[13]

The Iraqi case has vividly shown that even in the post-cold war world, prosperity and stability cannot be taken for granted. In a more uncertain world, a world with risks of turmoil in Europe and conflicts beyond, Germany will be something less than a world power. At home, it will be preoccupied with the immense task of politically, economically and psychologically bonding what was the GDR to the Federal Republic. Moreover, German politicians of all stripes will be acutely sensitive to awakening old fears on the part of close neighbours. A united Germany will thus be more proud and patriotic, but careful not to flex its new muscle in the name of a new nationalism. Indeed, it is very likely that its allies, especially the United States, will complain more loudly than ever that Germany is still unwilling to protect Western global interests with military power. The alternative, a more assertive Germany pursuing its interests independently, may emerge as a result of the current turmoil, but then the problem will be more difficult: to restrain rather than goad the newly confident ally.

In some respects, then, the unification of Germany means that modern German history has gone full circle – not back to 1871 when Germany was first unified by Bismarck, but to 1949 when the Federal Republic formally came into being. Then, as now, the Federal Republic needed to give first priority to economic development and democratisation; it needed to reassure its neighbours by contributing to a new European framework and it needed to work with the United States to help guarantee global security. Needless to say, this strategy worked. This time around, the tasks will be every bit as difficult. The process of rebuilding what had been the GDR will not only be prohibitively expensive, but there will be a dangerous tendency to become exclusively preoccupied with domestic affairs at the expense of the new and different responsibilities that the global community expects Germany to assume. In Europe, the problem will be to continue the ambitious programme of economic and political integration with the EC while simultaneously pursuing a broader programme aimed at developing the East and moving toward a united Europe. In other regions, particularly the Middle East, the task will be to develop a more active role in seeking diplomatic solutions but, working closely with other Europeans and the United States, projecting the necessary military power to back up this diplomacy. As Germany succeeded in the tasks it confronted in the early 1950s, it should be able to succeed with the new challenges it faces in the early 1990s.

Writing about the amazing changes that have led to German unification, Fritz Stern has said: 'Something quite rare has happened for Germany – it has received a second chance.'[14] As we have seen, the Federal Republic did a great deal, through its cooperation with Europe and the United States, to earn its second chance. If it now turns inward, then Germany could squander its magnificent new opportunity. On the other hand, a liberal, forward-looking internationally engaged Germany has the opportunity to play a major role in shaping a new, more diverse and less dangerous international order.

Notes

1. Stanley Hoffmann, 'Reflections on the "German Question",' *Survival*, July–August, 1990, p.293.
2. Fritz Stern, 'A New Beginning in Germany', *The Washington Post*, 29 July 1990, p.C7.
3. 'Bonn Tightens Grip on Trade in Chemical Weapons Gear', *The Wall Street Journal Europe*, 20 August 1990, p.3.
4. 'Waking Up in the New Europe – with a Headache', paper by Thomas Killinger.
5. 'Follow My Leader', *The Economist*, 11 August 1990, p.28.
6. Karl Kaiser, 'From Nuclear Deterrence to Graduated Conflict Control: German Unification and the Departure from Current NATO Strategy', *Survival*, November–December, 1990.
7. See 'Europe Does Its Bit', editorial in *The Financial Times*, 23 August 1990, p.14. See also 'Kohl Says He's Willing to Send Ships to Gulf, Sign West Germany Seeks More Global Role', *The Wall Street Journal Europe*, 16 August 1990, p.2.
8. Craig Whitney, 'From Germany's Neighbors: Respect and Then Acceptance', *The New York Times*, 27 September 1990.

9. Stanley Hoffman, op. cit., p.298.

10. Helmut Kohl, 'A United Germany in a United Europe', speech to the American Council on Germany, 5 June 1990, **XIII**, No. 15.

11. 'Bonn, Leery of Larger Role, Considers Joining Task Force', *The Washington Post*, 15 August 1990, p.3.

12. Fritz Stern, *Ibid*.

13. Ilya Prizel, 'Germany Is No Superpower', *The Christian Science Monitor*, 16 August 1990, p.17.

14. Fritz Stern, *Ibid*.

3 Germany, the Alliance and out-of-area crises

Gregory F. Treverton

With unification, Germany has become a normal country. It has also become a strong country in a strategic context that is unusual historically: Russia is relatively weaker than it has been for a hundred years, nuclear weapons aside, and Eastern Europe is essentially a vacuum. At the same time, Germany is enmeshed in institutional arrangements that are also unusual historically. Of these NATO is probably less important over the long run than the European Community (EC).

With unification, 'little Germany' has come to an end. It has been ending slowly over several decades, but unification concludes the process. The new Germany begins from an introverted base but will become less reticent in articulating its national interests. That will be true beyond Europe as well as within it. It will be uncomfortable for Germany's allies, but there will be advantages as well, for with normality will come responsibility. Germany will no longer be able to deny being a great power, saying 'we're just a trading nation', a kind of European Japan.

Ever since there has been a Germany, it has been Eurocentric; given geography, perhaps it could not have been otherwise. That will continue; it will be abetted by Russian weakness and Eastern Europe's vacuum. In particular, Germany's entanglement in Eastern Europe will limit both its reach and its grasp beyond Europe. The Iraqi invasion of Kuwait provided a foretaste of that: preoccupied with digesting East Germany, the Federal Republic was slow to take a role, however non-military, in the Gulf.

This chapter hints at Germany's future role beyond Europe. One guide to the future is continuity, the recent past, in the case of the Federal Republic. Yet this Federal Republic is not the same as its predecessor; continuity in name and form of government cover considerable discontinuity in fact. Thus hints from older German history are also suggestive, along with speculations about future interests. One element of continuity does seem predictable: in the future as in the past, the focal point of issues beyond Europe will be the Middle East and the Gulf.

A place in the sun

Germany was a relatively reluctant colonial power, especially so while Bismarck remained in office – a history which illustrates the country's European preoccupation. Until the 1880s, Bismarck encouraged other nations' colonial efforts while keeping his attention focused on Europe, thus avoiding a direct challenge to Britain. Britain could have political primacy; German traders would settle for money, a preference upset by the depression of 1871 and ensuing tariffs. A 'little Germany', the holder of the balance within Europe and mere trader beyond it, gradually gave way to a 'big Germany' which sought dominance in continental Europe and 'a place in the sun' beyond it.

Perhaps more so than for other European states, colonialism was less a policy than a reflection of the cross-currents in domestic politics. In particular, the tariffs of 1879, which cemented Bismarck's 'iron and rye' coalition of Junker landowners and newly-rich industrialists, hurt German traders, who feared being cut off from raw material sources through British and French retaliation.

Colonies were an outlet for domestic energies in a relatively closed system which had come late to industrialisation. That was all the more true after Germany deferred expansion in the most logical European direction, south-east, by staying true to Bismarck's famous dictum that the Balkans – the 'Eastern question', in the language of the times – involved no interest for Germany 'that was worth the healthy bones of a Pomeranian musketeer'.[1] Moreover, once nationalism permeated down through the social order, colonialism was a way to make it compatible with the right to leave Germany, especially for those frozen out of the tight domestic 'establishment'.[2]

Germany was also becoming a great power, and colonies were a part of the great-power game. Once established and recognised by the other European powers in the Berlin Conference of 1885, however, Germany's colonies in Africa and Asia were initially run solely by the trading companies. Formal colonial administration came only with the departure of Bismarck and the demise of the trading companies; with state administration came a push for German settlers in Namibia, especially, and also East Africa.

The colonies never were much of an economic success. Namibia was rich in potential, especially after diamonds were discovered in 1908, but it was also costly to pacify; Germany's own bloody repressions undercut its criticism of Britain's harsh methods during the Boer War. Samoa and Togo were modest successes, as was Germany's last colony, the Chinese port of Kiaochow which was strictly a trading post and not a point of settlement. It was run by the navy, not the colonial office. It was Kiaochow that occasioned Kaiser William II's line during the Boxer Rebellion: 'It will not be my duty to see to it that this place in the sun shall remain our undisputed possession.'[3]

Throughout, the debate over colonies somewhat paralleled that over *Mitteleuropa* (middle Europe). It pitted those who saw colonies only as commercial ventures for raw materials and markets against those tempted by land for settlers. Needless to say, the *Mitteleuropa* debate was far more critical; Hitler proved the point in 1938 by refusing to accept the return of all Germany's colonies in exchange for withdrawing from Czechoslovakia – another illustration of Germany's preoccupation with Europe. In Europe, capitalists and Junkers envisioned politically independent countries taking the place of the Austrio-Hungarian and Russian Empires, opening the Baltics, Balkans, Eastern Europe and the Ukraine to Prussian industrial and agricultural domination. Thus, Germany could have both economic fruits and political legitimacy without directly challenging British interests. Needless to say, the Nazis saw the world differently.

The Alliance out of area

Defeated and reconstructed as the Federal Republic, West Germans again became 'little Germans'. Preoccupied with economic growth and the fate of fellow Germans in Europe, 'out of area' – that particularly infelicitous term even for an alliance in which jargon abounded – referred to beyond Europe, very far indeed from German consciousness, let alone priorities. The connotations of an area, Europe, with the remainder 'out of' it are not especially attractive, particularly to those defined as out (although sometimes that status must have appealed to those who could remain so). But for the Federal Republic, the term, reflecting the geographical limit of NATO to areas north of the Tropic of Cancer, has suited perfectly.[4]

The out-of-area label has covered a diverse set of issues; in that sense it confuses more than it enlightens, for there is no actual place called 'Out of Area'. One category of out-of-area issues is disputes over former or remaining 'colonial' territories such as the Falklands/Malvinas. These disputes have diminished almost by definition but will still arise, unpredictably. Other nations mostly hope that they go away quickly.

A second set covers those particular issues regarded as critical by one or another member indirectly related to security as a whole – such as Central America in the 1980s. Allies of the nation directly concerned have had an incentive to mute their criticism if they disagree, for their other stakes have usually been greater. So it was with Central America. It will be less so in the future, for Germany and for other European states, as the imperative of unity against a Soviet threat disappears. But the change seems likely to be gradual, not dramatic.

The third, and most important, issues will continue to be those which both the United States and its friends in Europe would agree have direct effects on their joint security, even if they disagree about what to do. For the near future as the recent past, this category will comprise the Gulf and Middle East. Only there, will the elements of strategic importance come together: adjacency to NATO members and to both residual CIS military power and to the turbulence of the former Soviet Union's disintegration, the imperative of oil coupled with differing European and American vulnerabilities and the presence of Israel as a friend, even a strategic ally, for the United States in particular but also for Germany. Following the disintegration of the Soviet Union, the fates of its southern republics will link 'out' and 'in' areas.

West Germany's most extensive involvements beyond Europe were in Africa. That involvement, however, came late and did not amount to all that much.[5] Until 1965 Bonn was constrained by its Hallstein Doctrine, which stipulated that it would not have diplomatic relations with any nation that had them with East Germany. The doctrine crumbled in 1965, when Tanzania recognised East Germany and encouraged other states to do likewise. What had been intended to isolate East Germany ran the risk of isolating West Germany instead.

Most German assistance to Africa has been in the form of private capital, and much of its business has been with South Africa. The link to South Africa originally reflected German sympathies for the Boers against the British; more recently, the link has mainly been a commercial one, especially trade in South African minerals. Accordingly, the Federal Republic was reluctant to impose economic sanctions; Bonn tended to tuck in behind the greater British reluctance as the Community gradually tightened its sanctions.

There was the risk of some tensions over sanctions between America and Europe, but even before the Soviet Union's retrenchment the issue did not look like a major one. It is much less likely that it could become so today. Neither the differences among the United States and its allies nor the stakes of any of them are particularly great.[6]

The out-of-area issue is hardly new. In fact, in a very real sense, it was just such an issue, the Korean war, that touched off the American military build-up and allied cooperation that transformed NATO from a set of security guarantees into a real military alliance, even though NATO as an institution was not involved in Korea. That said, however, NATO has never been very united over out-of-area issues. On the other hand it has never let those disagreements tear the basic fabric of alliance cohesion. In the early days, the Europeans exhorted Washington to pay more attention to security issues beyond Europe, but the United States hung back, fearing it would be drawn into the residual colonial conflicts of the major European powers.

Indeed, the original geographic limitation of NATO came at American, rather than European insistence. France, for example, pushed for the inclusion of Italy. At the time this was problematic because the French wanted to extend NATO into the Mediterranean, thus strengthening the argument for the inclusion of then-French Algeria. There was also the notion of an alliance with three categories of members: a core group, plus associate members either linked by strictly military relations (Portugal) or given one-way aid in return for limited cooperation (Sweden). In addition there would have been a more peripheral category of, for example, former colonies. The idea appealed to some Europeans and also to some Americans, but for different reasons. It would have provided for a differentiated link especially to Portugal, an ideological outcast from which the allies in any case only wanted real estate.

However, American Undersecretary of State Robert Lovett derided the idea as 'resident members, non-resident members and summer privileges', and it never was a starter.[7] Leaders at the time recognised that it would have permitted countries to have most of the benefits of full membership at less cost and responsibility – thus institutionalising temptations toward free-riding.

The United States declined to intervene beyond Europe again and again, despite Korea: in 1949–50 it resisted a British call for a commitment to defend South-east Asia; in 1954 it decided not to come to the aid of the beleaguered French garrison at Dien Bien Phu; and still later in the decade it rebuffed General de Gaulle's call for a *directoire* of Britain, France and the United States to set common global policies. Suez was the most searing episode of this series, given both the special Anglo–American connection and the fact that Britain and France were entangled in a regional war. Here was NATO's pre-eminent power not just opposing its European allies but doing so in connivance with Moscow.

By the time of the Vietnam War, the pattern of the out-of-area issue had changed. Now it was the United States exhorting its allies to become involved. Writing in 1965, Henry Kissinger's words could have been those of any American official for the next generation:

United States spokesmen often exhort our Allies to play a more active global role with the argument that their resources are now adequate for such a task. But the problem is more complicated. The availability of resources does not guarantee an interest in assuming world-wide responsibilities as is demonstrated by United States policy prior to World War II. The same is true today for almost all our European Allies . . . If our Allies give assistance, it will be token in nature, and the motive will be to obtain a veto over United States actions. The thrust of their recommendations will be to avoid a direct showdown and even the semblance of risk.[8]

To caricature only slightly, in any crisis the United States asked first what Europe was prepared to contribute, while Europe first sought assurance that the crisis would not be permitted to upset the stability of Europe. When Washington found the European answers wanting, it did what it felt it had to, usually without much consulting its allies. For instance, the United States several times drew upon its garrison in Europe to send troops to Vietnam, and it continually robbed operating budgets in Europe to finance the war in Asia.

During the 1973 Middle East war, it asked permission to re-supply Israel through bases in Europe. Even Britain was reluctant, occasioning Kissinger's bitter remarks: 'Britain did not have to refuse permission because it was plain that the United States "should not ask" . . . [the allies were] acting as if the alliance does not exist.' The 1973 war evoked the awesome prospect of escalation beyond the region when the Soviet Union seemed to threaten to intervene to save the Egyptian army and the United States responded with a global nuclear alert – again without consulting its allies.

The consensus of the willing

After the Soviet invasion of Afghanistan in 1979, American President Jimmy Carter declared that the Gulf was a 'vital' American interest and that an assault on it would be 'repelled by any means necessary, including military force'. That idea was expanded by the Reagan administration. The Rapid Deployment Force (RDF) was ultimately turned into a full-fledged command, the Central Command (CentCom), located in Florida for want of Gulf locations. It does not 'own' forces but 'borrows' forces in crises, thus underscoring the link between out of area and Europe since any forces assigned to CentCom would otherwise be available for Europe. The RDF was derided as neither rapid, nor deployable, nor a force.[9] Yet it is far from clear that the epithet still applies – a point demonstrated by the response to Iraq's invasion of Kuwait.

The Europeans took the point that out-of-area issues mattered, at least because they did so to the United States. NATO's first Defence Planning Committee communiqué after Afghanistan, for example, said:

The stability of regions outside NATO boundaries, particularly in the South West Asia area, and the secure supply of essential commodities from this area are of crucial importance. Therefore, the current situation has serious implications for the security of member countries. The altered strategic situation in South West Asia warrants full solidarity and the strengthening of Allied cohesion as a response to the new challenges . . . It is in the interests of members of the Alliance that countries which are in a position to do so should use their best efforts to help achieve peace and stability in South West Asia.[10]

The key phrase was 'in a position to do so', the consensus of the willing and able. The language reflected what had been true since the beginning of NATO:

only a few countries were in a position to do much of anything outside Europe. But it also reflected new circumstances. NATO attempted, in its South-west Asia Impact Study, to come to grips with the need to offset possible diversions of American efforts to the Gulf.

Crises of the late 1970s and 1980s illustrated both the benefits and the limits of this 'consensus of the willing'. In the run-up to the American bombing of Libya in April 1986, for instance, the United States identified a problem and framed a response. The major European states agreed, more or less, with the identification of the problem but expressed reservations about the response; those nations then moved, over time, to take more action – although still less than the United States desired – as much from a desire to forestall an American military strike as from conviction that the action made sense; and in the end they got just the military strike they had feared.

During the inter-allied discussion over protecting Kuwaiti and other tankers during the Iran–Iraq war, Europeans were better at criticising than proposing: what, they asked, was the point of protecting the Kuwaiti tankers? More pointedly, why did the administration seem to be trying to pick a fight with Iran? To be fair, these questions were ones Europeans shared with American critics of the action, most notably in the Congress. Iranian attacks on tankers *en route* to or from Kuwait disrupted only one per cent of Gulf oil. Indeed, over the course of the Iran–Iraq war, Pentagon statistics recorded ninety-three Iranian attacks on Gulf shipping but 223 by Iraq. For their part, not surprisingly, it did not take long for Americans in Congress and elsewhere to ask what the Europeans were doing to help. Why not a multilateral force? After all, the oil supposedly being protected was pre-eminently that of the allies.

At the same time, the value of some cooperation, loosely organised among the 'willing', in military deployments beyond Europe was apparent well before the Iraqi invasion of Kuwait. The allies shared facilities in American use of British-owned Diego Garcia and British use of the American base at Ascension Island during the Falklands/Malvinas war. The United States airlifted French and Belgian troops into the Shaba region of Zaïre during 1978, suggesting that out-of-area cooperation need not be limited to the Gulf.

During the early stages of the Iran–Iraq war in 1980, the United States, France, Britain and others maintained a naval presence in the region. That served to deter any expansion of the war. Equally important, the multinational character of the presence diminished concerns of local states that would have been aroused by an American-only force – that it was, for instance, merely camouflage for an attack on Iran. In August 1984 the Egyptian and Saudi governments asked the United States, Britain, France, Italy and the Netherlands to mount minesweeping operations in the Gulf of Suez. In 1987–8 escort operations in the Gulf, originally begun by the United States at Kuwait's request, eventually came to involve ships from six NATO navies.

In all these cases the cooperation was military-to-military, much of it behind the scenes. The Europeans were thus able to skirt public opposition to any formalised 'allied' effort; for its part, France could retain its independence, insisting that any cooperation, especially with the United States, was great powers consulting as equals.

The multinational force (MNF) in Lebanon initially sent in the summer of 1982 by the United States, France and Italy, and redeployed in the autumn – that time also including a small British contingent – at first had some of the same virtues of quiet cooperation. For a time it contributed some stability to that ravaged country, though changing circumstances in Lebanon made the enterprise a disaster in the end, when huge bombs killed 241 American Marines and fifty-eight French in October 1983. Still, despite its chaotic end, the MNF episode provoked suprisingly few recriminations among the allies.

The MNF underscored one powerful European incentive to participate in military measures beyond Europe: it gave them a claim to share in American decision-making. The MNF foreign ministers met frequently at the margins of other meetings, and working groups of civilian and military officials produced guidelines for allied action and provided a discreet opportunity to air differences. In other cases the incentive was more negative: Europeans have felt compelled to support American policies they did not particularly like lest they be excluded altogether from decisions, thus running the risk of American policies they like even less. That was the case during the 1986 American confrontation with Libya and earlier during the Iranian hostage crisis when most of the Europeans went along in some measure, albeit reluctantly, with American-sponsored economic sanctions against Iran. (In both cases, Europeans did get what they liked even less – military action.)

Germany: from non-role to role

From the beginning the Federal Republic shunned involvements beyond Europe. West Germany's constitution, its Basic Law, was drafted to permit the country to join NATO.[11] The language is not so restrictive, but its interpretation came to be that German forces could be deployed only for NATO purposes and thus only within NATO's territorial limits. The restraint was a legacy of World War II, imposed by the victors but now deeply embedded in the politics of the vanquished. With unification came agreement across the political spectrum that if this practice were to be changed, even to permit German participation in UN peacekeeping, changing the Basic Law would be required.

There was a certain irony in the German position in that West Germany had been the beneficiary of events out of area. The Korean War, the stimulus to convert NATO from a security guarantee into a military alliance, settled the debate over German rearmament by enhancing the value of those prospective armed Germans. Once armed and admitted to NATO, however, West Germany's founding father, Konrad Adenauer, expressed the concerns echoed by his successors: Germany could neither afford the risk of 'guilt by association' involved in out-of-area ventures nor of diverting energy from Europe.

Accordingly, Adenauer argued that the French decision, in March 1956, to move 200,000 soldiers from the central front to Algeria was a threat to German security, and he was blunt in criticising Britain and France a few months later for their Suez invasion. By the same token, when American and British troops transited West German bases *en route* to Lebanon and Jordan in 1958, the chancellor's office expressed

regret for the gaps in the treaties with the West that permit forces to fly into and over the country at their pleasure . . . [and] . . . the lack of a common constructive political policy for the future, not only in the Middle East but also in Africa and Asia.[12]

Similarly, in the 1960s when Lyndon Johnson gently asked Adenauer's successor as chancellor, Ludwig Erhard, whether Germany might contribute soldiers to Vietnam, he got the ritual negatives. Deploying the *Bundeswehr* (German armed forces) 'beyond the zone of German defence', Erhard apparently said, would contravene the 'spirit' of the German Basic Law.[13]

Germany became a part of the out-of-area history only with the 1973 war.[14] All America's NATO allies save Portugal refused to allow the United States to resupply Israel during the war through American bases on their territory. Germany permitted resupply for a time but apparently through inadvertence; when it learned what was afoot, it, too, refused the United States permission to use German bases for Middle-East purposes.[15]

The only time the Germans themselves used military – paramilitary, to be precise – force outside Europe during the 1970s was in 1977. Twenty-six members of the West German anti-terrorist squad, GSG-9, aided by two British Special Air Services soldiers, rescued a Lufthansa airliner controlled by hijackers at Mogadishu airport in Somalia.

Interestingly, one other West German out-of-area venture, its participation in the five-nation UN Contact Group over Namibia, was not an outgrowth of its earlier colonial past. Rather, the Federal Republic just happened to be serving a term on the Security Council when the issue of Namibian independence arose, and so was a 'Western member' by convenient chance. After completing its term, however, it stayed on the Contact Group until the latter's demise in 1983,[16] it was not a major player in the group.

The Federal Republic's special stake in East–West relations in Europe was apparent in the aftermath of Afghanistan and continued to be evident. One example of the special, and particularly delicate, German relations eastward was Bonn's practice of buying East Germans their freedom. Between 1964 and 1989, 33,000 East German political prisoners and their families were released in return for indirect payments that started at about $10,000 per head and ended at around $60,000; the payments were deliberately calculated not to be a round number and so to look less like a charge per head.[17]

For the Federal Republic more so than for other European states, events in the Middle East or elsewhere were viewed through the lens of Europe. In the aftermath of the Soviet invasion of Afghanistan in 1979, for example, German and other European officials constantly echoed the view that the Soviet invasion was a grave matter and that the West had to react strongly. Yet another view of the threat, although seldom explicit, broke through the surface of the debate. According to that view, Afghanistan mattered but did not change the basic East–West balance. Soviet weaknesses remained. Besides, the invasion owed something to Western policy: to signals of disinterest in the fate of Afghanistan after the April 1978 coup and to America's inability to provide much by way of positive incentives for Soviet restraint in Soviet–American *détente*, for instance by getting SALT II ratified.

This view also stressed the interest in protecting European *détente* even in a time of superpower tension, an obvious reflection of the different stakes between Europe and America. The West should not be the first to import tension into Europe from outside it.[18] As Hans Apel, then the West German defence minister, put it in 1982, the American effort in south-west Asia 'must not jeopardize the balance of forces in Europe. For Europe, the stability of East–West relations is the foundation of its security. The global commitment of the

United States and regional stability in Central Europe must be harmonized with each other'.[19]

So, American requests and German responses focused not on what Germany could do to help in Asia but rather on how its actions might compensate in Europe for the diversion of American efforts. That turned out to be hard enough. Providing more reserve forces for European contingencies ran into German demographics. Germans came to worry, as they and the other Europeans had during Vietnam, that American attentions were being too diverted by south-west Asia.

Bonn did agree in principle to let the United States overfly German territory or use German bases for out-of-area contingencies. But permission would be case-by-case, not automatic: shades of 1973. The most visible fruit of this debate was the 1982 wartime Host Nation Support Agreement, in which Bonn agreed to build up support and rearguard security if American forces in Europe were redeployed to south-west Asia. In return, the United States committed additional forces to the rapid reinforcement of Germany in the event of a war with the Warsaw Pact.

There was some internal debate over changing the interpretation of the Basic Law, at least to permit German participation in UN peacekeeping activities. Even that, however, ran into Germany's sensitivities, its general disinclination to be seen as interested in too wide a role, and its specific concern lest German soldiers confront Israelis during peacekeeping operations. German criticism of American out-of-area actions, like the air raid on Libya in April 1986, was, however, relatively restrained.

The other line of German response was to increase its foreign aid and target it on countries of particular strategic interest – Greece, Turkey and Portugal. By the mid-1980s German development assistance came to 2.6 per cent of the federal budget – twice the percentage of the United States – and included contributions to Egypt, the Sudan and Pakistan.

As the 1987–8 escort operations in the Gulf expanded to become a major effort in allied cooperation, Germany stretched the limits of its self-imposed restraint. While stressing to its partners in the Western European Union (WEU) that it could not deploy forces beyond Europe, it sent several warships to the eastern Mediterranean to fill in for the forces of other navies diverted to the Gulf.

Out of area after the cold war

The 1990 Iraqi invasion of Kuwait was the first post-cold war out-of-area crisis. It seemed to suggest that, between the United States and its Western European allies at least, not so much had changed as met the eye. For all the talk of American decline and European resurgence, when push came to shove, only the United States could put together a military response. Britain tagged along, as did France, more slowly. Indeed, the episode first seemed to suggest that, if anything, the only change was that the United States no longer had any competition as a superpower; the Soviet Union followed the American lead, first cautiously then openly.

The invasion caught Germany in the middle of reunification. It was just in the process of agreeing to some $7.5 billion in assistance to the Soviet Union – the 'bill' for Soviet acquiescence to unification. And so it was slow to respond in the usual way, with money not military force. The contrast between generosity for Moscow and niggardliness for Washington was not lost on members of the American Congress.

Accordingly, Bonn expanded its role, first providing $280 million to those countries hardest hit by the UN embargo on trade with Iraq and several minesweepers to the eastern Mediterranean, then adding a number of civilian planes and ships to ferry other nations' troops and supplies to the region. Eventually, its total support was reckoned to be around $2 billion, including Germany's share of EC assistance. Chancellor Kohl openly called for changing the constitution, or at least the prevailing interpretation of it:

The current situation on the basis of our Constitution is in no circumstances bearable for the future. I know there are different opinions here [in Germany], but we must not allow the situation . . . if the judgment around the world was that if there is money to be made they're here, but if the issue [is] taking responsibility, they evade it.[20]

Because it caught Germany in such special circumstances, the most recent instance is no sure guide to future German behaviour out of area. The Kuwait invasion and subsequent war does seem, however, to confirm the Middle East and Gulf as the critical area 'out of area'.

In the Middle East, the stakes of all the allies are greater. So are the risks of political divisions among them. For instance, Europeans are more dependent on Gulf oil than the United States, though the difference is less than it was a decade ago. The United States and its major European allies all depend on oil for slightly under half their total energy requirements – 42 per cent for the United States, and 44 per cent for the Federal Republic.[21] However, virtually all of Germany's oil is imported, while about half of America's is, a percentage that has been rising. Gulf oil accounted for only six per cent of total American oil imports in 1985 but rose to 23 per cent in 1989 – primarily reflecting a big increase in Saudi imports but also a smaller one in Iraqi supplies. West Germany in 1989 took about the same percentage of its imports from the Gulf while France became more dependent on that region. Germany also took significant percentages from Algeria and Libya.

Unified Germany will need more imported oil, and given the world oil situation, that will mean more Gulf oil. East Germany had achieved its own brand of energy 'independence' but at the cost of ecological disaster. Based on not very reliable statistics, East Germany had reduced its dependence on imported energy to about 30 per cent of its consumption. Almost all its home-grown energy, however, was provided by lignite, which requires enormously scarring open-pit mines to acquire and whose sulphur made East Germany the world's leading polluter per capita.[22]

Oil accounted for 13 per cent of East German energy; four-fifths of that was imported from the Soviet Union through the Friendship pipeline. Those imports no doubt will continue, even increase despite stagnant oil production in the former Soviet Union, for a unified Germany will pay for oil in hard currency; the Soviet Union had been providing 8 per cent of West German oil imports. But as oil becomes more important in eastern Germany's energy balance, that oil will be pre-eminently from the Gulf.

As oil prices declined in the 1980s, attention to the Gulf waned, especially in the United States. Indeed, a cynic (or a Marxist) would point to oil prices as the key determinant of attention, or lack thereof, to security issues in the Gulf. No doubt attention will increase with oil prices in the 1990s. If the Europeans remain more dependent on imported oil – particularly oil imported from the Middle East and Gulf – than the United States, that should make them even more attentive to threats to the supply of Gulf oil, hence more prepared to take action to address those threats. Or so Americans will be tempted to believe; they have before.

On the other hand, the invasion of Kuwait was a case in point of how little the Europeans can do about military threats in the Gulf. That is especially so for Germany and will remain the case if the constitution is changed to permit German participation in UN peacekeeping. Germany, like other Europeans, will be tempted to try carrots instead of sticks, hoping to curry special favour with oil producers. Such was French policy after 1973, a policy that irritated the United States, but was not necessarily irrational from France's perspective.[23] In the past, Europeans, Germans included, have been tugged into action by the United States lest American sentiments lead to retaliation, perhaps by reducing American forces in Europe. With the end of the cold war, both that (implicit) threat and its cost to Europeans and Germans if carried out are lessened.

A particular feature of German policy in the region is the West German relationship to Israel, one which merits being called 'special'. In that sense it is the European connection to Israel most akin to that of the United States. There is no need to rehearse it in detail in this chapter.[24] Suffice to say that in the early years after 1952 the connection gave Germany moral approval when it was doubted and Israel's standing was high. Later, Germany from time to time risked its relations with other nations, especially in the Arab world, on behalf of Israel. Until 1965 its unilateral transfers to Israel were greater than those of any country, and after 1966 it gave more development aid to Israel per capita than to any other nation.

Chancellor Helmut Kohl's inaugural address in 1983 outlined the special relationship:

Our policy in the Middle East is based on respect for the legitimate interests of all peoples and countries in the region, some of them in conflict with one another. In addition, we are particularly attached to Israel and we support Israel's right to live in freedom and security. We will intensify our friendly relations with Israel and we will expand our traditional friendship with the Arab world. Together with the United States and our European partners, we will help to bring about a settlement of the Middle East conflict. Our policy on the Middle East is based on Israel's right to existence, the right of the Palestinian people to self-determination and the principle of mutual renunciation of force.[25]

To be sure, the tone of the relationship has changed with personalities. In the late 1970s and early 1980s, the then chancellor, Helmut Schmidt, tangled openly and sharply with Israeli Prime Minister Menachem Begin. With the arrival of Kohl the rhetoric returned to friendlier language.

Beneath the changes in tone, however, the relationship seemed to be growing more distant, even before German unification, as the distance from the Holocaust grew; and with time the memories of what had brought the two countries together initially became dimmer in the mind of the body politic.

Moreover, as West Germany became a major power, it had less need for the moral approval of its link with Israel; and as Israel's actions eroded its own moral position, that approval became less valuable.

The West German press, like its counterparts in Britain and France, is basically pro-Arab, whereas Israel's friends, like those in the United States, avoid public statements of opposition while making their views known privately to their Israeli counterparts. A February 1983 Allensbach poll hinted at a growing distance in German–Israeli relations, but it should be remembered that the poll came in the wake of the Israeli massacres at the Sabra and Shatila refugee camps in Lebanon the previous summer. Fifty-two per cent of respondents agreed with the following: 'We should not place our good relations with Israel above all else. The Arab countries are important for our oil needs. Therefore, we should not become enemies of these countries on Israel's account.' Only 18 per cent agreed with the opposite statement: 'It is still important today for the Federal Republic to attend to its especially friendly relationship with Israel. We have brought on ourselves too much guilt concerning the Jews.'[26]

To be sure, West German attitudes toward Israel are ambivalent. Criticism of and support for Israel co-exist. In the same poll, a majority believed the Palestinians should have their own state, while a plurality opposed recognising the Palestine Liberation Organization (PLO).

Similarly, the West German government both strongly condemned Israeli actions in Lebanon *and* acted within the European Community (EC) to temper concrete retaliations. The EC called the original Israeli invasion 'a flagrant violation of international law and of the most basic humanitarian principles'.[27] Bonn, however, argued against a French proposal for economic sanctions, and the resulting EC action – postponing several measures of EC–Israeli cooperation – were relatively mild, too mild for the Arab states. After the refugee camp massacres, the EC expressed 'profound shock and revulsion', but did not take new retaliatory measures.

On the surface, a unified Germany should be more self-confident, more willing to express its national interests and one step further removed from Nazi guilt. It is therefore likely to distance itself further from Israel, or, put more precisely, the tug of the Israeli connection should be less of a constraint in dealing with Middle-East issues. That does seem the safest bet.

At the same time, however, beneath the surface the conflicting currents of opinion will continue to run. On this issue as others, exactly how they will be affected by the addition of eastern German politics is hard to foresee. On one hand, those eastern politics have been suffused by none of the special connections to Israel of their western counterpart – quite the contrary. On the other, having been artificially absolved of Nazi guilt for forty years, eastern Germans will now discover it as they work their way through their recent history.

The new Germany out of area

In one respect a unified Germany will surely behave differently with regard to out-of-area issues: it will not have an eastern half competitively undermining it. In the 1970s East Germany replaced Czechoslovakia as the most important supplier of military support to friendly developing countries. Most of this support was in the form of providing training for military and intelligence services, not arms.[28] Such support as well as the East German aid to and sanctuary for terrorists will also end. This will be in line with other Eastern European states, most notably Czechoslovakia, producer of the plastic explosive Semtex, which the country's new president, Vaclav Havel, stated had been shipped to Libya between 1974 and 1981.[29] Before unification, Germany had already begun unravelling links between the former East German government and terrorists, especially the home-grown Red Army Faction.[30]

More generally, if a 'Big' Germany is more assertive in the future, as seems predictable, it will also behave more like a great power. It will be less of a freerider on existing structures, less able to call itself a mere trading nation. In that connection, the case of the Libyan chemical plant at Rabta, outside Tripoli, is instructive.

At the end of the Reagan administration, American officials charged that German corporations had assisted Gaddafi in building the plant. Kohl at first responded defensively, denying firm evidence of German complicity. By mid-January 1990, however, it did emerge that loopholes in German laws and export controls had permitted several German firms to collaborate in the plant. Still more embarrassing to the Kohl government was the assertion by the head of German intelligence Hans-Georg Wieck that his service had evidence against the corporations that would stand up in court and had had it for six months before the dispute with Washington came out into the open.

The official German report on the incident, released to the Bundestag on 15 February 1990, indicated that Kohl and Foreign Minister Hans-Dietrich Genscher had not been informed of the German companies' role until May 1988. But the government, including Genscher's foreign office, had known of possible participation by one company as early as 1985, while intelligence had vague reports of Libya's intention to build a chemical weapons plant with German help in 1980.[31]

The government promised tougher laws and more overseers. But the implications of the affair ran far beyond chemicals and Libya. Business was business and, it seemed, none of the government's business. On paper, the Federal Republic has stringent constraints on weapons exports, barring them to 'areas of tension'. In fact, the constraints have been diminished, sometimes for explicit foreign policy reasons, such as the sales to Saudi Arabia. But arms and weapons-related technology have seeped through owing to loopholes in the categories or lax supervision: for instance sales of submarine blueprints to South Africa in 1984–5; ammunition for Iran in 1987 (stopped at the last minute); or 1989 reports that German companies had helped Libya with mid-air refuelling technology.

That pattern seems likely to change in the new Germany, if perhaps not fast enough to suit the United States. More generally, Germany will be less able to plead 'special limitations' of constitution or history when crises arise and joint action seems indicated. It will have much less by way of specific stakes in German people or a German state in Eastern Europe. And so it will be less able to argue that confrontations should be muted out of area for fear they will poison East–West relations inside Europe.

There are not that many ethnic Germans left in Eastern Europe or the Soviet Union after the large migrations of recent years – 400,000 in 1990 excluding

East Germans who crossed to the West. Those remaining in Europe's east are estimated to number some three million, with the largest single group, those in the lands of the former Soviet Union, accounting for two-thirds of that total. Many of those, moreover, like the ethnic Germans in Poland, are more and more marginal in their 'German' ethnicity. They are more economic migrants than returning diaspora.

The new Germany will remain fixed in Europe, and it is likely to become more and more entangled in Eastern Europe, whether it likes it or not. For it, as for the other European countries, new waves of immigrants, from the east but also from the south, will test its homogeneous society. But those entanglements will be unrelated to most crises in the Middle East and the Gulf.

On the other hand, Germany will have less to fear by way of American responses to perceptions that Germany is not doing enough. It will be able to say 'no' if it chooses and will do so with less reticence than in the past. The greater responsibility will more than balance the greater willingness to say 'no'. Officials of allied countries, especially the United States, will not always see it that way; German decisions will be made with a degree of table-thumping that is more characteristic of older German history than of the postwar Federal Republic.

For the near future, any out-of-area military crisis in the heavily armed Middle East and Gulf will be dominated by the United States. In the short term, Germany will not have much to contribute militarily. It will remain constrained by its inhibitions in the use of force long after the change in the constitution. That inhibition will be enhanced by the remnants of the special relationship with Israel. No German politician will want to countenance the prospect of German soldiers confronting Israelis.

The Gulf War: the German response

The broader challenge of out-of-area crises was demonstrated by the Iraqi invasion of Kuwait and the Gulf war. The war in the Gulf was like pressing the 'fast forward' button on a video player: it sharpened the trends and highlighted the ambiguities in German politics identified above. The timing could not have been worse, competing with the immediate domestic pressures of unification and preoccupation with the forthcoming German election. German leaders first acted as if they thought there was an implicit trans-Atlantic 'deal' – that Germany would take care of Eastern Europe and the Soviet Union while America tended the Gulf.

Belatedly, Germany recognised the importance of the Gulf – not least to George Bush who had staked his presidency on it – and provided significant financial assistance, nearly $11.4 billion. This consisted of $9.7 billion in military hardware, services and cash payments to the allied coalition and Israel, and $1.7 billion in economic assistance to Egypt, Turkey, Jordan and other neighbouring Arab states. About $5.5 billion of this was earmarked for the United States. Germany also sent Patriot missiles to Israel and 'Fox' chemical warfare detection vehicles to the coalition in Saudi Arabia.

Bonn followed the UN resolution for a total embargo against Iraq and worked throughout the crisis to close remaining loopholes. Germany was also committed to the American presence in the Gulf and aware that military force was an option; it, like the other Europeans, gave Washington permission to use European bases and European-based troops for Gulf purposes.

In early January 1991, Turkey, a NATO ally, asked for treaty protection against Iraq. Bonn/Berlin responded clumsily, treating its allies to a Bundestag debate over whether Iraqi Scud missiles were a threat under the treaty and whether Turkey had somehow provoked the threat by letting coalition aircraft use its bases for attack on Iraq. In the end, though, Germany did send planes, eighteen Alpha jets and several hundred German personnel. Its participation in postwar relief efforts among the Kurds in Turkey and Iran was another sign of a widening German role.

Had the war been longer and bloodier, there would have been more arguments in the Congress against spilling 'American blood for European oil'. There would also have been more awkwardness over Germany's past role as a source of technology for Iraq: how could a nation whose citizens wait patiently for the little green man to appear on a street-crossing signal not be able to prevent lethal exports to Libya or Iraq?

In addition to hastening Germany's enactment of laws and processes to stop 'suspect' exports, thus assuming the responsibilities of a 'normal' country, the war intensified the debate about 'out-of-area' issues both within Germany and in Europe. The possibility of a military role 'out of area' continued to be a divisive issue politically, and the debate remained confused. The Christian Democratic government first agreed with the Social Democratic opposition that a change in the constitution was required. It then altered tack, fearing that the opposition would have its way, and the change would limit Germany's role beyond Europe to 'blue helmets' – UN peacekeeping – an even more restrictive situation than the current state of affairs.

So, too, the war underscored the need for Germany to play a role in European approaches out of area more commensurate with its weight, but solutions have remained elusive. The idea, for instance, of a European rapid reaction force, perhaps under the Western Europe Union (WEU), to which Germany might contribute once its constitutional disposition changed, has remained in the air. The Bush administration has seen this as the beginning of a slippery slope to an EC role in defence and has been engineering a NATO rapid reaction force – thus subject to NATO's restrictions of geography. The one sure bet is that neither the issues nor the debate will soon go away.

Notes

1. Bismarck used this line first in 1876 and repeated it often; later 'grenadier' replaced 'musketeer'. Quoted in A.J.P. Taylor, *Bismarck: The Man and the Statesman*, New York, Knopf, 1955, p.167.
2. See Woodruff D. Smith, *The German Colonial Empire*, Chapel Hill, University of North Carolina Press, 1978.
3. Speech to the Reichstag, 18 June 1901. He repeated the line in July 1908 as 'Germany must have her place in the sun'.
4. This limitation is in Article 6 of the North Atlantic Treaty.
5. For background, see Ernst-Otto Czempiel, 'Germany and the Third World: the Politics of Free Trade and the Free Hand', in Wolfram F. Hanrieder (ed.), *West German Foreign Policy 1949–1979*, Boulder, Westview Press, 1980; and Elizabeth Thompson,

'Mirror of a Century of Afrikapolitik', in Peter H. Merkl (ed.), *West German Foreign Policy: Dilemmas and Directions*, Chicago, Chicago Council on Foreign Relations, 1982.

6. See, for instance, my edited volume, *Europe, America and South Africa*, New York, Council on Foreign Relations, 1988.

7. For the Lovett quote and more detail, see Alan K. Hendrikson, 'The Creation of the North Atlantic Alliance, 1948–1952', *Naval War College Review*, **32**, No. 3, 1980.

8. *The Troubled Partnership*, New York, McGraw-Hill, 1965, p.9.

9. For a variety of early perspectives on the RDF and its possible mission, see Jeffrey Record, *The RDF and U.S. Military Intervention in the Persian Gulf*, Cambridge, Mass., Institute for Foreign Policy Analysis, 1981; Congressional Budget Office, *RDF: Policy and Budgetary Implications*, Washington DC, 1983; Joshua M. Epstein, 'Soviet Vulnerabilities in Iran and the RDF Deterrent', *International Security*, **6**, No. 2, 1981, pp.126–58; and Kenneth N. Waltz, 'A Strategy for the RDF', *International Security*, **5**, No. 4, 1981, pp.49–73.

10. 13–14 May 1980.

11. Article 24 says the nation 'may join a system of mutual collective security . . . which will bring about and secure a peaceful and lasting order, in Europe and among the nations of the world'.

12. Quoted in *The Economist*, 26 July 1958, p.301.

13. See Catherine Kelleher, 'The Defense Policy of the Federal Republic of Germany', in Douglas Murray and Paul Viotti (eds), *The Defense Policies of Nations: A Comparative Study*, Baltimore, Johns Hopkins University Press, 1982, p.293.

14. That is evident from two recent books on the out-of-area issue; West Germany figures only slightly in both books and then only after 1973. See Douglas T. Stuart and William T. Tow, *The Limits of Alliance: NATO Out-of-Area Problems Since 1949*, Baltimore, Johns Hopkins University Press, 1990; and Elizabeth D. Sherwood, *Allies in Crisis: Meeting Global Challenges to Western Security*, New Haven, Yale University Press, 1990.

15. See Sherwood, *Allies in Crisis*, p.139.

16. For background on the Contact Group, see A.W. Singham and Shirley Hune, *Namibian Independence: A Global Responsibility*, Westport, Lawrence Hill & Co, 1986.

17. The figure was released by the interim non-communist East German government in July 1990. See the *New York Times*, 1 August 1990.

18. See, for example, the articles by Theo Sommer in *Die Zeit*, 22 and 29 February, and 27 June 1980.

19. Quoted in Sherwood, *Allies in Crisis*, p.173.

20. As quoted in the *New York Times*, 10 September 1990.

21. Cambridge Energy Research Associates, *World Oil Trends, 1988–89*, p.20.

22. See Vladimir Baum, 'Marriage of Opposites', *Petroleum Economist*, July 1990, pp.16–19.

23. For more discussion, see Robert J. Lieber, 'Economics, Energy and Security in Alliance Perspective', *International Security*, **4**, No. 4 , 1980, pp.139–63.

24. See Chapter 5, and also Lily Gardner Feldman, *The Special Relationship between West Germany and Israel*, Boston, Allen and Unwin, 1984.

25. Cited in ibid., p.xiii.

26. Institute für Demoskopie, *Allensbacher Jahrbuch der Demoskopie, 1978–1983, Band VIII*, Munich, K.G. Saur, 1983, p.648.

27. This and the subsequent EC statement quoted in Feldman, *Allies in Crisis*, p.xi.

28. Roger E. Kanet, 'East European States', in Thomas H. Henrikson (ed.), *Communist Powers and Sub-Saharan Africa*, Stanford, Hoover Institute, 1981, p.44.

29. See the *New York Times*, 6 April 1990.

30. For background, see 'Die terroristische Vereinigung', in *Die Zeit*, 29 June 1990.

31. The report is summarised in the *Wall Street Journal*, 16 February 1990.

4 Germany and the Middle-East conflict

Helmut Hubel

One hundred and twenty years after 1871, German unification has taken place for a second time. What Imperial Chancellor Bismarck achieved through 'blood and iron' (Prussia's military victory over France) and an undemocratic 'revolution from above', Federal Chancellor Kohl managed to accomplish under exceptional international circumstances – the collapse of the Stalinist system in the Soviet Union and the peaceful revolution in East Germany – and through the determined, skilful diplomacy of his Foreign Minister, Genscher, backed by the prosperous West German economy. All Europeans were winners at the end of the cold war, among them the East Germans who became free, after decades, to determine their future. They chose a united Germany. The Wall and the Iron Curtain had divided both Germany and Europe. Therefore, unification of Germany is an integral part of European unification.

Since Bismarck, Germany's weight and central location in Europe has posed particular challenges. Like the 'iron chancellor', any German leader has to use all his skills to reconcile unified Germany with the existing European system by credibly reassuring her neighbours. The major difference and decisive advantage for Germany in the late twentieth century is that the Federal Republic, including the 'new Eastern Bundesländer' (federal states), is an integral part of the West – its economic, military, political and cultural structures. At the same time, because of her proximity to and historical engagement in East Europe, including the former Soviet Union, united Germany will regard the development of all European structures – a genuine 'European home' – as her special mission.

Bismarck's strategic orientation was to secure Germany's place in Europe by deflecting her rivals' ambitions towards the 'Third World'. In the age of imperialism and during the gradual breakdown of the Ottoman Empire, French, British and Russian energies were to be consumed particularly in the Middle East.[1] As a consequence, Bismarck did not try to acquire major colonies.[2] Only during the rule of Emperor Wilhelm II did Germany try seriously – an endeavour which contributed to World War I.

What role will a late-twentieth-century unified Germany play outside Europe? Since the game is no longer about conquering foreign territories but rather safeguarding raw materials and export markets *vis-à-vis* sovereign states and maintaining stability in an interdependent world, Germany as a 'civilian power' cannot afford to neglect crucial regions such as the Middle East. But what does this general interest mean for her attitudes and behaviour toward the oldest and most troublesome conflict of this region – the Israelis' and Palestinians' rivalry over the same land and the problem of Israel's existence in the Arab–Islamic world?

41

Any assessment of future German attitudes should be based upon past experience. After summarising the lessons of history, I shall investigate the impact of unification on these factors. First, I shall discuss the basic determinants shaping the Federal Republic's perceptions and behaviour toward the Palestine conflict. I shall try to demonstrate that there is no particular policy but rather a set of norms leading to typical behaviour which is fundamentally moulded by the legacy of Germany's recent past: Hitler's genocide of European Jews and the postwar division of Germany. This behaviour is also the consequence of two 'special relationships' the Federal Republic managed to build – with Israel and the United States.

Second, I shall briefly discuss the GDR's role under communist rule and the changes which have taken place since November 1989. Finally, I shall explore the possible impact of the two unification processes in Europe on Germany's future role in the Arab–Israeli conflict.

In my final analysis I shall argue that Bismarck's basic problem and parts of his solution will remain. Preoccupied with herself and Europe, a united Germany will no longer be a 'political dwarf' in world politics but will remain a 'splendid isolationist' in the Middle-East conflict.

The Federal Republic and the Middle-East conflict

The Federal Republic was a child of the cold war. Bonn's major purpose, particularly in the 1950s and 1960s, was to liquidate the consequences of Hitler's war: to return Germany to the ranks of the civilised nations, to regain (West) German sovereignty through integration with the West and to overcome the division of the country (a goal which, in all honesty, many West Germans no longer cared about in the 1980s). Chancellor Adenauer managed to pursue the two principal goals by providing material compensation to those Jews who had survived and granting economic and military aid to Israel from 1952.[3] These initiatives were primarily driven by a moral imperative. Adenauer recognised that a new beginning was possible only after publicly recognising German guilt.[4] Nonetheless, *Realpolitik* certainly played a role. Aid to the Jewish survivors of the Holocaust and to the young state of Israel made a favourable impression on important American decision-makers who, in turn, supported badly needed credits for West Germany's own recovering economy.

The special relationship between West Germany and Israel which has evolved under these particular conditions is, on the one hand, the consequence of a century-old common history and many human, cultural–religious and political bonds.[5] The special relationship is nurtured, on the other hand, by a grave moral predicament which many Germans sense even today. Ashamed by what Germans did during the 1930s and World War II, many Germans – politicians, business leaders, journalists, and 'people on the street' – developed a special feeling of responsibility for the state of Israel.[6] Many founding members of the Jewish state, who were predominantly European, responded favourably. Some Israeli leaders (certainly not all) have shown an inclination to exploit this situation for concrete political purposes.[7] In German–Israeli relations the memory of human crimes and *Realpolitik* continue to coexist in an uneasy manner.

This special relationship complements the other central relationship the

Federal Republic has managed to establish. Vitally dependent on the American military presence and its nuclear guarantees, Bonn traditionally has sought to avoid any serious disagreement with Washington. Since pro-Israeli sentiments and policies in the United States were established fact, Bonn's support of Israel fitted in well. Gestures, let alone policies, which contradicted principles of American Middle-Eastern policy did not.

At first glance then, the Federal Republic's support for Israel seems unequivocal, but in reality the factors impinging upon Bonn's Middle-Eastern policies are more complex. First, the perennial volatility of the Middle East only compounded West Germany's vulnerability as a front-line state between East and West, facing, as it did, nearly 400,000 Soviet soldiers in the GDR. In addition, the United States' European Command (USEUCOM), based in West Germany, was responsible for Israel, Syria, and Lebanon.[8] Thus, American–Soviet confrontation in the Middle East might have spilled over and directly affected German security. West German decision-makers, therefore, viewed the problem of a potential 'horizontal escalation' – as it was called in the early 1980s – with particular concern. Bonn tried to deal with this problem, particularly during the 1967 and 1973 wars, by claiming neutrality.

Second, there was the imbalance between Israel and her numerous Arab neighbours. Bonn could not ignore the behaviour of the members of the Arab League in international organisations, particularly because West Germany was engaged, in the 1950s and 1960s, in a diplomatic struggle with the GDR over the claim to represent all Germans (the so-called '*Alleinvertretungsanspruch*'). Many Arab leaders regarded Germany, the former rival of the colonial powers in the Middle East and a traditional economic and cultural partner, as a 'natural ally'.[9] They were, therefore, all the more furious when they learned about secret West German weapons' deliveries to Israel. In 1965 ten (of the then thirteen) Arab States severed diplomatic relations with Bonn. Moreover, in 1969 many of them recognised the GDR – an obvious breakdown of Bonn's '*Alleinvertretungsanspruch*' and an indication of how much Arab–West German relations had deteriorated. Only between 1971 and 1974, after the Brandt–Scheel government abandoned the claim to represent all Germans[10] and West Germany halted arms deliveries to Israel, were political relations resumed.

As a consequence of these diverging responsibilities and interests, Bonn has pursued a characteristically cautious policy towards the Palestine conflict. When Israel was proclaimed and Arab states attacked the Jewish state in 1948, the Federal Republic was not yet established. In 1956, during the Suez crisis, Bonn's attention was absorbed by the Soviet intervention in Hungary. Moreover, the Suez crisis resulted in grave tensions between Bonn's new allies: the United States on one side and France and Great Britain on the other.

During the 1967 war West German sentiments were essentially pro-Israeli, while the official position of the government can be characterised as 'benevolent neutrality'. Shortly before Israel's pre-emptive strike and the six days of hostilities, the Federal Republic decided to respond favourably to Tel Aviv's urgent request and delivered 20,000 gas masks to the Jewish state.[11] In the media the war and its outcome was largely characterised as a fabulous victory like the Biblical fight of David against Goliath.[12]

The primary impetus for the shift in West German diplomacy toward a more 'balanced approach' was provided by the two oil crises of the 1970s and the combined West European efforts to deal with their consequences. Although there had been a growing awareness of West Germany's energy dependence[13] since the late 1960s, Bonn, like the other European capitals, was taken by surprise when the Arab states decided to use oil deliveries as a 'political weapon' in 1973.

The change in German perceptions was less the result of actual Arab black-mail – only the Netherlands had to face a reduction of supplies -- than of a growing awareness that cheap energy supplies could no longer be taken for granted and that economic and social aspects were integral parts of security.[14] Nevertheless, relations with oil-rich countries had to be improved on all levels; therefore, the Palestinian problem, a concern of all Arabs, had to be taken more seriously.

Since West Germany was basically in the same boat as the other EC and OECD members, she did not seek a national answer. Together with the United States and other West Europeans – except France which tried to secure her energy imports bilaterally – Bonn joined the International Energy Agency. The Federal Republic shared their basic aim which was to counter OPEC's cartel by joint consumer action.

Politically, Bonn also sought a multilateral framework. The European Political Cooperation (EPC), the foreign policy coordination instrument among the members of the European Community, was already established in December 1969. 'Speaking with one voice' was a logical consequence of West European economic integration. The economic and political challenge from the Middle East accelerated this process. It was no accident that cooperation on the Arab–Israeli conflict was one of the EPC's major topics. In 1971 the EPC produced the first declaration on the Middle-East conflict which was to be followed by many others. The Federal Republic shared the general desire of France and Great Britain to demonstrate a more active posture in foreign policy and followed their lead in using the West European framework to demonstrate more understanding for the Palestinian viewpoint.[15]

During the final stage of the 1973 October war Bonn was confronted with the discomfiting disclosure that the United States, without consultation, had used weapons stored on German soil for resupplying Israel. Shortly after the UN Security Council had ordered an Arab–Israeli ceasefire, Deputy Foreign Minister (*Staatssekretär*) Paul Frank told the American chargé d'affaires on 24 October that the Federal Republic had declared 'strict neutrality' in this war. It could not permit weapons' deliveries from its territory and 'assumed that US transfers had been concluded'.[16] This incident reminded the Germans that they could become involved, against their will, in a future major war in the Middle East.

The West Germans' search for a more 'balanced approach' ('*Ausgewogenheit*', as it was called) produced only verbal results. The Federal Republic was the first EC member to stress the Palestinian 'right of self-determination';[17] since the Federal Republic claimed 'self-determination' for all Germans, it could not logically refuse this 'right' to the Palestinians. Nevertheless, in subsequent declarations Bonn made the fulfilment of this principle more or less dependent on Israel's existence in 'secure borders'.[18] Although in 1981 Chancellor Schmidt and others claimed that the Germans bore historical responsibility not only toward the Jews and Israel but also toward the Palestinians – because it was Hitler's genocide which aggravated, to say the least, the Arab–Israeli conflict –[19] this argument did not lead to major political consequences.

During the 1970s and 1980s, relations with the PLO remained markedly low key. Unlike the French president, for example, no leading West German politician has ever met with Yassir Arafat or other high-ranking PLO officials.[20] In the discussions of the European Political Cooperation on the Middle-East conflict, Bonn sometimes saw its special mission as reconciling the quest for an 'independent European position' with the American approach and Israeli sensitivities. Whereas France, Greece and other Europeans did not hesitate to criticise the Camp David agreements and the Egyptian–Israeli peace treaty of 1979 as being insufficient and neglecting the crucial Palestinian problem, Bonn was careful not to offend anybody.

The famous Venice declaration of 13 June 1980 is illustrative of Bonn's 'mediating' role between the two positions. In this declaration, the West Europeans stressed the Palestinians' right of self-determination and the necessity to include the PLO in the negotiations on a peaceful settlement. However, in accordance with Bonn's suggestions, they also made sure not to contradict the United States directly or openly to criticise Israel.[21] The European initiative was not put to the test in reality; it remained declaratory. Its impotence was obvious when Israel annexed East Jerusalem on 30 July 1980, only a few weeks after 'Venice'.

Some months later, Western European determination was tested when the United States government and Israel asked for participation in the Multinational Force and Observers in the Sinai (MFO) which essentially meant to consolidate the Egyptian–Israeli peace under American leadership. France, Great Britain, Italy and the Netherlands participated. West Germany did not. Pointing to its Basic Law, which it interpreted to prohibit the presence of German troops 'outside NATO territory', Bonn declared itself unable to participate directly in any peace-keeping mission.[22]

Israel's war in Lebanon in 1982 took place without any concrete German reaction. For the same reason cited in the MFO case, Bonn did not participate in the American–West European Multinational Force (MNF, 1982–4). However, this war seemed to change German perceptions of Israel and the Palestinians. It was now all too obvious that the 'David' of 1967 had become 'Goliath'.[23] The Jewish state was no longer fighting for sheer survival, it was acting as a kind of regional superpower. However, this change in public perception did not have political consequences.

Because there was no threat of a new 'oil weapon', German–Arab trade was in decline, and Israel had lost her glorious reputation, there was virtually no pressure to conduct a more coherent and dynamic policy. Despite some attempts by German scholars and political foundations to contribute to the 'peace process' by promoting the Israeli–Palestinian dialogue, Bonn's attitude toward the conflict can be best characterised as 'benign neglect'.

The West German debate over arms' exports has been closely linked with the Arab–Israeli conflict. As mentioned above, secret German arms' deliveries to Israel in the early 1960s created a major diplomatic crisis with the Arab states. As a consequence, Bonn decided to tighten official export rules and not to deliver arms to 'zones of tension'. The test of this principle came in the early 1980s when Saudi Arabia asked for German Leopard II battle tanks. During the second oil crisis Saudi Arabia, by increasing her oil production and thus helping to keep the price explosion under control, was very responsive to Western needs. Bonn regarded West German–Saudi Arabian relations as crucial for safeguarding the Federal Republic's economic security. The Saudi Arabian leadership considered the Leopard II to be a 'test of friendship'.

Chancellor Schmidt, visiting the Kingdom in April 1981, seemed prepared to go along with the sale. He was supported by the business community and the majority of conservatives, including the head of the Bavarian Christian Social Union (CSU), Franz Josef Strauss. For the advocates, the sale was not only an important instrument for safeguarding German economic interests but also the symbol of a new, more independent role the Federal Republic was to play in world politics.

The proponents of the sale were opposed by a 'coalition' of different groups with various interests. The friends of the Jewish state, represented in all major political parties and supported by Israel's embassy in Bonn and a series of critical comments in the media, vigorously opposed the sale. These friends, who often joined the opponents of armament in general,[24] were particularly outspoken within the Social Democratic Party, Chancellor Schmidt's party. Foreign Minister Genscher, later chairman of the Liberals, opposed the sale as a matter of principle. Selling some of the most sophisticated technology would be a major revision of a policy which had stood the test of time; it would provoke a series of requests from other countries which would be difficult to refuse.[25] Chancellor Schmidt did not manage to push the sale through his own party. His successor Kohl, aware of the internal obstacles, did not fight for it.

Whereas official arms sales' policy did not change substantially,[26] statistics prove that West German arms sales to the Middle East were not insignificant. One rather spectacular case was the British sale of Tornado fighter aircraft to Saudi Arabia. Since more than a third of the plane's components are produced by German companies, the Federal Republic was involved. Politically, however, it was London which took the lead.

The Federal Republic has maintained a certain military relationship both with some Arab states and Israel. The Bundeswehr has been a customer for Israeli weapons, including firearms and sophisticated radar devices. Moreover, it was very interested in obtaining information on Soviet weapons, some of which were captured by the Israeli Defence Forces, for example from Syria during the 1982 Lebanon war. On the other hand, several German companies have been active in oil-rich Arab countries, building weapons factories and delivering components, for example to manufacture chemical weapons. The case of the Libyan chemical plant Rabta, built with the secret support of the German industrialist Hippenstiehl-Imhausen, is well known. German press reports have claimed that other German companies are involved in similar projects in countries such as Iraq. It was only after the Rabta scandal, which generated some friction with Washington and strong criticism from the American press, that on 1 July 1990 the Bundestag passed a law to tighten the control of sensitive export items.[27]

Whereas these cases demonstrate that West Germany, highly industrialised and very export-orientated, played a certain role in the Middle-Eastern arms market, they do not invalidate the basic conclusion that German arms sales were of rather negligible *political* significance. A comparison with French arms sales to the Middle East, for example,[28] would prove this thesis in detail.

To sum up: West Germany's attitude towards the Arab–Israeli conflict was determined by two special relationships – with Israel and the United States. The Federal Republic's strategy to deal with the repercussions of this conflict was basically twofold. Diplomatically, the European Political Cooperation provided Bonn with an 'evenhanded' declaratory approach which did not commit it to concrete action.[29] Economically, Bonn was anxious to promote trade relations while working actively toward a reduction of West German dependency on 'Arab oil'. Some arms sales took place, mainly because of economic interests.

The GDR's role in the Middle East

Germany's postwar division resulted in two different states and two principally opposed Middle-Eastern policies. Since the 1950s, the GDR's primary foreign policy goal had been to gain legitimacy. In order to fight the West German '*Alleinvertretungsanspruch*' (Bonn's claim to represent all Germans), East Berlin was anxious to develop contacts with the Third World, notably the Arab countries. In the Middle East, East Berlin did not have diplomatic relations with Israel. Unlike the Federal Republic, communist GDR officials never admitted any responsibility for German atrocities against the Jews. When the Soviet Union and its East European allies severed relations with Israel shortly after the 1967 war, East Berlin shared with them the same official 'non-relationship'.[30]

The GDR supported Israel's Arab enemies in close accordance with the policy of the Soviet Union and the other members of the Warsaw Treaty Organisation.[31] East German relations with the PLO were developed from the early 1970s. In 1973 (more than a year before the Arab Summit of Rabat!), the GDR recognised the PLO as the sole representative of the Palestinian people.[32] Like Moscow, East Berlin regarded relations with the Palestinian political representation as a means to promote its political influence in the Middle East. It made sure to balance its contacts with the PLO with other important relationships, with Syria, Iraq, and Libya. Depending on the often changing intra-Arab relationships, the GDR's political and material support was not unequivocal.

When in 1985 the new Soviet leadership under Gorbachev opened contacts with Israel, Hungary and Poland followed quickly. Characteristically, the Honecker regime did not react. It was only after the 'November revolution' that the new, democratic government decided to address the problem of relations with Israel. East Berlin first of all acknowledged responsibility for Germany's past and declared itself ready to talk about material compensation for the 'victims of Fascism'. On 12 April 1990 the East German parliament unanimously passed a resolution in which it asked 'the Jews of the world to forgive us'.[33] A few weeks later the GDR and Israel started negotiations on establishing diplomatic relations.[34] In this respect it was of symbolic importance that in late June 1990 Rita Süssmuth and Sabine Bergmann-Pohl, the Presidents of the two German parliaments, visited Israel together. Also in June 1990 the East German prime minister, Lothar de Mazière, met Jewish officials during his visit to the United States.

Thus, one of the first foreign policy initiatives of democratic GDR was to follow the early 1950s example of the Federal Republic – to demonstrate its good will to restore contacts with the Jewish people and to open relations with the state of Israel. There were no official comments on the Palestinians or the Arab states.

Unifying Germany and the Arab–Israeli conflict

The Federal Republic and the GDR were integral parts of the postwar system. The process of German unification marked the end of this period. However, not only Germany but Europe as a whole is unifying. Given the complexity of this process, it will take many years, probably decades. What will the consequences be for Germany's attitudes toward the Middle East in general and the Palestine conflict in particular?

First of all, any potential player has to take note of the basic change which has already taken place in American–Soviet relations. With the end of East–West confrontation, the Third World has lost its significance as a 'proxy theatre'. Its conflicts have always been, of course, primarily indigenous. However, the manner in which these confrontations took place was, to a considerable degree, shaped by superpower (and their respective allies) rivalry. Today, most regional conflicts of the 1980s have lost their international significance; they simply no longer 'disturb' superpower relations and world politics in general.

This qualitative change is evident in the Middle East where the former Soviet Union is no longer the 'natural ally' of the Arabs; American unconditional support of Israel is no longer beyond any doubt. The Western allies of the first superpower – the second 'super' power no longer has allies – no longer feel obliged to act in close cooperation. As a general rule, one could say that all players – if they are interested – are free to act according to their own preferences.

This general statement, however, is valid only as long as tensions in the region can be kept under control. If one of the simmering conflicts should again escalate to a military confrontation, most West Europeans would once again be inclined to act in close cooperation with the United States. Given the more devastating and longer-range weapons at the disposal of Israel and several Arab states, the Europeans and the countries of the former Soviet Union could be seriously affected by any new war.[35] On the other hand, if East and West would act in concert – if present circumstances continue – even a new Arab–Israeli war would not necessarily lead to renewed East–West tensions. International behaviour would more likely follow the example of the 1948 war rather than the military confrontations of 1967 and 1973. As a consequence, there would be less German concern about potential 'spill-over effects'.

The second basic observation relates to Europe. There, most energies will be absorbed by keeping the two processes of unification, Germany's and Europe's, in synchronisation. To alleviate her neighbours' apprehension and to bring German unification to a successful conclusion, Germany will have to invest considerable political energy and material support in European integration. If problems of military security continue to recede, the West Europeans will no longer fear increased dependency on Eastern European energy. On the contrary, Eastern European raw materials, to be paid with hard currency for world market prices, constitute the major item to be traded for West European technology and know-how. Germany, already receiving considerable quantities of natural gas, would be the most important partner. Increased energy deliveries could be all the more welcome in the later 1990s when the OECD countries' dependence on the Middle East is expected to reach a new peak.

Politically, the West Europeans would certainly also welcome measures which could prevent a repetition of the Arab oil threat of the early 1970s. Germany would feel less economic pressure to pursue a more active, essentially pro-Arab policy which would conflict with her special relationships with Israel and the United States. If this hypothesis is correct, there is little reason to expect any major change in German Middle-Eastern policy for economic reasons.

Third, as far as West European (and later probably East European) political cooperation is concerned, one could imagine growing differences of interest. Whereas the southern Europeans will increasingly feel the repercussions of Middle-Eastern problems, the northern Europeans will probably tend to focus their interest on the developments in the eastern part of their own continent. France, Greece, Italy, Portugal and Spain in particular will be increasingly affected by the demographic, social, economic and political tensions in the Mediterranean.[36] Muslim 'fundamentalism' and problems of unemployment and social integration will heavily affect their internal policies. France and Italy will probably be the exponents of an active European policy for dealing with these new challenges. From this point of view, the Palestinian issue continues to be one of the major stumbling blocks for developing a more stable relationship with the Arab–Islamic world.

Germany, Denmark and the Benelux countries will probably be more affected by changes in the East. Since these northern countries would tend to focus on Eastern Europe and want to deal with the social, economic and ethnic problems there, growing political tensions within the European Community might be the consequence. Great Britain, still harbouring some particular interests in the Middle East and feeling isolated by the unification processes on the continent, will have a difficult choice.

One can imagine that Europe's diplomats will find some appropriate formula to square the circle, a 'European division of labour' for example. The basic problem will remain, however. France and Germany could become the respective leaders of two different perceptions and regional policies. Future French–German cooperation would have to carry the burden of reconciling Europe's eastern and southern mission.

Regarding the Palestine conflict, it seems probable that France will continue to be the proponent of an active, essentially more 'pro-Arab' policy.[37] Germany, because of her historic burden and the other factors mentioned above which determine the special relationship with Israel, will continue to prefer a much less ambitious role. Germany's other special relationship, with the United States, will continue for many reasons. Germany, having renounced the possession of nuclear weapons, will still need some American nuclear guarantees. Since the Federal Republic is now, in the early 1990s, Washington's privileged partner in Western Europe, a united Germany will be very interested in preserving this relationship. A continuation of Bonn's 'policy' toward the Palestine conflict would be most appropriate.

Nevertheless, despite all the factors of continuity, a gradual change in Germany's attitudes could be imagined. With the unavoidable generational change taking place, fewer and fewer younger Germans will accept personal guilt for the past. Future German politicians will reiterate Chancellor Kohl's repeated statement of the 'mercy of late birth' (*Gnade der späten Geburt*). Much will depend on the manner in which Israeli politicians deal with this new self-confidence which does not necessarily neglect the continuing special character of the relationship.

But little change can be expected regarding the other side of the conflict.

Bilateral German–Arab relations, based on mutual economic interests and comparatively generous German aid for the poorer countries, will continue to function rather smoothly. The Palestinians will continue to receive German understanding for their desires – all the more when they respect Israel's existence – but they can hardly expect any decisive German action. Now that the East Germans have been able to exercise their right of self-determination, it remains to be seen how important Germany will consider the same right for the Palestinians. There might be more than a grain of truth in the statement by the PLO's representative in Bonn: 'We know that the Germans are preoccupied with German unity and have hardly any capacity to deal with other problems in the world.'[38]

For many years to come, German political energies will be absorbed in Europe. Moreover, the historical legacy will continue to dampen any German ambition to play a major role in the conflict between Israel and the Arabs.

The 1990–91 Gulf War

Germany's attitudes and reactions during the Iraq–Kuwait crisis of 1990–1 confirm the basic argument of this chapter. Completely absorbed by the unification process, the formations of the government after the first national elections in the unified country and the dramatic changes in Eastern Europe and the Soviet Union, German political leaders were unprepared to deal with the war in the Gulf.

Despite the impression of German hesitancy, Bonn provided the allies with prompt and comprehensive logistical support. However, politicians did not stress their support clearly, publicly and in time. Self-constrained by its decision not to dispatch German armed forces outside the 'NATO area', the government left political initiative to a minority of 'peace groups' who often not only failed to distinguish between the aggressor and the victim but also used double standards in criticising the air attacks against Baghdad and ignoring the Iraqi attacks against Tel Aviv and Riyadh. This quandary led to a situation in which the German government felt obliged to pay an amount of money to its allies and friends, totalling almost DM18 billion.

The latest Gulf War has intensified the debate about Germany's future role in world politics. While there is general agreement among the major political parties that Germany should participate in UN peacekeeping operations, a two-thirds majority in parliament which could reinterpret the Basic Law's restrictions on Germany's military role, is not in the offing at the time of writing. However, the question is not a legal but a political one as the government, with the agreement of the Social Democratic opposition, demonstrated in March 1991. Before the formal ceasefire, some Federal Navy minesweepers were dispatched to the Gulf in a 'humanitarian mission'. In April 1991 units of the Federal Army were also heavily engaged in efforts to alleviate the sufferings of the Iraqi Kurdish refugees in Turkey – and in Iran, which is clearly 'outside the NATO area'.[39]

It is probably too early to call this engagement a precedent for any future German participation in a peace-keeping mission to consolidate an eventual Israeli–Palestinian agreement. Even if the German government were ready to dispatch observers, it seems questionable whether many Israelis – for well-known historical reasons – would welcome a German role.

Notes

1. See L. Carl Brown, *International Politics and the Middle East*, Princeton, Princeton University Press, 1984, pp.18, 272, analysing Bismarck's famous statement that the 'Eastern question' was 'not worth the bone of one Pommeranian musketeer'.
2. The case of Namibia, the former 'Deutsch-Südwestafrika', and the German presence in places like China are rather exceptions!
3. West German secret military deliveries to the Jewish state began after Shimon Peres, then general secretary of the Israeli defence ministry, had visited West German Defence Minister Strauss and asked for military aid in late 1957. In the following years Israel received transport planes, helicopters, artillery, and anti-tank weapons, worth DM300 Million, without payment. See Franz Josef Strauss, *Erinnerungen*, Berlin, Siedler, 1989, pp.341–5.
4. See Lily Gardner Feldman, *The Special Relationship Between West Germany and Israel*, Boston, Allen & Unwin, 1984, pp.39–41.
5. German visitors to Israel are usually surprised to find so many elderly people among the Ashkenasim population speaking German. The German–Jewish history of science and arts does not need to be described in detail: names such as the religious philosopher Martin Buber and the nuclear physicist Albert Einstein speak for themselves! German churches also have a very special interest in the Holy Land. Moreover, in politics there is a close relationship between the Social Democrats and the trade unions of both countries. For many West (and now also East) German members of Parliament and other 'political tourists', Israel is probably the number one foreign country to visit. For a comprehensive study see Gardner Feldman, *op. cit.*
6. In this respect one could apply Thomas Friedman's statement, referring to American citizens, also to the Germans: 'Israel occupies a place in the American psyche, in American civilization, that no other country really does.' ('US Media and the Middle East' in Shai Feldman, *U.S. Middle East Policy: the Domestic Setting*, Boulder, Westview Press (for the Centre for Strategic Studies, Tel Aviv University), 1988, pp.36–9.
7. Noteworthy were the accusations of Prime Minister Begin against Chancellor Schmidt in 1981 when he called the latter 'arrogant' and 'impudent', denying that 'a German' had the 'right to give advice' to Israel. On 30 April 1981, Schmidt had spoken about the Palestinians' 'moral right' to self-determination and to establish an independent state. After Begin's charges, Schmidt never repeated his statement about the Palestinians. For a detailed description of the Begin–Schmidt controversy see Amnon Neustadt, *Die deutsch-israelischen Beziehungen im Schatten der EG-Nahostpolitik*, Frankfurt, Haag+Heerchen, 1983, pp.475–503; 492–5.
8. For a more comprehensive analysis see Dore Gold, *America, the Gulf and Israel: CENTCOM (Central Command) and Emerging US Regional Security Policies in the Mideast*, Tel Aviv, 1988 (Jaffee Centre for Strategic Studies, JCSS Study, No. 11).
9. A fact Hitler exploited in supporting Palestinian leader Haj Amin al-Husseiny against the British. See Nicholas Bethell, *The Palestine Triangle. The Struggle between the British, the Jews and the Arabs 1935–48*, London, A. Deutsch, 1979.
10. Bonn accepted the GDR as a second state in Germany but not as a 'foreign country'.
11. See Amnon Neustadt, *op. cit.*, pp.75–6. There is no need to elaborate on the symbolic importance of gas masks after Auschwitz. The problem remains virulent, as Israeli and Jewish–American accusations against German business interests selling chemicals to Arab dictators demonstrate.
12. See Kenneth Lewan, *Der Nahost-Krieg in der westdeutschen Presse*, Cologne, Pahl-Rugenstein, 1970; Friedemann Büttner, 'German Perceptions of the Middle East

Conflict: Images and Identifications during the 1967 War' in *Journal of Palestine Studies*, Winter, 1977, pp.66–81; and Friedemann Büttner and Peter Hünseler, 'Die politischen Beziehungen zwischen der Bundesrepublik Deutschland und den arabischen Staaten. Entwicklung, Stand und Perspektiven' in Karl Kaiser and Udo Steinbach (eds), *Deutsch–arabische Beziehungen*, Munich and Vienna, Oldenbourg, 1981 (Schriften des Forschungsinstituts der Deutschen Gesellschaft für Auswärtige Politik), pp.111–52.

13. In 1972 72.5 per cent and in 1979 55 per cent of West Germany's oil imports came from Arab countries: see Ernst Eberhard Hotz, 'Die Bedeutung des arabischen Öls für die Bundesrepublik' in Kaiser and Steinbach, *op. cit.*, pp.303–14.

14. See Wolfgang Hager, *Westeuropas wirtschaftliche Sicherheit*, Bonn, Europa Union, February 1976 (Forschungsinstitut der Deutschen Gesellschaft für Auswärtige Politik, Arbeitspapiere zur Internationalen Politik, No. 6).

15. Economic interests certainly played a role, and there was indeed pressure from the German business community. Nevertheless, it would be primitive to assign the evolution of German policy simply to the 'oil factor' and neglect the overriding political reasons. Interestingly, after the second oil crisis the Federal Republic considerably reduced its dependency on Middle-Eastern oil – particularly from the Gulf – much more than France which was indeed more susceptible to Arab, for example Iraqi, pressures. Chancellor Schmidt, personally concerned about this problem, played a major role in this shift.

16. Quoted by Neustadt, *op. cit.*, pp.213–4 (my translation). The Israeli author claims that this statement was a reaction to the 'Arab oil threat'. I was assured by a former high-ranking German diplomat, personally involved in this affair, that such threats did not play any role. In the Foreign Office, the American shipments were regarded as a matter of principle violating the Federal Republic's officially stated neutrality. See also the memoirs of Paul Frank, *Entschlüsselte Botschaft*, Stuttgart, DVA, 1981 (2nd ed.), pp. 267–72.

17. See the West German ambassador's speech to the General Assembly of the United Nations on 19 November 1974 (United Nations, General Assembly Official Records, Meeting No. 2291).

18. On 1 September 1979 Foreign Minister Genscher, while visiting Egypt, stated the Palestinians' right to self-determination and a home land. However, only ten days later – after Israeli Foreign Minister Dayan had visited Bonn – Genscher declared this right to be dependent on the 'consent of all parties involved' – which included Israel. See Büttner and Hünseler, *op. cit.*, pp.142–3 and the critical remarks of Walter Jesser, former German ambassador to several Arab States in his lecture 'Die Bundesrepublik Deutschland und der Palästinakonflikt', 3 July 1986, mimeo.

19. Susan Hattis Rolef, *The Middle East Policy of the Federal Republic*, Jerusalem, 1985 (Hebrew University, Jerusalem Papers on Peace Problems, No. 39) p.26, arguing that Israel would have been created even without Hitler and the Holocaust, strongly disagrees with this thesis.

20. It was only on 16 October 1989 – some months after the PLO had accepted all UN declarations on the Arab–Israeli conflict and thereby recognised Israel – that Staatssekretär Jürgen Sudhoff (assistant secretary of state in the Foreign Office) received Arafat's personal adviser, Bassam Abu Sharif.

21. Personal information from a high-ranking West European diplomat. For the text of the declaration, and a collection of official statements to German Middle Eastern policy, see Auswärtiges Amt (ed.), *Die Bundesrepublik Deutschland und der Nahe Osten. Dokumentation*, Bonn, 1988, pp.61–2. For analyses from different perspectives see Thomas Oppermann, 'Israel und Palästina – Reifeprüfung der Bonner Aussenpolitik' in *Europa-Archiv*, No. 14, 1980, pp.435–47 and Ilan Greilsammer and Joseph Weiler, 'European Political Cooperation and the Palestinian–Israeli conflict: an Israeli Perspective' in David Allen and Alfred Pijpers, *European Foreign Policy-Making and the Arab-Israeli Conflict*, The Hague, Nijhoff, 1984, pp. 144–6.

22. This policy was reversed for the first time only in 1989 when Bonn provided border police units to supervise free elections in Namibia, the former German South-west

Africa. In 1978 Bonn had supported the creation of UN peace-keeping forces in southern Lebanon (UNIFIL) by providing transport planes for airlift. Given the continuing Israeli touchiness against German soldiers, there is little reason to expect any direct German participation in a hypothetical peace-keeping force consolidating an Arab–Israeli peace settlement.

23. A detailed analysis of West German press reactions, particularly in comparison with the war of 1967, would prove this thesis.

24. One should not forget that this controversy took place during another passionate arms debate, the issue of Intermediate Nuclear Forces.

25. Personal information.

26. On 28 April 1982 the Federal Government approved new political principles concerning arms transfers. The new regulations permitted arms exports to countries outside NATO only if 'vital interests' of the Federal Republic were at stake. Essentially, the new rules allowed case-by-case decisions and confirmed the existing practice. See Joachim Krause, 'Trendwende in der deutschen Rüstungsexport-Politik?' in *Europa-Archiv*, No. 17, 1982, pp.527–34 and Joachim Krause and G.A. Mattox, 'West German Arms Sales to the Third World', *Atlantic Quarterly*, No. 2, Summer, 1984, pp.171–82.

27. To understand West German behaviour, one should not forget that Bonn has traditionally been a proponent of free trade (for example in the Western debates over COCOM). As a consequence, the authorities supervising exports did not have the capacity to deal with all dubious cases.

28. Since the first oil crisis French policy deliberately directed at creating special political relationships with the major oil-rich Arab countries – first Iraq, later Saudi Arabia and other members of the Gulf Cooperation Council – by essentially exchanging oil for industrial products, including sophisticated weapons. See Helmut Hubel, *Frankreichs Rolle im Nahen Osten*, Bonn, Europa Union, 1985 (Forschungsinstitut der Deutschen Gesellschaft für Auswärtige Politik, Arbeitspapiere zur Internationalen Politik, No. 37) and Edward A. Kolodziej, *Making and Marketing Arms: the French Experience and its Implications for the International System*, Princeton, Princeton University Press, 1987.

29. See the statement of one of the best Western observers of the Middle East: 'Declarations alone, even if periodically repeated, are no policy. To become policy, they have to be materialized by action.' (Arnold Hottinger, 'Rahmenbedingungen deutscher Nahostpolitik' in *Aus Politik und Zeitgeschichte*, supplement to the weekly *Das Parlament*, Bonn, Nos. 7–8, 1985, pp.23–7, my translation).

30. See Bernard von Plate, 'Der Nahe und Mittlere Osten sowie der Maghreb' in Hans-Adolf Jacobsen, Gert Leptin, Ulrich Scheuner, Eberhard Schulz (eds.), *Drei Jahrzehnte Aussenpolitik der DDR*, Munich and Vienna, Oldenbourg, 1979 (Schriften des Forschungsinstituts der Deutschen Gesellschaft für Auswärtige Politik, Reihe, Internationale Politik und Wirtschaft, Band 44), pp.675–98.

31. Recently, an unconfirmed press report, based on former 'secret documents', claimed that the GDR provided Egypt and Syria with military equipment (fighter jets, missiles and possibly also tanks) during the 1967 war. (See *Süddeutsche Zeitung*, 7–8 July 1990).

32. See Plate, op. cit., pp.678–9.

33. 'We feel sad and ashamed and acknowledge this burden [the genocide particularly of the Jews] of German history. (See excerpts of the statement in *International Herald Tribune*, 13 April 1990.) To understand this declaration, it is worthwhile mentioning that a high percentage of the new members of government and Parliament are officials of the Protestant Church.

34. It may be assumed that the problem will be solved only by the government of united Germany.

35. See Helmut Hubel, 'Neue Waffen in der Dritten Welt und Ihre Folgen' in *Europa-Archiv*, No. 15, 1990, pp.453–60.

36. For a description see Claude Nigoul, 'Die wirtschaftlichen und sozialen Herausforderungen' in Helmut Hubel (ed.), *Nordafrika in der internationalen Politik,*

Munich, Oldenbourg, 1988, pp.5–33 (Schriften des Forschungsinstituts der Deutschen Gesellschaft für Auswärtige Politik, Reihe, Internationale Politik und Wirtschaft, Band 55).

37. As long as Socialist President Mitterrand is in power, Israel's basic interests will definitely not be touched. This might change, however, if his Gaullist rival Jacques Chirac became his successor.

38. Abdallah Frangi, *Palästina Bulletin*, 21/90, 25 May 1990, p.1 (my translation).

39. For a more comprehensive assessment, see my *Der zweite Golfkrieg in der internationalen Politik* (The Second Gulf War in International Politics), Bonn, Europa Union, 1991, (Deutsche Gesellschaft für Auswärtige Politik, Arbeitspapiere zur internationalen Politik, No. 62), pp.52 ff.

5 Unique dilemmas of German–Israeli relations: a political avoidance of tragedy*

David Witzthum
(Translated from Hebrew by Peretz Kidron)

What is past is not dead, it is not even past. We cut ourselves off from it; we pretend to be strangers.

Christa Wolf, *Kindheit's Muster* (*A Model Childhood*)

Everyone discovers, in the course of their lifetime, that perfect happiness is an impossibility; but few consider that the opposite is equally true: one cannot be utterly miserable. That which precludes the two extreme states is of a single nature: our human existence is in contradiction to the infinite.

Primo Levi, *'Se questo e un omo?'* (*If this is man?*)

Preface

The annals of German–Israeli relations are rooted in World War II and the Holocaust which descended upon the Jews of Europe. The story comprises elements too numerous for exploration in the space of a single chapter. Even in the narrow sphere I have chosen, I intend to restrict discussion to two non-contingent periods to present one single thesis: namely, that the relationship between Israel and Germany has indeed been unique; but that, contrary to sporadic claims by those who shaped it and charted its course, it was not a 'special relationship'. I shall attempt to sketch out that which was unique and that which was created in reaction and opposition to that uniqueness – the latter being principally a separate uniqueness, of Germany and of Israel, rather than of the relationship forged between them.[1]

Furthermore, from the outset of their relations each of the countries surrendered some of the uniqueness to which history had condemned them – whether out of sheer necessity, as in the case of Israel's need to forge relations so as to receive material aid from Germany; or out of a sense of relief, as in the case of Germany, whose uniqueness lay in its enormous guilt for World War II and the Holocaust, and whose principal ambition after the wartime debacle was a 'return to normalcy'.[2]

I believe that the rationale of the relationship forged between Germany and Israel, in defiance of the obstacle offered by the looming, oppressive shadow of war and Holocaust, is *Realpolitik*. That obstacle seemed to dictate an absence of any relationship whatsoever or a quest for a totally unique basis for such a relationship.

* Special thanks to Professor Moshe Zimmermann, Head, Koebnor Centre of German History, The Hebrew University, Jerusalem, for his kind advice.

Both those options were considered – and rejected. Ultimately, the character of those relations, their course and durability, was dictated by interests and needs; possibly, too, it was 'the cunning of history'.

In this chapter, I shall attempt to illuminate several processes in the Israeli–German relationship while rejecting the rhetoric of some of its architects and offering a critique of its character. Overall, I shall examine two periods I consider crucial and illustrative, concomitantly analysing the claims put forward.

The first period is from 1949–65. This stretches from the foundation of the GDR (and of the DDR), one year after the establishment of Israel, until the year the two countries established diplomatic relations. This period moulded the postwar international order and, with it, the relationship between the two countries. The second period is from 1989–91. This period saw the collapse of inter-bloc rivalry in Europe, German reunification and the Gulf war and its context in the Middle East and the international arena. Commencing with this period, a different world order is emerging which I believe will generate a fundamental change in Israeli–German relations.

The choice of these periods rests on the contingency of the bilateral relationship upon the international environment and the interests and needs arising therefrom and similarly upon other factors not inherent to the perceptions of the two countries, whether of themselves or of one another. In other words, the decisive factors were not an offshoot of the 'uniqueness' of the relationship; rather, they stemmed from the international context and current realities.

During the first of the periods I shall consider, the postwar order was moulded, the two states came into being and embarked upon an interrelationship culminating in full and overt diplomatic relations. The second period witnessed the eclipse of East Germany and the emergence of a single German entity. The novel international circumstances will, I believe, require a fundamental change in policy on the part of Germany and of the whole of Europe; ultimately, too, a change in Israel's policies and international links. In consequence, I foresee a fundamental alteration in Israeli–German relations. Such a change did not come about *between* the two periods because international circumstances did not require – indeed, they blocked – far-reaching change in the global arena, in the characters of the two countries or in their interrelationship. All of these were determined in the earlier of the two periods under consideration, and the changes commenced during the later period.

During the earlier period, I believe that the character of the relationship was shaped by various factors. In Germany, these factors were the wartime defeat and the country's partition, along with its rapid and total integration – political, military and economic – into the Western alliance; the hegemony of the United States as the leading power both in defeating Germany and in legitimising the 'new' Germany's restoration to the international community; the mutual rivalry between the two Germanys, extending beyond Europe into other regions such as the Middle East; Germany's transformation from wasteland to economic superpower; the Federal Republic's efforts to achieve internal stability ('Bonn isn't Weimar') by political dissociation from the Third Reich, while preserving its formal and legal rights and obligations as successor thereto and simultaneously playing down the significance of the institutional and social continuity marking the transition from Hitler's Germany to Adenauer's Germany. In the early years Germany tried to depict this transition as an abrupt *Stunde Null*; research proves unequivocally that this 'zero hour' was a myth.[3] Within the new international order, Israel was perceived as marginal, its importance to Germany stemming from a grasp of its centrality to the Jewish community in the United States and the world at large – to a lesser degree, from the interest displayed by European political elites, for example the German SPD (as Shafir proves in his wide-ranging research on the subject) which adopted a different and conscientious approach.[4] But the SPD was not in power; and when it did attain office, it did not substantially modify its predecessor's policies towards Israel. In fact, diplomatic relations between the two countries reached their nadir during the SPD's tenure of office in Bonn.

In Israel, the relationship was shaped by the following factors: the political travails of a state founded in conflict with its neighbours, placing it in urgent need of external support, both military and diplomatic; the enormous economic difficulties stemming from the necessity to resettle Holocaust survivors and subsequent waves of immigrants, while simultaneously creating an economic infrastructure, a welfare state and a modern army; pressure from world Jewry, and from within Israel itself, to demand compensation for Nazi crimes against the Jews before it was too late; and, finally, perception of Germany as a rising power in the Western bloc, as a country politically accessible by virtue of its past history, and important for its political and economic potential in contrast to Israel's position of marginal isolation.

The thesis suggested regarding the character of bilateral relations, and the abovementioned underlying elements, consequently denies the view that the predominant factors in shaping those relations were morality, the lessons of the past, a wish to atone or a willingness to forgive. In the discussion to follow, I shall attach little importance to the discourse within and between the intellectual elites of the two countries, to the public rhetoric of personages official or unofficial, to the media or the fluctuations of public opinion. However, I will examine that discourse, whether intellectual or day to day, particularly in the context of the second period under consideration. The deduction to be drawn is that its importance increased progressively in advance of and during the second period.

Hence, my view also rejects the central role attributed to traumatic collective memories of World War II and the Holocaust in forging and maintaining relations between the two countries. There is of course no overlooking the centrality of that trauma, and its psychological and political components, in mutual perceptions of Israelis and Germans. But I shall argue that the trauma enhanced the unique nature of each of the two states but not the link between them. From the outset, that link was constructed and defined as a *response* to that uniqueness, not as an offshoot, or expression, of the trauma.

Furthermore, alongside my central thesis, I shall argue that although apparently stemming from a shared experience, the trauma was interpreted differently in each country, and dealt with in different ways.

In Israel, the Holocaust became the core of a myth, national and Zionist, whose ahistorical context links it with the destiny, heroism and existential tragedy of the Jewish people. Almost from the outset, the Holocaust was depicted as a cosmic event which could be neither compared nor measured against other human cataclysms, previous or subsequent; and was likewise not connected with the historical circumstances prevailing in pre-Nazi Europe, the character of totalitarian regimes in general or the political realities of Europe and the new Germany.

In Germany, the trauma of the past entailed its repression: formally, by creation of a 'new' Germany (West and East); and psychologically, by a lack of ability, will or need to confront the dreadful conclusions. It was only in the seventies or eighties that significant intellectual trends began grappling with the past in historical and political terms, leading to conclusions regarding foreign policy (pacifism or anti-Americanism on the left and neo-nationalism on the right). However, it was not the trauma, or its political interpretations, which effected changes in German policy; nor did they accelerate reunification. Politicians and intellectuals, whether of the left or right, did not bring about reunification, nor did they wish it or even foresee it.

Discussion of the second period (1989–91) will therefore take account of asymmetrical developments in perceptions of the past, together with the considerations of international *Realpolitik* already noted. The growing weight of considerations stemming from the past, along with an erosion of the uniqueness of the two states – as viewed by themselves, each other and the surrounding international audience – have yet to bring about a significant change, though I consider it liable to upset the delicate equilibrium in bilateral relations.

In Germany, the Nazi past – as a period bordering upon the present and directly influencing it – has disappeared. Today's direct 'past' is the forty-year period of division which followed World War II. In reunited Germany, the 'return to history' marks the start of a confrontation with the new 'past': the division imposed from without and reunification, likewise virtually imposed from without through the collapse of the inter-bloc European order. German foreign policy may be expected progressively to stress the country's geopolitical position between East and West; its national and economic power and its cultural tradition.

In its effect on German policy towards Israel, this shift is likely to replace rhetoric with expressions closer to the German consensus and interests, as well as influencing the lessons drawn from the confrontation with the more remote, and therefore less oppressive, past represented by the Third Reich. Support for Israel (as for the United States, or the West overall) may be expected to become less automatic than hitherto, while moral considerations will stand out more through the need, in view of the eclipse of the ideologies and of the alliances that gave them expression, to forge an independent foreign policy. On the other hand, Europe, and Germany with it, is liable to slide into a period of instability – political, economic and social. Gone are the calm shallows in which Bonn paddled under the hegemony of the United States, NATO and the European Community. The internal stability which characterised the Federal Republic (and the GDR) is no guarantee of a similar stability in the reunited Germany. Sharp shocks are liable to have a paralysing effect – possibly inclining to nationalist isolationism – on Germany's policies.

Israel has undergone changes – demographic, biological, ethnic and religious – effecting radical shifts in the political spectrum. In the recent past, changes within Israel (the *intifada* in particular) and in the Middle East (the traumatic vulnerability shown up in the Gulf war, and its effect upon the perceived existential threat to Israel) have gravely fractured the consensus internally, though not with regard to the United States and Europe, including Germany.

With the disappearance of the Soviet Union as a regional superpower, Israel's dependence upon the United States has increased, its economic dimension reinforced by Soviet Jewish immigration. Concomitantly, Israel's importance as a Western ally (never very great) has further declined.

In my view, the divorce of Israel's foreign policy from the national myth of the Holocaust facilitated an unfolding relationship with Germany which, commencing in reaction and opposition to a hostile public opinion, and in defiance of Israel's self-view as 'unique', continued as a faithful expression of interests and consensus. But within that broad consent to relations – normal initially, close later – lay an implied consent to waive the claim to uniqueness *vis-à-vis* Germany. After several years of rhetorical mishaps, which led to nothing beyond a sense of bad taste, Israel's foreign ministry can no longer put forward claims regarding the uniqueness of Israel or of Germany – or of their bilateral relations – as substantial claims bearing political relevance. Should there be any change in German–Israeli relations, it may, temporarily at least, be unilateral: Israel is unprepared for political somersaults and its government is presently unequipped to deal with them. The end of the postwar era, and the new period now in its place, do not mark the end of the bilateral 'special relationship', which in my view never existed: one can speak only of the end of the uniqueness of the two states which came into existence as a result of a global crisis and the new order it entailed. They now enter a new era stripped of their uniqueness, and, with it, of many of the traditional assumptions underlying their national existence and international contacts. Germany is preparing for the change, though there is no knowing whether it will be effected successfully. Israel, as yet unprepared for change, and with no interest therein, is fearful of gambling with the unknown.

The first period

The date marking the onset of German–Israeli relations is, in my view, 27 September 1951, when the Bundestag in Bonn heard Konrad Adenauer read a written declaration whereby Germany effectively shouldered responsibility for 'moral and material restitution' for Nazi crimes against the Jews; crimes committed – in the expression which was to figure in the political lexicon of the Federal Republic – 'in the name of Germany' because, in Adenauer's words 'the majority of the German people was revulsed by these crimes and took no part in their commission'. Adenauer concluded his statement as follows:

With regard to the extent of the reparations – a momentous problem in view of the enormous destruction of Jewish values by National Socialism – the limits imposed on German ability to pay through the bitter necessity of caring for the innumerable war victims and the support of refugees and expellees must be considered. The Federal Government are prepared, jointly with representatives of Jewry and the State of Israel which has admitted so many homeless Jewish fugitives, to bring about a solution of the material indemnity problem, thus easing the way to the spiritual settlement of infinite suffering. They are profoundly convinced that the spirit of true humanity must once again come alive and become fruitful. The Federal Government consider it the chief duty of the German people to serve this spirit with all their strength.[5]

The Bundestag members rose to their feet to hear the declaration; it was approved unanimously. That same day, an Israeli government spokesman issued a statement which, acknowledging the German declaration as 'an attempt' to recognise the existence of the problem arising from Nazi crimes against the Jews, and stressing the urgency and extent of the need for material restitution, compensation and reparations, concluded as follows:

It is imperative, furthermore, that the German people undertake a measure of collective restitution to the Jewish people by making a major contribution towards the absorption and rehabilitation of the survivors of Nazi persecution, the bulk of whom have found new homes in Israel. The Government of Israel has notified the Occupying Powers of its claim to such restitution. The claim of the Jewish people, which suffered infinitely more from the brutality of the Nazis than any other people that fell under their sway, stands in a category of its own and calls for special and comprehensive satisfaction.

The Government of Israel will study the German Chancellor's declaration and will in due course make its attitude known.[6]

The two statements were issued after several months of tentative contacts between representative leaders of Jewish organisations, headed by Nahum Goldman and officials of the Israeli government acting on instructions from David Ben Gurion with representatives of the West German government of Konrad Adenauer. The purpose of the declarations was to launch negotiations on compensation and reparations to the Jewish people and the state of Israel.[7]

Research literature dealing with Israeli–German relations focuses, naturally enough, upon those preliminary 'feelers', and the leading actors on both sides. Adenauer and Ben Gurion were the decisive and predominant personages, and the research examines their motives, utterances and deeds against the background circumstances in the two countries and the international arena.

However, the full story somehow evades the texts which convey it to us across a forty year gap, following the second shock which has rocked the international scene since 1989. The documents and accounts, and their attendant commentaries, strikes one today as a kind of footnote to the history of Germany and Europe in the period after World War II, and to the history of the state of Israel in its own part of the world, the Middle East, rather than a substantive component thereof.

With regard to Ben Gurion and Adenauer, the architects of relations between the two countries, history may have charged them with a 'mission impossible'. The only way of creating those relations lay in avoiding any direct confrontation with the substance of the mission, but alternatively, in the words of Gershom Scholem, 'to build a bridge over the abyss'. There was no way to meet within the abyss gaping between Jews and Germans says Scholem; the special characteristic of the annals of the two peoples is the impossibility of their ultimate realisation.[8] I shall argue that in the first period under discussion, consciously or not, that is precisely what the two countries contrived to do. It was the 'cunning of history': the course of circumstance and international realities and the unique nature of the two states which contributed to the non-uniqueness of their relationship.

From the distance of those forty years, any description of the start of the relationship and the events at their conclusion, must address the discrepancy between the enormity of the calamity (then yet to be fully revealed) and the flimsy 'bridges' that the representatives set about constructing at that time. Israel had imposed an almost total boycott on any person or artefact of German origin; public opinion, the press, the cultural and political elite – all demanded revenge or, at the very least, a total dissociation between Israelis and Jews, and Germans. From the outset, the representatives of the Jewish organisations and the Israeli government faced officials and politicians some of whom – including some of the leading figures – had served in the administration of the Third Reich and were former members of the Nazi Party. From the outset, the Jewish and Israeli representatives encountered a German public largely indifferent, and in part overtly hostile, to the demands for reparations and for the institution of relations, of one kind or another, between Germany and Israel.[9] In illustration of the opinions then prevalent in Germany, Wolffsohn mentions a poll regarding reparations, which was conducted in the American sector in September 1952. The results were as follows: 11 per cent were in favour; 24 per cent were in favour 'as long as the sum is not excessive'; 44 per cent were against any compensation to the Jews(!); 21 per cent expressed no opinion. Shortly before the official declarations, there were protests from Nahum

Goldman, Moshe Sharett and others, over utterances and manifestations of a neo-Nazi nature in Germany, over the leniency of sentences imposed upon Nazi criminals, and the rapidity of German rearmament. The atmosphere surrounding the preliminary contacts was oppressively tense and hostile. It was only the international circumstances, rendering the talks marginal in relation to what was in train about them, and the interests of the two countries, which ultimately shaped the course and outcome of the largely confidential negotiations, and engendered progress in the negotiations and the initial agreements.

First, let us consider the texts already quoted, particularly the German declaration.

In the draft text sent to Jerusalem for study and approval, Bonn made absolutely no mention of the state of Israel.[10] When the Israelis insisted on its inclusion, it was mentioned merely as the country offering the refugees a new home, not as the representative of the Jewish people, as it perceived itself (some of the Jewish organisations also objected to such a wording) or as that people's national home. The Israeli government statement likewise makes no such mention. From this important, possibly crucial, aspect, the two statements run a close parallel.

From the outset, the rationale and the extent of the reparations were rendered subject to the contextual policies, resources and interests – internal and external – of Germany; in other words, they were not a value in their own right, or a moral act autonomous in rationale, justification and extent. The declaration's opening paragraph reflects its character as response to public opinion, while clearly emphasising that the past, dead and gone, has no bearing upon the very different present:

Recently world opinion has concerned itself repeatedly with the attitude of the Federal Republic towards the Jews. Doubts have been expressed here and there as to whether the new state has been guided in this momentous question by principles that do justice to the frightful crimes of a past epoch and put the relationship of the Jews to the German people on a new and healthy basis.[11]

The German draft sent to Jerusalem stated further that 'West Germany shares in defence of the free world against Communist onslaught'(!) – an assertion whose thrust Ben Gurion would certainly have approved; but the purpose Israel sought was, of course, very different. Similarly, Germany's mention of limited resources, and the needs of its own refugees and deportees, reflects the German view of restitution payments – and, later, of diplomatic relations – in German policy *vis-à-vis* Israel. For its part, Israel – out of a mixture of pragmatism, lack of choice, domestic pressures and hopes for the future – accepted the German wording, and its own position in the Federal Republic's foreign policy from this highly symbolic opening of relations between the two states. In particular, Israel accepted the affirmation – formal but crucial – that, in relation to reparations, Israel is not the representative of the Jewish people, merely the home of some of its adherents. Israel's unique status, the underlying foundation of its national self-perception, was never presented or accepted as such by the Federal Republic. The German opposition, headed by the SPD, attempted to submit a resolution to this effect to the Bundestag on 21 February 1951. A draft was referred to a committee where it remained for several months but after some futile deliberations, it was shelved and forgotten. For the Israeli side, Nahum Goldman recalls Ben Gurion and Sharett telling him that the talks must be held primarily with the Jewish *people* because the Nazis' victims were annihilated as Jews, not as Israelis. They said: 'Personally, we cannot stand out too far, because the Herut party has already turned the matter into a political issue.'[12]

Furthermore, by the mere fact of initiating negotiations, the Federal Republic succeeded in presenting itself to its Israeli co-locutors precisely as it wished to be seen in its future foreign relations. In formal legal terms, it was the successor of the Third Reich, with the same borders, rights and obligations, but, simultaneously, a Germany 'different' in social organisation and regime and recognised as such even by the people who had suffered particularly horribly at the hands of the Third Reich – and was recognised as such by the state of Israel.

The context: American hegemony

The superpowers under whose protection the two German states sheltered, endowed them with legitimacy without requiring them to fight for it. Subsequently, both also gained it from the divided world around them, and finally, in the seventies, from one another. From the beginning of the period, the international context left the two Germanies no real options: both blocs exploited their respective portions of Germany, rapidly restoring them to the arena of a cold war which had commenced before either was created – indeed, before the termination of World War II hostilities. Israel, too, was born during this period of European reconstruction with its renewed ideological and national division and extension of inter-bloc rivalry beyond the continent's confines into the Middle East.

In every decision – political, military, economic and ideological – that West Germany adopted at its birth, the superpower which played the decisive role was the United States. The Federal Republic's relations with the United States were of total dependency, underlined by the trauma of occupation. For its part, the United States sought to restore Germany quickly and deliberately to the role of partner in the Western alliance in Europe. America's political and economic aid to Germany was without precedent. As for Adenauer, he embraced all of Washington's fundamental ideological positions and sought, from the outset, to depict himself, and his country, as loyal and trustworthy allies. However there were obstacles, principally press reports and voices from American public opinion – Jews in particular – questioning whether Germany had indeed changed in view of neo-Nazi manifestations, the hasty return to a normal agenda by occupation authorities and Germans alike – whether in punishing Nazi criminals or with regard to West German rearmament. Apprehension over the effect of this hostility upon American public opinion, and over the Eastern bloc's propaganda offensive which dangled the bait of reunification in exchange for neutrality, further heightened Adenauer's determination to win over not merely the administration in Washington but also American public opinion. Above all he wanted to reassure the sceptical American Jewish leadership which he regarded as wielding particularly extensive political power. An address to that Jewish public, as well as to the state of Israel, therefore appeared necessary, if not vital.[13]

Throughout the months of the restitution negotiations, Adenauer twisted the arms of critics, invariably – as sharply portrayed in Feldman's book on Israeli–German relations – in response to external pressures.[14]

As the superpower exercising hegemony over both states – granting decisive assistance to their security, development and the legitimacy they ultimately gained in the international arena – the United States assumed the role of mediator in Israeli–German relations. However, as I shall argue in the second part of this chapter, the United States offered a kind of reverse model in Israel's unfolding relations with Germany. From the early years of its independence,

Israel developed a growing dependency – political, military, economic and, later, cultural – upon the United States. From the viewpoint of American foreign policy, Israel was marginal, and even played a disruptive role in the administration's relations with the Arab states, as in the 1956 Suez campaign. At the same time, Israel, with the overt support of American Jews, occupied a position of growing importance in American public opinion, the media and Congress. With regard to Germany, matters were reversed. Washington's political choice was to aid Germany so as to draw upon German support in the inter-bloc stand-off. Successive administrations, the state department and the CIA were Germany's natural allies, conferring on that country legitimacy. By contrast, public opinion, the media and Congress viewed Germany with suspicious reserve.

For its part, Germany contrived to interpret its foreign policy decisions – which did not reflect a domestic consensus as one did not exist – as a response to American demands.[15] Adenauer himself never made a secret of this approach, which was construed in Germany as expressing dependence upon the United States. Simultaneously, however, it achieved an additional objective: no mere expression of dependency but its intensification.

Grave rifts emerged in the Western alliance and in American hegemony as a result of the Vietnam war in the late sixties, the Arab oil embargo in the seventies, the NATO nuclear missiles stationed in Germany in the eighties, and latterly with the outbreak of the 2nd Gulf war. However, the Federal Republic never made any moves towards withdrawal or dissociation from the Western alliance. The 'anti-Americanism' prevailing in the German left (as well as portions of the far right) has not hitherto proved sufficiently virulent to undermine American–German relations.

At the margins, Germany's dependency – part shotgun wedding, part marriage of convenience – led to reservations with regard to Israeli policies, which were viewed as an offshoot of American policy in the Middle East. Particularly at the extremities of the German political spectrum, Israel's dependence upon the United States, and American sympathies towards Israel, were perceived as a symmetrical relationship between policy-makers in the two countries. In fact, American foreign policy in relation to Israel reflected the attitudes of American public opinion and the Congress, rather than *Realpolitik* of the Administration or the state department.[16] From Israel's side, relations developed in a different manner: political, military and economic dependency (existing to this day) were backed up by cultural dependency and unreserved sympathy on the part of Israel's general public and its intellectual elite. In this sense, Israel and the United States do indeed have a special relationship. This relationship has however faced a grave test recently, with a bitter confrontation between Congress and the President over Israel's request for loan guarantees for resettling Russian Jewish immigrants. The United States has maintained its full hegemony in the international arena, but the American ability to impose a new international order – upon Germany or even on Israel – is now highly questionable.

Germany, Israel and the cold war

Reverting to the context of the inter-bloc rivalries of the early fifties, the assumption of direct relations between Israel and the Federal Republic found both countries in the process of entering the Western alliance, with Israel in a more marginal position. Political views in Israel were still divided between support for the West and sympathy towards the Soviet Union – in spite of Soviet anti-Semitism, Stalinism and Moscow's overtly pro-Arab policies. Ben Gurion set himself the political objective of attaching Israel to NATO and the Western bloc, dismissing the leftist parties and the other unrealistic option. From the start, Israel's course was charted towards Bonn, not the GDR. An Israeli note to the occupying powers about restitution never received a reply from the Soviet Union, whereas the three Western powers directed Israel to approach Bonn directly.[17]

Even after the September 1951 declarations from Bonn and Jerusalem, both sides were clear that diplomatic relations were, as yet, out of the question. The mere existence of contacts with Germany, and the Knesset debate on the reparations agreement, sufficed to spark off the gravest political crisis Israel has ever faced. In January 1952, Herut party leader Menachem Begin came close to proclaiming a rebellion. Mobs laid siege to the Knesset, hurling stones into the building. There were injuries and the whole country plunged into a painful domestic crisis whose bitter memories took many years to recede.

A recent book by Tom Segev, exploring Israeli attitudes to the Holocaust, shows how – throughout debate and action on this vital aspect of the Israeli experience – the pivotal role fell to Ben Gurion, the key figure in the early years of Israel's independence. Despite Ben Gurion's numerous utterances on the issue, and his acts, there is an enigma surrounding his attitude towards Germany. Segev depicts Ben Gurion's resolve in drawing Israel towards the West and its leader, the United States, even though Washington initially displayed little enthusiasm for taking Israel into its sphere of influence. According to Segev, Ben Gurion grasped that the cold war, and Israel's needs, required identification with the West.

That is the global context of the effort towards closer relations with France and Germany. Ben Gurion suffered no moral qualms, and likewise appears to have experienced no emotional hesitation. His moral and emotional criteria were moulded almost exclusively by the interests of the state of Israel as he grasped them . . . So it was prior to the Holocaust, so it was at its height, and it naturally remained so after the creation of the state.

In retrospect, Segev adds, most Israelis supported him.[18]

To this day, Ben Gurion's attitude towards the Holocaust remains a bone of bitter contention among Israeli historians. However, his attitude towards the 'new' Germany has hitherto lain beyond controversy. It may be the nature of *Realpolitik* to bypass the abyss of emotion in the name of interests. Ben Gurion tipped the scales with the fiery vigour he threw into the battle for political and economic needs and interests, against the feebleness – as seen in retrospect – of his vociferous opponents, who spoke in the name of moral imperative. That self same resolve may also underlie the enormous complexity of Israel's decision to forge diplomatic ties with Germany. In effect, Israel, or Ben Gurion, went further than mere diplomatic relations, embracing the German myth – more wish than reality – about the 'zero hour' which allegedly occurred at the downfall of the Third Reich and accepting Adenauer's claim about the total dissociation between the Germany of the fifties and that of the forties. Furthermore, in exchange for the reparations – and diplomatic relations – extended to Israel, Ben Gurion was willing to pay the true price Bonn demanded: legitimacy in the eyes of the United States and recognition as 'the sole representative' of the German people and nation without being required –

or offering – to grant Israel similar recognition as sole representative of the Jewish people. Thus the non-unique relationship between Israel and the Federal Republic was formalised, reaching its lowest and most astounding ebb in the mid-fifties, when the German Foreign Ministry resolved to reject Israeli feelers about instituting diplomatic relations.[19] Germany contrived to postpone diplomatic ties for close on ten years, until forced into them by Walter Ulbricht and Gamal Abdel Nasser.

Sequence and motives

The developing relationship between Israel and Germany was marked by chance and intuition, coincidence of circumstances, interests and pressures, all occurring despite – or, perhaps, because of – the uniqueness of the two countries, mutual perceptions of that uniqueness and the attendant international circumstances. Commencing with the initial bilateral contacts over reparations, right up to the inauguration of diplomatic relations, we find the pressures and responses of the two sides conditioned by circumstances arising out of international realities, rather than by any substantive programmatic perceptions.

In early 1952, after months of wrangling over the extent, form and scheduling of reparation payments, the talks reached a kind of dead end. Coinciding with the negotiations with Israel, Bonn was involved in London talks with the Powers over their own demands for German reparations. Furthermore, in May of that year, Germany was due to sign an agreement effectively restoring it to the Western alliance by means of the creation of a 'European Defence Community'. It was only the express threats of the Jewish representatives headed by Nahum Goldman, backed by American administration representatives in Germany – and not the negative, often sullen, attitude of the Israeli delegation – that induced Adenauer to overrule his delegation to the talks with Israel. Their swift conclusion would help, argued Adenauer – correctly as it would transpire – in winning American public opinion over to the view that Germany was indeed worthy to join the Western alliance; furthermore it would assist Germany in keeping down the reparations demanded by other countries. Similarly, the form of payment ultimately boosted the German economy: Israel's consent to receive part of the reparations in the form of German industrial products helped the rapid reconstruction of the Federal Republic as well as banishing notions about restrictions, or an embargo, on German goods and exports.[20]

From the early fifties onwards, Israel thus received considerable material aid from Germany. Scholars who have studied the effect of reparations on Israel's society and economy are unanimous in their conviction that the impact on the construction of Israel was great. (There is less stress – in fact virtual silence – on the effect of reparations on Germany's policy and economy.) Certainly, the mere preoccupation with such a matter (Segev quotes one of the Israelis involved who heard his child ask: 'How much will we get for Grandpa and Grandma?') was humiliating, personally and nationally, and involved a heroic gritting of the teeth. Be that as it may; when the public furore had receded after the violence of the exchanges in the Knesset, the street and the press, and Ben Gurion had gained the consent of his Mapai party and the government, Israeli diplomats and representatives reverted to their grim, convoluted task at the negotiating table. Tom Segev offers the following estimate of the failure of the opposition under Menachem Begin:

Begin sought to foster the legacy of the Holocaust into a virtual religious creed. The lesson of the Holocaust as depicted by Begin was to serve as a guideline for formulating national policy, a political, ideal and emotional substitute for Ben Gurion's pragmatic get-things-done philosophy . . . He set the legacy of the Holocaust against the state itself, just as the Orthodox parties set against the state the divine commandments, and as Mapam and Maki briefly set against it the creed of Karl Marx. Everyone identified himself with history, clung to absolute, all-embracing truths: everyone tried to impose them upon the state and everyone failed, Begin too . . . He failed primarily because he was capable of perceiving in the Holocaust nothing but a national experience and a chapter in the annals of the people . . . but not of grasping that, at that time, the Holocaust was still, first and foremost, part of the individual biographies of its survivors, the private calamity of each and every one of them.

A further illustration of the tone of the debate, and of Segev's claim that Begin was ahead of his time in exploiting the Holocaust for political ends, can be found in the following description by writer Haim Beer, a child growing up in Jerusalem at the time of the reparations demonstrations:

The following day, it was discussed in my father's grocery. Many people were against reparations, people who came from the camps – that was how they called it, 'the camps', not 'the Holocaust' – people with fears who bought a quarter packet of butter and half a loaf so as not to take on too far-reaching a commitment. Their objections were understandable, but even then, I thought instinctively that the thugs [the demonstrators] were trying to make capital from others' pain and fear and dread.[21]

That was how matters unfolded in Israel. But relations with Germany, in all their aspects, were never again seriously questioned, being effectively divorced from the national Holocaust trauma.

It is harder to pinpoint an answer concerning German motives overall. With regard to Adenauer, there is a measure of artificiality in the hypothesis put forward by scholars who credit him with a blend of profound moral feeling and political pragmatism.[22] Profound moral feeling does not jive with the pressures, delays and timing which characterised the progress of the negotiations. Nor can it be reconciled with his initial offer, whether with regard to the draft declaration that launched the negotiations, or the sum of reparations he originally offered prior to the onset of the negotiations and before he adjusted his assessment of their importance for Germany's political future. Interviewed in 1949 by the German Jewish weekly *Allgemeine Wochenzeitung der Juden in Deutschland*, he suggested a sum of DM ten million ($2 million).[23] I see no need to comment on the offer – a charitable view would surmise a printing error; it wasn't.

Gunther Gillessen, having likewise puzzled over the question, disagrees with Nahum Goldman's virtually unqualified admiration for Adenauer as a man of 'moral and political principle, as well as enormous political wisdom', adding that Adenauer was 'a cynic'.[24] Gillessen finds insufficient evidence for the charge that the purpose of the agreement with Israel rested entirely upon political pragmatism; indeed, scholarly literature which does so draws on the circumstances, rather than Adenauer's own utterances. Gillessen concludes that, behind the hazy blend of motives, lay a sense of 'honour, of conscience, and of sympathy for the victims of Nazism'.[25] That, supplementing Adenauer's own testimony regarding his reflections on the day the reparations agreement was signed in Luxembourg, leads one to conclude that it was indeed 'the cunning of history', and not Adenauer's own renowned guile, that guided him to the bridge over the chasm rather than into the chasm itself.

Adenauer's memoirs vividly recount those reflections: he thought of the day in 1933 when the Nazis dismissed him from his office as mayor of Cologne and simultaneously froze his bank account, leaving him effectively penniless. Two friends – an American, Danny Heinneman, and a German, Professor Kraus, on his way to exile in the United States — offered him money. Adenauer accepted Heinneman's offer of ten thousand marks – a large sum at that time – and adds: 'As long as I was mayor of Cologne, I had numerous friends.' Heinneman and Kraus were alone in offering assistance; both were Jews. In my view, there is no conventional way of categorising or analysing this story. In retrospect, I regard it as a kind of intuition which ultimately led to the only way of establishing German–Israeli relations under the prevailing circumstances: shutting eyes tightly and groping one's way by instinct over the chasm that history had opened up between the two peoples and the two states.

From the outset, the German negotiating team was saddled with the thankless role of 'bad guys', while Adenauer reserved for himself the task of final arbitrator, overruling his own officials from the chancellor's office and the foreign and economics ministries. From time to time, whenever there was a crisis, the sides appealed for his intervention.

After the conclusion of the reparations agreement, economic ties – and, later, military and political links – began taking on a conventional form.[26] The first Israeli feelers on diplomatic representation appeared in 1956, but Adenauer was preoccupied with Germany's immediate cold war problems, and his foreign ministry was waging a bitter struggle against GDR attempts to win international recognition. West Germany fully and punctiliously fulfilled its obligations under the reparations agreement. Any further *démarche*, essentially political, was predicated upon formulation of an appropriate policy. That step was taken in May 1956, at a confidential meeting of Bonn's ambassadors in the Middle East, held in Istanbul under the chairmanship of Walter Hallstein, state secretary in the chancellor's office, who stood in for Foreign Minister Brentano.

May 1956 was therefore a kind of watershed in Israeli–German relations, and a significant turning point in the histories of the two Germanies: the Istanbul meeting set down the rules of the 'Hallstein doctrine' and, dialectically, the guidelines for Bonn's policy on the Middle East – Israel included. Subsequent changes in Bonn's policy *vis-à-vis* Jerusalem were basically variations on an immutable motif. Briefly, the decisions adopted under Hallstein's chairmanship were as follows: first, West Germany would regard establishment of diplomatic relations with East Germany on the part of any other country as a hostile act, and break off relations with any country so doing. Second, in view of the fact that the Arab states were liable to sever their relations with Bonn and establish links with East Germany, should Bonn forge diplomatic ties with Israel? Bonn was dutybound to consider its steps towards Israel in that context.[27]

Until rendered anachronistic by changing relations between the superpowers, and between the two German states, the principle laid down in Article 1 of the doctrine guided Bonn's foreign policy over several years (but did not prevent Germany – at Adenauer's personal instigation – from maintaining diplomatic ties with the Soviet Union, the effective ruler of East Germany). Article 2 dominated Bonn's subsequent relations with Jerusalem, the policy it specified being in essence indistinguishable from the policies towards Israel of most of the other countries of the world, then and now.

The relationship between the respective leaders of the two countries became increasingly remarkable, their personal ties offering a kind of bulwark against the prosaic, often difficult, social and political realities in the two countries and the surrounding world. Following upon the Suez crisis of 1956, Adenauer promptly and firmly rejected the demand from United States Secretary of State Dulles to institute sanctions against Israel.[28] He took care to foster and extend his country's ties – economic and, particularly, military – with Israel. At his historic meeting with Ben Gurion in the United States in March 1960, Adenauer went so far as to offer a hand in Negev development projects.[29] Nevertheless, the two countries still maintained no diplomatic relations while painful and disturbing manifestations and events surfaced: such as the anti-Semitic wave which swept Germany in the winter of 1959–60, the Eichmann trial, the debate in Germany over the 'statute of limitations' with regard to Nazi crimes and the affair of the German scientists in Egypt.

Throughout the public debate on these matters, in Israel and Germany, and unrelated to the traumatic tide inundating public opinion in both countries, Adenauer and Ben Gurion contrived to maintain an unreal status quo of relations hovering somewhere between artificial rhetoric and the practice of expanding economic links, particularly with regard to military aid. On various occasions they even took steps to play down issues which threatened to invoke crises in bilateral relations. Their efforts subsequently drew attention, particularly in relation to the most striking instance, the Eichmann trial. Segev relates that, after a private talk with Franz-Josef Strauss in Paris, Ben Gurion favoured playing down the role in Eichmann's exploits played by Hans Globke, Adenauer's adviser and previously a principal architect of Nazi race policy. He notified Adenauer that the prosecution would make use of documents linking Globke to Eichmann's crimes. According to Shenar's account, 'Adenauer was unenthusiastic, but displayed understanding.' In the course of the trial, Attorney-General Gideon Hausner took pains to minimise Globke's role.[30]

It was thus Adenauer's successor, Ludwig Ehrhard, who proclaimed the establishment of diplomatic relations with Israel. The step, taken in retaliation for the invitation extended to GDR leader Walter Ulbricht to visit Egypt, was adopted over the express objections of the German foreign ministry under Gerhard Schroeder. Inge Deutschkron offers a graphic description of the way Ehrhard adopted his decision: 'I remained alone', he told her, describing his rift with the foreign ministry on this point. He announced his decision at a dramatic press conference convened on 7 March 1965 (a Sunday – a timing without precedent). The course of events was stark and simple: incidental to its stand-off with the GDR, West Germany's relations with Egypt were plunged into a grave crisis; as one of its reprisals against Cairo, Bonn established diplomatic ties with Israel.

The German announcement did not resort to any rhetoric regarding the character of the projected relations with Jerusalem which featured third in the list of political and economic countermeasures undertaken to punish Nasser for his invitation to Ulbricht: 'The Federal government strives to establish diplomatic relations with Israel. This step is designed to contribute to normalisation of the circumstances. It is not aimed against any of the Arab states.'[31]

Later, the word 'strives' was replaced by 'proposes'. It was unclear – deliberately, perhaps – what 'circumstances' Ehrhard referred to in speaking of 'normalisation'. Be that as it may, Israel, though taken totally by surprise, showed considerable gratification. The German foreign ministry regarded the step as a major setback for its Middle-Eastern policy. Seemingly a leap forward, the *démarche* nevertheless bore a rider dolefully familiar in its political context. In addition to its justification – as reprisal rather than as a positive expression of unfolding bilateral relations – the proclamation was seized upon by Germany as an excuse to specify Israel as lying in an 'area of tension' and consequently to halt its arms shipments to Israel, (the extent of which had come to light a short time before, sparking an outcry in both countries and in the Arab world). Bonn's relations with the Arab world – ruptured immediately after Ehrhard's proclamation – were progressively restored. But Bonn's new definition of Israel as belonging to an 'area of tension' has remained in force ever since.

The resumption of military aid to Israel was now assumed by the United States, and Germany sent its first ambassador to Tel Aviv: Rolf Pauls, a Wehrmacht officer during the Third Reich. A diplomat accompanying Pauls was Alexander Toeroek, alleged to have belonged to Hungary's Nazi Party.[32] Pauls was accorded an angry reception, with thousands of demonstrators protesting against the newly created political *fait accompli*. But the furore rapidly subsided and it was not long before Pauls began, openly and fearlessly, to criticise Israeli policy while simultaneously forging social ties with Israelis.[33] Israel's first ambassador to Germany, Asher Ben Nathan, arrived in Bonn simultaneously, in August 1965. Official German rhetoric now dropped the term 'special relationship' in portraying its ties with Israel. Indeed, bilateral relations, their diplomatic status having been delineated in 1965, continued right up to the second period described below. There was no notable disruption, and, in retrospect, there was an almost paradoxical stability in view of the historical burden, the national trauma and the psychological and political phenomena characterising both countries. All of these coexisted, as long as the existing order remained in place in Europe and – regardless of wars and other upheavals – in the Middle East.

The second period

The second period for examination hinges roughly upon the years 1989–91. This period witnessed two events which had a profound impact on Israel and Germany and on the rest of the surrounding world. I claim that these global changes have already far outstripped any other factor in generating a profound change – in effect, the first substantive shift – in relations between the two countries; and that, moreover, this change will extend further in the future.

In conjunction with this claim, I shall attempt briefly to sketch the parallel discourse in train between Israel and Germany. In my view, its significance does not fall short, and may even exceed, the somewhat banal and routine course of diplomatic and economic ties. I refer to the intellectual discourse whereby both countries attempt to confront the past, and, consequently, its link with the present day, including the political present. Likewise I refer to the day-to-day discourse between Germans and Israelis which, though finding no obvious expression in research literature, accompanied the two other forms of discourse I shall depict – the formal–political and the intellectual. Up to the end of the period surveyed, formal bilateral relations had not been shunted from their course by these two latter forms of discourse. However, their growing importance, in contrast with the recently collapsed foundations of the two countries' policies, endows them with added weight in discussing the future.

The German context

The forty-year existence of two Germanies (1949–89) proves that the two systems, in East and West, functioned as long as the surrounding European and international order remained intact. The two sides, adjusting to their circumstances in a more or less satisfactory manner, conducted a peaceful coexistence. In fact, the Berlin Wall was not torn down by freedom fighters of either side, nor by right-wing nationalists. Whether East or West, left or right, Germans not only held back from fighting for reunification, they didn't even foresee it: when it came about, it took them utterly by surprise.

As in the rest of Europe, the changes in Germany were instigated by Ronald Reagan, Mikhail Gorbachev and George Bush. The signals – and subsequently, the pressures – came from Moscow in the form of *perestroika*, and later from the Soviets' need of massive German aid in combination with Washington's European policy of benign neglect. These initially sent hundreds of thousands of East Germans into neighbouring countries and, later, hundreds of thousands more into the streets of Dresden, Leipzig and Berlin. West Germany settled for rhetoric and a measure of apprehension. The slogan of the demonstrators in the East, 'We are the people!' could be construed to mean: what we are, is simply 'the people' – neither avant-garde, nationalists, rebels, ideologues nor dreamers – nothing but 'the people'. Only subsequently, in the final months of the GDR's downfall, and on the margins, did the banners change to 'We are *one* people!' and did the neo-Nazis appear. Above all, those demonstrations conveyed hope rather than an expression of reality. Right to the end, the Germans lacked the ability – or the awareness or the courage – to seize the initiative to change the status quo as happened, for instance, in Poland. Certainly, they never envisaged scenarios like those played out in Romania, the Baltic countries, Yugoslavia or Russia, all of which peaked later. The West Germans never thought of shunting matters on to that course or extending active assistance. Bonn was content with the Western system of alliances and communities which also offered a haven from the dark and complex past. From both sides, the Wall was perceived as a decree of fate which could be tolerated, yet offered a framework for possible improvements.[34]

Although reunification was specifically designated as an objective in the German constitution, concrete notions of a reversal to a 'greater' Germany were perceived as nationalism and chauvinism – irreconcilable with Germany's own past or with the postwar division of the world. In true innocence, West Germany's Left believed in the right, and even the value, of the existence of a socialist Germany because it was different and an antithesis to the right wing and the capitalist way of life. They believed this in spite of the GDR's corruption, the arbitrary Stalinism of its leaders, and its hankering, in its later years particularly, after Prussian national emblems.[35]

The two states accordingly reached a tacit agreement not to disrupt the existing order, domestic and international; a few years after the erection of the dividing wall, they discarded the trappings of rivalry and began cooperating on a whole range of matters, in so far as the international framework permitted.

After deliberations and proposals discussed in the fifties and firmly rejected by Adenauer, the idea of reunification progressively receded from the sixties onwards, as West Germany focused its political efforts on expanding exports and forging intimate ties with its partners in the European Economic Community, particularly de Gaulle's France. Later, under SPD governments, the Federal Republic also embarked upon building bridges towards Eastern Europe. Although accepting the new world order politically, Bonn never formally recognised it as final, for example in relation to its new Eastern border, the Oder–Neisse.

Notwithstanding the leading role played by the German foreign ministry in fostering the changes that Gorbachev wanted in his own country and in the map of Europe; and in spite of Gorbachev's astounding popularity in Germany, events immediately preceding reunification, within the context of a rapidly disintegrating European order, moved at too rapid a pace. All the same, reunification was accomplished in a manner swift, resolute and controversial. Creatures of the old order, the two German states disappeared. The new Germany, united and sovereign, was born into a Europe and an international community as yet unprepared – without even the semblance of a plan – for a different international order. The first test of that reunited Germany came earlier than expected, before a new international order could be created.

Preceding Germany's formal reunification by two months, the international crisis surrounding the second Gulf war dredged up traumas, mindsets, uncertainties and interests hitherto without expression in German foreign policy. The latter now encountered new international realities which, in my opinion, pointed up the need for change which Germany must now face: a sharp modification of its foreign policy and a quest for a different continuity, not stemming from the recent past but rooted in German history predating the ideological wars and revolutions of the first half of the twentieth century.

In a particularly critical article on German policy during the Gulf crisis, Alan Sked wrote:

. . . it is now clear that the defense of liberty cannot be entrusted to a European federal state [a term employed during the Gulf war by Helmut Kohl and his foreign minister, Genscher] dominated by an inward-looking, provincial and pacifist Germany; a Germany which may yet establish a special relationship with Moscow rather than Washington. The free world will simply not remain free for very long if the American eagle is obliged to mate with a teutonic, double-headed European ostrich.[36]

These harsh words are merely a sample of the sharp responses to the first test confronting the foreign policy of reunited Germany. Within Germany itself, demonstrations against the war and the debate on Bonn's policy were equally fierce and sharp.[37] For the first time since World War II, Germans found themselves required to chart their own course.

The Israeli response

With regard to Israel, the two aforementioned developments influenced its policies, and its relations with Germany, in an asymmetrical manner. But their impact will be greater in the longer term than in the period surveyed here.

The collapse of the old order in Europe is already bringing to Israel a number, without precedent since the fifties, of Jewish immigrants, from the former Soviet Union in particular. The disappearance of the Soviet Union as a major player in the Middle East undermines regional stability, which rested upon a balance between the superpowers; it also strips Moscow of its moderating role vis-à-vis its allies in the region, Syria especially. Similarly, the Soviet Moslem republics, removed from Moscow's control, are liable to slip away perhaps toward the sphere of influence of Iran, and the world of Islamic politics, including fundamentalism.

German reunification has confronted Israel with a dilemma of a kind also unfamiliar since the fifties: the need to redefine its attitude towards Germany. In this sense, Israel made its decision virtually instantaneously. After a few utterances reflecting fear and apprehension, Israel's foreign minister was despatched to Bonn to express Israel's support for the process of democratisation sweeping Europe, including German reunification.[38] Certainly, few Israelis shed tears over the demise of the GDR, which had done its utmost to harm Israel, from providing aid and training for the most hardline of Palestinian terrorists and their German sympathisers to supplying weapons, know-how, gas and intelligence to the Arab states.[39] After brief reflection, Israel therefore elected to pursue the policy of Ben Gurion, with a total consensus emerging between the prime minister, a follower of Begin, and the president, a member of the opposition Labour party.

In the Knesset debate held in May 1990, Yitzchak Shamir expressed himself in the spirit and terms of his illustrious predecessor Ben Gurion: 'It is not for us, but for the Germans themselves, and the other nations, to decide thereon. Anyone wishing to atone for what happened in the Holocaust must take care to buttress the state of the Jews.'[40]

When I interviewed Israeli state president Haim Herzog in a television programme on German reunification on 6 October 1990, he put it in even clearer terms:

Of course Jews entertain doleful thoughts [regarding reunification]. How could it be otherwise? . . . But we should recall that we are in the midst of a revolution, not merely in Germany; a worldwide revolution centred upon everything that has happened in the Soviet Union. Ben Gurion laid down Israel's policy towards Germany, and that is the applicable policy to this very day, even with Germany reunited. In other words, the most precious asset the Jewish people has is the state of Israel, its future and its security. That was the basis of his policy with regard to Germany in the past, and it ought to continue with regard to the future.[41]

This broad Israeli consensus was also reflected in opinion polls conducted after reunification, and even in the immediate wake of the allied war in the Gulf.

In spite of emerging revelations about Germany's role in the sale of arms and military know-how to Iraq, and in spite of the anti-American demonstrations with their concomitant display of hostility towards Israel, the issue of relations with Germany remained independent of the profound crisis overtaking Israeli and German intellectuals. This crisis concerned their own identity and their perceptions of each other's identity or the views of opposition groups – particularly at the extremities of the political spectrum – with regard to the relations between the two countries, and their respective country's foreign policy.[42]

These two external events – the European upheaval and the Gulf war – have subjected the Israeli–German relationship to a substantive change far transcending the prosaic continuity exhibited by unfolding bilateral relations or internal developments within each country between the two periods being considered.

Shortly after the exchange of ambassadors between the two countries, West Germany witnessed the emergence of a broad consensus with the SPD joining the government for the first time. It marked the beginning of a break with Adenauer's traditional rule that denuded Bonn's foreign policy of any values he considered irreconcilable with American policy.[43] Under the influence of the SPD, hitherto unrepresented in the decision-making process, the German consensus shifted. At the margins, the extra-parliamentary opposition began to play a role, with the students' rebellion leaving its imprint on Germany's intellectual development. The marginal groups – from the outset fiercely critical of the political systems of the Federal Republic, the United States and Israel – were hostile towards Israel, which they identified with the United States. At the same time, Germany's general public began taking a sympathetic view of Israel. The 1967 war marked a peak in support for Israel.

But the seventies – with the Arab oil embargo and initial European efforts to formulate a joint foreign policy *vis-à-vis* Israel, the Arab world and the United States – progressively eroded the positive attitudes of the sixties. There was a total lack of communication during the terms of office of Chancellor Helmut Schmidt and of Prime Minister Menachem Begin[44] – the selfsame Begin who had once resisted the reparations agreement, but now, as a statesman in the eighties, never for a moment considered severing relations with Germany. Begin's utterances about Schmidt's past with the Wehrmacht, matched by Schmidt's arrogant refusal to visit Israel or include the Jewish people or Israel in the list of nations to whom Germany owed a moral debt, combined to create a nadir in both countries. However, practical relations remained unimpaired. The first great tests confronted the two countries towards the nineties, with conflicting trains of thought exhibited in each as it confronted its past.

The trauma and the German intellectuals

In a significant article which contributed to the weighty debate on Germany's identity and past, philosopher Jurgen Habermass quoted the conservative historian Michael Stuermer as he launched what was subsequently known as 'the debate of the historians', the effective onset of the intellectual exchange surrounding the demise of the Federal Republic as moulded by Konrad Adenauer. Stuermer says: 'A loss of the sense of direction, and a quest for identity, are interconnected. Anyone believing that these are without effect upon politics and the future, does not take into account that in a land without history, the present [will be won by] those who replenish memory, coin expressions and interpret the past.'[45]

The debate commenced shortly after the joint visit of Helmut Kohl and Ronald Reagan to the Bitburg cemetery which houses the graves of SS men. The visit sparked off a storm in Germany, in the Jewish communities in the United States and in the world at large. There was slightly less reaction in Israel.[44] Not long after Bitburg, new ideas came to flower on the conservative right wing, which included historians and intellectuals with no direct political affiliations. Stuermer, Joachim Fest and others turned to discussing the essence of the past, and the way to the future. A fundamental element of this controversial debate was the historisation – and so-called 'relativisation' of the Nazi past: in other words, setting that past within the context of other historical processes such as Soviet Stalinism and presenting it from a viewpoint unlike that of historians from 'the winning side' in World War II. This was extended to comparisons with the present, to analogies drawn with other events before and after World War II such as Cambodia and (in extreme cases) the issue of the Palestinians in the territories occupied by Israel.[47] Comparisons of the last mentioned had been drawn in Germany (and elsewhere, including Israel itself) long before the debate which commenced in Germany in the latter half of the eighties. All the same, the simplistic thesis presented earlier, especially on Germany's extreme left and right, and, obliquely, even by Helmut Schmidt, was a slogan with no profound political or philosophical significance. The start of the more acute debate about the past laid the ground for questions about German identity, and was able to look at the past with greater clarity and deduce its political lessons for Germany's future path. The trauma which Germany had sought hitherto to evade, affecting its identity at a psychological level, now became a concrete 'past', more comprehensible, capable of being compared and measured and with a correspondingly greater role as what Stuermer terms '*Sinnstifter*' (provider of significance).[48] Habermass's opposing thesis of *Verfassungspatriotismus* (patriotism to the Federal Republic's constitution) was ultimately defeated. The Federal Republic, not founded for that purpose, was unable to provide anything more than temporary shelter (the German expression is '*Provisorium*', or, the expression employed by Professor Arnulf Baring, 'a doll's house').[49] However, that doll's house, and its Eastern counterpart, were not demolished by the intellectuals – of left, right or centre – nor did they even inspire its demolition. History itself chose a different course for the process of reunification.

Alongside the philosophical debate about German history, other schools of thought began to emerge, dealing with present and future. Some, led by the ecological movement, the Evangelical church and the peace movement, sought to change Germany by directing their gaze beyond its borders. They began to mould politics in Bonn and, to a lesser degree, in East Germany too. The changes, particularly noticeable among the younger generation of Germans, and the transition of the '1968' movement to other channels, were signalled by the Greens' 1983 success in gaining a foothold in the Bundestag and the growing political weight of the German peace movement and the Evangelical church. Yet, the ultimate inability of these movements to offer Germany a political and intellectual alternative, or generate genuine change, stems in part from their flight from a past which still represented trauma rather than history. The issues they emblazoned on their banners were, they claimed, connected with the future, not connected with German history, which they rejected lock stock and barrel. Instead, they drew from the past a number of negative lessons, that is the results of its rejection such as outright pacifism, a pursuit – a virtual deification – of nature, universalism bordering on exoticism, together with hostility towards materialism and 'Americanism' (and hence to Israel), a sidelong glance towards anarchism, tolerance towards acts of terrorism. They also included a quest among ideologies including East and West, and left and right, for a kind of *Sonderweg* (unique path) – a peculiarly German concept whose connotations

were explained by the Greens' numerous critics, including their own supporters, without disabusing most of them of adherence to its charms.[50]

The Greens did include several friends of Israel but were, on the whole, its
severest critics. The party leadership endorsed positions drawn directly from
Palestinian organisations more extreme even than the PLO. For the sake of the
Middle East, some party members called expressly for Israel's liquidation.[51] On
the eve of a visit to Israel, one of its leaders, Christian Strobele, declared that the
Scud missiles fired at Israel by Iraq in January 1991 were 'the logical, inevitable
outcome of its policy in the occupied territories'. Though forced to resign after
this statement, Strobele was not alone in that view.[52]

However, these movements did not tip the domestic scales. Failing to confront the problem of their identity, as well as offering an unattractive electoral
alternative to the economic and social success of the Federal Republic, they
never won over a majority of the German public. Good relations with the United
States and the EC, successes in Federal organisation, in the economy, in
education, culture, workers' rights and pay, stability of the currency and
exports, the relatively low level of unemployment, the relative but progressive
amelioration in living conditions in the GDR – all these preserved both German
states from fundamental upheavals. Up to the eve of the fall of the Berlin Wall,
Germany witnessed no turnabout of any kind, psychological or political. The
most serious confrontation commenced only with the national and economic
collapse of Eastern Europe, in the Soviet Union particularly, and when the
enormous economic and social cost of reunification became evident.

The Israeli trauma

Israel emerged from the shadow of the Holocaust, inheriting the trauma, the
memory, the lessons, the needs – material, psychological, historical and political
– as a chain of processes and events which accompanied and unsettled it
throughout its years of existence: the impotence of the Jewish *Yishuv* (community) in Palestine, and of world Jewry – in the United States especially – in
saving the Jews of Europe; the rift among Zionists, in Palestine and elsewhere,
as to the priorities between building up the Jewish *Yishuv* and total mobilisation
to save Jews; the feasibility and justification of negotiating with Nazi Germany
to that end; issues surrounding what was termed 'like sheep to the slaughter', in
contrast with manifestations of heroism; the philosophical and theological
meaning and interpretation of the Holocaust; and above all, the enormity of the
calamity, unprecedented, indescribable and inexplicable, enfolding millions of
private calamities. All of these, and numerous other issues linked with the
Holocaust were, from the outset, closely connected with the annals of the state
of Israel and the Jewish people. Tom Segev's detailed and critical recent book
traces the phases from this beginning right up to the contemporary period; he
concludes that the confrontation between Israelis and the Holocaust followed
two principal lines:

One line led from national seclusion, verging upon xenophobia, to universal humanistic
openness. The second line led from Israeli identity to Jewish identity. As the Holocaust
receded, its presence struck deeper roots as a personal and family trauma which
determined the life's course of the Israelis, their personal weave, and their outlook on

life, a source from which they drew the components of their identities as individuals and group.[53]

Holocaust awareness in Israel thus pursued a quasi-circular track from personal traumas with no political application, by way of an attempt to construct a national Zionist myth bonding the collective Israeli and Jewish memory, to conclusions about the present and future, while fusing it with other national elements. These included the dual term 'Holocaust and Heroism'; Holocaust commemoration day, marked close to the memorial day for the IDF dead and Israel's Independence Day; and rites of a Jewish religious nature. In recent years, preoccupation with the Holocaust has reverted to a more individualist character, although Israel's schools continue to foster the collective myth and the Zionist conclusions, including their political, or in Orthodox circles, theological aspect. Segev writes: 'Demonisation of Nazi evil freed the textbooks of the need to explain the crimes of the Nazis, and above all, freed them of the need to confront the possibility that the horrors were spawned in a normal human environment.'

Segev quotes a survey by sociologist Uri Fargo showing that school pupils draw most of their knowledge of the Holocaust from television, films, books, commemorations and study days. As a source of information about the Holocaust, the pupils placed their school history lessons last![54]

Space prohibits details about the centrality of the Holocaust in Israeli public life. Segev's book, which provides these, is, in effect, an intellectual history of the state of Israel. The elements mentioned here are included only for contrast with the elements I noted in the German consciousness and its attitude towards the selfsame historical trauma. Shaul Friedlaender writes:

On a symbolical level, one can speak of the Jewish memory of Auschwitz, and of the German memory of Auschwitz. The discrepancy between these memories may expand and grow sharper; but they are inextricably interwoven in what historian Dan Diner of Essen University terms a 'negative symbiosis'. Every reworking of this memory will directly influence the other's memory; any attempt at obfuscation casts an overall shadow of oblivion. Neither Germans nor Jews can relate to their own memory, without touching upon the others' memory.[55]

Professor Moshe Zimmermann perceives centrality – psychological and political – in the role of the traumas in shaping the mutual relations of the two peoples, and more so: 'The memories, the responsibilities, and the hangovers of the two peoples, became the property of the younger states, not only in their own eyes, but also in their awareness of each other and towards each other.'[56]

On this point, the veteran editor of *Ha'aretz*, Gershom Shoken, again quotes Bermass, who stated that the German–Israeli relationship eternally hinges on 'the scenes from that platform' – the platform at Auschwitz.[57] But in my opinion, those selfsame scenes unfolded asymetrically in the two countries, ultimately playing no major role in their policies towards one another, nor in shaping their own political courses. The treatment of the subject – intellectual initially and then political – enabled Germany to grapple with the past in a manner that made it possible to live with and thus diminish the oppressive sense of uniqueness which weighed upon Germany since the creation of its two states. In Israel, the Holocaust was transmuted, by means of its attachment to the national Zionist myth, into a unique, virtually ahistorical, chapter of Jewish destiny, linked less and less to the realities and consciousness of the history of modern Germany and Europe.

Here are two brief examples of the unique discourse between Israelis and Germans, alongside their diplomatic and economic discourse.

The two countries' different modes of dealing with the past are exemplified by the creative avant-garde in each. I am not acquainted with any notable artistic or cultural creation generated in the new Germany about life or culture in Israel or the new Judaism. The same applies to Israel: the subject was left to journalists, columnists, academics or producers of documentary films – not writers, play-wrights, painters or poets. Adorno's remark about 'the barbarism of poetry after Auschwitz' did not preclude extensive – and agonised – preoccupation, artistic and cultural, with the history of the Holocaust. With that, there is an evident difference: German culture and art has dealt, almost obsessively, with Germany and the Germans. Israelis, too, were preoccupied with themselves. If there was any mutual recognition of each other's art, it was via translation and observation of colleagues on the other side, particularly of the more critically-minded, as is only natural. (An especially interesting example of this dialogue, from the viewpoint I am discussing, is Professor Shaul Friedlaender's book *Kitsch and Death*).[58] Ultimately, this hazy discourse has led both sides into a blind alley. The post-Gulf war encounter between Gunther Grass and Yoram Kanyuk, in a television programme recorded before a Berlin audience, was a dialogue of the deaf. Kanyuk, a member of the Israeli peace movement, spoke of his lessons from the Holocaust – moral, national, and unique, like the national essence of the state of Israel. Gunther Grass spoke as a man for whom the lesson of World War II – and the Holocaust, as an historic event of that period – permits comparisons and criticism, *vis-à-vis* his own country, Germany, and towards Israel and its policy, for example on the Palestinian issue.[59] In Israel too, particularly since the *intifada*, voices recalling that debate join in the discourse around the lessons of the Holocaust, scrutinising the historical environment and its circumstances, not necessarily, as hitherto, concentrating on its conventional and numbingly final conclusion – Auschwitz. In this sense, there are the beginnings, which will certainly continue, of a new and more critical discourse whose contribution to Israeli policy – on the Palestinian issue, for example – is as yet marginal.[60]

Day-to-day discourse

Lying at the other extremity of the field of Israeli–German discourse is a sphere which scholars have scarcely touched: day-to-day discourse between citizens of Israel and Germany. Throughout this period, opinion polls were conducted in both countries, questioning specific sectors such as school children or socio-economic cross-sections of the population.[61] From years of experience as an Israeli journalist in Germany and a frequent visitor there, and as a regular participant in the public debate in Israel on these questions, I can affirm that the full story has eluded research projects and the opinion polls.

Germany is a distant land to Israelis. Most have never been there, and some, not necessarily Holocaust survivors or members of their generation, even refuse – on principle – to visit. A considerable proportion of the Israeli population comes from Asian or African countries quite unconnected with European culture; recent trends do not incline towards that culture; on the contrary, they mark a return to Jewish roots. The Orthodox sector has joined in the Israeli discourse in a manner entirely precluding anything not directly connected to the Jewish religious creed (*halacha*). The German language is rarely heard in Israel; the old generation of 'Yekkes', as the German Jews were nicknamed, is departing this world without leaving a deep imprint on Israel's culture or society. The media show a tendency – not necessarily deliberate policy – to avoid use of German; the works of Wagner and Richard Strauss are still not played, and few seem to care.

Many Israelis portray Germany paradoxically: on the one hand, there is (still) admiration – even to excess – for the German traits of efficiency, diligence, punctuality, courtesy and technical and cultural attainment. On the other hand, there is an oppressive feeling verging on fear with regard to negative traits and processes reported by the media, particularly television from which the majority of the population draws its foreign news. Manifestations of neo-Nazism, xenophobia, isolationism, hostility towards the United States or Israel – whether from left or right – are seen in a far graver light than their impact or political influence merits; they are viewed as a direct threat to Jews, to Israel or even to world peace, almost heralding a 'Fourth Reich'. Germany is invariably seen as far stronger and more menacing than other countries, even if, over the years, and with the continuity of diplomatic relations which have expanded into cultural and other links, these sentiments have remained hazy, scarcely achieving significant political formulation. Similar phenomena may be found in Germany: questions directed at me or my Israeli colleagues and surveys conducted in that country often show Germans to be convinced that their country contains hundreds of thousands of Jews whose public and political influence is 'excessive'.[62] In fact, there are just over 30,000 Jews living in Germany, and I am not acquainted with any Jew wielding political influence there.[63]

Germany's extensive aid to Israel – and Israelis – has expanded in recent years to generate a kind of cornucopia: alongside the embassy, there are other German bodies, semi-official or otherwise, like the Goethe Institute and foundations administered by German political parties or trade unions. Others are funded by German industry, academia, municipal authorities and sundry states (*Lander*), and so on and so forth. A very considerable number of Israeli groups and individuals have received some form of German financial support. The Israeli public frequently hears this dependency condemned, on a variety of grounds. One view holds that massive reliance upon German money reinforces the mutually negative feelings of donor and recipient, and the stereotypes of prejudice and trauma, again depicting the Jews as moneygrubbers and the Germans as handing out cash to expiate their guilt. There have also been instances of German money serving unworthy purposes.[64] Alternatively, some seek to address the German market, alleviating the German trauma by criticism of Israel, authored by Israelis and paid for by Germans. Furthermore, embarrassing revelations are sporadically published about the criminal, or dubious, deeds of Jews or Israelis visiting or permanently resident in Germany. The extent of official embarrassment in dealing with these cases is equalled only by the extensive and sensational publicity such episodes gain in the media of both countries, as glaring proof of the (moral) non-uniqueness of the Jews, or, conversely, the (sinister) non-uniqueness of the Germans.[65] Often enough,

Israelis arrested by the German police – even for mere traffic offences – invoke memories of the Holocaust to get themselves freed. Conversely, anti-Semitic remarks or macabre jokes are common in Germany, even by persons not involved, hostile or critical towards Israel, particularly the young, and doubly so when alcohol has been imbibed or at soccer stadiums – and again, without hitherto having any effect beyond the sphere of everyday discourse.

Set against the hobbled sterility of bilateral political discourse, the largely oblique and forced cultural discourse, and each people's limited acquaintance with the other, these sensations, apparently originating in apprehensions insufficiently worked through, have not inhibited curiosity. German literature in Hebrew translation is very popular in Israel. Events in Germany gain attention and receive proper coverage. Germans are equally familiar with events in Israel. Reporters sometimes show an unsavoury tendency to draw on terms from the Nazi lexicon – from one side, to make comparisons about Israeli actions; from the other, as an implied charge that Germany has not changed.[66] This was often done by critically minded columnists on both sides, particularly in editorials which attempted to highlight the past and transfer the day-to-day discourse to the sphere of bilateral political discourse. Most of these attempts failed.[67]

The end of the past

Anticipating the fortieth anniversaries of Israel and the Federal Republic policy-makers in both countries were in a position to draw up summaries which principally patted backs – their own and those of their counterparts. Bilateral relations seemed to be flourishing and their extent and quality in the ascendant, to the benefit of both sides and the irritation of almost no one in either land, or beyond.

In terms of German political practice, Israel was, indeed, a 'special case'. Israel got more German aid, more frequently, than other countries.[68] But that is not my main point. The emphasis, rather, is on the principle delineating each side's policies towards the other. Germany, for example, never went beyond the political line dictated by broader interests, such as its links with the United States, the European community or the Arab world; or the interests of its own economic policies or industry.

Israel likewise perceived Germany as a special case. Anti-German utterances, some extremely fierce, were frequently heard in Israel, whether from politicians, public opinion or the media. However, Israel too treated Germany in accordance with its own needs and interests, frequently diverging from the line adopted by Jewish organisations. This distinction between the voice of organised Jewry and the voice of official Jerusalem, already finding clearcut expression in Ben Gurion's time, continued throughout the years up to and including German reunification and the Gulf war: Israel and world Jewry continued to speak in different voices.[69]

Germany itself refrained from officially calling its relationship with Israel 'special' – other than in the sense employed by Feldman, who claims that German–Israeli relations were 'special, not unique';[70] that is with a special quality but basically resembling either country's relations with others. In this case, I find semantics of great significance: there is virtually no parallel this century with the uniqueness of Israel or the two German states created after the

Second World War and the Holocaust. Under the circumstances, any German–Israeli relationship would therefore be special. But the relationship created in practice attempted to pursue interests and needs – material or otherwise – while bypassing the unique character of each country. Weaker in the material aspect though apparently holding the moral advantage, Israel was forced to accede to Bonn's characterisation of the relationship as material rather than moral.

Along with the beginnings of change in the Soviet Union, and some two years before German reunification, the territories occupied by Israel in 1967 witnessed the onset of the Palestinian uprising, which progressively polarised Israeli society. Other issues like the state, religion and ethnic problems and questions of culture and identity were shunted aside, along with moderate views on either side of the political spectrum. Israelis, their dependence upon the United States now decisive, became less and less preoccupied with Germany and Europe. But through its political representatives, European public opinion began showing growing sympathy for the Palestinians, their political organisation and their demands for self-determination.

Within the now firmly institutionalised framework of the European Community, Germany had contrived throughout the eighties to maintain its policies towards Europe, on the one hand, and *vis-à-vis* Israel and the Arabs on the other, without letting matters reach crisis point. In the final years before reunification Hans-Dietrich Genscher, Germany's foreign minister, excelled himself. A political acrobat of the first order, he contrived to extend consistent support to Israeli interests *vis-à-vis* Germany, or Europe, or through German mediation in other spheres of diplomatic activity (for example, with regard to the problem of Soviet Jews, before the Kremlin opened the exit gates). But he simultaneously supported EC policies towards Israel, even when Brussels' decisions angered Jerusalem. The Europeans understood German sympathy towards Israel, and the Israelis recognised Europe's importance to Germany, even when Germany joined Community sanctions against Israel after the closure of universities in the occupied territories. Israelis and Europeans alike were long accustomed to the fact that political resolutions adopted in Brussels were not exactly the outcome of a genuine change of policy, or indications of a real crisis; rather, they reflected a consensus between a dozen foreign ministers convening to draw up convoluted resolutions, mostly without teeth and motivated above all by the wish or need – for reasons totally unrelated – to achieve that consensus.

Had the German foreign ministry taken diplomatic action, for example, to impose unilateral sanctions against scientific cooperation with Israel, it would have sparked an immediate crisis in bilateral relations. But the EC was the perfect instrument, permitting Bonn to impose sanctions (and many similar quasi-diplomatic *démarches*) upon Israel, without directly affecting relations with Israel. Among other diplomatic successes, Israel could count upon Bonn's regular and consistent support for its requests, and it was gratified to receive reports from its representatives at the EC's Council of Ministers about Bonn's positions, which were benign relative to those of other European states. It was made plain to Jerusalem that Germany was less hostile than its partners, and if Bonn had failed to tilt the balance, it was a pity, but such was the way in Brussels. Germany never vetoed a European resolution connected to Israel, and was never required to choose between Brussels and Jerusalem. But Jerusalem knew what Bonn would choose, and Israeli foreign policy has become progressively more cautious in recent years.

At the same time, Bonn was expanding its links with the Arab world, particularly those states without direct or close links with the United States. German industry contrived to export to countries such as Iran, Iraq, Syria and Libya whose relations with the West were strained. Before taking office as FDR deputy foreign minister, Jorgen Moellmann was president of the German–Arab Friendship Association. Bonn's ministries of foreign affairs, finance and economic cooperation spoke, with evident gratification and growing self-confidence, of the Federal Republic's skilful manoeuvring in a complex world of political and economic interests. Simultaneously, in defiance of German export regulations, and certainly in defiance of Germany's past or the uniqueness – or whatever remained thereof – of Israel (target of most of the weaponry channelled to the Arabs, other than that destined for the Iran–Iraq war), they shut their eyes to the aggressive export policies of German firms which sold the Arab states components, products and know-how in spheres liable to have military application. These sales went ahead despite Germany's moral vulnerability to accusations of involvement in any wars or conflicts.

On the eve of the great upheavals in Europe and the Gulf, the situation appeared entirely unthreatening. The prevalent German view (expressed in many books about the two Germanies' forty-year history published in 1989, and in numerous articles in the German and world press) was that the Berlin Wall would remain in place for a further fifty or a hundred years and that that was not necessarily a bad thing. Germany's political leadership held similar views.[71] The German political system largely functioned on the model of Francis Fukuyama's views on 'The end of history'. Up to the very last moment before the Wall's collapse, German leaders never suggested, to themselves or their people, that after a kind of forty-year lull, the history of Europe, and of Germany therein, would recommence in November 1989 even though, in retrospect, the prognosis was written in foot-high letters all along the Wall.

Israel, it must be admitted, showed far greater scepticism. The fierce domestic crisis surrounding the issue of Palestinian nationalism, the cultural struggle between Orthodox clericalism and a secular majority, the looming military threat posed by the reinforcement of the eastern front after the end of the Iraq–Iran war in mid 1988 particularly in view of Saddam Hussein's increasingly threatening tone towards Israel – all these precluded Israel's adherence to the German view of history's imminent end. Israel gave no heed to the era of bureaucracy lying around the corner for a kind of world-wide 1992, as sketched by Jacques Delors, or the 'common European home' of Mikhail Gorbachev (the most popular politician in Germany, far outstripping leaders of the West or of Germany itself).[72] Europe in general, and Germany in particular, willingly accepted the vision which sought to replace political and ideological history with bureaucracy, even justifying the process as the progress of the human spirit as envisaged by Hegel who, in his own lifetime, laid the ideological foundations for the Prussian state as the incarnation of the human spirit.

But matters unfolded differently. Unexpectedly, history began making fools of Fukuyama and his followers. From the Soviet Union, to Eastern Europe to Berlin, Europe reverted to history, with Germany at the focus. As it transpired, this was just the beginning. Two months before the formal reunification of Germany, the Gulf crisis erupted, and after repeated attempts to evade taking a stand, official Germany was forced to announce a quasi-solidarity with the Western states, in spite of the constitutional ban on sending forces beyond the

NATO domain (a view currently disputed, though there is no disagreement over Germany's political reluctance to do so).[73] When the first Scud missiles fell on Israel, Foreign Minister Genscher was sent there to take the flak. And there was plenty of it with reports of German assistance to the Iraqi arms industry (conventional, chemical and nuclear); of Germans helping Iraq develop gas weapons designed for mass annihilation; and of German know-how bringing Israel within range of the Scuds – set off by the gigantic anti-American demonstrations held in Germany. In addition there was the position adopted by the left (and the embarrassing picture of the former chancellor, Social-Democrat Willy Brandt, anti-Nazi and friend of Israel, on a placatory visit to Baghdad where he shocked Israelis by embracing Yassir Arafat). Finally there were marginal but striking gestures – like neo-Nazis volunteering to help Saddam annihilate the Jews.[74] All these were blows that Genscher suffered 'willingly' as he scuttled from Jerusalem government offices to scenes of Iraqi missile devastation.

Genscher and Kohl promptly pledged the only help they had: money and arms. Naturally enough, Israel was equally prompt in deciding what it wanted. Within days, a shopping list was drawn up including military items previously considered but deferred through budgetary or other constraints (such as construction in German shipyards of two submarines for the Israeli navy). Thus, after swopping declarations about the shock and pain over the threat to Israel, and the dreadful connotations surrounding the word association Germany–gas–Jews, the two sides hastened to the diplomatic and economic negotiating table to proceed with the agenda. With regard to formal ties between the two countries, this Gulf war exercised a merely marginal effect, despite the Israeli trauma – the sealed rooms, the gas masks and the collapse of confidence in the IDF's ability to protect the civilian rear and deter Israel's enemies; and despite the German trauma – political paralysis between East and West, Germany's internal divisions over support for the United States, apprehensions that German lettering would be found on mass annihilation weapons deployed against Israel and so on.

I believe that the thesis presented throughout this chapter – that both states' claim to uniqueness has rendered their mutual relations non-unique – also stands up to a scrutiny of their positions in the Gulf crisis – which, however, may have been that claim's final test. The Gulf war exposed Germany and Israel – each for different reasons – to their uniqueness, possibly for the last time, in a quasi-transitional stage between the demise of the old world order and the necessity of adjusting to a different order, without it being self-evident, as it was after World War II, what that order actually will be. It remains unclear whether that 'new order' will be anything more than a euphemism for a quest for stability in a world where the collapse of ideologies has left national and economic power the sole objective. The strongest world power is the United States, but no one foresees Washington being able to dictate to Berlin in the future international arena. Israel is comprehensively dependent upon the United States, but one cannot automatically conclude that it will in future agree with the White House, or even Congress or American public opinion.

The world order has already changed; the Gulf war was the final test of Germany and Israel, the two states created by the old order. The war ended the era of their uniqueness, and that process may enhance the influence, on their policies and their interrelationship, of other forms of discourse.

I have depicted some of those forms, with the agony, the apprehension and the curiosity they represent. Israel remains tied to Europe by political and economic interests. In my view Israeli–German relations in their new phase, whenever it appears, will rest, not upon the existing formal infrastructure, but on internal changes within both countries, and the emergence of hitherto non-existent elements in the official discourse between them. I do not foresee continuity in the relationship but change – and indeed, change that may be unilateral initially. Germany is already considering its course and policies.[75] In Israel, as noted, that is as yet a remote prospect: internal division paralyses any ability to conduct a creative foreign policy. Other options – beyond dependency upon the United States and continuation of the occupation in the absence of a political solution – seem too remote to come to fruition. The United States has wrestled Israel into regional political negotiations, and the recent EC proposals – offering Israel a status comparable to that of the EFTA countries – will draw a positive response from Jerusalem. But in any event, the process will be lengthy. That still does not exhaust the Israeli–German relationship. Whenever created, the new infrastructure must try, after over forty years of disguise and dissembling, artificiality and evasiveness, to confront the substance, the essence and the extent of the historical tale and message the two peoples have to relate to each other and to themselves. Hitherto, both states have endeavoured, successfully, to evade the task, possibly with a measure of justification. In future, they will have no cause to do so, and they may even wish to face up to it.

Notes

1. The term 'Germany' will relate particularly to the German Federal Republic – West Germany – and, subsequently, reunified Germany. Any reference to the DDR will be specified as such.

Germany's partitioning, and its formal dependence upon the occupying powers, facilitated matters for Israel in the early period of their relations. In its role of successor state, Bonn's formal identification with the German nation, while proclaiming itself a 'different' Germany in spite of that continuity, played an important role in forging relations with Israel. The first formal contacts between Israel and the GDR, commencing in 1990 shortly before the latter's eclipse as a sovereign entity, remained meaningless.

2. The expression is drawn from Guenther Hoffman: 'Sehnsucht nach Normalitaet', *Die Zeit* No. 10, 28 February 1986.

3. Professor Moshe Zimmermann affirms that the mythical nature of 'Stunde Null' is now generally accepted. To quote just one example: in 1948, over 50 per cent of the Germans in the American sector believed that Nazism was 'a good idea applied badly'. M. Zimmermann, 'The Memory of War and Holocaust in Germany' in M. Zimmermann (ed.), *25 years of Israeli–German Relations*, Jerusalem, Magnes Press, forthcoming.

In another article, Zimmermann argues that the German trauma comprises two elements: 'The damage Germany inflicted upon itself, and the damage it inflicted upon others – the reason for Germany's disgrace. The seven evil years 1941–8 are the ones constituting the German trauma to this day – not necessarily the dozen years between 1933 and 1945. *Total war, Auschwitz, the collapse, the deportations, the humiliation, the post-war helplessness and the partitioning of Germany* are the traumatic elements in the day-to-day experience of the inhabitants of the Federal Republic, old and young alike.' (p.9 of 'The Phoenix in Trauma – the FRG' in *Germany after 1945: Overcoming the Trauma*, Moshe Zimmermann and Michael Toch (eds), pp.9–36, Jerusalem, Magnes Press, Jerusalem, 1984. See also (p.12): 'The peak hour of the trauma is what German literature calls 'Stunde Null'; it was termed thus, not particularly because it appeared as the beginning of a new period, but because it was the hour of chaos and *uncertainty*' (italics in the original).

See also the renowned address by the president of the Federal Republic, Richard von Weizsaecker, on 8 May 1985, the fortieth anniversary of the victory over Nazi Germany: 'Es gab keine "Stunde Null", aber wir hatten die Chance zu einem Neubeginn.' ('There was no "zero hour", but we had the chance of a new beginning.')

4. Shlomo Shafir, *An Outstretched Hand, German Social Democrats, Jews and Israel, 1945–67*, Tel Aviv, Zmora Bitan, 1986, Chaps. 3–6, pp.46–103.

5. *Documents on the Foreign Policy of Israel vol. 6. 1951*, State of Israel, Jerusalem, Israel State Archives, 1991, p.665.

6. Ibid., companion volume, p.289.

7. Regarding contacts and the reparations, see especially: Nana Sagi, *German reparations: A History of the Negotiations*, Jerusalem, Magnes Press, 1980; Lily Gardner Feldman, *The Special Relationship between West Germany and Israel*, Boston, George Allen and Unwin, 1984; P. Eliezer Shinnar, *Under the Burden of Necessity and Emotion, Israel–German Relations 1951–66*, Shoken, 1967; and Inge Deutschkron, *Israel und die Deutschen*, Cologne, Verlag Wissenschaft und Politik, 1983. Also, Shafir, as above.

8. Gershom Scholem, 'Jews and Germans', *Ha'aretz*, 14 September 1966 in the book *Words of Relevance*, Tel Aviv, AM OVED, 1975, see particularly pp.112–13.

9. Michael Wolffsohn, *Deutsch–Israelische Beziehungen: Umfragen und Interpretationen, 1952–1983*, Munich, Bayerische Landeszentrale für Politische Bildung, 1986, p.34.

See too, Shafir, pp.84–5. Other opponents included Franz-Josef Strauss, Germany's ambassadors to the Arab states, experts on Arab affairs, and financial and economic circles.

After the November 1952 American elections brought a Republican victory in Congress and the presidency, the German assessment foresaw diminished influence for the Jewish organisations. Accordingly, delaying tactics were employed. Shafir quotes the German journalist Marion Doenhoff from the liberal newspaper *Die Zeit* who said: 'All German payments and shipments should be delayed until peace is made between Israel and the Arab states.'

With regard to the debate in Israel and its domestic fallout see: Tom Segev, *The Seventh Million: Israelis and the Holocaust*, Jerusalem, Domino, 1991, particularly Section D, pp.173–236.

10. Segev, op. cit., p.186.

11. Documents, op. cit. As will be recalled, the 'past epoch' had ended six years prior to the declaration.

12. Deutschkron, op. cit., p.22; Nahum Goldman, *Le paradox juif*, Tel Aviv, Massada Press, 1978, p.106. Shafir relates that objections to conceding Israel's 'uniqueness' came from the Christian Democrats and the Liberals, who feared negative reactions from a considerable portion of the German public and did not want the moral credit to fall to the SPD, who had frequently spoken out on the issue. There was also opposition from Jewish organisations world-wide. Ronald Zweig shows that this opposition, stemming from fear of an Israeli monopoly of the reparations and coming also from anti-Zionist positions, influenced Israeli decision-makers. See: Ronald Zweig, 'German Reparations and Israel–Diaspora Relations', *Zionism*, anthology 14, 1989, pp.232–9.

Segev reveals that Herut leader Begin consented to Israel's request to the occupying powers to demand reparations from Germany when the note was sent in early 1951. It was only later, when it became a matter of direct contacts with Bonn, that he changed his mind and took up a position of furious opposition to reparations. See Segev, pp.205–7.

Internal attitudes in Germany, Israel and the Jewish organisations reinforced political guidelines on both sides. Israel from the outset waived any insistence on sole representation of the Jewish people *vis-à-vis* Germany.

Yeshayahu A. Jelinek presents a thesis he calls 'the Locarno concept' – the Federal Republic drew away from Eastern Europe to integrate with the West under American leadership. In Jelinek's view, the phrase 'restoration to the family of nations' was a code denoting 'Bonn's integration into the anti-Communist bloc, under cover provided by the tacit consent of former victims of the Third Reich'. Politicians – American, British, German, Jewish and Israeli – used the term to vindicate the verbal and financial gestures towards victims of Nazism. East European victims received no compensation whatsoever because the Federal Republic adhered to the 'good guys' (the West) against the 'bad guys' (the Communists).

The Locarno conference (1925) marked out the western borders of the Weimar Republic, whereas there was no agreement over its borders with Poland and Czechoslovakia. In similar fashion, Jelinek holds, compensation and restitution were granted to the Jewish people and Israel, whereas the claims of Germany's eastern neighbours gained no response. 'The agreements permitted Germany to join the Western camp. But it ultimately transpired that this course – and the Hallstein doctrine that supported it – was erroneous, giving ammunition to the East Germans and Arabs, and bedevilling Israeli–German relations right up to its final abandonment.' Yeshayahu Jelinek, lecture, Hebrew University, Jerusalem, 1990. See also his article, 'Political Acumen, Altruism, Foreign Pressure or Moral Debt', *Tel Aviv Jahrbuch für Deutsche Geschichte*, 1990.

13. See Feldman, op. cit., Chapter 3, particularly pp.52–8; Deutschkron, op. cit., 32–3; Shafir, op. cit., Chapters 3, 5.

14. Feldman, op. cit., chapter 3, see particularly pp.52–8.

15. See, for example, Edwina S. Campbell, 'Dilemmas of an Atlantic Dialogue' in Gale A. Mattox and John H. Vaughan Jr. (eds), *Germany through American Eyes: Foreign and Domestic Issues*, Boulder, Westview Press, 1989, pp.3–75, particularly p.5.

16. Two of the many articles are: Dan Halperin, 'States and Union', *Politika*, 12, 1987, pp.64–6; 'What Next in the Sphere of US–Israel Relations?', *Tatzpit*, No. 3, Davies Centre for International Relations, Hebrew University, Jerusalem, May 1990: 'Admittedly, there was never complete harmony between the US and Israel, but likewise, there has never been so great a rift between the two countries as there is today.' The Gulf war and events in Eastern Europe further accelerated these processes, see Avraham Ben Tsvi, 'The possibility of American Pressure on Israel' in *War in the Gulf: Implications for Israel*, report of Jaffee Centre for Strategic Studies, Tel Aviv University, 1991, pp.89–103.

17. See *Documents*.

18. Segev, op. cit., p.175.

19. Shinnar, op. cit., pp. 93–116 relates the entire episode; also Deutschkron, op. cit., pp. 89–98.

20. Shinnar, p.22. The letter with Adenauer's first mention of payment in kind was written on 6 December 1951 to Nahum Goldman in his capacity as chairman of the claims conference, following the aforementioned declaration to the Bundestag. Shinnar claims that Professor Ludwig Ehrhard, then economics minister, played a key role in this matter: 'From an economic–political viewpoint, the final outcome [of payment in goods] was that the wages and profit remained in the German economy.'

21. Haim Beer, in 'People shouted Gas! Gas!', from the weekly *Jerusalem*, 13 September 1991. The term 'Holocaust' in the sense subsequently used was not yet in circulation: there were 'camps', painful personal memories which remained untranslatable. See also: Segev, op. cit., p.207.

22. See Feldman, op. cit., pp. 60–6; Michael Wolffsohn, *Ewige Schuld? 40 Jahre Deutsch Israelische Beziehungen*, Munich, Piper, 1988; Hans Peter Schwartz, *Die Aera Adenauer, 1949–1957: Gruendjahre Der Republik* (Bd. II of 'Der Geschichte der Bundesrepublik Deutschland') Stuttgart, Deutsche Verlag Anstalt, 1981, pp.184–7; Konrad Adenauer, *Errinerungen*, Bd. II, 1953–1955, Stuttgart, Deutsche Verlag Anstalt, 1966, pp.132–62, especially pp.157–9.

23. Shafir, op. cit., p.53. The interview was given on 14 November 1949 to Karl Marx, editor of *'Allgemeine Wochenzuietung der Juden'*.

24. Gunther Gillessen, *Konrad Adenauer and Israel*, Konrad Adenauer Memorial

Lecture, 1986, St. Antony's College, Oxford. Oxford University Press. p.18.
25. Ibid., p.19.
26. Shinnar, op. cit., especially pp.57–70.
27. Ibid., pp.98–9. Deutschkron, op. cit., p.91; see also, Yelinek, op. cit.
28. Shinnar, op. cit., pp.63–4.
29. Ibid., pp.84–8.
30. Segev, op. cit., pp.321–2. The most pointed criticism voiced at that time came from Hannah Arendt, *Eichmann in Jerusalem, a Report on the Banality of Evil*, New York, Penguin, 1977 (1963). See particularly Chapter 1, 'The House of Justice', pp.3–20. Arendt also refers to the failure to summon Globke to testify at the trial.

Michael Bar Zohar's *Hunt for the German Scientists*, Shoken, 1965, pp.218–19 portrays the confidential action undertaken by Israel and Germany to maintain a low profile in relation to the trial to avoid harming bilateral relations, particularly the arms deal and German aid to Israel. The same was true for the episode of the German scientists assisting Egypt to build missiles; revelations about Israeli arms sales to Germany sparked a government crisis in Israel in the summer of 1959. In 1962, Issar Harel, head of Israel's intelligence services, submitted his resignation to Ben Gurion on this issue.

Adenauer was particularly apprehensive over the use East Germany would make of the link between Nazi crimes and the Federal Republic; likewise with regard to the anti-Semitic outbreaks recorded in Germany in the winter of 1959–60 (Shafir, op. cit., Chapter 10, pp.158–62 and Chapter 11, pp.169–73).

Shafir writes that 'Ben Gurion's moderation on the German issue ultimately caught up with him in the episode of the German scientists in Egypt, and was one of the main reasons for his isolation and downfall' (p.172). Nevertheless, Ben Gurion's successor, Levi Eshkol, pursued the identical policy. The controversies undermined Ben Gurion's position but not the continuity of Israeli policy nor the character of bilateral relations. See also Jelinek, op. cit.
31. In an interview to Deutschkron in March 1975, Ehrhard related: 'I told the ministers: "I don't need you anymore"' (pp.284–6). This was after the controversy intensified, and the cabinet was divided for fear of Arab reaction. For the German statement in entirety, see Shinnar, op. cit., pp.110–12.
32. Regarding Toeroek, see Deutschkron, op. cit., pp. 318–9. He served in the Hungarian embassy (representing the Horthy regime) in Berlin during the Nazi era. At the time, his appointment to the German embassy in Israel upon its inauguration was a particularly startling step.
33. See Feldman, op. cit., who quotes Pauls extensively, pp.164–6.
34. In 1990, the two Germanys reunited without attempting – indeed, it is doubtful whether they seriously desired to – to implement the selfsame reunification provided for forty years previously in their respective constitutions (though the GDR had deleted the relevant article from its constitution in 1974).

Parts of the aforegoing analysis stem from background interviews in Germany: in this context, with Professor Arnulf Baring, Berlin, July 1991. See also Michael Stuermer, 'Germany, A Nation of Two States in Slow Motion', *International Herald Tribune*, 17 November 1988, where he precludes any possibility of Soviet consent to German reunification in the foreseeable future.

A new Stalin-type note offering unification on Soviet terms, as in 1952, is not on the cards. Anyone who expects such a move from Mr. Gorbachev is falling victim to the legend of missed opportunities. In the real world, German reunification as a Soviet gift and in isolation from the West would be a revolutionary transformation of the European map that would make Bismarck's policy of 1866–71 look as banal as a change of nameplates over a store . . . Any Soviet leader seriously playing the card of German unity would run the risk of being dismissed as an adventurer, as was Nikita Khrushchev.

35. Conversation with Professor Karl Dietrich Bracher, Bonn, summer 1989.
36. Alan Sked, 'Cheap Excuses', *The National Interest*, summer 1991, pp.51–60.

37. In relation to the Gulf war, I will not extend the discussion beyond several references, particularly to the debates in the February 1991 editions of *Der Spiegel* and *Die Zeit*; also Helmut Hubel, *Der Zweite Golfkrieg in der internationalen Politik*, Bonn, Forschungsinstitut der Deutschen Gesellschaft für Auswaertige Politik, May 1991, pp.52–64 particularly; Dan Diner, 'Dem Westen Verstehen, Der Golfkrieg als Deutsches Lehrstueck', *Kursbuch 104*, June 1991, pp. 143–53,

In Germany the Gulf war functioned somewhat like an internal alienation from the West, towards a stronger identification with self, a kind of unique path – '*Sonderweg*' – of political culture. Whereas anti-Slavic resentment was transformed into a notorious anti-Communism during the Republic's early years, the traditional dislike towards the West, further reinforced by the Second World War, but without scope or real objective, was given oblique expression. The political integration of the Federal part-state into Western institutions lay too deeply in the genuine interests of the population. Now, after unification of the German part-states, and the end of the ideological contradiction between East and West, the resentful distancing *vis-à-vis* the West can be released. This need was met by the Gulf war. To that extent, it was also a German war' (p.153).

With regard to Israel, see M. Zimmermann, 'Lethal Pacificism', *Ha'aretz*, 7 February 1991, Rolf Pauls, 'Hitler's Curse', *Ha'aretz*, 4 March 1991.

German delegations travel to Israel to bring what we always bring when we wish to insulate ourselves without knowing: money. The Israelis want Patriot missiles. That requires consideration. Have we not grasped yet that in the present situation, saying a swift Yes can be the only answer? . . . Within a few weeks, a credibility built up over 40 years – credibility of a decent Germany – has been demolished by self-intoxicated, tearful peace demonstrators who do not comprehend that their pacificism helps only persons like Saddam, who misuse unbridled power . . . We are turning ourselves into strangers within the alliance of which we are members, and we will howl and condemn others when we find no further understanding for our own security. The Americans and our other allies will not forget that, in an hour of travail, when they fought for the right of survival of Kuwait and Israel, we offered them nothing but money and words. The Jews will despise us as they despised us 45 years ago, and we will have to bear that burden.

38. An interview granted to the present writer by Defence Minister Moshe Arens (Israel Television, February 1990). Earlier, in November 1989, Prime Minister Yitzchak Shamir said that should the Germans become 'the strongest nation in Europe, in the world perhaps, they will try to repeat their actions [during the Holocaust]'. Subsequently, the government reconsidered the matter, in full coordination with Bonn.

39. I will not elaborate on Israel–DDR relations. During the final months of its existence, the East German parliament issued a 'declaration of contrition' over GDR policy towards Israel, and its share of responsibility *vis-à-vis* the Jewish people. All Israeli *démarches* towards the DDR were carefully coordinated with Bonn, including the question of establishing a diplomatic legation there. (Source: conversations with Israeli officials.)

40. Quoted in *Ha'aretz*, 11 May 1990: 'Poless: Israel confronts a United Germany'.

41. Interview for the programme 'One Germany', Israel Television.

42. A few examples from surveys conducted at the time:

A *Dahaf* survey sponsored by the Anti-Defamation League and held 7–10 September 1991: 68 per cent of Israelis believe that 'Germans have not changed since the Second World War'; however, 66 per cent believed that to improve relations with Israel Germany should prosecute companies that supplied military technology to Iraq, as against a mere 7 per cent who thought aid to Israel would improve relations.

Germany came last in a list of ten European countries that Israelis 'like', but 62 per cent wanted good relations with Germany; 26 per cent did not desire such relations; 12 per cent were neutral.

In a PORI poll sponsored by the Hebrew University's history department, and conducted immediately following the Gulf war, the question: 'Do you think presentday Germany is different?' drew the following responses: yes – 55.7 per cent; no – 34.5 per cent; no response/don't know – 10 per cent. 'Do you think Israel–German relations can be defined as normal?' Yes – 51.9 per cent; no – 35.9 per cent; no response/don't know – 12 per cent.

Of the responses overall, those aged up to eighteen showed particular reservations: yes – 41.7 per cent; no – 43.6 per cent. Native-born Israelis were less favourably inclined: yes – 49.6 per cent; no – 39 per cent. In other words, Holocaust survivors and those with personal memories of the past did not necessarily offer the harshest judgement.

For comparison: a previous PORI poll for the Hebrew University's history department (March 1990) asked: 'Are you for or against German reunification?' Against – 33 per cent; for – 26 per cent; depends on circumstances/don't know – 41 per cent. In other words, a majority of the Israeli public either did not oppose reunification or was indifferent.

43. Jelinek, op. cit., p.11.

44. See a description in Yohanan Meroz, *Was it in Vain?*, Sifriat Hapoalim, 1988, pp.56–68. In October 1980, Schmidt privately characterised Begin as 'a danger to world peace' (Wolffsohn, *Ewige*, pp.41–3). In retrospect, the Begin–Schmidt controversy comes across less as a major event than a reflection of two complex personalities with traumatic memories.

45. Quoted from Juergen Habermass's article, 'Eine Art Schadensabwicklung: Die Apologetischen Tendenzen in der deutschen Zeitgeschichtsschreibung', *Die Zeit*, 11 July 1986.

46. Yitzchak Ben Ari, then Israel's ambassador to Bonn, attended the memorial service Reagan and Kohl held just before their visit to Bitburg, but other Jewish representatives, including representatives of Germany's Jewish community, boycotted the ceremony. (I covered the event, in May 1985.)

47. The controversy spilled over into newspapers, periodicals and public statements inside Germany and elsewhere. For a summary see *Historikerstreit*, No. 816, Munich, Piper Verlag, 1987.

And in Israel – see particularly Shaul Friedlaender, 'The New German Nationalism: the Controversy Sharpens', *Ha'aretz*, 3 October 1986.

48. Habermass claims that 'whosoever wishes to recall the Germans to a conventional form of their national identity, destroys the sole reliable basis of our adherence to the West'.

49. Conversation with Baring, (*ibid*, Note 34): the expression is 'Puppenheim'. In an interview granted to me on behalf of Israel Television (October 1990) Professor Friedlaender also said that the Federal Republic offered its citizens an efficient social and economic system, but did not intend, nor was it able, to grant them an identity transcending the ability of that system.

50. Among the principal critics: Henryk Broder: *Der Ewige Antisemit*, Frankfurt-am-Main, Fischer, 1986; and Henryk Broder: *Ich Liebe Karstadt*, Augsburg Oelbaum Verlag, Augsburg, 1987, but there were numerous other critics from all portions of the political spectrum, from the Communist Left to the Conservative right and among the Greens themselves.

51. See, for example, a draft paper submitted to the Greens faction on the Palestinian issue by Ellen Olms and Dietrich Schulze-Marmeling, on 11 September 1987: 'A solution of the Palestinian problem is truly feasible through *elimination* of the Israeli nation-state, with its repressionist and expansionist tendencies' (p.9). This is one of numerous examples. See particularly the public debate surrounding despatch of a Greens' delegation to Israel in December 1984 and the paper submitted by its leader, Juergen Reentz, at the time in charge of the Greens' international contacts.

52. The interview was published in *Semit* 5, February 1991, under the title, 'Die Treudeutschen Dummheiten des Gessinungsidioten'; the interviewer was H. Broeder. See also *Die Zeit*, 'Unfiede unter den Pazifisten', which argues that many more concur with the views of Strobele. For the opposite view see D. Diner, op. cit., Zimmermann, 'Fatal Pacificism' op. cit., and Hubel, op. cit.

53. Segev, op. cit., p.469.
54. Ibid., p.438.
55. *Ha'aretz*, ibid., Note 47.
56. Zimmermann, 'The Memory of War and Holocaust'.
57. Gershom Shoken, 'The Scene of that Platform and Business as Usual', *Politika*, No. 12, January 1987. Ever since the establishment of diplomatic relations, Shoken writes 'formal Israel–German relations are indistinguishable from Israel's relations with any other state maintaining relations with Israel' (p.23). Naturally, he notes numerous differences betweeen formal diplomatic relations and other aspects of relations between the two peoples.
58. The aforementioned passage may constitute a kind of challenge to debate or rebuttal. Shaul Friedlaender's *Reflections on Nazism: an Essay on Kitsch and Death*, Keter, Jerusalem, 1982, is a dual example. The Israeli philosopher–historian observes – from his own viewpoint – the new German discourse relating to Nazism. Friedlaender mentions one of the prominent German participants in that discourse, the theatrical director Hans Juergen Syberberg. Syberberg's book, *Vom Unglueck und Glueck der Kunst in Deutschland nach dem letzten Krieg*. Munich, Matthes and Seitz, 1990, sparked off a storm in Germany. Syberberg stated that the Jews, the Left and the United States in concert paralysed and devastated German culture; he calls for its historic renewal: 'The American–Israel axis determines the external boundaries of this culture; Judaism, its content and direction, particularly its technological–materialistic substance, without sense or meaning (*ohne Geist und Sinn*)'. See especially pp. 14–15, 78–9 of this astounding book. Critical reviews and discussions of the book appeared at the end of 1990 in Germany and in the *New York Review of Books*, 20 December 1990.
59. The debate, summarised in Yoram Kaniuk, 'Dreieinhalf Stunden und funfzig Jahre mit Gunter Grass in Berlin', *Die Zeit*, 21 June 1991, was held in February 1991, immediately after the Gulf war. For the opposing German viewpoint, see 'Der Golfkrieg, Deutschland und Israel', *Die Zeit*, 22 February 1991 by the German–Jewish philosopher Ernst Tugendhat: 'There are people, and states too, which play with virtuosity, as on a piano, on the other's irrational guilt feelings; that is what the Israelis do with the Germans.'
60. The new Israeli discourse began engaging public attention shortly after the outbreak of the *intifada* in the occupied territories, though having been in muted progress long before. Dr Ilana Hammerman, in a lecture on 'The Holocaust and presentday Israeli Society – Further Reflections about the Controversy over Comparison' (Holocaust Day, 1989, Beersheba University) mentions the case of Adi Ophir, jailed for refusing a military reserve posting to the occupied territories. Ophir claimed that 'whosoever places obedience to orders beyond debate effectively agrees with Eichmann'. In response, journalist Dan Margalit wrote that 'Ophir's attempt to plant a Nazi analogy into the Israeli debate can be answered with something taken from his own set of images – that this is propaganda of the variety that would not have shamed Josef Goebbels' (*Ha'aretz*, 25 July 1988).
   Another instance: in an interview with *Newsweek*, (17 October 1988) Israeli writer A.B. Yehoshua, referring to Israeli silence over what is happening in the occupied territories, says he can understand how the Germans could say they didn't know; many Israelis similarly refuse to know what is going on in the territories. In Yehoshua's words, the Holocaust was more than Auschwitz; it was 'a terrible network of humiliation and torture of people – the old, women and children'. This made it possible to draw analogies.
   The response from writer Aharon Meged, 'Words without Truth', *Ha'aretz*, 14 October 1988 (*Newsweek* appears before the date it bears) follows D. Margalit's response to A. Ophir in drawing upon Holocaust terminology: 'Possibly the powerful urge to see in our own visage the visage of our worst persecutors is merely one more psychic aberration, one of those stamped into us by the Holocaust itself.'
   Hammerman quotes Holocaust survivor and writer Primo Levi: 'At the edge of

consciousness is the feeling that every stranger is foe and enemy.' She adds that the danger noted by Levi, whereby this feeling becomes systematic thought, looms over Israel, where 'legality' has become a camouflage, and there is growing acceptance over the state of human rights in the territories. That is the danger: this is not direct analogy; rather, an attempt to learn.

In his instructive critique of Uriel Tal's *Political Theology and the Third Reich* (Tel-Aviv, Sifriat Hapoalim, 1991), Professor Zimmermann says that Tal warns of manifestations comparable with the Holocaust. Comparisons can be drawn; these comparisons alone register the historic uniqueness of the Holocaust. That is also the conclusion drawn by Primo Levi in *I sommersi e i salvati*, Turin, Giulio Einaudi, 1986.

Segev expands upon the Israeli public debate on the subject in recent years. The most important article is Yehuda Elkana's 'In Defence of Forgetfulness' (*Ha'aretz*, 2 March 1988):

Each people, the Germans included, decides in its own way, and for its own considerations, whether it wishes to remember. We, by contrast, should forget. I see no political or educational task more important for the leaders of this nation than taking a stand on the side of life, to dedicate themselves to constructing our future, and not engage, morning and night, in symbols, ceremonies and lessons of the Holocaust. It is up to them to root out the control the historic 'Remember!' exercises over our lives.

Professor Elkana claims that the existential fear prevailing in Israel is 'Hitler's tragic and paradoxical victory'; atrocity pictures can be construed as incitement to hatred; and events in the territories – particularly the actions of IDF soldiers – stem from the profound existential anxiety fostered by the historical 'Remember!'

Segev quotes from a research work which discovered that the Holocaust has become an event common to all Israelis, irrespective of disparities in origin and culture (op.cit. p.472). For this, see also Professor Shimon Redlich, 'The Holocaust as against the Uprising', *Ha'aretz*, 11 June 1989: 'To my regret, the subject of the Holocaust is possibly the last remaining subject which unites us unquestionably.' But now, with the state at an historic crossroads owing to the Palestinian uprising, Redlich says 'there has to be some rethinking on the subject'. The rethinking has indeed commenced. In September 1988, the poet Nathan Zach said: 'The consensus on the subject has been smashed', after his utterances on the subject drew condemnation from the Israeli Writers' Association (*Ha'aretz*, 20 September 1988). But the debate's effect on public opinion remains marginal, being confined particularly to the Israeli Left. On the other hand, as indicated by the surveys and studies quoted here, conventional concepts are unconnected with atttitudes towards Germany.

61. See particularly: Wolffsohn, *Deutsch.*

62. A poll conducted by SINUS in October 1980 showed this claim to be highly characteristic of the German far Right; Jews wield 'excessive influence over Germany's economy and politics'. 'Rechtsextreme Politische Einstellungen in der Bundesrepublik Deutschland', Heidelberg, 1980, p.55.

According to a poll by *Stern* magazine (April 1986, p.35) that is the view held by 26 per cent of Germans.

63. The relationship between Germans and Jews – German Jews in particular – is a separate issue which cannot be considered here; on this subject, see especially Wolffsohn, *Ewige*, Chapter IX, pp.138–81.

64. For example money 'laundering' in party funds.

65. See particularly, Broder, *Der Ewige* and *Ich Liebe.* Broder's conclusion – he claims to quote 'a wise Israeli' – is that the Germans will never forgive the Israelis for Auschwitz (*Der Ewige*, p.130).

66. During the Lebanon war, the Ansar detention facility was depicted as 'a concentration camp'; the Israeli invasion was portrayed as an attempt towards *Endloesung* (final solution) of the Palestinian problem. A commentator on German television described

'Operation Solomon' (which brought Ethiopian Jews to Israel) as a *'Selektion'* among the starving. Graffin Marion Doenhoff compared the siege of Beirut with the siege of the Warsaw ghetto. During the Lebanon war, the ARD local programme network Berlin Station SFB screened a film showing a Palestinian woman and her family who had fled from Beirut to live in a hostel in Berlin against extracts from Anne Frank's diary. (*Der Ewige*, p.128.) See also the report on a theatre piece entitled *'Anna and Hanna'*, a musical dialogue (!) performed in 1991 at the annual Jewish festival held in Berlin, depicting Israeli children's impressions of the Gulf war contrasted with dialogue from Anne Frank in her Amsterdam hideout; the sealed rooms of the Gulf war paralleled Anne Frank's room, 'the gas is the same gas, the Germans are the same Germans, and the Israelis are in fact the same Jews who were herded to annihilation' (Yigael Avidan, 'From Anna to Hanna', *Davar*, 7 June 1991). See also, ibid., 'Professional Jews, Sickening Success' by Miri Paz.

67. Zimmermann, *The Trauma*, argues that the boomerang effect of harnessing the Holocaust to political ends has become irrelevant since the Lebanon war. In his view, ever since the great controversy between Schmidt and Begin, declarations, films, plays, opinions, analogies etc. have all failed to restore the Holocaust to the focus of Israeli–German relations. Not even the *intifada* caused any perceptible turn for the worse in German public opinion towards Israel (pp.9–10). I argue, similarly, that the Gulf war did not produce any perceptible turn for the worse in Israeli public opinion *vis-à-vis* Germany.

68. Interview with Benjamin Navon, Israeli ambassador to Germany. Navon:

There is a positive consistency in Germany's attitude towards Israel in the European context; that is the special aspect of the relationship. It is Israel's experience – and expectation for the future – that Germany, as the European state most sympathetic to Israel's needs, interests and political objectives, will persist in this line.

With that, Navon agrees that Bonn has never adopted towards Israel a position conflicting with Germany's own basic interests; the assessment of circles in Jerusalem is that, contrary to hopes of continuity, what lies in store – particularly if the SPD should achieve office – is a significant worsening of bilateral relations, exacerbated by isolationist trends, pacificism and economic difficulties stemming from Eastern Europe and east Germany.

69. In a TV programme on German reunification (*ibid.*, Note 49, 6 October 1990) as well as utterances to the press, a note of remarkable reservation and caution was sounded by Eli Wiesel. In Israel, too, cautionary voices came from representatives of Jewish organisations like Yitzchak Arad, director of Yad VeShem, and institutions concerned with Holocaust commemoration, or newspaper editors, particularly Gershom Shoken of *Ha'aretz* and Ido Dissenchik of *Maariv*.

70. Feldman, op. cit., p.276, defines a certain type of relationship which she terms 'special'; see Chapter 12 and Conclusion, pp.276–88.

71. There are numerous examples. See for one, Michael Stuermer, op. cit. Another by Margarita Mathiopoulos, 'Peace would Settle the German Question', *International Herald Tribune*, 1 November 1989.

If West Germany really wants to see freedom and reforms in East Germany, the preconditions would be formal renunciation of reunification and final recognition of a second German state and of East German citizenship . . . Citizens in East Germany do not want reunification. The thousands who leave do so because it seems to them at present to be the only way to gain freedom. If there were hope of change, they would prefer not to leave their work, homes, relatives and friends.

A final example: Gert Krell, 'Germanys: Reunification isn't today's problem', *International Herald Tribune*, 19 October 1989. 'Certainly, reunification is not the major German question today; it is much too early to discuss it; it is even politically harmful.'

Or from a politician: SPD leader Egon Bahr, quoted in *Ha'aretz* (22 May 1989) from the *New York Times*, said that 'reunification is a strange item, with no present relevance'. A survey quoted in the same article had 95 per cent of Germans convinced that the Berlin Wall would vanish within 100 years, but 70 per cent believed it would still be in place in the year 2000! The statement that 'the Wall will stand another 50–100 years' was made by Erich Honecker in January 1989. At that time, and on this point, most Germans – in East and West – agreed with him.

72. See, for example, the *Der Spiegel* poll, 16 September 1991. In recent years, Gorbachev was the European leader most popular in East and West Germany (Germany's own leaders included).

73. See especially: Sked, op. cit. and Hubel, op. cit.

74. The report was screened on 'Panorama' on NDR, German TV's first channel and on Israel Television in January 1991. It sparked off a public storm and vigorous political protests. Prime Minister Shamir, Foreign Minister Levy and Knesset members raised the issue with German delegations then visiting Israel. Bundestag members were fiercely critical of my decision to screen the report. In response to my explanations, Bundestag member Reiner Eppelmman (CDU) alleged: 'The arguments you put forward draw on the same arguments as those of Eichmann and Himmler' (conversation in Jerusalem, May 1991).

75. In conversation with Germany's ambassador to Israel, Otto von der Gablentz (September 1991), he said that 'the elements for change in German–Israeli relations henceforth are greater – perhaps for the first time since relations were established – than the elements of continuity'. On first arriving in Israel, after reunification, Gablentz introduced himself as Bonn's eighth ambassador to Israel; today, he regards himself as the first ambassador of a Germany belonging to Europe, and different from the past. In his view, bilateral relations will undergo 'Europisation'. The Holocaust will remain the 'test case' for gauging the authenticity of Germans' attitude towards their own history, and that is the element of continuity; but changes – in the world, in Europe and in Germany itself – now overshadow the elements of continuity in determining the future of bilateral relations.

Gablentz believes that these changes will require Israel to change its economic deploy-ment, as well as its diplomatic goals, so as to open the way for its integration into Europe. In his view, the European interest requires a strong Germany, because only a strong Germany can face up to the challenge of reconstructing East Germany and Eastern Europe. 'No one is interested in a weak Germany', says Gablentz, certainly not Israel, where Germany maintains what he terms 'a helpful presence' – referring, of course, to German aid – economic, cultural, scientific, municipal etc. – which, he claims, coincides with German interests.

6 German society and foreign policy

Stephen F. Szabo

A new Germany

The domestic context of German policy toward the Middle East will alter dramatically in the 1990s owing to the changes in East–West relations which occurred in the wake of the revolutions of 1989. The most significant change in the German context is obvious, namely the reunification of the nation after forty-five years of forced division. There will no longer be West and East German polities and policies but only a German polity and German policies. This raises some significant questions about the impact of the amalgamation of the diverse political cultures upon attitudes toward the Middle East and other key regions.

Second, Germany will remain a medium power but will move ahead of the other key European medium powers, Britain and France, in both population and economic power. The new Germany is likely to think more like a significant power than did the smaller German states, particularly if European integration continues to develop and a Europe led by Germany becomes an effective international actor.

Third, the relationship with the United States is likely to change significantly as the need for American protection in Europe will be dramatically reduced. This implies that support for American policies in the Middle East will diminish to the extent that it was based on East–West considerations. This more autonomous posture is congruent as well with the development of a growing feeling of 'sovereignty' or 'normalcy' among the new generation of German leaders coming to power in the 1990s. Combined with a growing Europeanisation of European foreign policies, a greater German–European self-assertiveness is likely to characterise the relationship with the United States in the future. Divergences in European and American policies may be enhanced by economic competition spawned by the integrated European market after 1992.

Finally, the Mediterranean is likely to become an area of increased political and security interest to Europe and Germany as the military threat in Central Front recedes. The demographic expansion of the Mediterranean basin combined with political instability and a growing gap in living standards will promote growing tensions between Christian Europe and the Moslem countries of the Middle East. The proliferation of chemical and nuclear weapons in the region will only heighten the German perception of threat as will the continued dependence of a growing German economy on Middle-East oil and the vulnerability in areas of vital national interests that this creates.

The strategic culture of a divided Germany

The strategic culture of the Federal Republic of Germany was shaped by the division of the nation, the threat of a short-warning Soviet military threat and the political legacy of the Third Reich. As a result of these factors West German foreign and security policies emphasised dependence upon the United States and its extended nuclear deterrent for national security and on multinational frameworks for its foreign policies.

The strategic culture of West Germany was almost completely preoccupied with the problems associated with the division of the nation and of Europe. Its policies toward the Middle East reflected this Central European preoccupation. German policies toward the region were characterised by a 'double dependency'.[1] One dependency was the FRG's need for oil to fuel its economic machine, with a good deal of this oil coming from the Gulf. The Germans were also dependent upon the United States for security in Europe. West German policies toward the region were subordinated to this larger interest of maintaining the Atlantic Alliance and the American security commitment.

When these two dependencies clashed during the Arab–Israeli war of 1973, the Germans resisted the use of American bases in the Federal Republic for resupply of Israel. However they chose to continue to support an American-led response to the Arab oil embargo rather than a French-led effort to create a separate European response.[2] The same pattern continued after the Iranian crisis of 1979–80.

The historical legacy of the Third Reich also had a powerful influence on West German attitudes and policies toward the region. The responsibility for the Holocaust created a 'special relationship' with Israel and limited German options *vis-à-vis* the Arab states.[3] This historical legacy, combined with the smaller size of a divided Germany, also promoted multilateral approaches to the Middle East. The Germans were the best Europeans in this regard, preferring whenever possible to conduct policies within the larger context of the EC.

The historical legacy also limited the German role in terms of arms exports and military intervention. The West German Basic Law contains a number of provisions which prohibit or limit actions that threaten international peace and stability, including arms exports.[4] Throughout the early 1980s the West Germans consistently pursued policies which prohibited export of arms to areas of 'tension'. In addition West German governments consistently argued that the West German Basic Law and limitations placed on it by the provisions of the Western European Union prohibited the use of German forces outside of the NATO area.[5] Rather than deploying their forces outside of the NATO treaty area, the West Germans have preferred to offer aid to Turkey and Pakistan and to have their forces 'fill in' for American forces pulled out of NATO to deal with Middle-East contingencies. The most dramatic example of this was during the Iran–Iraq war when the United States and a number of European nations in 1987 deployed naval forces to the Gulf. For the first time the FRG deployed naval forces to the Mediterranean for joint NATO manoeuvres to fill the gap left by American forces deployed to the Gulf.[6]

All of these policies found broad support both within public opinion and among the political parties. The West German public, especially the postwar generations, eschewed military instruments as legitimate means for German statecraft and were sensitive to any approaches which could be viewed as 'nationalistic' or 'militaristic'.

Germans were opposed on moral and historical grounds to the use of force to solve disputes and sceptical about the efficacy of force in dealing with the complex problems of the Middle East. When the Reagan administration launched air strikes on Libya in 1986 in response to Libyan-sponsored terrorism, the German public condemned this action although it believed that Gaddafi sponsored terrorism.[7] The German sentiment was summed up by Chancellor Kohl who reportedly told President Reagan that no German chancellor could support the use of military force.[8]

This strong cultural antipathy to power politics was strengthened by the New Peace Movement of the 1980s. With its origins in the ecological movement and the Greens, and with the Euromissile issue as its catalyst, the New Peace Movement reinforced, among the young especially, a scepticism about the use of power and nurtured an apocalyptic fear of the destructiveness of technology. Although centred on nuclear weapons and Europe, the Peace Movement and the Greens introduced a strong North–South perspective into the strategic culture. Peace and environmental activists stressed not only the destructiveness of the arms race but also its diversion of resources from the fight against poverty in the Third World.

Realist arguments about countering the Soviet threat, in Europe or the Middle East, were rejected by a new sensibility which discounted any meaningful Soviet military threat and which stressed various indigenous roots of political instability in the Third World. This sensibility spread from the Peace Movement to key sectors of opinion among the better-educated young in West Germany.

Finally, another legacy with implications for the German role in the Middle East was 'Erhardism', an economic philosophy which combined a social market economy at home with a free-trade policy abroad. Postwar German energies were directed toward rebuilding a devastated nation and in making the Federal Republic a trading state rather than a military power. The German economic miracle was export-led and German prosperity has continued to rest upon substantial trade- and current-account surpluses. As a result, the West Germans have consistently been among the leading exponents of free trade in the European Community.

Among a more conservative part of opinion in the Federal Republic, German economic interests in the Middle East were the dominant concern. The strong role of banks and of free-trade ideology in the German approach to the Middle East combined with a deep dependence on oil from the Gulf tended to foster a more pro-Arab attitude among conservatives.[9] This led to a situation where German firms exported numerous items to the region, especially in the chemical sector, with little or no government control.

The political and strategic culture of a unified Germany

All in all German attitudes and politics regarding the Middle East have been relatively stable and have been subsidiary to the German preoccupation with Europe and the national question. Much of this is likely to change over the next decade as Germany emerges as a single nation and a leader in a revived and reassertive Europe. Change will not occur rapidly because Germans will be absorbed for at least the next five years in the myriad tasks of reunification and state-building as well as with the broad challenges of building a new Europe. But after the foundations for a new Europe and a new Germany are laid, German leaders are likely to become more active in policies which deal with the rest of the world, especially those involving the Middle East. Which changes are likely to be the most significant and how is the new Germany likely to view the Middle East?

A shifting threat

Following unification Germany will have a new geography. It will no longer be a front-line state with little strategic depth in Central Europe facing 400,000 Soviet forces directly across its border. It will now have Poland and Czechoslovakia as buffer states between it and the largest potential military threat to its security, Russia. It is likely to continue to follow a policy of *détente* with the countries of the former Soviet Union with the goal of creating a cooperative security system in Europe.

Unification will also mean that the latter will have lost an important lever to use with the West Germans; and following the reconstruction and integration of the former East Germany, German leaders will no longer have the preoccupation of the national division. While German policies are likely to remain largely Eurocentric, they will be less concerned with a threat from the East and more with economic and technological competition and cooperation with the West.

The main threats or problems likely to preoccupy German foreign and defence policy-makers are instability in southern Europe and the Mediterranean. With the collapse of the Second World in Europe, the First World is living next door to the Third. As the economies of Western Europe grow from the double stimuli of 1992 and German unification, they will be magnets for immigrants from central and southern Europe and from North Africa.

The need for foreign workers will grow because of the demographic stagnation of Germany and Western Europe. Before unification, birth rates in both Germanies were declining and projections were for a decline in the West German population from sixty-two million in 1990 down to fifty million in the early part of the next decade. Given current birth rates, a unified Germany in 2025 may have a population only about as large as that of West Germany in 1990. With an economy which is expected to grow over the next decade in the east at rates of seven per cent or more, and overall at three to four per cent annually, there will be a need, even allowing for over-optimistic projections, for more immigrants or for greater foreign investment, or both.

North Africa and the Middle East, in contrast, are facing population explosions combined with little prospect for economic growth at rates near those of Western Europe. In 1950, for example, Western Europe had 358 million people compared to 138 million in Eastern Europe and 278 million in North Africa and the Middle East. If current demographic trends continue, the Islamic population will exceed Western Europe's by the year 2001 and all of Europe's by 2015.[10]

In addition Germany will continue to be dependent for a substantial portion of its petroleum requirements on the Middle East. It will have to respond, as well, to the potential threats it may face because of missile, chemical and possibly nuclear proliferation in the region. It is significant that the first post-Cold War crisis took place in the Gulf following Iraq's invasion of Kuwait and this may be a harbinger of things to come.

Instability is likely as well in southern Europe. The prospects for economic and democratic development seem far better in Hapsburg Europe (Poland, Czechoslovakia, Hungary and Austria) than in Ottoman Europe (Romania, Bulgaria, Serbia, Albania). The former have better ties to Germany and to the European Community and are likely to have better access to Western European support than the latter. Ottoman Europe also has a substantial Moslem community and faces real dangers of Moslem–Christian conflicts, in Yugoslavia and Bulgaria and unravelling of state structures in the Balkans.

Germany and the rest of Western Europe may, in summary, be entering a more dangerous period than they faced during the Cold War, living on the edge of an arc of crisis to the south without the military forces to deal with problems which are less disciplined by the bipolarity of the East–West conflict. The remainder of this chapter will provide a profile of the domestic context of the new Germany and the factors likely to shape German responses to this new environment.

Sovereignty and the return to 'normalcy'

The most obvious and important change after unification is the return of Germany to full sovereignty. Berlin is no longer a divided city under Four-Power occupation status, the forces of the former Soviet Union will be out of eastern Germany by the end of 1994 at the latest and the foreign military forces which remain in western Germany will do so on the basis of bilateral agreements. German leaders and public alike will insist that Germany is not 'singularised' or treated any differently than France, Britain or any other European nation.

This return to 'normalcy' of the German nation means that the political statute of limitations which has applied to both German states will end. Future leaders of the new nation will not accept the application of a separate standard of behaviour solely because of the crimes of Hitler. This change did not come with reunification but will certainly be accelerated by it.

The signs of this return to normalcy could be seen first in the chancellorship of Helmut Schmidt and more clearly in that of Helmut Kohl. Schmidt, although having served in the German army in World War II, was the first West German chancellor to assert German national interests self-consciously and to challenge the right of the United States to set European security and economic policy. Among other actions his shaping of the European Monetary System (EMS) in cooperation with Giscard d'Estaing, and their joint attempt to salvage *détente* in Europe during the crisis set off by the Soviet invasion of Afghanistan and the imposition of martial law in Poland, marked him as the chancellor of a self-confident Germany. He represented 'a new Germany . . . one which was internally fortified and self-conscious in its foreign policy'.[11]

Schmidt personified the end of the period when, as Willy Brandt described it, West Germany was an economic giant and a political dwarf. Foreign policy after Schmidt would no longer be founded on the need for reconciliation or moral rehabilitation. Instead it would be based increasingly on *Staatsraeson* and on pragmatic and largely economic considerations.[12] Although a solid supporter of the Atlantic Alliance, Schmidt also represented the growing separation of German and American interests and viewpoints. This was captured most dramatically in his characterisation of his role during the superpower crisis of the early 1980s as an 'interpreter' in the American–Soviet conflict, raising the image of a Germany between the superpowers.

In many ways an 'Americanised' chancellor who knew the United States well and respected it in his early career, during his chancellorship Schmidt lost confidence in the two American presidents, Carter and Reagan, with whom he had to deal. His growing disdain for the amateurism and unpredictability of American politics and policy, linked as he saw it to the decline of the influence of the Europe-orientated east-coast foreign-policy establishment, both exacerbated and reflected a disillusionment with America among broad segments of the German elite and public.

It was during the Schmidt years that a belief began to take hold that the United States was in many important ways equivalent to the Soviet Union in its foreign policy behaviour. Both superpowers came to be seen as part of the problem rather than solely the Soviet Union as had been the case previously. The chancellor's acerbic criticism of Carter and (to a lesser extent) Reagan – and the serious policy clashes over Afghanistan, the Soviet–West European gas pipeline and the Iranian crisis of 1979–81 – fed a view, especially among the opinion shapers in West German society, that the Federal Republic had to defend its vital national interests from damage by American policies.

These attitudes were clear regarding the Middle East. In his memoirs, Schmidt writes of his disagreement with the Camp David agreement and the isolation it would bring to Egypt within the Arab world as well as the increasing alienation from the Saudi leadership which would also result. He criticises both administrations for their poor judgement and weak leadership and for tying American policy so closely to that of Israel. While the Europeans had better insights into the region based on longer experience in it, they were unable to influence policy because of their lack of adequate military and economic means.[13]

Kohl's chancellorship, while probably the most pro-American since Erhard's, continued and expanded this new sense of sovereignty. Although an Atlanticist, as chancellor Kohl had to deal with a changed political culture reshaped by the Peace Movement and the Social Democrats. He and his party had to respond to the expectation that they would defend German interests against the Americans.

Beyond this need was also a new disillusionment with American policy. A sense of victimisation which began on the left in the early 1980s spread to the right by the end of the decade. Conservative Christian Democrats, led by the CDU parliamentary leader, Alfred Dregger, felt betrayed by the Soviet–American INF treaty and the Reagan administration's movement away from extended deterrence. It was this wing which coined the phrase 'singularisation' in response to American pressure to modernise short-range nuclear weapons (SNF) after the INF treaty signing. They viewed American policy after INF as aimed at reducing the nuclear risk to the United States while enhancing the risk of limited nuclear war for the Germans.[14]

Associated with the politics of resentment on the right was the rise of a new right party, *Die Republikaner*, in 1988–9. While the party faded in electoral significance after the movement toward unification began in October and November 1989, some of the themes it evoked have longer-term implications. The rise of this new nationalist party came after the controversial visit of President Reagan to Bitburg in 1985 and the so-called Historians' Debate which followed.

The significance of the Historians' Debate lies less in its impact on historiography and more in what it says about the changing political and strategic culture.[15] The Historians' Debate was in essence a debate over German identity in the 1980s. It centred around the uniqueness of the Holocaust and the uniqueness, therefore, of German guilt. The purpose of the conservative historians who reopened this question was to establish moral equivalence by balancing Auschwitz against the fire-bombing of Dresden, and Hitler against Stalin. The deeper purpose was to transcend an 'obsession with guilt' and to repair Germany's broken identity.

The need for identity and a re-establishment of historical continuity to German history was another sign of a growing self-confidence in the political culture. The *Historikerstreit* was triggered in part by the neo-nationalism of the left.[16] The left's sense of victimisation, its drawing of moral equivalence between the United States and Nazi Germany during Vietnam and of equivalence of the two superpowers, as well as its view of both Germanys as occupied countries, was now duplicated by a segment of the right.

These were themes picked up by the *Republikaner* and their leader Franz Schoenhuber in 1989. In an early communique Schoenhuber wrote:

Only one who is sovereign can be a reliable ally. Each state must have control over weapons on its territory. . . . We can't live either internationally or domestically in a State of Emergency. We want to be a normal nation. That means a decriminalization of our history as a precondition for a self-confident national consciousness.[17]

Schoenhuber's foreign policies were not the main reason for his electoral appeal, which was based rather upon anti-Semitic sentiment and anti-immigrant resentments. However, the significance of Schoenhuber and the 'Reps' did not lie in any realistic prospect that they would come to power, but in what they have said about new emerging undercurrents in the political and strategic culture. The 'Reps' do not represent a return of Nazism but rather of nationalism. Gordon Craig identified this meaning when he concluded an essay on Schoenhuber with the following assessment:

his place in the history of German politics will be not that of a new *Fuehrer* but rather that of an *animateur de la victoire* of a new nationalism, the cunning exploiter of irritations that have accumulated since the fight over the Pershings and Bitburg . . . Schoenhuber may indeed turn out to be the man who made the public expressions of national ambition and national defiance respectable again.[18]

The *Republikaner* faded from the scene after Kohl seized the national issue in November 1989, but they had an important impact on the chancellor's policies. Until the spring of 1990 there seemed to be a good chance that they would capture more than five per cent of the vote in the Bundestag election of 1990, raising the prospect that they might deny the Christian–Liberal coalition a majority. This was enough to cause conservative politicians to be cautious about alienating the right. Theo Waigel, Strauss's successor as chairman of the Bavarian affiliate of the Christian Democrats, the Christian Social Union (CSU), revived the old issue of the Polish–German border, keeping open for a while at least, the possibility of a return of former German territory lost to Poland and Czechoslovakia. It was widely assumed that Chancellor Kohl's lingering reluctance to state clearly that the Oder–Neisse border would be the final border of a unified Germany was due to a desire not to cede what could be crucial votes to the 'Reps'. A few percentage points can upset the delicate balance of coalition politics in the Federal Republic and thus Kohl could not disregard the 'Reps'' limited appeal.

Finally, even before the rise and fall of Schoenhuber, Chancellor Kohl and his party were much more assertive on the openness of the German question than Schmidt had been. Kohl spoke emphatically and often about the German 'Fatherland', even during his trips to Moscow. Although his government continued the *Ostpolitik* of the Social–Liberal coalition, the new coalition spoke of 'two states in Germany', rather than of the 'two German states' of the Schmidt government.

This new self-confidence and national assertiveness had implications for German policies in the Middle East. The German–American controversy over the Libyan chemical plant in early 1989 was largely the result of this new assertiveness. For months the Kohl government resisted clear American intelligence information that West German firms were materially assisting the Libyan effort to build chemical weapons. This resistance was founded on Kohl's desire not to appear as 'Reagan's poodle', especially after the strong German public reaction against the American air raid on Libya in 1986. The charge of William Safire in a column for *The New York Times* of 'Auschwitz in the Sand', and that the Germans of all people should stay out of the poison gas business, only fuelled a nationalist response by Chancellor Kohl who complained about being treated like a 'banana republic'.

Another American columnist, Richard Cohen, captured the essence of Kohl's dilemma well.

The trouble with indictments such as Safire's is that, rather than dealing with the issue of a single company, they make it a question of national character. Germans, from Chancellor Kohl on down, feel unfairly singled out. As with Bitburg, they dig in their heels and emotionally deny what the State Department says is obvious: Incontrovertible evidence that a German firm has aided Libyan efforts to make poison gas.[19]

The Kohl government came around to taking some limited actions against German firms which had aided Gaddafi, and public opinion polls in the Federal Republic indicated support for the American position, but the long resistance of a pro-American government to the American-provided evidence was indicative of a certain tension.

This new autonomy is bound to become more dominant once unification is not only an accomplished legal fact but a political, economic and social one as well. Unlike western Germans who can associate foreign involvement with economic prosperity, military security and national rehabilitation, eastern

Germans conjure up memories of domination, exploitation and the suppression of national identity. The east Germans lived under a foreign-dominated regime for four decades. The key reason for the rapid disintegration of the GDR after October 1989 was the removal of Soviet support for the Honecker regime. Once it became clear that the Soviets would no longer sustain the rule of the East German Communists, the system was finished. Resentment against both the old regime and toward Soviet troops in the GDR was deep and raises questions about the degree of latent support which exists for nationalist themes and movements. It seems predictable that the sixteen million citizens of the new German republic who lived in the former GDR will be even more sensitive to issues concerning national and local self-determination than are the west Germans.

The new Germany is the largest state in terms of population and economic power in Europe. Its population of 78 million eclipses those of its major European partners (France, Britain and Italy all have populations around 55 million). Its trillion dollar economy will make up about 35 per cent of the GNP of the EC. Given its limited military capabilities, it may not be a superpower but along with Japan and the United States it will be one of the three key global economic centres. Clearly its perspective will change. As Stanley Hoffmann has observed,

. . . the most serious concern is likely to be the prospect of a Germany, even harnessed inside a 'tight' European Community, that yields to the 'arrogance of power' that has been a characteristic of so many major states in history. Under these circumstances, Germany might behave less like a wise 'hegemon', understanding the need to take account of the interests of lesser powers, than like a selfish player concerned above all with relative gains and insensitive to the claims and fears of others.[20]

One concrete area where change is likely is in the area of Germany's role outside of Europe. The self-imposed limitation on German military operations to the NATO treaty area came under strain immediately in the Gulf crisis of 1990–1991. Kohl gave indications early in the crisis that he would deploy German naval forces to the Gulf to assist European and American forces. While he and other Christian Democrats argued for Germany to support American efforts both in gratitude for American backing for German unification and to avoid a view in the United States that the Germans were free-loaders, a deeper reason was a new psychology of an emerging new nation. The Chancellor's national security adviser Horst Teltschik expressed this attitude when he said, 'The role that Germany is playing in the world has a new quality. The problem is that most Germans haven't recognized it yet. We must take more responsibility ourselves. The world expects more of us.'[21]

Among other measures, German minesweepers were sent to the Mediterranean, and the government allowed American planes to use American bases in Germany for Gulf operations. Kohl's efforts to send German minesweepers to the Gulf, however, were blocked by FDP and SPD opposition. Genscher and his Liberal Party continued to argue that the Basic Law forbade any deployments outside of the NATO treaty area, although he and his party agreed to change the constitution to allow future German participation within a UN peacekeeping force. This was in conflict with the CDU's desires to support alliance and American policies in the Gulf.[22] The Social Democrats had decided at their party congress in Münster in 1988 that 'every military mission of the Bundeswehr outside the Alliance's sphere of influence' is constitutionally inadmissible and had consequently rejected German participation in UN peacekeeping missions. [23] However the party and its candidate for chancellor, Oskar LaFontaine, agreed during the initial stages of the Gulf crisis to consider a change in the constitution after unification which would allow Bundeswehr involvement in UN peacekeeping forces. The Greens rejected any German deployment to the Gulf on the general grounds that behind such a move lay an attempt, in the words of the party's spokeswoman in the Bundestag, to 'establish Germany as an emerging great power, and also as an internationally functioning military power'. She added that the Iraqi aggression had 'regrettably' proved to be an opportunity for NATO to 'rig up' a new legitimation for its own, and the Bundeswehr's, continued existence. All parties in the Bundestag with the exception of the Greens finally supported a change in the constitution after unification which would allow German forces to take part in UN peacekeeping operations.[24]

It is significant that the new German assertiveness continues to prefer multinational frameworks to a unilateral approach. This is further evidence that German leaders and the broader public as well have no desire to go-it-alone or to be seen as acting in an overtly national way. Not only does the nation lack the military means, particularly the naval forces, to act independently, but German leaders remain sensitive to the impact of a high German profile on the outside world.[25]

It is also important that the multinational contexts discussed do not centre on NATO, but rather upon the EC, the WEU (the West European Union) and the UN. Those, especially in the United States, who looked to the Gulf crisis of 1990 as the beginning of a new role for NATO and a means for solving the Alliance's post-cold war identity crisis through developing a mechanism for defending Western interests beyond the East–West arena, are likely to be disappointed by the Germans.[26]

Although both the Kohl government and the opposition supported the American deployments to Saudi Arabia, the legacy of the 1980s is not likely simply to be forgotten. Germans will remain very sensitive about the use of military force to solve crises in the Third World and are unlikely to trust American policy if it is seen as aggressive or unilateral. The fear that an American president may drag Europe into a war through reckless policies remains just below the surface. The resistance of the Free Democrats and the Social Democrats to Bundeswehr deployments to the Gulf is based as much on these considerations as they are upon 'strict constructionism' in interpreting the Basic Law.[27] As the need for American protection in Europe fades, German leaders will be less rather than more keen to rely upon an American-led alliance to pursue European interests in the future.

Because of the lack of military capabilities and the deep aversion to *Realpolitik*, especially among the postwar generations, future German leaders will emphasise the diplomatic, political and economic instruments of statecraft and will remain averse to the use of military force.[28] If force is felt to be necessary, a large international organisation like the UN, or a European one like the WEU, will be seen as a more appropriate means of using military power and will be more compatible with the interests and self-image of a unified Germany than will the American-led NATO, an alliance which is likely to be seen as anachronistic in the post-cold war era.[29]

'Normalcy', anti-Semitism and foreign minorities

A unified Germany runs the risk of being less tolerant toward foreign minorities and Jews than was the Federal Republic. The Historians' Debate, the rise of the *Republikaner* and the influx of large numbers of refugees from Eastern Europe and the Third World raised concerns both within and outside Germany that prejudice was increasing in West Germany. The incorporation of East Germany only adds to these worries.

The GDR, unlike the Federal Republic, did not accept responsibility for the Holocaust and the crimes of the Third Reich until after the election of its first and only democratic government in March 1990. The Communist leadership maintained that as the GDR was a socialist state it was liberated from Hitler and was not consequently responsible for the crimes of Fascism. The responsibility lay with capitalism and with the 'unreconstructed' Federal Republic. The East German regime refused to pay reparations to Jews or to Israel and supported the anti-Israeli line of its Soviet ally.

The legacy of these policies upon the political culture of a unified Germany is unknown, but it is probable that there is not much of a reservoir of support for a special relationship with Israel and that the contrary may in fact be the case. Forty years of consistently anti-Israeli propaganda combined with a pre-Communist history of anti-Semitism and a broad anti-religion campaign have left their mark. People living in east Germany face an enormous identity crisis and are more susceptible to nationalist appeals than their west German compatriots.[30] Finally, there is a widespread sentiment in the former GDR that the east Germans have been the real German losers of the war and have paid more than their share of reparations to the Soviets. Given the daunting task of rebuilding a collapsed economy, few will be sympathetic to pleas from Israel for reparations and restitution. The potential exists, on the contrary, for anti-Israeli sentiment to grow.

There is, as well, a broad anti-foreign sentiment directed especially against Moslem 'Guest Workers' from Turkey and refugees from the Third World. While resentment against the more than four million foreign workers (in the Federal Republic) has been present at least since the recessions of the 1970s, it has intensified in the last few years as West Germany became a haven for political and economic refugees from Asia and Africa as well as latterly from Eastern Europe. It was this resentment which finally set off the wave of support for the *Republikaner* in 1988–9. In many ways this parallels the phenomenon of *Le Penisme* in France. In east Germany Vietnamese and African workers have become the focus of this prejudice.

These resentments have been centred in the lower middle class and the working class in large cities with big foreign populations (Berlin, Frankfurt and the Ruhr cities) and in Bavaria. They are likely to intensify as the single European market comes into effect in 1993 further reducing restrictions on the movement of labour in the Community.

The political impact of this *Auslaenderfeindlichkeit*, or animosity toward foreigners, is likely to be more restrictive laws on immigration and political asylum. Yet given the demographic trends mentioned earlier, it is probable that Germany will be even more reliant upon foreign labour in the future than currently. This opens up the possibility that a broad anti-Moslem sentiment could develop as part of a new exclusive national identity. And signs of this have been evident in 1992.

New generations and political change

Generations matter more in Germany than anywhere else in Western Europe.[31] Because of the sharp discontinuities in historical experience, the lessons learned by successive postwar generations have been quite different from the preceding ones. Postwar Germans (those born around the end of World War II) have been socialised in a stable, democratic, affluent and relatively secure country. Their parents, in contrast, lived through World War II, dictatorship and the bleak immediate postwar period which included the Soviet occupation and subjection of East Germany and the Berlin Airlift. Postwar Germans, while aware of their responsibility as Germans for Hitler's legacy, do not feel personally responsible for the crimes of the Third Reich. While aware of the concerns of other nations about Germany, they are unwilling to be treated differently than other Europeans.

The three postwar generations (the generation which came of age during the student protests of the 1960s, that which entered university age during the post-oil-embargo 1970s and that socialised during the 1980s), while different from each other in terms of ideological values and style, seem to share a mutual disillusionment with both the United States and Israel. Both Israel and the United States were presented as models for German rehabilitation and implied as well the continuing burden of guilt. Vietnam began the process of 'killing the father' in the case of the United States, a process which was continued during the Reagan years. The United States became an anti-model for many of the university-educated young in the 1960s, representing both an unjust capitalism and an aggressive world power, images reinforced in the Reagan 1980s.

The image of Israel went through a similar change, both because of the close ties between Israel and the United States and because of Lebanon and the *intifada*. As one close observer of German–Israeli relations concludes: 'The third postwar generation, born in the 1960s and touched most directly by youth exchange programs, is reaching political consciousness as world opinion seems to conclude that Israel has lost its moral fiber'.[32] While these generations are reacting to changes in both Israel and the United States, the devaluation of both serves an important psychological purpose as well, reducing as it does the weight of the German past on contemporary Germans. This is part of the 'relativisation' of the Holocaust apparent both in Bitburg and the Historians' Debate.

The political result of this aspect of generational change is to undercut the reservoir of good will which existed in the German political culture for both the United States and Israel. The image of the United States recovered somewhat with the return of *détente* and with American support for German unification, but the better-educated young remained more indifferent to the United States than did their elders. While polls show that Germans still side more with the Israelis than the Arabs, and the networks of personal contacts and exchanges remain thicker, the number of 'undecideds' or 'indifferents' concerning Israel has grown.[33] This also implies that economic and other 'realistic' interests will weigh more heavily in German attitudes toward the Middle East, and the restraints on German policies deriving from the responsibilities of the past will diminish although not vanish.

Value change is another broad aspect of generational change with important implications for the German role in the world. The university-educated segment of the postwar generations has developed a system of values which has been characterised as 'post-materialist'.[34] Post-materialists, having been socialised in a stable, secure and affluent environment tend as a result to emphasise non-material values such as self-fulfilment, civil liberties and quality of life over materialist priorities such as economic growth, law and order and security.

The emerging new leaders of Germany, at least those from the dominant western part of the nation, are more sensitive to these priorities than previous generations. They are especially concerned about environmental issues, for example, and have a strong and consistent aversion to the use of military force in solving disputes. They are more likely to be sensitive to the North–South relationship than were the East–West-fixated leaders of the postwar era. They will have both realistic economic and social reasons for this (energy, exports and immigration) and broader value motivations as well.

The parties

These trends are strongest on the left, within the new generations of Social Democrats and the Greens. Here the legacy of the peace and environmental movements and of 'post-materialism' is strongest. The Christian Democrats have not been immune to these changes but they are more likely to stress the materialist agenda. Nevertheless, they have had to accommodate the strong anti-nuclear concerns of the new generations, concerns which have found a wider public after Chernobyl and the revelations of the environmental catastrophe in the former GDR.

This emerging ecological agenda implies that Germany will not move much further in the development of nuclear power as an alternative to a petroleum-based economy and that it will remain heavily dependent upon imported oil for the medium to long term, much of which will continue to come from the Middle East.

The parties in general have maintained a broad consensus on German policy in the Middle East. Social Democrats, while critical of German business dealings in weapons and chemical and nuclear facilities with Middle Eastern and other Third World clients, agree with the Christian Democrats and the Liberals over the main outlines of German policy toward the region. The policies of the two Helmuts are similar in their desire to 'compensate' for what is believed to be a 'one-sided' American policy which favours Israel by leaning toward the Arab states, albeit within a European approach.[35]

While the SPD would be more resistant to a German military role in the region, it has agreed, after initial opposition, to German participation in UN peacekeeping forces. The CDU seems more willing to deploy German forces within a European context and to be more sympathetic to American policies in the Gulf, but these differences are matters of degree not kind. The prospect is rather for support for a more independent European approach to the region and a gradually reduced German dependence upon the American role in an area of vital German economic interests.

German politics and the future of German foreign policy

It is difficult to think of another country in which domestic and foreign policy have been so closely intertwined as in Germany. Foreign policy is often the extension of domestic politics by other means, but the reverse is also often the case. The forty-six-year division of the nation which ended in October 1990 was only the most dramatic example of how the fundamentals of German politics and society have been linked to the constellation of international forces and politics.

With the reunification of the German nation the balance is likely to shift more toward domestic factors since the Germans will have far greater autonomy in deciding their foreign policies than at any time since the destruction of the Third Reich. This change contrasts with the condition in Weimar Germany described by Otto Hintze, a condition which held for the divided Germany of the postwar era as well:

We are no longer a free and strong people; and the fundamental basis of all politics is thereby changed . . . The spirit of domestic politics depends upon the external existential conditions of a state. Our external existential conditions are today such that foreign policy is only possible within very narrow boundaries and deprived of military vigour. We have in essence moved from being a subject to being an object in world politics.[36]

The Germans will once again be subjects but subjects in a Europe where the nation-state has lost much of the meaning it had before World War II. They will react to the reactions of other European states. If the British and French in particular revert to a narrow nationalism, they could foster a revival of nationalism in Germany. But in spite of the revival of a new sense of sovereignty and normalcy in Germany, there are strong reasons to believe that the Germans are unlikely to revert to a unilateral and divisive nationalism.

The ambiguity of the German reaction to reunification itself is an indication that the nationalism which spawned two wars in this century has been tempered if not transformed. West Germans have not shown much enthusiasm for the concept of a 'Greater Germany', and the ambivalent and cautionary approach of the Social Democratic candidate for the chancellorship in 1990, Oskar LaFontaine, reflected a good deal of the impact of generational and value change upon the political culture. LaFontaine was not elected in the first all-German election of 1990, but his hesitation about the costs, both short and long term, of reunification struck a chord. The new German nation enters its new history without nationalist hysteria or hyperbole.

This ambivalence is part of the development of a post-national political culture in the western part of Germany, linked to a sense that national solutions are not really possible in a Europe with the EC and the prospects of further integration after 1992. While Germany may be first among equals in the new Europe, there is a predisposition to create a European Germany rather than a German Europe.

The domestic factor is likely to act as a moderating influence on the future of German foreign policy. For the first time in its history the nation has a well-developed and effectively functioning set of democratic institutions. Perhaps equally important, it has a mature democratic political culture. The German economy will remain export-orientated, fostering a world view which stresses interdependence and collective approaches to global economic management and conflict resolution.

The new Germany is likely to be more willing to assume the responsibilities of leadership which its new weight implies. Yet its new weight should not be exaggerated. It will be an economic power of the first rank but only because of its role in an integrated European Community; it will be a conventional military power of medium rank but will not possess nuclear weapons nor the conventional capabilities to act independently outside of Europe. It will, therefore, project its influence in non-military ways and through its role within the European Community. Only if the progress toward the building of a new Europe fails, or is deemed too costly, will Germany be faced with any realistic national option.

The German and European future are as open now as at any time since the other two major turning points of 1919 and 1945. How the new generation of German and European leaders react to the opportunities and challenges before them will be crucial not only for the future of the Continent but will have important consequences for the Middle East as well.

The Gulf War: reinforcing the trends

The German domestic reaction to the Gulf War highlights several of the themes set out in this chapter and reveals some important aspects of the emerging strategic culture of the new Germany. The fact that the crisis occurred so early in the history of united Germany, and at a time when Germans were preoccupied with the beginnings of rebuilding east Germany and reshaping a new nation, clouds the significance of the crisis for interpreting German political culture. As this chapter has noted it will take some time before the contours of the political and strategic culture of united Germany are clear; some indications for the future did, however, emerge from this experience.

First concerning 'normalisation', it was clear that being 'normal' has a different meaning for Germany than for other European nations. Chancellor Kohl said at the beginning of the unification process that his goal was a 'normal' Germany, by which he meant a Germany which would not be treated any differently from France, Britain and other European states. Yet the Gulf crisis demonstrated that normality for Germany would be different from that of other states. History and the lessons learned from it have proved to be durable with lasting consequences. Attitudes toward the use of military force and towards national identity are different in Germany than they are in France or Britain.

Although public opinion polls found a growing acceptance of the need for the use of force in the Gulf as the war approached, there was almost no support for German participation in the war. The collective memory of the destructiveness of war and the misuse of military power by the Third Reich as well as the learning of the lessons of demilitarisation taught by the Allies remains deep even among the generations born after World War II.

Normalcy has meant more than just an aversion to the use of force. It has also meant a parochialism which has turned Germans inward toward their own concerns and in defence of their prosperity and privacy. The massive demands of reunification have crowded out most international issues as east Germans are preoccupied by fear of unemployment and the desire to catch up with the West, while the west Germans worry over paying the costs. Opinion polls and behaviour both provide evidence of a lack of interest in international involvement. Some have termed this the 'Swiss syndrome' because of the desire of many Germans, expressed in a public opinion survey, to model their nation after Switzerland.

The revival of nationalism, set off by the Euromissile dispute and the desire to defend German interests against American demands, was undercut by American support for German unification, Chancellor Kohl's skilful handling of the process and the warming of American–Soviet relations. Support for the *Republikaner* was quickly siphoned off by the CDU and CSU as the major parties retrieved the national issue from the radical right. The Gulf crisis did not change the general German preference for multinational over unilateral approaches.

Yet the German aversion to force and the view of America as too prone to use force to solve international problems were reinforced by the Gulf War, but German conservatives lamented the restrictive constitutional view the Kohl government took on committing German forces outside of Europe. They attempted to open up a broader debate on the legitimacy of democracies using force to defend democracy and human rights. They argued that Germany had to assume new responsibilities with its regained sovereignty and international weight and that it could no longer stand aloof from the dirty necessities of international politics. Some also argued that Germany could not be fully European if it abstained from playing a military role in Europe and that it should help develop a credible European defence identity.

These arguments are not over but they failed to shake a broad public consensus against the involvement of Germans in such contingencies. The reluctance of the Social Democrats to go beyond accepting German involvement in UN 'Blue Helmet' operations seemed to be widely shared beyond that party's group of supporters. Young Germans in particular remained the most opposed to any more assertive German military role.

Anti-Americanism did make a brief return in some of the anti-war demonstrations which swept the country prior to the January outbreak of the war. Yet here the German political culture seemed more relaxed than it was during the INF years. The end of the cold war reduced if not eliminated the fear that a conflict 'out of area' would pull the Germans into a confrontation with the Soviets in Europe. In fact the extent of Soviet–American cooperation during the second Gulf War dampened whatever potential there was for new *angst* over war. The Americans may still be regarded as a bit trigger happy, but the consequences of such behaviour were now seen as far less dangerous.

The other 'special relationship', that with Israel, had a rougher ride. The young and the left continued to regard Israel with great suspicion and many of the demonstrations had anti-Israeli aspects to them, yet the Scud attacks on Israel and the role of German firms in providing missile technology and components for chemical weapons, severely chastened a good part of the German public. Israelis were victims once again and this had its impact, especially in creating a new sensitivity to the role of German exports to the region. Yet the negative public view of Israel remained after the war, and there is little reason to believe that the trends outlined earlier have been altered fundamentally.

In fact a new parochialism was evident in the anti-foreign sentiment, which remains at troubling levels in both parts of Germany. The feeling of being overrun by foreigners has been heightened by growing concerns over increased immigration and refugees from the troubled Eastern part of Europe as well as from the Middle East. In this respect both Arabs and Jews face problems with the German public.

It is safe to say that German leaders and the public do not believe that the Gulf War is characteristic of the kinds of problems which will be central either to a new world order or to European security architecture. The Yugoslavian crisis may be viewed as a better test both of the emerging new order in Europe and the German role in it. Here the German government took a leading role within the EC in shaping a response to the escalating violence in Yugoslavia. Despite criticism from outside about German motives and the opposition of a key ally, France, Germany took the lead within a multilateral framework to deal with a problem of central importance to Europe. This is likely to give a better picture of the new Germany than the Gulf war. Here, Germany felt confident to lead and required no prodding. It is unlikely to do the same in the Middle East, where multilateral cover is seldom available.

Notes

1. Harvey Sicherman, 'Western Europe and the Arab-Israeli Conflict', *Orbis*, 23, Winter, 1980 p.846.
2. See Alfred Grosser, *The Western Alliance: European–American Relations Since 1945*, New York, Vintage, 1982, Chapter 10; H. Sicherman, 'Politics of Dependence', and Hanns W. Maull, 'Western Europe: A Fragmenting Response to a Fragmenting Order', *Orbis* 23, Winter, 1980, pp.803–24. Maull concludes that the West European response to the energy crises of 1974–8 was, 'in general, the Europeans were once more content to seek shelter under the American umbrella'.
3. On this special relationship see Chapter 5 Lily Gardner Feldman, *The Special Relationship Between West Germany and Israel*, Boston, George Allen and Unwin, 1984.
4. See Chapter 8 and Frederick S. Pearson, ' "Necessary Evil": Perspectives on West German Arms Transfer Policies', *Armed Forces and Society* 12 Summer, 1986, p.531–7; and Pearson, 'Of Leopards and Cheetahs: West Germany's Role as a Mid-Sized Arms Supplier', *Orbis*, 29, Spring, 1985, pp. 165–82.
5. Most often cited.as prohibiting German military involvement outside of the NATO treaty area are Articles 24 and 87a. The key wording in Article 24 states: 'For the maintenance of peace, the Federation may join a system of mutual collective security; in doing so it will consent to those limitations of its sovereign powers which will bring and secure a peaceful and lasting order, in Europe and among the nations of the world.' The relevant sections of Article 87a reads: 'The Federation shall build up Armed Forces for defense purposes. Apart from defense, the Armed Forces may only be used to the extent explicitly permitted by this Basic Law.' In neither article does the wording seem clearly to rule out military involvement outside of the NATO area and, as will be discussed later, Article 24 seems on the contrary to open the door for such action.
6. See Catherine M. Kelleher, 'The Federal Republic of Germany' in Douglas J. Murray and Paul R. Viotti (eds), *The Defense Policy of Nations: A Comparative Study*, 2nd edition, Baltimore, The Johns Hopkins University Press, 1989, p.174; John A. Reed,

Germany and NATO, Washington, DC, The National Defense University Press, 1987, pp.176-7 and Janice Gross Stein, 'The Wrong Strategy in the Right Place: The United States in the Gulf', *International Security*, 13 Winter, 1988–9, p.160.

7. See United States Information Agency, 'Key West European Publics Believe Libyan Chemical Weapons a Threat, Support Trade Embargo to Close Rabta Plant', *Research Memorandum*, Washington, DC, USIA, Office of Research, 24 January 1989.

8. This sentiment was hardly limited to the Germans. Italian Prime Minister Goria in sending an Italian naval force to the Gulf in 1987 said it was being done 'without enthusiasm' because in Italy 'there is no one who dreams of military action, gunboat diplomacy, or any exhibition of military strength'. Quoted in James M. Markham, 'European Policy and the Gulf: A Striking Reversal', *The New York Times*, 16 September 1987.

9. See Ulrich Albrecht, 'The Policy of the Federal Republic of Germany Toward the South', in Ekkehart Krippendorff and Volker Rittberger (eds), *The Foreign Policy of West Germany: Formation and Contents*, London, Sage, 1980, pp.177–82.

10. David D. Hale, 'Deutsche Mark Uber Alles', *The Washington Post*, 1 July 1990, p.B4.

11. Christian Hacke, *Weltmacht wider Willen: Die Aussenpolitik der Bundesrepublik Deutschland*, Stuttgart, Klett, 1988, p.308.

12. See Hacke, *Weltmacht wider Willen*, p.306 and Theo Sommer, 'Helmut Schmidt' in *Die Deutschen Kanzler: Von Bismarck Bis Schmidt*, Wilhelm von Sternburg (ed.), Koenigstein, Athenaum, 1985, pp.451–3.

13. Helmut Schmidt, *Menschen und Maechte*, Berlin, Siedler, 1987, pp.235–43.

14. For more on this see Elizabeth Pond, 'Sind wir verraten und verkauft?', *Die Zeit* (North American edition) 3 July 1987, p.3 and Clay Clemens, 'Beyond INF: West Germany's centre-right party and arms control in the 1980s', *International Affairs* 65, No. 1, Winter 1988–9, p.60–4.

15. For a collection of the key documents in this controversy see *Historikerstreit*, Munich, Piper, 1987; for interpretations and critiques see Charles Maier, *The Unmasterable Past* Cambridge, Mass, Harvard University Press, 1988 and Richard J. Evans, *In Hitler's Shadow: West German Historians and the Attempt to Escape from the Nazi Past*, New York, Pantheon, 1989. A good short overview of the debate is provided by Dennis Bark and David Gress, *Democracy and its Discontents*, Stanford, Hoover Institution, 1989, pp.432–47.

16. See Josef Joffe, 'The Battle of the Historians', *Encounter*, June 1987, pp.75–6. Joffe writes

... the Battle of the German Historians and the War Against the American Missiles are clearly related – like two brothers fighting over patrimony or primogeniture. In both cases the real object of conquest was the past that would not pass away ... [the left's] progressive purpose – national reassertion and the reclamation of moral worth – was no different from the quest of the revisionist historians ...

17. Quoted in Claus Leggewie, *Die Republikaner: Phantombild der Neuen Rechten*, Berlin, Rotbuch Verlag, 1989, pp.62–3.

18. Gordon A. Craig, 'The Rising Star of the German Right', *The New York Review of Books*, 15 June 1989, p.24.

19. Richard Cohen, '. . . And the Germans', *The Washington Post*, 10 January 1989, p. A23. See also Josef Joffe, 'In Bonn, Echoes of Kaiser Wilhelm', *The New York Times*, 17 January 1989, p. A25.

20. 'Reflections on "the German Question"', *Survival*, 32, No. 4 July–August 1990, p.295–6.

21. Frederick Kempe, 'Kohl is Willing to Order Ships to Gulf, Signaling Readiness for a New World Role', *The Wall Street Journal*, 16 August 1990, p.10. Teltschik's views were echoed by Helmut Schaefer, minister of state in the foreign office and a close aide of

Minister Genscher, when he said 'considerably greater things' will be expected of a united Germany and that Germans will have to change their constitution to allow participation in UN peacekeeping forces. 'Official Opposes Sending Army Units to Gulf', Hamburg DPA reprinted in *Foreign Broadcast Information Service (FBIS): Daily Report: West Europe*, 10 August 1990, p.6.

22. 'Disagreement Within Bonn Coalition About Deploying Bundeswehr in Gulf', *Frankfurter Allgemeine Zeitung*, 16 August 1990, p.2, reprinted in *FBIS*, 17 August 1990, p.10.

23. 'Bundeswehr Under UN Command?', *Die Welt*, 19 August 1990, p.1 and reprinted in *FBIS*, 20 August 1990, p.16.

24. Marc Fisher, 'Kohl Seeks German Role in a U.N. Force in Gulf,' *The Washington Post*, 17 August 1990, p.A16; 'Kohl Fails to Win Support for Sending German Troops to Gulf', *The Washington Post*, 21 August 1990, p.A5 and 'Disagreement Within Bonn Coalition About Deploying Bundeswehr in Gulf', p.2.

25. One factor which prevented a more active role in the Gulf crisis was the continuing weight of the past. As one German foreign-policy analyst Jochen Thies put it, 'Germany's silence is revealing. It is the classic German problem. Because of our history, there is a hesitation to send German troops where Rommel has been.' Quoted in Fischer, 'West German Troops to Remain out of Gulf', *The Washington Post*, 10 August 1990, p. A30.

26. See, for example, William Drozdiak, 'NATO Redefines Defense Role', *The Washington Post*, 8 August 1990, p.A12 and Alan Riding, 'Allies Reminded of Need for U.S. Shield', *The New York Times*, 12 August 1990, p.14. The German view is closer to that expressed in an article in *Die Zeit*: 'The Federal Republic could not and can not in the future play the role of deputy sheriff of a superpower, which in addition to its role as the leading power of NATO also represents itself as a world policeman.' The author goes on to argue that Germany is part of the international collective security system and has a responsibility to make a contribution through the UN. He notes that the importance of the UN grows with every day of the crisis as the end of the era of East–West confrontation has opened up opportunities for it, implying that NATO has lost its meaning in this new situation. Hans Schueler, 'Wider den Tyrannen: Deutsche Raeumboote in den Golf?', *Die Zeit* (North American edition), 24 August 1990, p.4.

27. The key provision in the Basic Law often cited by opponents of German involvement outside of the NATO area, Article 24, clearly provides for such involvement if the political will is there. See the wording in footnote 5.

28. The new Germany, as part of the price it paid to the Soviets for reunification, has agreed to limit its forces to 340,000 men and to continue to renounce the possession of nuclear, chemical and biological weapons. 'Excerpts from Kohl–Gorbachev News Conference', *The New York Times*, 17 July 1990, p.A8 and 'German Vows Limit on the New Force', *The New York Times*, 31 August 1990, p.A7.

29. Reunification is likely to increase scepticism about NATO. Public opinion surveys taken in the spring of 1990 in East Germany indicated that support for NATO was substantially weaker in East Germany than it was in West Germany. The poll found that a majority in the GDR supported a neutral Germany to one which belonged to NATO. See *Der Spiegel*, 23 April 1990, p.103.

30. For a survey of anti-Semitism and the GDR's policy of dealing with the Nazi past see Friedrich Ebert Stiftung, *Zur Bewaeltigung der NS Zeit in der DDR: Defizite und Neubewertungen*, Bonn, Friedrich Ebert Stiftung, 1989 in the series, *Die DDR: Realitaeten-Arguemente*.

31. For a comparative analysis see Stephen F. Szabo (ed.), *The Successor Generation: International Perspectives of Postwar Europeans*, London, Butterworth, 1983.

32. Lily Gardner Feldman, 'German Morality and Israel', in Peter H. Merkl (ed.), *The Federal Republic of Germany at Forty*, New York, New York University Press, 1989, p.459.

33. Michael Wolffsohn, 'Deutsche–israelische Beziehungen im Spiegel der oeffentlichen Meinung', *Aus Politik und Zeitgeschichte* 46–47/84, 17 November 1984, p.21. See also

Feldman, *The Special Relationship Between West Germany and Israel*, p.210. A comparative survey conducted in the United States and West Germany in March 1990 found that on a scale going from −5 for a country the respondent did not like much to +5 for one which was viewed very favourably, Israel was given 0.9 by the American public and 0.3 by the West Germans. This put Israel just ahead of Poland (0.1), the country with the lowest rating in the survey of Germans. Friedrich Naumann Stiftung, *Public Opinion in the USA and the Federal Republic of Germany: A Two Nation Study*, Bonn, Friedrich Naumann Stiftung, typewritten, 1989, p.5.

34. For a full exposition of the concept and its impact in advanced industrial societies see Ronald Inglehart, *Culture Shift in Advanced Industrial Society*, Princeton, Princeton University Press, 1990.

35. Peter Huenseler, 'Der arabische-israelische Konflikt' in Karl Kaiser and Hans-Peter Schwarz (eds), *Weltpolitik: Strukturen-Aktuere-Perspektiven* Stuttgart, Klett, 1985, p.522.

36. Otto Hintze, 'Liberalismus, Demokratie und auswaertige Politik (1926)' in *Soziologie und Geschichte* Goettingen, 1982, and quoted in Hacke, *Weltmacht Wider Willen*, p.445.

7 Economic relations with the Middle East: weight and dimensions

Hanns Maull

West Germany's postwar development has in many important ways been shaped by its economic successes. These successes have turned it into the world's leading exporter of manufactured goods and the *economie dominante* of the European Community, of Western Europe and soon perhaps it might become the dominant economy of Europe as a whole. At the same time, this West German economic weight has become ever more deeply embedded in the European context. An analysis of Germany's economic relations with the Middle East from that point of view represents in many ways an analysis *pars pro toto*, in which Germany stands for the European Community as a whole. The focus of the following analysis will therefore be as much on the broader picture as on bilateral economic relations. It will begin, however, by sketching some unique historical and political factors which have shaped West Germany's involvement in international economic relations in the postwar world. The second part looks at developments during the 1970s, while the third part considers the 1980s. In the final section, I shall try to draw some tentative conclusions for the future of economic relations between united Germany and the Middle East: the latter region is here generally taken to stretch from Egypt to Syria, Iraq and Iran and the Arabian peninsula. I will also consider the German reaction to the Gulf War of 1991.

Germany and the Middle East: determinants of economic relations

Economic relations between Germany and the Middle East have largely been shaped by the forces of history and politics and by the abundance of low-cost oil in North Africa and the Gulf. Germany's colonial and imperial ambitions in the region were shattered in World War I, and its second, even more disastrous attempt to impose its dominance on the whole of Europe which brought German armies to North Africa in a vain attempt to shake Britain's imperial positions, finally ended the European war, in which Germany had played such a crucial role, for good.

Out of the ruins of World War II arose a new Germany and a new Europe, both split into two halves along the great divide of the East–West conflict. The luckier part of Germany and Europe came under the tutelage of the United States, whose far-sighted postwar policies pursued one Janus-headed central objective – the 'double containment'[1] of both a resurgence of German revisionism and, more urgently, of the threat of Soviet expansionism: while the god's face of war (read: national security) was turned towards the Soviet Union, that of peace (read: Atlantic partnership) was turned towards West Germany. The former enemy was helped to its feet economically and politically; at the same time it was firmly enmeshed in a web of institutionalised cooperation and supranational integration.

West Germany benefited hugely from those arrangements. At the time that was perhaps not entirely obvious: to regain full political sovereignty from the Western occupying powers, West Germany had to accept a simultaneous transfer of key elements of this sovereignty to new international institutions, primarily to NATO (in the realm of security) and to the European Coal and Steel Community, later to develop into the European Community (in the realm of economics). Through NATO, West Germany essentially entrusted what is the core interest of any state, the guarantee of its security, to its allies; and it accepted that its own contribution to the common security of NATO should be fully integrated into a common military force. Through the European Coal and Steel Community, West Germany accepted international control over key heavy industries.

Thus, from the beginning of its postwar history, West Germany internalised the realities of interdependence and learned to see them as an asset rather than as a liability. What had originally been demands by the allies were quickly taken up by West Germany itself, which abrogated aspirations to the traditional grandeur of a nation-state in favour of exploiting the advantages and opportunities provided by interdependence. To be sure, there was the objective of reunification, of overcoming the division of Germany. But Adenauer firmly held that integration into the Western alliance and the European Community had to be given priority over reunification. The national objective of German unity thus gradually faded into the background – still enshrined as a key national objective in the constitution and vehemently upheld at political rallies but more and more remote in real terms given the realities of the division of Europe and the world.

The national issue had thus lost its salience by the end of the 1950s. NATO provided West Germany with the required security at rather low cost, thus freeing resources for other, economic purposes. The European Community (and again NATO) made West Germany acceptable to its neighbours, enormously facilitating economic expansion. West Germany's collective energies could thereby be channelled away from the traditional ambitions of the 'territorial state' to new ones of the 'trading state'.[2] This was clearly where the future lay. In this way West Germany developed from the great scourge of Europe to its economic powerhouse; it became a model, a prototype of the new world of European supranationalism – although with the unresolved issue of national unity and identity still lurking in the background. By the autumn of 1989, that issue was to resurface with a vengeance.

The patterns of much of West German postwar foreign and foreign economic policy emerged from this historical background: Germany had destroyed the old Europe in the World Wars and had murdered six million Jews. The price it had had to pay was national division and the abrogation of national autonomy in the traditional sense. This meant that West Germany was unable to pursue a 'Middle East policy' in the traditional sense of a great power. But the burdens of the past also offered vast opportunities – the opportunities of interdependence. West Germany seized them and used them well.

What, then, in this blend of old legacies and new approaches were the particular factors shaping relations with the Middle East? Economics defined dependence and vulnerability, but history and politics determined the responses.

At the most basic level, Germany's economic relations with the Middle East have been, and will continue to be, shaped by two simple facts: the *industrial strength of Germany* as a key producer and the number-one exporter of manufactured goods – having however to rely largely on imported raw materials and energy – and the *abundant and low-cost reserves of oil in the Middle East* which can provide this energy.

Beyond that economic complementarity, history and politics take over. Thus, the *Jewish Holocaust* established a special West German relationship[3] with Israel which included – apart from compensation payments to individuals totalling some $970 million between 1953 and 1965 – substantial reparations, development assistance and military support for the Jewish state. The legacy of Nazi extermination policies also shaped West German policies towards the Israeli–Arab conflict until the 1970s. West Germany has consistently taken a particular interest in the security of the state of Israel,[4] and its secret arms supplies to the Jewish state led to an almost complete political rupture with the Arab world between 1965 and 1972. Since 1970, however, West Germany has found an alternative to a national policy towards the Israeli–Arab conflict through European Political Cooperation. Israeli–German relations continue to be close and sensitive, however, and the process of German reunification has revived some of the strong emotions the Holocaust inevitably left behind.[5]

The *division of Germany* introduced elements of competition for recognition in the relationships of the two German states with the Middle East during the 1950s and 1960s. Both tried to use trade and aid relations with Middle Eastern countries as a lever in the struggle over recognition of East Germany. The *Ostpolitik* of the Brandt–Scheel coalition government after 1969 cleared the way for cross-recognition; as a consequence, the rivalry between the two Germanies in the Middle East faded away. Elements of the East–West conflict, however, lingered on in the patterns of economic interaction between the two Germanies and the Middle East. The end of the division of Europe and the reunification of Germany can also be expected to have a substantial impact on the region.

Supranationalism has become a cornerstone of Germany's relations with the outside world. As the birth of the Federal Republic was intimately linked to a substantial transfer of sovereignty, so the process of reunification in 1989–90 went hand in hand with a deepening of Western European integration and with a firm support for NATO – despite the dissolution of the East–West confrontation in Europe. West Germany has learnt to pursue its 'national interests' within and through the networks of alliance ties. In the economic realm (and to some degree also in the realm of foreign policy), this means above all the European Community. Within those alliance contexts, Germany's influence and weight have undoubtedly grown and are likely to grow further with unification. At the same time, however, this should not simply be equated with a rise of German 'power'. German influence – and indeed even the formulation of its objectives and interests – has become intricately tied into networks of institutionalised cooperation and thus represents power and national interests of a particular kind: 'soft' or 'co-optive' power, to quote Jo Nye,[6] and 'national interests' which in their very formulation incorporate the realities of interdependence in the context of the European Community. In many ways, the Community, rather than Germany, has thus been the economic partner of the

Middle Eastern countries and will continue in this role. Even the concept of a 'German economy' has become misleading, given the seamless economic space which today more and more characterises the Community.

'Crisis and promise': trends and issues in economic relations between West Germany and the Middle East during the 1970s

The 1970s were, of course, the decade of the first oil crisis; paradoxically, it was also a period of great promise. In substantive terms, the decade in 1970 began with Libya's successful pressure on American oil companies to raise prices; it ended with the Iranian revolution in 1978–9 which once more pushed the world oil markets into turmoil. In between, in October 1973, there was the successful use of the oil weapon by the Arab producers which caused oil prices to quadruple almost within a few weeks – from $3.01/barrel in September to $11.65/barrel by the end of the year.

The promise of this decade rested on two factors: one was the enormous increase in capital available to the Arab states and Iran as a result of higher oil revenues. This allowed governments to design and implement large budget increases for consumption and investments and to set up ambitious development plans to tackle, by way of crash programmes, the huge tasks of development in the region. The result was an enormous boom: the GDP of the Arab world rose from $41 billion in 1970 to $406 billion in 1980.[7] The second factor was less tangible but at least as important: the Arab world and Iran now appeared determined to take its fate into its own hands. Libya had shown this resolve *vis-à-vis* the oil companies; Egypt and Syria showed it in their military assault on Israel in the Yom Kippur war, which was to break the diplomatic stalemate in the Israeli–Arab conflict imposed by Israeli intransigence and superpower neglect; Saudi Arabia and most other Arab oil producers demonstrated it in their use of the oil weapon and through OPEC's takeover of the world oil market.

This willingness to act for themselves, even if confronted with apparently superior forces, went hand in hand with remarkable moderation. By and large, Middle Eastern countries were prepared to turn their attention towards solving their internal problems of underdevelopment and instability and to seek regional and international cooperation as a means to provide the necessary external conditions for peace and regional stability. Politically, the Arab world from 1973 to 1978 was largely dominated by Egyptian–Saudi Arabian cooperation and the Gulf region dominated by Iran, with Saudi Arabia as a junior partner. All three countries cooperated closely with the United States to maintain and strengthen the regional status quo. Strengthening this conservative status quo, however, required two things: progress in settling the Israeli–Arab conflict and genuine economic and social development.

In terms of economic relations with the West, the implications were an effort to expand cooperation, albeit on a new and more balanced basis. The Middle Eastern countries had – with the support of other OPEC members – successfully demonstrated the power of oil. Through this power, they had managed to establish a new regime for the international oil market and thus a new relationship between producers and consumers. In the process, they had acquired huge amounts of money, now available for enhanced cooperation with the West. Yet dependence was far from one-sided: the Middle Eastern countries also needed Western support to turn petrodollars into real and sustainable social and economic development.

The West in general, and the Federal Republic in particular, had had the opposite experience, the revelation of their vulnerability to oil-supply disruptions and price increases. Access to oil supplies at reasonable and stable prices suddenly became a real and urgent security issue. The huge oil price increases had also produced a massive swing into the red of the trade balances of most industrialised countries. There were thus strong incentives to expand exports into oil-producing countries generally. For the companies, there was the lure of newly wealthy buyers; for economic planners in the government, expanded exports could correct trade imbalances though in the case of West Germany, those imbalances were only bilateral.' Overall, the German export industry continued to clock up surpluses even in 1973 and 1974, and for those officials concerned with security of supply, strengthened ties with producers could reasonably be expected to contribute to this objective.

The new wealth of the Middle East thus produced a sizeable increase and diversification in economic interaction, while considerations of security of oil supplies gave new urgency to political approaches to the Middle East. Those political approaches took various forms – bilateral agreements, association agreements with the EC (in the framework of the EC's Mediterranean Policy) and the Euro–Arab Dialogue – but all tried to secure access to oil through closer relations without tackling the key regional political issue, the Israeli–Arab conflict. The Arab side would not accept this, of course, and thus the Europeans more or less reluctantly shifted their position so as to accommodate a genuine political dialogue about this conflict. There had always been those in the Community who saw the Israeli–Arab conflict in itself as a threat to regional stability, including the stability of oil supplies, arguing as a consequence that Europe should take initiatives to resolve the conflict. In reality, however, it was doubtful whether the European countries – even if they had been united in their approach – would have been able to contribute effectively to a solution. There was also American and Israeli opposition to any such independent European role – and both countries wielded particular influence in Bonn.

While the political dialogue between West Germany (as part of the European Community) and the Arab world thus never amounted to much in substantive terms, economic relations intensified rapidly, reflected mainly in the shopping spree of new wealth and the lure of new, rich markets. But there was also political support for such a development along the lines mentioned above. A web of interdependence and mutual advantage would, it was hoped, blunt the oil weapon and domesticate oil power or – to put it more diplomatically – create strong vested interests in stable and growing economic relations between Europe and the Middle Eastern oil producers. Behind this logic, there were two key assumptions which turned out to be highly problematical. The first assumption was that this new interdependence between the Middle East and the Western world would turn out to be mutually beneficial and germane to effective and genuine development of the former. The second assumption was that interdependence would create – or simply benefit from – domestic and regional political stability and a regional order which would provide the security prerequisite for beneficial economic interaction.

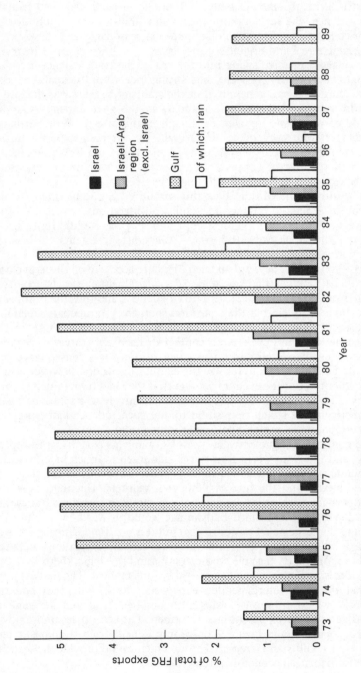

Figure 7.1 West German exports to the Middle East

The expansion of economic ties was most obvious in trade. With regard to exports to the Middle East, West Germany, together with Japan and Korea, proved itself to be particularly nimble in capitalising on the new circumstances: West German industry launched an impressive attack on OPEC markets, which produced swift results. As Figure 7.1 shows, there was a very strong expansion of German exports to the Middle East. Exports to the Gulf rose from 1.48 per cent of total West German exports in 1973 to 5.12 per cent in 1978. In that year, Iran alone accounted for 2.37 per cent of German exports. The expansion was less dramatic but still considerable, in the case of the Arab countries in the Israeli–Arab region – reflecting the sizeable spillover effects of the oil boom in the region. While the Middle Eastern countries thus gained in relative importance as West German export markets, Israel slipped back.

During the same period (1973 to 1978) West Germany also managed to gain market shares in manufactures in key Middle Eastern countries at the expense of other suppliers. Taking Libya, Algeria, Iraq, Kuwait and Saudi Arabia together, West Germany pushed up its market share there from 9.05 per cent in 1970 to a peak of 17.84 per cent in 1975; by 1979, this share had declined to a still very respectable 16.69 per cent.[8] The strongest surges came in machinery and transport equipment and chemicals, the traditionally strong sectors of the West German export economy.

After 1973 exports to Middle Eastern countries clearly took on a new priority for West German industry and government. The determined push into these markets was rewarded. As a result, those markets modestly gained in overall importance to the West German economy, though this importance should certainly not be overestimated. West Germany was also more successful than others in supplying those new markets, as shown by the substantial gains in market share in several Middle Eastern and North African countries in 1974–6.

The vast amounts of petrodollars flowing from 1973 into the Middle Eastern producers' treasuries could not be spent on higher imports immediately: infrastructure bottlenecks initially limited their capacity to absorb higher imports. This gave rise to the recycling problem. The problem really consisted of two aspects: first, the petrodollars accumulating unspent in bank accounts and other forms of highly liquid assets had to be channelled into productive investments. Second, petrodollars had to be recycled from oil exporters to importers creating balance of payments' problems. Germany was not affected by the latter problem, as its balance of payments remained in the black throughout the 1970s. German banks nevertheless played an important part in the recycling efforts of countries with balance of payments' problems, and they also secured some important Middle Eastern investments for West Germany. Most famous among those were the Iranian investment in Krupp and the Kuwaiti purchase of minority shares in Daimler-Benz, Hoechst, Metallgesellschaft and ASKO. Total Middle Eastern direct investment in the FRG rose from DM53 million in 1973 to about DM1539 million in 1979.[9] In addition, portfolio investments no doubt also grew substantially.

The politically critical element in the economic equation, however, clearly continued to be oil. The Middle East, in 1973, supplied 49.3 per cent of total West German oil imports; by 1978, this had fallen slightly to 47.3 per cent (see Figure 7.2). Oil also continued to account for the bulk of imports from Middle Eastern countries, which singularly failed to develop alternative sources of export earnings.[10]

'Failure': developments and trends in the 1980s

The promises of the 1970s were rudely shattered in 1978–9 by two major political developments in the region which were to change economic interactions between West Germany and the Middle East profoundly. The first of those processes was the Iranian revolution, which overthrew the regime of the Shah and replaced it with a theocracy led by Ayatollah Khomeini. Revolutionary Iran rapidly drifted into confrontation with its Arab neighbours, and especially with Iraq, which in September 1980 launched into war in the erroneous assumption that Iran's new system would not be able to withstand such an attack. The result was a long and bloody war which ended only in the summer of 1988. The second process which undermined regional stability was the peace agreement between Egypt and Israel resulting from American mediation at Camp David. This effectively isolated Egypt from the Arab mainstream for almost a decade, profoundly changing the political alignments and the relative strength of moderates and radicals in the Arab world.

The two processes exposed the brittle domestic and regional foundations on which Middle Eastern stability had rested during the 1970s and shattered many of the assumptions which had guided Western policies and economic relations with the region in the past. The second oil crisis, triggered initially by strikes of Iranian oil workers, and then by a radical revision of Iran's oil policy under the new revolutionary regime, demonstrated that security of supply was threatened not only – and not even primarily – by the 'oil weapon', that is by deliberate manipulation of supplies and prices by producer governments but also by domestic and regional instability. Bilateral efforts to cultivate special relationships between producer and consumer governments turned out to be worthless at best, dangerous at worst.[11] The European–Arab Dialogue practically came to a halt in 1978, and the results of the Community's Mediterranean Policy also turned out to be meagre in practical terms, as preferences accorded to some of those countries within the context of this policy were of limited importance and subject to erosion due to the proliferation of preferential access agreements between the Community and other countries or groupings.

None of those activities made any substantial difference with regard to security of supply. Nor was the International Energy Agency, the organisation set up by the industrialised countries (with the exception of France) to protect member countries against supply shortfalls, able to prevent another steep oil price increase in 1979–80. The essentials of oil security were now demonstrably to be found in the ability of the West to defend production sites and supply lines against military attacks, and in the mechanisms of the international oil markets and the self-interest of its major players.

The capacity to protect supplies against military attacks consisted essentially in the military power projection capabilities of the United States (though the much more limited capabilities of France and Britain also played a useful role). In both the Iran–Iraq war, and again in the aftermath of the Iraqi invasion of Kuwait, those capabilities were mobilised successfully against the threat of a spillover of hostilities on the Arabian peninsula proper, that is, in a significant way into Saudi Arabia.[12]

Beyond the *ultima ratio* of military force, Western access to oil in the 1980s was shown to depend largely on the mechanisms of the international oil market and the slow but relentless evolution of the world energy system in response to price changes. While market mechanisms at the beginning of the 1980s were responsible for another huge, and economically much more damaging round of price increases, they began to work more and more in favour of oil-importing nations from 1982 onwards. In 1986, they produced a steep decline in oil prices and effectively broke OPEC's power. Cumulatively, the oil market changed from a seller's to a buyer's market; in the process, the market lost many of its unique features and thus became more and more like any normal commodity market.

Above all the swing in the relationship of forces in the market back to the buyers reflected large gains in energy efficiency, achieved in response to higher energy prices throughout the 1970s and 1980s. Additionally, there were successes in substituting other sources of energy (natural gas, coal and nuclear energy) for oil and in diversification efforts away from (low-cost) Middle Eastern oil to (high-cost) oil supplies from the North Sea, Alaska and a number of other producing regions. In the light of long lead times, however, most of those gains took time to materialise, meaning that their cumulative impact only became visible largely in the 1980s.

The cumulative effects of those changes are demonstrated in Figure 7.2. Between 1973 and 1980, West Germany's energy demand increased by 3.1 per cent and between 1981 and 1989 by 1.5 per cent, while Gross National Product rose in real terms by 10.9 per cent during the 1970s and by 19.1 per cent from 1981 to 1989. Oil demand declined by 9.1 per cent between 1973 and 1980, and by a further 6.9 per cent between 1981 and 1989. Finally, oil imports declined by 11.4 per cent between 1973 and 1980 and by a further 16.8 per cent from 1981 to 1989. Oil imports from the Middle East went down by 22.6 per cent from 1973 to 1981 and by a further 56.6 per cent from 1981 to 1989. In this period, the fall from the import peak year 1974 (with 57.2 million tonnes) to the low in 1985 (with 7.7 million) was a truly dramatic 86.5 per cent. The principal beneficiaries of this shift were the North Sea and other non-OPEC producers.

While the West German change in energy-supply patterns was particularly pronounced, it reflected the general trend in Western Europe and Japan, while in the United States the decline of domestic production and a rise in demand for oil in the second half of the 1980s produced a new rise of imports in that period. Overall, however, the Middle East's share in world oil production went down from 53 per cent in 1973 and 47 per cent in 1980 to 29 per cent in 1985 and 37 per cent in 1989; its share in world oil exports declined from 30 per cent in 1980 to a low of 19 per cent in 1985 and 26 per cent in 1989. When OPEC failed in 1986 to reduce output in line with falling demand, oil prices rose from $2.83 in 1973 (per barrel Arabian light) to a peak of $35.69 in 1980 and then collapsed to $12.97 in 1986; thereafter, they rose only modestly to $15.69 in 1989.[13]

The impact of falling oil demand and the price collapse of government oil revenues was truly dramatic, as is shown in figure 7.3. To take the most dramatic example, Saudi Arabian oil revenues between 1972 and 1981 rose from $3.1 billion to $113.3 billion, and then slumped to $20 billion in 1986. In terms of purchasing power per barrel of exported oil, the slump was, of course, even more pronounced, as import prices continued to rise and the dollar lost much of its value as a result of exchange-rate fluctuations. Even without the effects of the dollar depreciation, the purchasing power of one barrel of oil, if set at 100 in 1973, fell from a peak of 483 in 1981 to a low of 150 in 1988 and 180 in 1989.[14]

The change from a seller's to a buyer's market in the international oil business

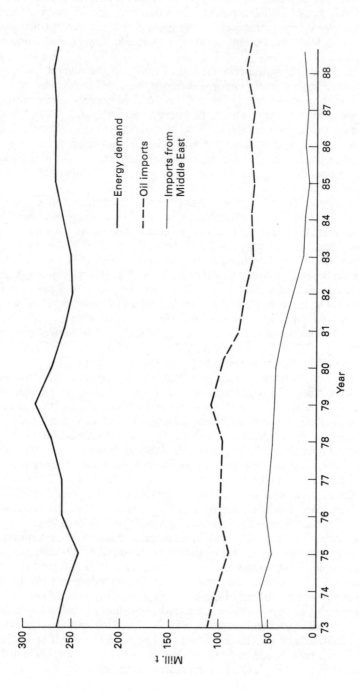

Figure 7.2 FRG Oil Imports and Energy Demand, 1973–1989

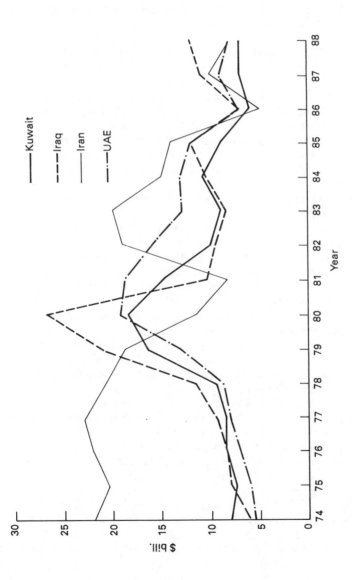

Figure 7.3 Middle East oil revenues

had a lot to do with changes in market structures. The vertical integration of the world oil industry, which had survived the first oil crisis in the form of long-term contractual ties between producer countries and the international oil industry, was smashed by the second oil shock in 1979. Moreover, by the mid-1980s, as Edward Krapels has persuasively argued, the OPEC governments and the oil companies had lost much of their previous financial independence: OPEC government revenues came under the severe squeeze noted above, while the industry was invaded by a whole set of new actors such as Wall Street investment banks.[15] This development, in turn, was related to the growing importance of new market mechanisms such as future and forward markets and the much expanded role of spot prices which made the international oil market look much like any other commodity market. By the late 1980s, the largest 'paper' market for oil, the New York Mercantile Exchange, routinely traded daily volumes of 200 million barrels, ten times the actual physical world oil trade.[16]

The sum of all those developments was that the pursuit of oil security was no longer sought through courting the producers. Relations between the Middle East and the Western world accordingly lost some of their urgency. During the 1970s, those relations had, in more than one sense, become inflated by the impact of the first oil shock. During the 1980s, as oil power waned, so its role was more and more discounted, and relations returned to 'normal'. Politically, this meant a continuing concern with the threat of regional instability (which could demonstrably threaten security of supply) and with possible Western responses to those threats in the form of efforts to contain, and perhaps even to settle, the region's most virulent conflicts (the Iran–Iraq war and the Israeli–Arab conflict). Economically, it meant 'doing business', rather than a special economic relationship.

Thus, the illusions of the 1970s were now rudely shattered. The assumption that the injection of massive oil income could buy real and sustainable development in a short period of time proved ill-founded: not one of the major oil exporters achieved a substantial diversification of its economic base, and while the picture looked somewhat brighter in some of the non-oil Middle Eastern countries, the overall progress towards sustainable development was modest at best there, too. The reasons for this failure were manifold: lack of cohesive and effective development planning, lack of regional cooperation and less than favourable indigenous conditions for entrepreneurial development. But the overwhelming cause for this failure was political instability and violence – as epitomised in the Iran–Iraq war. From 1980 to 1985 alone, the costs of this war have been estimated at $417 billion of which Iraq bore $176 billion ($94 billion for military expenditure, $56 billion in loss of oil export revenues and $26 billion in GNP loss) and Iran $241 billion overall.[17] The war produced a whole range of negative economic impulses – the destruction of human lives and economic resources; the massive drain on available resources from the war effort; the dislocation of the workforce through the shift from productive activities to military service; the flight of capital and skilled labour; neglect of agriculture and severe damage to the climate for foreign investment.

The net effect of all this was a severe recession. From 1982 onward, growth rates declined, often severely. Hardest hit were the Gulf Cooperation Council members on the Arabian peninsula: annual GDP losses from 1980 to 1987 averaged 1.3 per cent in Kuwait, 4.3 per cent in the UAE, and 5.3 per cent in

Saudi Arabia. But other Middle Eastern countries also suffered: during the same period, GDP growth slowed to an average of 4.3 per cent per annum in Jordan and 0.3 per cent in Syria.[18]

The principal mechanism for the transferral of oil revenues from producers to other countries in the region is through foreign workers and their financial transfers to their home countries.[19] The impact of declining oil revenues, recession in the Gulf and falling workers' remittances created a vicious cycle: while revenues from oil and workers' remittances declined – and non-oil exports could not compensate for this decline due to lack of capacity and the growth of protectionist barriers world-wide – most imports were hard to cut without severe political or economic repercussions or both. The results were a rapidly growing debt burden both at home and abroad and recurrent balance of payments' difficulties. The total debt of the Arab world rose from $68 billion in 1982 to about $180 billion in 1988, representing a rise from 52.5 per cent of GNP to 65.8 per cent. By 1988, for the two principal debtor countries in the region, Egypt and Jordan, debt had exceeded GNP.[20]

War and recession had a severe impact on economic relations between the Middle East and the West, and the West German experience illustrates this perfectly. Excluding Israel, total West German exports to the Middle East declined from DM33.4 billion in 1982 to DM19.5 billion in 1989. Exports to the Gulf states, Iran, Iraq and the GCC members declined from DM25 billion in 1982 to DM10 billion in 1987. Export orders from the Middle East for German construction companies slumped from DM10.5 billion in 1981 to DM1.7 billion in 1985, those for turnkey plant suppliers from DM9.7 billion to DM1.7 billion. Imports also went down dramatically, reflecting above all declining volumes and values of oil supplies. Overall, imports from the Middle East went from DM19.8 billion in 1982 to DM8.5 billion in 1988 and DM11 billion in 1989. For the Gulf oil states (GCC plus Iran and Iraq), this contraction was even more severe: imports from those countries slumped from DM16.4 billion in 1982 to DM3.8 billion in 1986 and DM3.7 billion in 1989. As a percentage of total West German export trade, the share of the Gulf region fell from a peak of 5.76 per cent in 1982 to 1.64 per cent in 1989 and that of the Israeli–Arab region (excluding Israel) from 1.2 per cent to 0.46 per cent to almost exactly that of Israel which, however, had remained roughly constant around 0.45 per cent throughout the 1980s (Figure 7.4). Imports from those countries fell from 0.40 per cent in 1982 to 0.24 per cent in 1989 – that is, below the share of Israel which had gone from 0.32 per cent to 0.26 per cent of total West German imports, and had thus overtaken the group of Egypt, Syria, Jordan and Lebanon in importance as a trading partner of West Germany (Figure 7.5).

At the political level, trade relations between the Middle East and West Germany were now fully within the hands of the European Community. With the Euro–Arab Dialogue dormant for much of the 1980s, attention shifted to possible cooperation between the newly founded Gulf Cooperation Council (which tried to emulate the European Community model on the Arabian peninsula) and the Community. In June 1988, the two groupings signed a non-preferential cooperation agreement as a means to 'contribute to political stability, economic development and regional integration' on the peninsula (in the words of the Preamble to the Cooperation Agreement). The Joint Cooperation Council and a Ministerial Meeting were convened in March 1990 to discuss both economic and political issues but were unable in the former arena to agree on a

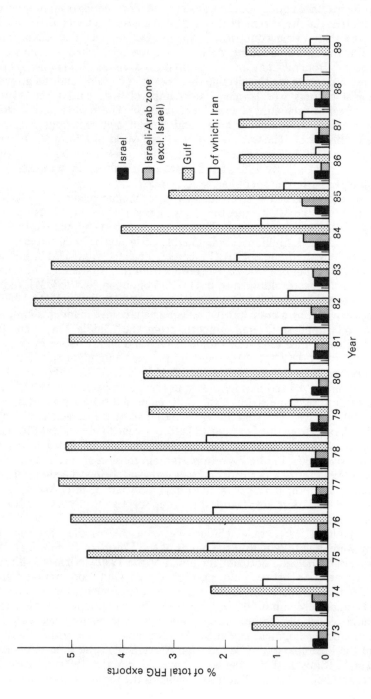

Figure 7.4 West German imports from the Middle East

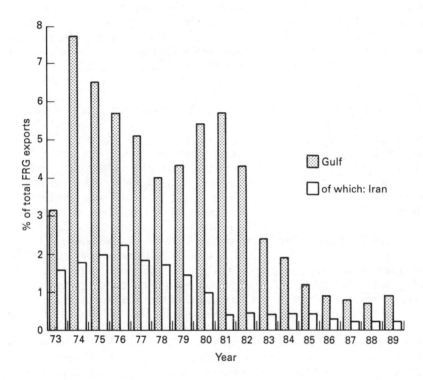

Figure 7.5 West German imports from the Middle East: Gulf region

preferential trade agreement for GCC petrochemicals, the most important substantive concern for the Arab side.[21] Vested industrial interests in the EC were
easily strong enough to override any residual political concerns about building
special ties to the GCC countries, and the GCC members provided them with a
perfect excuse by being unable to agree on a common external trade policy
among themselves. Internal divisions within the Arab world once more contributed to poor results.

West German investment in the region also largely came to a halt and a
substantial number of direct investments were dissolved. Only in 1987 and 1988
did net direct West German investment in the Gulf region exceed DM100
million (with DM172 and DM151 million, respectively); even in those years,
this was not much more than 0.1 per cent of total West German foreign direct
investment. For the Israeli–Arab region (but excluding Israel), the peak year in
the 1980s was 1982, with direct investments of about DM292 billion, representing 0.3 per cent of total West German foreign direct investment in that
year.[22]

With the Iran–Iraq war overshadowing the whole region, military supplies
loomed large in trade relations. Iran's total arms imports in the period 1982 to
1986 were estimated at $8.405 billion, those of Iraq at $34.740 billion, or 12 per
cent and 48 per cent of total imports, respectively.[23] In this trade, West
Germany supposedly played a subordinate role, given its traditionally restrictive
policies on arms exports.[24] Indeed, ACDA data show only relatively modest
sales of West German arms to Iraq, Kuwait and Oman and some smaller deals
with other countries in the region between Mauritania and Iran, totalling some
$1.425 billion over the period. Cumulatively, West Germany's share in the
Middle East and North African arms market from 1982 to 1986 came to 1.3 per
cent, representing about 22 per cent of total West German arms exports. By
comparison, France supplied arms worth $16.310 billion or 15.3 per cent of the
total market, representing almost 80 per cent of its total arms exports.[25]

West Germany's role in the military sector of the Middle East nevertheless
turned out to be rather ominous, with revelations in 1988, 1989 and 1990 about
a major involvement of West German industry in Iraqi and Libyan efforts to
procure nuclear and chemical weapons capabilities and long-range delivery
systems.[26] As discussed elsewhere in this book, it appears that German companies – in violation of West German export laws, but benefiting from less than
stringent controls on sensitive exports – substantially contributed to the proliferation of weapons of mass destruction into the region and to some of the new
risks to West Germany's own security of oil supply.

Overall, the relative economic importance of the Middle East to West
Germany has (with the exception of Israel!) declined dramatically during the
1980s. The oil security problem had shown itself to be largely different in nature
from one in which cultivation of close ties with countries in the region would
make much difference; what mattered above all was domestic and regional
stability in the region. Sea changes in the international oil market also reduced
the vulnerability of importers to supply disruptions and efforts at price manipulation and eventually shifted bargaining power back to the consumers. This in
turn contributed to a massive decline in oil revenues and a severe recession in
the whole region, which negatively affected West German export markets in the
region. Finally, the Iran–Iraq war seriously reduced and distorted trade and
economic relations with the region – and when this war had finally ground to a

halt, and hopes for a modest reconstruction boom seemed to bear fruit, the region was again thrown into turmoil by the Iraqi invasion of Kuwait and the subsequent war.

The only remnants of a West German special relationship during the 1980s may have been the relationship with Iran. Due to the perseverance of German companies and the circumspect attitude of the Foreign Office, West Germany managed to keep lines to Iran open despite the turmoil of the hostage crisis, the Iran–Iraq war and other shocks. Together with Italy and Japan, which had also been able to maintain reasonable links with both combatants in the war, West Germany repeatedly tried to mediate in this war, and to promote a ceasefire. Bonn apparently also played an important role in the drafting of UN Security Council Resolution 598, which eventually formed the basis of the ceasefire in 1988. Even this relationship with Iran, however, must be seen more in the light of West German foreign-policy objectives than as a reflection of economic interdependence. Bonn was reluctant to see Tehran isolated for political reasons, but when Khomeini called for the murder of author Salman Rushdie in 1988, it was Foreign Minister Genscher who led the hard line against Iran within the Community (See Chapter 12).[27]

The 1990s and beyond: perspectives for the future

In December 1987, the Palestinian *intifada* in the occupied territories shook the Middle East and dramatically transformed the outlook for the Israeli–Arab conflict. As a result of the *intifada*, the United States restarted its efforts to mediate a solution to the Israeli–Arab conflict and began a direct dialogue with the PLO, which had substantially moderated its stance. Once more, there appeared to be a chance for progress on this most protracted of all Middle Eastern conflicts. Then, in the summer of 1988, the Iran–Iraq war finally drew to an end. There had been massive loss of life and enormous material damage: estimates suggest that the two countries together experienced over a million casualties and damage to their infrastructure of at least $188 billion in the case of Iraq and $369 billion for Iran.[28] The cease-fire and subsequent peace negotiations under UN auspices again appeared to offer new opportunities for a shift of attention to reconstruction and internal development. Those opportunities were quickly dissipated, however, and when Iraq started to turn its military power against its Arab neighbours in August 1990, the Middle East was once more thrown into turmoil. The new decade was off to an ominous start with the subsequent war of 1991, which however decisive in military terms, remained more ambiguous and muffled in its political repercussions.

Meanwhile, Germany was also experiencing profound changes, but of an entirely different nature. While the Middle East remained steeped in political violence, domestic instability and regional turmoil, the whole of Europe was transformed by the ramifications of Mikhail Gorbachev's 'new thinking' in foreign policy. The Soviet Union accepted defeat in the cold war and sought to put East–West relations on an entirely new basis of interdependence and cooperation. In the process, Moscow accepted the *de facto* demise of the Warsaw Treaty Organisation and the reunification of Germany. By October 1990, the two halves of the country had come together under the auspices of the West

German constitution and continued German membership in NATO and the European Community.

Somewhat paradoxically, West Germany, which *de facto* had found itself a new vanguard role in international politics as a 'trading state' with a strong supranational orientation, was now presented by sheer luck with an opportunity to re-establish national unity. This opportunity was seized upon by the political leadership, but it represented an integration of East Germany into the West German polity, including its strong supranational bias. German reunification in fact provided additional impetus to the process of European integration, just as the entry of West Germany into the Western alliance in the 1950s had pushed Western Europe towards closer cooperation and integration.

It seems highly unlikely that a united Germany will turn away from its postwar orientation towards Western Europe, the Atlantic Alliance and the politics of interdependence and opt instead for the traditional nation-state path of power politics. Economics will thus continue to play a central role in West German foreign policy; economic interdependence will shape political relations but also provide the means and opportunities to pursue national interests.

Unfortunately for the Middle East, the dynamics of interdependence have shifted during the 1970s and 1980s in directions which are highly unfavourable for this region. This shift was geographic: the deepening of interdependence took place largely within and between the three major industrialised regions of North America, Western Europe and East Asia. And it was functional: while international trade flows – the traditional sinews of interdependence – continued to grow during the 1970s and 1980s (and particularly so within and between the regions identified above), their role as the spearhead of global economic integration was taken over by dramatically expanded flows of capital and technology across borders. In this changing world, the assets of the Middle East were rapidly diminishing: technological innovation was relentlessly reducing the energy intensity of economic growth, while the rapidly vanishing Middle Eastern petrodollar assets were replaced by Japanese and West German capital surpluses as the engines of international financial markets.

Oil continues to be of critical (if somewhat reduced) importance to the functioning of industrialised countries, but the essence of the oil security problem had, as it turned out, been largely misperceived in the 1970s: the problem was not the deliberate manipulation of oil prices, the oil weapon, it was rather the notorious instability of the Middle East as a producer region. This offered the Middle Eastern countries at best modest opportunities for instrumentalising those vulnerabilities. Moreover, Germany (and the Western world as a whole) will in the 1990s and beyond confront a new kind of economic security threat: the former Eastern bloc countries, Eastern Europe and the republics of the former Soviet Union are now all on a highly dangerous trajectory away from authoritarian command politics and economics to political pluralism and market economies. Economic setbacks and crises could produce far-reaching and dangerous ramifications; as the 1930s amply demonstrated, those ramifications could ultimately also threaten the security of Western Europe and particularly West Germany.

Attempts to deal with this new security concern will undoubtedly involve very substantial economic resources from the West in terms of financial assistance, foreign direct investment and technical aid. They will also clearly involve new institutional links for Eastern Europe and the former Soviet States with the

European Community, the OECD, the IMF, GATT, the World Bank and other international bodies. Within this context, preferential economic treatment will also be granted. The West is thus looking at Eastern Europe and the former Soviet Union in ways which resemble attitudes towards OPEC countries in the mid-1970s: the objective is to establish firm bonds of interdependence to pre-empt potential threats, and it is assumed that both sides have an intense interest in cooperation and that this cooperation can offer both sides what they want – enhanced welfare, genuine development and prosperity. The stakes of success and failure, however, are much higher in the case of Eastern Europe. So, perhaps, are the chances for success, for most of these countries share the West's scientific–technological culture as well as much of Europe's economic, political, cultural and social traditions.

West Germany will no doubt have to play a particularly important role in the transition of Eastern Europe. Its first task will be the construction of a viable economy, ecology and society in eastern Germany. This, in itself, will involve a substantial expansion of economic interaction with Eastern European countries and especially Russia and the Ukraine. Much of east German industry was geared to Eastern European markets and will hope to continue those ties as a means to stay afloat in a new, severely competitive climate. Moreover, Germany agreed to compensate the former Soviet Union economically for its acceptance of reunification and for any costs which it would incur as a result of this process. This will involve, *inter alia*, importation of oil and continuation of east German supply contracts. Finally, Eastern European markets will lure German industry, which has traditionally had a strong interest in those markets.

In addition to the huge challenges in Eastern Europe, and the western parts of the Commonwealth of Independent States which will place heavy demands on all kinds of German resources, the German economy will also have to ensure that its shift of attention towards the East is balanced by enhanced ties with the Western world. There are important political reasons for this but also strong economic arguments: Germany will continue to be the pivot of the Western European economic system, and will thus have to keep step with economic and technological developments in North America and East Asia, the other two major poles of world economic activity. Enhanced German economic interaction with Eastern Europe will thus have to be balanced by enhanced efforts at European integration and the globalisation of the European economy.

The continuation of past trends towards a globalisation of international economic relations involving three major growth centres, and the new challenges of Eastern Europe bode ill for German relations with the Third World in general, and the Middle East in particular. Despite official rhetoric to the contrary, Germany's commitments to the Third World are bound to suffer in political and material terms. In the future, relations with the South will mostly be shaped by the latter's success or failure to compete successfully in world industrial and service markets, rather than by effective trade preferences or development aid. The efforts to catch up with the advanced economies, and to secure markets for themselves, will essentially have to come from those countries themselves. The East and South-East Asian NIEs (Newly Industrialising Economies) have demonstrated that such a course is possible.

While such limited and select cooption of Third World economies may suggest a decoupling between North and South, this is unlikely actually to happen. The transmission belts of global interdependence have become too manifold for the North to be able to insulate itself effectively from the South. Thus, to the extent Third World countries fail in their quest for development and growth, the fallout of this failure is likely to recouple North and South in the form of increased security threats arising from immigration pressures, ecological deterioration, drugs and terrorism as well as the old security problems of regional instability and turmoil.

What does this imply for relations between Germany and the Middle East? First, contrary to a widely held view, I do not believe in a resurgence of Middle Eastern oil power, short of a very substantial political move towards unity in the Arab world. Such a political transformation seems at present unlikely, though it could be the end result of prolonged failure. For the time being, however, there is no discernible ideology, nor any political force, which would seem capable of uniting the Arab world. This suggests that the political matrix surrounding the international oil market in its Middle Eastern component will continue to be shaped by weak or brittle domestic political structures, regional rivalries and lack of purpose. In such circumstances, the weaknesses of the Middle Eastern oil position are unlikely to overcome its strengths.

Those strengths are well known: about two-thirds of proven world oil reserves, and ultimately probably even more, are contained in this region. Much of this oil can be produced at very low cost, and domestic demand will continue to be limited by the relatively small populations of the Gulf countries; thus the high per-capita oil reserves give the Gulf countries a unique ability to produce for export. Partly for this reason, world oil export capacity will increasingly be concentrated in the Gulf, with the concomitant opportunities for cartelisation. According to recent estimates for the period up to 1995, declines in production capacities in the United States and the former Soviet Union will be offset essentially by additions from other industrialised and non-OPEC developing countries, leaving extra demand to be met by OPEC. Within OPEC, substantial capacity increases will only be possible in Venezuela and Nigeria, and in Libya and the Gulf.[29]

Against those strengths of the Middle Eastern oil position are its weaknesses. According to Krapels,[30] oil-market power requires four major assets, three of which are unlikely to exist in sufficient degree in the Middle East during the 1990s: spare capacity; financially and politically strong hands to control it; vertical integration of the industry; and the existence of an effective mechanism of market control. Middle Eastern countries are unlikely to recover their strong financial and political position of the 1970s and early 1980s, if only because pressure for redistribution of oil wealth within the Arab world is likely to grow after the Iraqi invasion of Kuwait and the ensuing Gulf War. The vertical integration of the industry has been smashed for good, and the new markets and actors (such as forward markets and brokers) are here to stay. Finally, the OPEC mechanism (or some new grouping of producer countries) will be insufficient to achieve market control.

This view does not deny the possibility of a tightening of oil markets and rising oil prices for some time. The Middle Eastern oil industry may recover somewhat from the bottom of 1986 and so may oil prices. But this in itself does not constitute a comeback of oil power as we have seen it in the 1970s. To achieve this, world oil demand would have to rise strongly – and this is unlikely for two major reasons: first, consumer governments have just been reminded by the Gulf crisis of 1990–1 that they must not allow themselves to become too dependent on insecure Middle Eastern oil. And second, environmental considerations will in the future probably provide strong additional impetus for higher taxes on oil consumption. This combination of the crisis of 1990–1 and global environmental concerns will probably, yet again, substantially depress the world energy demand trajectory. Oil power may thus remain a chimera.

This leaves the Middle East in a less than happy position *vis-à-vis* the industrialised countries in general and Europe in particular. In normal times, it can expect at best limited attention, and it is unlikely to appreciate the kind of attention it will receive under conditions of crisis. Nor can it hope to secure preferential treatment or sizeable support for its development efforts, as the example of the treatment of GCC petrochemicals by the European Community illustrates. And, with the possible exception of Egypt, even development crises and breakdowns are unlikely to create strong new links between the Middle East and Europe: on the contrary they are more likely to make at least some of the relationships worse. European attention has already begun to shift and will likely continue to focus on the southern Mediterranean countries.

This sombre picture contains, however, at least one grain of hope. The Middle East will have little option but to find its future through its own efforts. Only if and when the region begins to take its fate into its own hands will it have a better future.

Reflections on Germany and the Gulf War of 1991

The events in the Middle East of 1990–1991, and the German reaction to them, only confirm several of the conclusions drawn above. For one thing, concern about security of oil supplies no longer constitutes a primary focus of German foreign policy but the security of Israel does. The threat posed to oil supplies by Iraq's invasion of Kuwait was hardly perceived in Germany: there was no panic, and Germany quickly fell in line with – indeed strongly advocated – comprehensive economic sanctions against Iraq which also meant a loss of Iraqi and Kuwaiti oil exports. The issue of Israeli security, on the other hand, intruded dramatically into the debate about Germany's response to the Gulf war. Germany's special responsibility for Israel, put into sharp relief by the nightmarish possibility of Jews once more being killed by gas made with the active involvement of German companies, continued to shape the foreign-policy response of the FRG.

True to form, the new Germany tried to resolve the dilemma of her special obligation to Israel through chequebook diplomacy and arms transfers. This was a response typical of the trading state Germany has become. The trading state acts primarily through economic instruments; it tends to pursue traditional foreign policy and security goals through cooperation with others in formal or informal arrangements of interdependence and to downgrade the role of military force (a tendency strongly supported by Germany's aversion to war resulting from its own experiences in World War II). The trading state is also prone to a subordination of political to commercial considerations – resulting in such troubling breakdowns of political control over transfers of military technology and equipment as happened in the case of German transfers to Iraq.

Finally, the outcome of the Gulf crisis of 1990–91 confirms the assessment that the Middle East will not be likely to benefit from its growing importance in world oil markets: the lack of political cohesion and purpose which has troubled the region for so long shows no sign of disappearing. The focus of Germany's foreign policy will thus continue to be directed elsewhere: to Western Europe, its principal political anchor and compass in the difficult transition Eastern Europe will face in the years ahead; to Eastern Europe itself, from where major threats to German social and economic stability may emanate; and finally across the Atlantic, where America may still continue to provide vital reassurance. The Middle East can expect little particular attention from the new Germany – this situation has not changed as a result of the Gulf War of 1991.

Notes

1. Wolfram Hanrieder, *Germany, America, Europe*, New Haven, Yale UP, 1989.
2. Richard N. Rosecrance, *The Rise of the Trading State*, New York, Basic Books, 1986.
3. Lily Gardner Feldman, *The West German Special Relationship with Israel*, Boston, Allen & Unwin, 1984.
4. Jitzhak Ben-Ari, 'Israel und die Bundesrepublik, Eine Bilanz besonderer Beziehungen', in: *Aus Politik und Zeitgeschichte*, April 6, 1990, pp.1–7; Niels Hansen, 'Verbindung in die Zukunft, 25 Jahre diplomatische Beziehungen zwischen Deutschland und Israel', in: *ibid.*, pp.8–18.
5. See *New York Times*, Nov. 13, 1989.
6. Joseph S. Nye, *Bound to Lead The Changing Nature of American Power*, New York, Basic Books, 1990.
7. Aziz Alkazaz, 'Die Okonomie in Nahost in den 8Oer Jahren' in: *Aussenpolitik* No.3/1988, pp.256–69.
8. *Ibid.*, p.39.
9. *Ibid.*, p.61.
10. Hugo Dicke/Hans H. Glisman, 'Die industrielle Entwicklung der OPEC-Staaten und ihre Ruckwirkungen auf die Wirtschaft der Bundesrepublik Deutschland', Kiel, Institut f. Weltwirtschaft 1985 (*Kieler Arbeitspapiere No. 231*).
11. France, which had gone in the direction of bilateral special relationships with Algeria and later with Iraq and Saudi Arabia most forcefully, was later on to suffer particularly from its economic and political overexposure to Iraq. When Iraq invaded Kuwait in August 1990, it finally decided to cut its losses and throw its weight behind the efforts to contain Iraq's threat to regional stability.
12. One may argue whether this was achieved in 1987/88 through competence and sound policies or sheer luck. For the case of incompetence, see Janice Gross Stein, 'The Wrong Strategy in the Right Place, The United States in the Gulf', in: *International Security*, Winter 1988/89, pp.142–167. For the counterarguments, see my, 'Alliance Cooperation and Conflict in the Middle East: The Gulf Experience', in: Hanns W. Maull and Otto Pick (eds), *The Gulf War*, London, Pinter Publishers, 1989, pp.152–169.
13. *BP Statistical Review of World Energy*, London, BP, different years.
14. Data taken from *Nah- und Mittelostverein*, Annual Report, various years.
15. Edward N. Krapels, *The Commanding Heights, Control over International Oil from the 1980s to the 1990s*, Washington, D.C., unpublished MS, pp.190 ff.
16. *Ibid.*, p.197.
17. Alkazaz, *op.cit.*, p.262.
18. World Bank, *World Development Report 1989*, Oxford, OUP, 1989, Table 2.
19. Those remittances in 1984 covered 88 per cent of the Jordanian trade deficit, 79 per cent of that of North Yemen, and over 50 per cent in the case of Egypt, Syria and South Yemen (Alkazaz, *op.cit.* p.267).
20. *Handelsblatt*, 17 February 1990.

21. Agence Europe, 13 March 1990; cf. Achim v. Heynitz, *Die Beziehungen zwischen dem Gulf Cooperation Council und der Europaischen Gemeinschaft*, Ebenhausen, Stiftung Wissenschaft und Politik, IP 2645, March 1990.

22. Data taken from *Nah- und Mittelostverein*, Annual Reports, Hamburg, NuMOV, different years.

23. Data taken from *Arms Control and Disarmament Agency, World Military Expenditure*, Washington, D.C., ACDA, 1989; and *CIA Handbook of Economic Indicators*, Langley, VA, CIA, 1989.

24. See Alan A. Platt, 'Arms Transfer to the Middle East: European and Other Suppliers', in: Steven Spiegel *et al.*, *The U.S.–Soviet Competition in the Middle East*, Lexington, Mass., Lexington Books, 1990.

25. Hanns W. Maull, 'The Arms Trade With the Middle East and North Africa, 1990', in: *The Middle East and North Africa Yearbook*, London, Europa Publications, 1990, pp.126–133.

26. Michael Brzoska, 'Behind the German Export Scandals', in: *Bulletin of the Atomic Scientists*, July/August 1989, pp.32–35.

27. See Thomas Koszinowski/Hanspeter Mattes (eds), *Nahost-Jahr-buch 1989*, Opladen, Leske & Budrich, 1990, p.17f.

28. See Kamran Mofid, 'After the Gulf War', in: *The World Today*, March 1989, p. 49.

29. Krapels, *op. cit.*, pp. 279f.

30. *Ibid.*, ch. 6.

8 A necessary evil or the best of all worlds? German arms sales to the Middle East

Efraim Karsh*

In discussions of German arms exports to the Third World in general and to the Middle East in particular, it has become commonplace to present this policy as extremely restrictive. Although not supported by the evidence, this perception of German policy is not difficult to understand. During the 1960s and the 1970s German arms sales were subjected to probably the most restrictive export regulations placed on any Western country; even after the liberalisation of these regulations in 1982, the Federal Republic has 'deftly cultivated its image as a country intent on avoiding a purely economically motivated, politically indiscriminate arms export policy'[1] by limiting the export of major weapons systems to the barest minimum and concentrating instead on the supply of less visible weaponry. The low-keyed nature of the FRG's export policy in relation to the other major producers has also been illustrated by the small share of arms sales both in overall defence production (10 per cent as compared with 33 per cent in Britain and 45 per cent in France)[2] and in the Republic's total exports (less than one per cent as compared with 1.78 per cent in Great Britain, 3.15 per cent in France and 4.46 per cent in the United States).[3]

Yet this apparent circumspection is somewhat misleading. Not only has Germany developed during the past two decades into the world's fifth largest arms exporter, but her restrictive arms exports policy has been subjected from the outset to a continuous process of erosion in which 'compromises were made, loopholes were created and regulations were not enforced'.[4] This trend holds good for the Middle East where German exports still lag behind those of the United States, the former Soviet Union and France yet are anything but negligible. Indeed, it is arguable that since drawing a clear line between government arms aid programmes and commercial sales in the mid-1960s, the FRG has enjoyed the best of all worlds, namely, the ability to expand her arms exports significantly without incurring most of the adverse consequences attending this type of export, particularly in volatile areas like the Middle East. By withdrawing to the back of the stage and assuming the role of a 'watchdog' over the arms trade, the Federal government has managed to give the German arms industry the necessary breathing space while distancing itself from its activities whenever these seemed to embarrass the Republic. Yet, as illustrated by the most recent revelations of the role of German companies in the development of Iraq's chemical, nuclear and ballistic missile programmes, the involvement of

---

* The author gratefully thanks Philip Sabin for his incisive criticism of an earlier draft.

the Federal Republic in the trade of deadly weapons in the Middle East runs far deeper than it would like the international community to believe.

The evolution of the FRG's arms export policy

West Germany's entry into the club of arms exporters was slow and hesitant. Following World War II the German arms industry was dismantled by the victorious powers and for some time it seemed that the general fear of the colossus, which twice this century had made a bid for the mastery of Europe, would preclude the re-arming of Germany. This widespread anxiety struck a responsive chord within the German leadership which was extremely reluctant to revive the ominous image of German militarism by re-establishing the FRG's formidable military industry. Finally, the Germans would not invest significant resources in defence when they faced the Sisyphean task of economic recovery.

Yet, as wartime memories were transcended by the advent of a new perceived threat from the East, the Western powers could ill-afford to leave such a glaring vacuum at the heart of the continent. Hence, in 1951 German arms manufacturing was legitimised and by the time the FRG was linked to NATO in 1955 she had already re-established her arms industry,[5] though not before the West European Union (WEU) had constrained German military power in certain important respects. These included a prohibition on the manufacture of nuclear, chemical and biological weapons, as well as long-range and guided missiles, warships (except for smaller vessels for purely defensive purposes) and strategic bomber aircraft.[6]

These international restrictions were augmented by elaborate domestic legislation which reflected Germany's trepidation when she came to re-enter the arms field. Article 26 of the German constitution (1949) forbids 'acts tending to and undertaken with the intent to disturb the peaceful relations between nations, especially to prepare for aggressive war', and clearly stipulates that 'weapons designed for warfare may not be manufactured, transported, or marketed except with the permission of the Federal Government'.[7] This statement of intention was further reinforced by the War Material Control Act (*Kriegswaffenkontrollgesetz*) and the Foreign Trade Act (*Aussenwirtschaftsgesetz*) of 1961 which aimed to restrict Germany's integration into the world arms market. According to the former the export of weapons of war (included in an extensive special list, periodically revised) was subject to government approval. The government, for its part, could prevent such sales whenever it deemed them harmful to the FRG's foreign relations. Specifically this meant: a prohibition of exports to countries at war or close to war; sales which would violate Germany's obligations under international law; 'peace-breaking action' might ensue from the arms' recipient; or when the agent applying for the export licence was considered unreliable.

The Foreign Trade Act complemented the War Material Control Act both by covering strategic goods which might have otherwise evaded the former law (for example, components and know-how), and by expanding the restrictions on the export of such goods to include situations which 'endanger the security and the foreign relations of the Federal Republic' or disturb the 'peaceful relations among nations'.[8] In June 1971 the Social Democratic (SPD) government went a step further in tightening its control over the arms industry by prohibiting arms exports to 'areas of tension', a stipulation which implied the virtual cessation of arms transfers outside the NATO alliance.[9] Another constraining amendment to the War Material Control Act was introduced in 1978, making it compulsory for West German companies acting as agents for foreign companies or countries and based outside Germany to seek government approval for their deals.[10]

These regulations notwithstanding, the 1970s witnessed the growing circumvention of arms export restrictions through a variety of loopholes such as the supply of components for assembly abroad; the provision of machinery and know-how for armament production (and even the export of entire plants); the sale of production licences; and, finally, the entry into European multinational ventures. This last means of circumvention has become especially attractive to German industry not only because it blurs the line of responsibility for decisions on arms exports and enables German companies to shelter behind countries with less restrictive export policies but on account of its attendant economic benefits as well.[11] The growing evasion of the export regulations was also facilitated by the decentralised nature of the German arms industry which, unlike those of other European countries, has neither a nationalised sector (it consists solely of private corporations) nor a governmental or quasi-governmental mechanism for the promotion of German arms exports. This, in turn, has forced German arms producers to display greater initiative in their dealings with both the German authorities and external clients and has expanded their room for manoeuvre.[12]

Also, the vagueness of the term 'areas of tension', together with the lack of effective parliamentary control over arms exports, enabled the government to interpret this concept in a highly flexible fashion: judged by the pattern of German arms transfers, South and Latin America should be considered among the most stable and peaceful regions in today's world! Moreover, in reflection of the deeply rooted German commitment to the notion of free trade, the Foreign Trade Act of 1961 clearly states that 'controls . . . have to be configured so that there is as little limitation to the economic activity as possible'. This, in turn, has given arms exporters the right to decide for themselves whether an application for an export licence is necessary, as well as affording them a wide latitude *vis-à-vis* the authorities in the case of legal action.[13] Finally, by defining the 1971 restrictions on arms exports as 'political principles' instead of nailing them down in the form of law, the Federal government clearly signalled to the industry that these regulations would be susceptible to cabinet revision in the future.[14]

Indeed, recognising the greater untenability of the 1971 restrictions and eager to exploit to the full the widening prospects of arms exports, in April 1982 the Federal government revised these regulations by replacing the clause which required permission to export arms whenever the *vital foreign policy and security interests required such an act*, with the controversial *ban on arms exports to areas of tension*. Under the amended regulations, arms recipients were grouped into three distinct categories:

(a) NATO members, who are subject to few restrictions but are supposed to provide assurances that the supplied weapons would not leave the NATO zone;
(b) non-NATO countries, whose procurement relations with the FRG depend on the latter's vital interest in them;
(c) COCOM-listed states which have been prohibited from receiving arms supplies from Germany.

It should be noted, however, that while the 1982 principles opened the door for a more aggressive German export policy to hitherto restricted regions such as the Middle East, they also contained some visible elements of continuity. For example, arms exports to countries which were likely to engage in armed conflict remained forbidden in principle, whereas the supply of war weapons and related military equipment was constrained by the general provision that they must neither heighten existing tensions nor endanger the security and foreign relations of the Federal Republic. The 1982 regulations also introduced a new category of restricted goods, items related to weapons of war (*Kriegswaffennahe Rustungstuter*) which included licences to produce weapons.[15] In short, German arms exports remain governed by the 1961 acts, though the interpretation of these regulations has become far more flexible, thus reflecting Germany's awareness of the requirements attending its burgeoning role in the international arms market: during the past two decades German arms exports grew fourfold from about one per cent of total world arms transfers to just above four per cent.[16]

German arms and the Middle East: from government aid to commercial sales

The re-establishment of the FRG's arms industry in the mid-1950s was predicated on the assumption that it would be predominantly geared towards meeting NATO's operational requirements, namely, satisfaction of the procurement needs of the German armed forces and support for NATO's weaker members such as Greece and Turkey. Arms supplies to the Third World in general, and to the Middle East in particular, played a minor role in the FRG's overall arms exports policy, thereby lending credence to the government's portrayal of itself as a 'restrictive exporter' and satisfying the widespread domestic opposition to arms exports outside the NATO zone. There were, however, a few exceptions to this low-keyed pattern. One was Turkey, which as a member of NATO is not viewed as an ordinary Middle Eastern country; another salient, and far more problematic exception was the FRG's rather extensive procurement relationship with Israel in the early 1960s.

German arms transfers to Israel can be traced back to the late 1950s when the FRG supplied the Jewish state with two patrol boats. Two years later Germany delivered to Israel twenty-four American-made Sikorsky S-58 helicopters, and in 1962 the bilateral procurement relationship was considerably enhanced by the conclusion of an arms agreement, followed in 1964 by an $80 million deal. Within the framework of these deals, Israel was to receive significant quantities of (mainly American-made) German surplus weapons, including 200 M-48 Patton tanks, transport, utility and trainer aircraft, helicopters, anti-aircraft guns, and anti-tank guided missiles (MBB Cobra).[17]

Apart from the desire to placate the United States by providing a channel for the supply of American surplus weaponry to areas Washington was reluctant to enter directly, there is little doubt that Bonn's rather exceptional decision at the time to extend military support to Israel was motivated by a sense of moral obligation towards this country following the massacre of six million Jews by the Germans during World War II. In the words of German Chancellor Ludwig Erhardt:

With the Arab world we had a historically and traditionally untroubled record of friendly relations . . . Our relations with Israel, on the other hand, were heavily incriminated. Germany was and is still guilty of the crimes committed by the Third Reich, and consequently has to carry out a high moral obligation . . .[18]

Yet it is in the nature of international politics that moral imperatives are often superseded by considerations of *Realpolitik*. Hence, when the secret German–Israeli deals were uncovered by the Arabs, resulting in ten Arab states severing diplomatic relations with the FRG (President Nasser even welcomed East Germany's Walter Ulbricht on an official visit to Cairo), Bonn ignored her 'high moral obligation' and, despite Israeli protests and threats of boycott by some American companies, quickly suspended (in early 1965) her military aid programme to Israel.[19]

Together with the revelation of an illegal transfer to Pakistan (in 1965) of ninety surplus American F-86 Sabre fighters sold by Germany to Iran, the Israeli episode was highly instrumental in generating a revision of the FRG's arms sales policy towards the Third World.[20] Until that period, German arms sales to the Middle East (and to the Third World in general) had been conducted as part of an official military aid programme motivated essentially by political considerations. First of all, Germany viewed arms exports as part of her contribution to NATO through sharing some of the financial commitments to that organisation and helping to contain Soviet penetration in the developing world. Second, the FRG perceived military assistance as an important lever in her tireless effort to deny international recognition to the German Democratic Republic. Finally, arms sales provided a useful outlet for surplus military equipment, particularly since they were generously rewarded by the United States which regarded these sales as part of the offset-payments for American troops in Germany.[21] With the political embarrassment attending the above-mentioned incidents and the abrupt realisation that military aid could jeopardise rather than promote the attempts to isolate the twin German state (as illustrated by Ulbricht's high-profile visit to Egypt in 1965), the government virtually surrendered the country's arms exports to the commercial sector, reserving to itself the position of a 'watchdog' over these sales.[22] In 1966, in response to pressures by the opposition SPD, the government adopted restrictions on arms sales outside the NATO area, and in 1968 the Bundestag passed a resolution requesting the Federal government to exercise stricter restraints on its arms exports.[2] Three years later this restrictive trend culminated in the 1971 regulations.

Although these regulations were ostensibly aimed at tightening German arms export policy, it has been argued that they virtually paved the way for a more active German role in the arms market by severing 'the links between arms and exports and foreign policy at a time when increased rather than less government involvement was required'.[24] Indeed, despite the SPD's public commitment (before coming to power in 1969) to halt all arms transfers to the Third World, the 1970s witnessed a three- to fourfold growth in German arms sales to this part of the world. The Middle East became the FRG's most prominent arms trade partner, accounting for 46 per cent of German exports to the Third World between 1973 and 1977.[25] Two interrelated factors underlay the Middle East's rise to prominence. First, the accretion of huge oil revenues in regional hands created an unprecedented demand for weapons, thereby offering the German arms industry far wider horizons for expansion. Second, arms exports seemed to offer a useful means for reducing unemployment in certain sectors such as the shipbuilding industry at a time when the FRG was sliding into economic recession.[26]

Be that as it may, the government's exercise of its restrictive powers during that period was essentially confined to high-visibility major weapons systems such as tanks. Thus, for example, in 1969 the FRG declined an Iranian request for 1,000 Leopard tanks but had little qualms in authorising the sale of equipment for tank maintenance and the establishment of ammunition plants in this pro-Western country a few years later.[27]

Naval systems constituted the main bulk of German direct arms exports during the 1970s. Given the depressed economic condition of the civilian shipbuilding industry and the absence of alternative sources of employment in the far north of the country, the Federal government not only failed to restrict the sale of naval weapons systems but encouraged the expansion of this category of export.[28] The main deals in this sphere involved an agreement to sell six Type 209/3 submarines to Iran[29] and the transfer of eight such submarines to Turkey, together with twenty other vessels. German naval equipment was also exported to Bahrain (two missile boats and two patrol craft), Lebanon (three patrol craft) and Tunisia (one patrol craft). Other direct exports included the sale of thirty-eight Dornier transport aircraft to Israel, $73 million worth of tank laser-range-finders to Syria and more than $538 million for plants for the manufacture of rockets and explosives in Algeria.[30]

But direct sales provide only a partial picture of German arms exports to the Middle East. As noted earlier, an equally impressive, perhaps even more substantial share of these exports from the 1970s onwards has come in the form of major weapons systems co-produced with other European countries. Franco–German joint projects figured most prominently among the FRG's multinational exports, mainly due to the ease with which they could be exported: in 1971 the two governments decided that there would be no German veto over the export of joint products but agreed to hold mutual consultations on the issue should the need arise.[31] Consequently, the anti-tank missiles HOT and Milan were sold in large numbers to Egypt (c. 7,000), Syria (c. 1,200), Kuwait (504), Iraq (360) and Lebanon (200). Another Franco–German co-production, the Alpha Jet trainer/strike aircraft, was ordered by Morocco (twenty-four fighters), Qatar (six units) and Egypt, which signed an agreement with France in 1981 for the assembly and licensed production of forty-five Alpha Jets, the first of which left the Egyptian factory in July 1982.[32]

Turkey remained the most important single client of German arms during the 1970s, receiving twenty F-104G Starfighter aircraft, a mixture of naval systems including four Type 209 submarines, 1,000 Milan anti-tank missiles and nearly 200 Leopard-1-A4 tanks.

Leopards, oil and morality

Just as arms supplies to the Middle East played a key role in the tightening of Germany's arms export regulations in the late 1960s and the early 1970s, so they were instrumental in loosening this policy a decade later; and here, too, it was the Arab–Israeli conflict which triggered the policy review in Bonn.

During a visit to Riyadh in the summer of 1980, German Chancellor Helmut

Schmidt apparently suggested to his hosts that the FRG might respond favourably to a Saudi request for German tanks.[33] In the autumn of that year Saudi Arabia indicated its interest in placing a large order for some 300 Leopard-2 tanks, 1,000 Marder armoured personnel carriers and Gepard self-propelled anti-aircraft guns; a few months later the British government requested German consent to sell the Tornado multi-role combat aircraft (co-produced by Britain, Germany and Italy) to Saudi Arabia.[34] The instinctive reaction of the Federal government to the Saudi overtures (an official request was not made) was largely positive. Schmidt saw the prospective arms deal as a golden opportunity to improve his precarious political standing which was beset at the time by economic difficulties and widespread opposition to the deployment of new medium-range missiles in Germany. He argued that the 1971 regulations (which he had strongly supported before) had become anachronistic since it was no longer feasible properly to define an 'area of tension'; he was supported in this view by his foreign minister, Hans-Dietrich Genscher, as well as by the opposition leader Helmut Kohl.[35]

Before long, however, a heated debate had begun within the German political system, with the proponents of the arms deal pointing to the abundant economic and political gains to be reaped while their opponents (mainly, but not solely, within Schmidt's Social Democratic party) underlined the attendant risks of such a deal. According to the former, Saudi Arabia's position as the FRG's foremost oil supplier (accounting for just over a quarter of German oil consumption), her largest creditor (with more than DM13.6 billion in outstanding loans) and the largest non-European buyer of German goods after the United States and Japan required that this request be given the most serious consideration, particularly since Riyadh was determined to judge Bonn's response to her defence requirements as a test case for the entire bilateral relationship. To decline the Saudi request was bound to tarnish Saudi–German economic ties, whereas a positive response entailed formidable gains.

For one thing, the proposed arms sales would ease Germany's tight budgetary constraints and give the arms industry a much needed boost, both by reducing unemployment and by expanding production lines, hence pushing down unit costs of weapons. This last benefit was particularly important in the case of the Tornado where the Federal government needed an extra DM1.3 billion ($600 million) to cover the production costs and related expenditure of Germany's 42.5 per cent share in the project.[36] More importantly, the deal could lead to an unprecedented expansion of the entire bilateral economic relationship by ensuring the annual supply of forty million tons of crude oil on favourable terms for a decade and by guaranteeing Saudi credits worth DM10 billion.[37]

Apart from the formidable economic gains inherent in the Saudi arms deal and the heavy losses incurred by its rejection, the enhancement of that country's military potential constituted vital Western strategic interest. Since Saudi Arabia was an island of moderation and stability in an increasingly turbulent Gulf, the stronger she became the greater her resilience to domestic upheaval and external challenges and, in turn, the weightier her contribution to the containment of the Iran–Iraq War. Moreover, the strengthening of Saudi Arabia would threaten neither her neighbours nor Israeli security, given the overwhelmingly defensive orientation of that country. In short, by arming Saudi Arabia the FRG would not only promote direct German interests but would also contribute to regional stability, thus serving wider NATO objectives and satisfying the American demand for a greater German contribution to Gulf security. Above all, since arms exports are the 'essential small change in the currency of power', the FRG could not dismiss them out of hand if she were to play any significant role outside the European continent.[38]

These arguments were countered by equally compelling reasoning. In the first place, it was argued that the Saudi requests were motivated less by security concerns than by considerations of status and prestige: the Iran–Iraq War posed no real threat to Saudi security since the more dangerous belligerent (Iran) was not in a position to expand the conflict whereas the other party (Iraq) had no intention of doing so. And in any event, Saudi Arabia was more than adequately equipped to ward off external threats (however remote) whereas her internal stability could hardly benefit from the requested weapons systems. Nor would the German economy suffer severely from the rejection of the Saudi request; both because the military sphere occupied a minor place in overall bilateral trade and on account of the mutually beneficial nature of the interrelationship: just as the West needed Saudi oil, so the Kingdom depended on the West as a major customer for its oil, as well as an indispensable source of technology for its development.

The political advantages of the proposed arms deal were no less dubious. Not only was the deal unlikely to promote Gulf security, but it might also embroil Germany in inter-Gulf rivalries. Moreover, the sale of Leopards could drive the Soviet Union to increase her arms exports to the Middle East while simultaneously antagonising Germany's NATO allies, France and the United States in particular, who were bent on preserving their prominent share in the Saudi arms market.[39] Nor was the belief that arms sales were 'the essential small change in the currency of power' empirically grounded; if anything, the historical record of both Western and Soviet arms exports in the postwar era clearly indicated their limited value as a foreign-policy instrument.

Last but not least, the prospects of financial gains should not deflect the FRG from her moral obligation towards Israel. Given Saudi Arabia's hostility towards the Jewish state and the fact that the Leopards were not essential for Saudi Arabia's own security, it was quite conceivable that, in the case of another Arab–Israeli war, German-built tanks would be used (directly or through their transfer to a third party) against Israel. Even if war did not ensue, some Israelis (such as the opposition leader, Shimon Peres) made it abundantly clear that if German arms were to be supplied to Saudi Arabia, Jerusalem would ask for them too. This, in turn, could draw the Federal Republic into the vicious circle of the Arab–Israeli conflict, since it was inconceivable that she would arm the Arabs while denying military support to the survivors of the Nazi attempt to exterminate the Jewish people.

The vigorous opposition to the proposed arms deal prevented Schmidt from following his inclinations and complying with the Saudi request. In a visit to the Kingdom in late April 1981 the chancellor told his hosts that it was not feasible for the FRG 'for the time being' to provide the requested weapons, owing to her restrictive regulations regarding the export of arms to 'areas of tension'. That the Saudis did not interpret Schmidt's evasive reply as a final 'no' was illustrated by the growing pressures on the Federal government during the months following the visit. In June 1981, for example, a German foreign office spokesman admitted that the Saudi ambassador to Bonn had spoken of a 'two-way street' for German–Saudi relations. Similarly, notwithstanding public denials of Saudi pressure, the Federal economics minister, Count Lambsdorff, conceded privately that Saudi Arabia 'naturally made the extent of economic co-operation dependent on German arms supplies'. This pressure reached its peak in late October when the Saudi Foreign Minister Crown Prince Fahd arrived in Bonn on a sudden visit to sound out the state of the arms deal.[40]

Nor did Helmut Schmidt consider his April visit as the finale to the Saudi episode. By way of signalling to Riyadh that the door to future German arms sales was not closed, in October 1981 he authorised a British export of the sophisticated FH-70 155mm towed howitzer, co-produced by Britain, Germany and Italy, to Saudi Arabia.[41] Moreover, in February 1981 the chancellor set up a governmental committee to review German arms export policy, and in April 1982, following a year of agonising national debate, the review process culminated in a governmental decision to revise the 1971 export regulations.

Even though there was little doubt that the Saudi request was the direct catalyst for the 1982 policy revision, the opposition to this arms sale was so fierce that Schmidt had to back off from the deal and to declare, in tandem with the passing of the new regulations, that Germany would not sell the Leopards to Saudi Arabia, nor had she ever entertained the idea of selling these tanks to any Middle Eastern country: 'No government of any status at any time in the Gulf region could have assumed that the Federal government would sell or would want to sell its battle tank either under the old or new rules.'[42] The British request for the export of Tornados to Saudi Arabia, though far less divisive than its counterpart, was similarly vetoed by the German government.

More than anything, the Saudi episode epitomises the main predicament confronting the FRG's arms export policy towards the Middle East, namely the inability to extricate current policy decisions from the heavy burden of the Nazi past. Not only does the uncompromising nature of the Arab–Israeli conflict preclude military support of one side without the automatic alienation of the other, but the acrimonious legacy between Germans and Jews still tends to overshadow all 'rational' calculations of the national interest; this, in turn, reduced the political debate in Germany on the Saudi deal to the blunt question of whether prospective financial gains should supersede the moral obligation towards a people on which the Germans had inflicted the most dreadful crime in modern history.

This dilemma was to become more acute during the 1980s, as the growing appetite of the German arms industry for petrodollars, and the diminishing governmental control over this sector, led to the FRG's involvement in some shady areas of military exports, most notably the development of chemical weapons in the Arab world. This did not fail to bring out the Nazi skeletons from the cupboard, to the deep embarrassment of the Federal government.

Losing control over arms exports?

In October 1982 Helmut Schmidt's government was replaced by a Christian Democrat (CDU–CSU)–Liberal (FDP) coalition, headed by Helmut Kohl. Given the CDU's long record of criticism of the timidity of the SPD's arms export policy, a further loosening of this policy seemed a matter of course. Indeed, although it did not officially renounce the FRG's restrictive arms export regulations (mainly due to unabated domestic opposition to such a move), the new government clearly indicated its more lax interpretation of these regulations. Within six months of coming to power, the new coalition doubled the number of permits for arms exports to non-NATO countries and reduced the areas and goods which were subjected to restrictions: ASEAN member states, for example, were exempted from a case-by-case scrutiny of licensing, and arms sales to these countries were granted a general clearance. In addition, the government reversed a decision made in May 1982 by the Schmidt administration of the need to inform a special parliamentary body of impending arms sales.[43]

The more permissive German policy rekindled Riyadh's interest in the Leopards, and in April 1983 the Saudi minister of defence, Prince Sultan, paid a visit to Bonn to explore the possibility of obtaining these tanks, only to discover yet again the intensity of German political sensitivity over the issue. In October 1983, during an official visit to Riyadh, Chancellor Kohl was no more accommodating towards the Saudi request than his predecessor, informing his hosts that the FRG would not supply the coveted Leopards. Yet he had a sweetener for the Saudis in the form of German readiness to sell the Kingdom alternative 'defensive weapons', apparently the Roland and Gepard anti-aircraft gun and the Marder armoured personnel carrier. This was a far cry from Saudi expectations but still constituted an important landmark in Germany's arms export policy since these systems had not previously been supplied to any Third World country.

In an attempt to deflect Israel's vehement opposition to this sale the Germans reportedly offered to sell Jerusalem some weapons systems, including the Rheinmetall 120-mm smooth-bore gun. In addition, during the debate in the Bundestag following his visit to Israel in January 1984, Chancellor Kohl emphasised that any decision on arms sales to Saudi Arabia would take into account the Israeli (but also Saudi and German!) interests and that under no circumstances would Germany provide the Saudis with offensive weapons.

Not only did Kohl fail to sooth the Israelis and the Saudis, but Bonn found itself drawing fire from both sides. Dismissing the differentiation between 'offensive' and 'defensive' weapons, the Israelis remained entrenched in their opposition to any German arms sales to Saudi Arabia on the grounds that such weapons would be incorporated into the overall Arab war effort against Israel; these apprehensions were further fuelled by the FRG's agreement in 1983 to waive her veto power over the export of the Tornado aircraft thereby paving the way for its sale to Saudi Arabia. The Saudis, for their part, adamantly rejected any limitations on the use of these weapons, threatening that the attachment of such restrictive conditions was bound to damage bilateral cooperation at all levels.[44]

The Saudi threat proved to be groundless. Although Riyadh decided in 1985 to abandon the hunt for the Leopards and to buy French and American tanks instead, bilateral cooperation did not suffer. On the contrary, drawing some comfort from the waiving of German veto power over the export of the Tornados, the Saudis capitalised on Kohl's expressed readiness to supply 'defensive' weapons and initiated preliminary talks with several West German companies (including the conglomerate Thyssen AG) on a DM6–9 billion deal for the delivery and assembly of a state-of-the-art munitions plant that would produce 105mm, 120mm and 155mm tank and howitzer shells.

While the official negotiations on the plant were not to be concluded before

1987, the unprecedented scope of the envisaged deal (the largest single foreign arms order ever placed in the FRG) generated a public row in Germany. As in the past, the opposition to the deal was spearheaded by the Social Democrats, supported this time not only by the Greens but also by many in the FDP, the junior party in the ruling coalition; even Foreign Minister Genscher was reported to harbour strong reservations about the deal.[45] The debate continued into the late 1980s with the proponents, such as the Bavarian premier, Franz Josef Strauss, openly arguing that the FRG should shed her inhibitions, redefine what constituted an area of conflict and compete more aggressively against the other mid-sized European exporters.[46]

Although the Saudi episode has undoubtedly been the most troublesome experience of the FRG's procurement relations in the Middle East, it has by no means constituted the only source of embarrassment to the Kohl government. A measure of uneasiness was caused in 1984 by the revelation that Krauss-Maffei, a subsidiary of the Flick concern which produces the Leopard tanks, was studying the possibility of developing a tank from the Leopard series for construction in Egypt, possibly with a view to re-exporting it to Saudi Arabia.[47] A no less embarrassing incident was related to the Jordanian attempt to buy the Tornado aircraft.

In the summer of 1986 Jordan indicated her interest in purchasing forty of the defensive version of the Tornado, but following a more realistic re-assessment of her financial situation, reduced the order to eight. Since even this modest quantity proved to be beyond the means of the rapidly deteriorating Jordanian economy, the FRG was called upon to help fund the deal by providing DM48 million in an export loan. Initially the Federal government gave a 'green light' to a state-owned bank to lead a consortium of German banks in providing the requested support, but, alarmed by the widespread public row over the issue, it quickly pulled out of the deal. Eventually, following a furious British response (expressed *inter alia* in an angry personal letter from Thatcher to Kohl) and after reported American pressure,[48] a compromise solution was found whereby a Bavarian state bank was allowed to step in and provide the credit.[49]

These public embarrassments notwithstanding, the Kohl era witnessed the rapid expansion of German arms exports to the Middle East. Despite the world oil glut which reduced the ability of many oil producers to maintain the high level of military spending they had adopted in the 1970s, on the one hand, and the significant strengthening of the German economy (DM75 billion trade surplus in 1985), on the other, German direct and indirect arms sales to the Middle East were rising consistently. Like many other arms exporters, the FRG did not shy away from exploiting the eight-year war between Iran and Iraq to reap substantial financial gains. According to the American Arms Control and Disarmament Agency (ACDA), the FRG was (after France) the second-largest West European arms supplier during the war, surpassing other mid-sized exporters such as Britain and Italy.[50] Within this framework Germany supplied the two belligerents with a large number of military trucks and other transport vehicles (which did not require an export licence), thus playing a crucial role in building Iraq's formidable fleet of tank transporters.

Since this involvement in one of the bitterest conflicts in the postwar era was the most blatant violation of the spirit of the FRG's allegedly self-restrained arms export policy, it was bound to add to the growing political embarrassment of the Kohl government. For example, the revelation (in the summer of 1984) that twenty-four German Bo-15 helicopters, manufactured under licence in Spain, had been supplied to Iraq aroused a wave of domestic criticism and marred a well-publicised visit to Tehran by Foreign Minister Genscher.[51] Equally embarrassing for the government were the disclosures in early 1987 that Messerschmitt-Bleokow-Blohm (MBB), the FRG's largest aerospace group, had been negotiating with Iran during the past year a $1 billion deal for the sale of twelve Transall military transport planes, co-produced with France; the government's contention that it had already blocked this deal in 1986 was received by many Germans with considerable scepticism.[52] Interestingly enough, the reported German involvement in the development of Iraq's ballistic missile capability (through the Condor Project) passed relatively unnoticed by German public opinion. But even the ending of the Iran–Iraq War did not terminate the FRG's series of embarrassments: in late 1988 the Pentagon attacked the attempts of a German company to sell a miniature submarine to Iran on the grounds that the prospective sale violated the COCOM regulations.[53]

The most galling aspect of German military exports to the Middle East, both during the Iran–Iraq War and its aftermath, was linked to the war material which, more than anything else, symbolised the essence of Nazi atrocities: gas. In the summer of 1984 it was revealed that a plant supplied by West German companies to Iraq, allegedly for the manufacture of agricultural pesticides, had in effect been used to produce chemical weapons for use in the Iran–Iraq War. Three years later, in 1987, a Munich-based German company delivered small amounts of biological warfare agents to Iraq.[54] Although the FRG responded to the 1984 disclosures by tightening the Foreign Trade Act to cover the possibility of exporting materials that could be used for the production of chemical weapons,[55] these restrictions were hardly heeded by the industry: on 1 January 1989, the *New York Times* broke the explosive story that West German companies had supplied Libya with a chemical plant capable of producing chemical weapons.

The news of German involvement in the Libyan plant, described by the American columnist William Safire as 'Auschwitz-in-the-sands' created a huge domestic outcry. 'Germans and poison gas', wrote *Die Zeit*, 'surprise is hardly warranted. Too often in the twentieth century this disastrous combination has made an indelible mark on the bodies and minds of an entire generation. Excuses can easily be found,' continued the influential magazine, 'other countries have used gas too . . . others would supply [the Libyans] if we did not. This may all be true, but we cannot simply shrug off the burden of German history. Our blood must curdle at the very idea of chemical weapons manufactured with German backing being fired at Israel on board missiles built in collaboration between Syria, Argentina and West Germany'.[56]

Paralleled by an unprecedented American reprimand, this domestic row drove the Federal government into panic-stricken behaviour. Helmut Kohl's initial reaction was a bizarre combination of alleged innocence and pious fury. 'I have said, not just here but through several American channels, that I find it intolerable for anyone to accuse the Germans without giving us the chance of seeing the proof,' he told the German newspaper *Die Welt*. 'That is not the way to behave among friends.'[57]

As the scandal unravelled rapidly, the Germans were grudgingly forced to admit that the Americans had given them far more than ample 'chance of seeing the proof'. In fact, it turned out that as early as 1980 the German secret service had informed the government of its suspicions regarding West German involvement in the development of a poison gas factory in Libya, and American government sources had been mentioning the issue regularly to the Germans since 1985. Neither these numerous reports nor a personal plea on this issue by Secretary of State Schultz, during Kohl's visit to Washington in November 1988, were of any avail.[58] It was only the haemorrhage of disturbing revelations in January 1989 which compelled the German government to try to take the heat off by ostensibly reversing a decade of extremely lenient arms export policy. In mid-February the government announced a 'drastic tightening' of control on military exports. Measures included the tripling of personnel in the government's export control office from seventy to 210, an extension of the list of chemicals that could not be exported and an increase from three to fifteen years in the maximum prison sentence for any West German convicted of helping to deliver chemical, biological or other 'extremely dangerous' arms or related technology.[59] At the same time the German customs authorities seized 255 tonnes of chemicals bound for Libya, and the Munich city prosecutor launched a criminal investigation against Imhausen-Chemie GmbH, the main German company involved in the Libyan scandal.

Conclusions and outlook

Although the Middle East has not always accounted for the lion's share of the flow of German arms outside NATO (during the 1980s, for example, Latin America surpassed this region as the primary recipient of German weapons), its impact on the evolution of the FRG's arms exports policy has exceeded by far that of any other Third World area. The Middle East was highly instrumental in the tightening of Germany's arms export regulations in the early 1970s, in the loosening of these restrictions a decade later and in the half-hearted new restrictions of the late 1980s. Two contradictory forces account for this disproportionate influence. On the one hand, the accretion of huge revenues in the hands of the oil-producing countries turned the Middle East into one of the world's most attractive target areas for arms exporters. On the other hand, the extraordinary volatility of the region constrained the growing German appetite for arms exports by putting the FRG's declared commitment not to sell weapons to areas of conflict to its severest test. This problem has been compounded by the unique and unparalleled German–Israeli relationship which has repeatedly thrown the FRG into an agonising process of soul-searching.

The outcome has been a schizophrenic policy – seeking to have the cake and to eat it: to reap substantial economic gains without being seen as shipping arms to areas of conflict; to arm Israel's adversaries without being perceived as jeopardising the security of the Jewish state. To square this circle, the government has chosen to confine itself to the role of watchdog, leaving the actual trade in arms to the commercial sector. Yet, the inadequacy of this evasive policy was glaringly exposed during the 1991 Gulf War as the horrendous spectre of mass killing of Jews by German gas for the second time in half a century loomed very large indeed. In these disturbing circumstances the Federal Republic felt unable to sustain its policy of formal aloofness and, in an attempt to allay Israeli irritation at the substantial involvement of German companies in Saddam's non-conventional weapons programmes, offered Israel $700 million in military aid (as well as $165 million in 'humanitarian aid'). Before the war was over, Israel had already taken the first delivery of German military supplies, (including antidotes to counteract the effects of chemical and biological weapons) and anti-missile Patriot missiles.

The question which is likely to preoccupy German decision-makers for the foreseeable future, therefore, is whether to continue their allegedly restrictive policy while violating it incessantly, or to embark on a straightforward course, either in the form of a 'normal' arms export policy or by pulling out of the Middle East arms trade. This dilemma is bound to gain particular impetus as a result of the German unification. On the one hand, the weighty economic problems involved in unification might increase pressures for a more aggressive arms export policy, especially in view of the decrease in arms sales from the former Soviet Union to the Third World which opens new opportunities for medium-sized exporters; indeed, leading industrialists have already urged the government to reverse its 1989 decision to curb arms exports.[60] Conversely, the FRG's eagerness to allay widespread apprehensions of the possible revival of German hegemonism following unification may result in a non-provocative policy, one that lowers the profile of German arms exports to the barest minimum.

This last consideration is particularly relevant to the Arab–Israeli conflict. The surge of anti-semitism in Eastern Europe (including the former East Germany), the special sensitivity of world Jewry to the question of German unification and the unflattering revelations during and after the Gulf War of the German role in Saddam's death industry – all these factors can be expected to ensure the FRG's continued sensitivity to Israel's security anxieties.

Given the delicate balance of hatreds, fears and hopes characterising the Arab–Israeli conflict, the FRG may find the task of satisfying both Arabs and Jews, while alienating neither, no more feasible than before. The best way of surmounting this formidable obstacle lies, perhaps, in a *scrupulous* adherence to the longstanding principle of non-involvement in areas of tension, namely, the cessation of German arms transfers to the Middle East. Whether or not this road will be taken remains to be seen.

Notes

1. German arms transfers to the Middle East: 1955–90.

	No. ordered	Weapon designation	Weapon description	Year of order	Year(s) of delivery	total del.
Algeria	..	Milan*	ATM	1982	1982	..
Bahrain	3	Bo-105C	Hel	1977–8	1978	3
	2	FPB-38	PC	1979	1981–2	2
	2	TNC-45	FAC	1979	1983–4	2
	2	TNC-45	FAC	1985	1986–7	2
	2	Type 62-001	Corvette	1981	1988	2
Egypt	38	Alpha Jet*	Trainer/strike	1980–1	1982–3	38
	2,976	HOT*	ATM	1975–81	1976–85	2,976
	4,000	Milan*	ATM	1975	1976–9	4,000
	2	Jetstar	Transport	1986	1987	2

Country						
Iran	90	Sabre 6***	Fighter		1966	90
	2	Bandar Abbas	Support ship	1972	1974	2
	3		PC	1974	1975	3
	6	Type 209/3	Submarine	1977–8	(renewed in '85)	
Iraq	360	HOT*	ATM	1976	1980–1	360
	23	Bo-105	Hel	1978	1979–83	23
	600	Roland-2	SAM	1981	1982–5	600
	6	BK-117	Hel	1984	1984–5	6
	6	BK-117	Hel	1984	1985	6
	..	Alpha Jet*	Trainer/strike	1986		0
Israel	2		PC		1956–7	2
	24	Sikorsky S-58***	Hel		1960	24
	200	M-48 Patton	MBT	1964	1964–6	200
	500	MBB-Cobra	ATM		1962–5	500
	25	Magister***	Trainer		1968	25
	15	Do-28D-1	Transport	1973	1974	15
	23	Do-27	Transport	1975	1976	23
	3	Dolphin	Submarine	1988		0
Jordan	8	Tornado**	Fighter	1988		0
Kuwait	504	HOT	ATM	1974	1975–7	504
	2	FB-57 Type	PC	1980	1983–4	2
	6	TNC-45	FAC	1980	1984–5	6
Lebanon	3		PC		1974	3
	200	Milan*	ATM	1978	1979	200
Libya	4	Benina	FAC	1982		0
	3	Jihan	FAC	1982		0
Morocco	24	Magister***	Trainer		1968	24
	2		FC		1968	2
	24	Alpha Jet*	Trainer/strike	1978	1979–81	24
	10	Do-28D-2	Transport	1979	1981–2	10
	..	UR-416	APC	1978	1978	30
	..	Cobra-2000	ATM	1978	1978	30
Oman	8	Tornado**	Fighter	1985		0
Qatar	6	Alpha Jet*	Trainer/strike	1979	1980–1	6
	..	HOT	ATM	1982		0
	..	Milan	ATM	1982		0
Saudi Arabia	3		FC		1969	3
	72	FH-70 155mm**	TH	1982	1983–5	72
	400	JPz SK-105***	ATK gun	1982		
	300	Gepard	AAV	1986	Ongoing neg.	
	60	Wildcat	AAV	1986	Unconfirmed	
	24	Tornado ADV**	Fighter/MRCA	1986	1986	2
	48	Tornado IDS**	Fighter/MRCA	1986	1986	4
Sudan	3	Do-27	Transport		1964	3
	20	Bo-105c	Hel	1977	1979–80	20
Syria	2,000	Milan*	ATM	1976		?
	216	HOT	ATM	1978	1980–1	216
	1,000	Milan*	ATM	1978	1978–9	1,000
	180	HOT*	ATM	1984		
Tunisia	1		PC		1961	1
	1		PC		1963	1
	1		PC		1969	1
	..	Milan*	ATM	1981	1981	100
Turkey	2	'Nasty' class	Torpedo boat		1959–60	2

	9		Motor launch		1960–1	9
	42	Republic F-84F***	Fighter		1964	42
	300	Cobra	ATM		1964	300
	15	Do-27	Transport		1966	15
	5	Do-28 B-1	Transport		1966	5
	42	Republic F-84F***	Fighter		1967	42
	2	Jaguar class	Torpedo boat		1968	2
	3	Do-27	Transport		1968	3
	18	Lockheed T-33***	Trainer		1968	18
	15	Siat 223 Flamingo	Light aircraft		1969	15
	2	'Nasty' class	Torpedo boat		1969	2
	79	M-48 Patton***	MBT		1969–70	79
	69	M-74***	MBT		1969–70	69
	8	Type 209	Submarine	1974	1978	8
	7	Jaguar class	Torpedo boat	1975	1975–6	7
	5	Vegesacy class	Minesweeper	1975	1975–6	5
	20	F-104G	Fighter	1975	1978	20
	13	33 Type	SAR	1976		13
	1,000	Milan	ATM	1976	1977	1,000
	193	Leopard-1-A4	MBT	1976	?	193
	1	Type 57	PC	1979		1
	148	F-104G	Fighter	1980	1980–8	148
	4	Meko 200	Frigate	1983		0
	8	Leopard	ARV	1988		0
	150	Leopard-1	MBT	1986	1988	50
	100	Leopard1-A4	MBT	1987		0
	6,250	Milan*	ATM	1981	1981–8	6,520
UAE	4	Bo-105CB	Hel	1974	1975	4
	3	Bo-105-L	Hel	1981	1981	3
	2	Type 62-001	Corvette	1986		0
	2	TNC45	FAC	1988		0

*   Joint production with France
**   Joint production with Great Britain and Italy (and Austria in the case of the SK-105)
***   Bundeswehr surplus equipment

Sources: SIPRI, *The Arms Trade with the Third World*, London, Paul Elek, 1971; *SIPRI Yearbook*, Stockholm, Almquist & Wiksell, various editions; M. Brzoska and T. Ohlson, *Arms Transfers to the Third World 1971–85*, Oxford, Oxford University Press for SIPRI, 1987; H. Rattinger, 'West Germany's Arms Transfers to the Nonindustrial World' in U. Ra'anan *et al.* (eds), *Arms Transfers to the Third World: The Military Buildup in Less Industrial Countries*, Boulder, CO, Westview Press, 1978, p. 231; International Institute for Strategic Studies, *The Military Balance*, London, various editions.

2. M. Bittelson, 'Cooperation or Competition? Defence Procurement Options for the Future', *Adelphi Papers* No. 250, London 11SS, 1990, p.2.

3. Figures are for the years 1977–87. See ACDA, *World Military Expenditures and Arms Transfers, 1988*, Washington DC, 1989, pp. 84–5, 106–7.

4. M. Brzoska, 'The Erosion of Restraint in West German Arms Transfer Policy', *Journal of Peace Research*, **26**, No. 2, 1989, p.166.

5. Lucas, *West Germany*, p.1; U. Albrecht, 'The Federal Republic of Germany and Italy: New Strategies of Mid-Sized Weapons Exporters?', *Journal of International Affairs*, **40**, No.1, Summer 1986, p.131.

6. These restrictions were lifted later with the exception of the ban on nuclear, chemical and biological weapons. Moreover, the WEU's Agency for the Control of Armaments, responsible for supervising the organisation's agreements with member states, has vetoed neither the expansion of the FRG's arms industry nor her military export decisions. SIPRI, *The Arms Trade with the Third World*, London, Paul Elek, 1971, p.298; M. Dillon, 'Arms Transfers and the Federal Republic of Germany' in C. Cannizzo (ed.), *The Gun Merchants: Politics and Policies of the Major Arms Suppliers*, New York, Pergamon, 1980, p.108.

7. J. Krause and G.A. Mattox, 'West German Arms Sales to the Third World Countries', *Atlantic Quarterly*, 2, No. 2, Summer 1984, p.172.

8. SIPRI, *The Arms Trade*, p.300; M. Brzoska and T. Ohlson, *Arms Transfers to the Third World 1971–85*, Oxford, Oxford University Press for SIPRI, 1987, p.91.

9. Special provisions were made, though, for the supply of arms to 'safe' countries such as Sweden, Switzerland, Japan, Australia and New Zealand.

10. Largely motivated by the anxiety to prevent German weapons from falling into terrorist hands, this amendment was also interpreted as prohibiting West German arms companies with production facilities abroad from selling or marketing these weapons from German soil.

11. A. Pierre, *The Global Politics of Arms Sales*, Princeton, Princeton University Press, 1982, p.112.

12. C. Christian, *Arms Transfers and Dependence*, New York, Taylor and Francis for UNIDIR, 1988, pp.101–2. This leeway of arms producers *vis-à-vis* the central authorities has been illustrated, *inter alia*, by the subordination of state exports to far harsher restrictions than commercial exports.

13. M. Brzoska, 'Behind the German export scandals', *Bulletin of Atomic Scientists*, July–August, 1989, p. 33.

14. Albrecht, *The Federal Republic of Germany*, p.130.

15. F.S. Pearson, ' "Necessary Evil": Perspectives on West German Arms Transfers Policies', *Armed Forces & Society*, 12, No. 4, Summer 1986, p.553; Christian, *Arms Transfers*, p.103; Brzoska and Ohlson, *Arms Transfers*, p.91.

16. SIPRI, *SIPRI Yearbook 1986*, Stockholm, Almqvist and Wiksell, pp.324–5; *SIPRI Yearbook 1989*, p.199.

17. H. Rattinger, 'West Germany's Arms Transfers to the Nonindustrial World' in U. Ra'anan, *et. al.* (eds), *Arms Transfers to the Third World: The Military Buildup in Less Industrial Countries*, Boulder, Westview Press, 1978, p.231.

18. SIPRI, *The Arms Trade*, p.312.

19. *Ibid.*

20. Another embarrassing incident which occurred in 1965 was the transfer to India of twenty-three Seahawk aircraft which had been exported to Italy.

21. Krause and Mattox, *West German Arms Sales*, p.173; Rattinger, 'West Germany's Arms Transfers', p.231.

22. Krause and Mattox tend to question the impact of these fiascos on Germany's arms export policy, arguing that 'even without the divisive issue of sales to Israel, Third World countries receiving military aid had shown no great willingness to follow the West German line in the so-called *Deutschlandfrage* on the issue of East German recognition'. Krause and Mattox, *West German Arms Sales*, p.173.

23. *Ibid.*; Pierre, *The Global Politics*, p.111.

24. G. Cowen, 'Arms Exports and Government Policy: The West German Experience', *ADIU Report*, 4, No. 4, July–August, 1982, p.6.

25. Pearson, *Necessary Evil*, p.529.

26. Brzoska, 'The Erosion of Restraint', p.168.

27. Rattinger, 'Germany's Arms Transfers', p.249.

28. *Ibid.*, p.531; Cowen, *Arms Exports*, p.7.

29. Concluded in 1979, the deal was shelved following the Islamic Revolution and renewed a decade later.

30. *Radio Free Europe*, 23 February 1981.
31. Brzoska, 'The Erosion of Restraint', p.170.
32. *Middle East Economic Digest* (hereinafter *MEED*), 16 January 1981; *SIPRI Yearbook 1983*, p.278.
33. Brzoska, 'The Erosion of Restraint', p.171.
34. *The Economist*, 28 February 1981.
35. *The Times*, 13 February 1981.
36. *International Herald Tribune*, 23 February 1981.
37. Albrecht, 'The Federal Republic of Germany', p.137.
38. *Financial Times*, 13 January 1981.
39. *International Herald Tribune*, 3 April, 27 September 1981; *The German Tribune*, 20 December 1981.
40. *Guardian*, 1, 2 June 1981; *Financial Times*, 28 October 1981.
41. *SIPRI Yearbook, 1984*, London, Taylor and Francis, pp.193–4.
42. *International Herald Tribune*, 28 May 1982.
43. Brzoska and Ohlson, 'Arms Transfers', p.94; *Guardian*, 26, March 1984.
44. *SIPRI Yearbook, 1984*, p.194; *Daily Telegraph*, 15 August 1983; *MEED*, 14 October 1983; *International Herald Tribune*, 12 October 1983, 28 January 1984; *Financial Times*, 15 February 1984; *Guardian*, 26 May 1984.
45. *Financial Times*, 7, 12 October 1985, 12 November 1985; *International Herald Tribune*, 7 October 1985.
46. *Jane's Defence Weekly*, 15 October 1988.
47. *Die Zeit*, 10 February 1984; 24 February 1984; *Financial Times*, 15 February 1984; *Guardian*, 26 March 1984.
48. The Americans were not willing to sell Jordan the F-16 aircraft but encouraged the FRG to do so in order to prevent the Jordanians from buying Soviet arms.
49. *Die Zeit*, 28 October, 4 November 1988; *Financial Times*, 7 June 1986, 29 October 1988, 23 January 1989; *Sunday Times*, 29 January 1989.
50. According to ACDA, the FRG supplied Iraq with $860 million of arms (figures regarding supply to Iran are not available), as compared with France's $6.7 billion, Britain's $570 million and Italy's $560. See *ACDA, World Military Expenditures, 1988*, p.22.
51. *Der Spiegel*, 6 August 1984; *Financial Times*, 7 August 1984.
52. *Frankfurter Allgemeine Zeitung*, 5, 6 January 1987; *Guardian*, 1 October 1987; *Financial Times*, 6 January 1987.
53. *The Times*, 10 October 1988.
54. *Financial Times*, 8 August 1984; *Der Spiegel*, 30 January 1989; *The Times*, 22 April 1989.
55. *Die Zeit*, 20 January 1989.
56. Cited by the *German Tribune*, 25 January 1989.
57. Cited in the *Washington Post*, 11 January 1989.
58. Brzoska, 'Behind the German export scandals', p.33; *International Herald Tribune*, 15 January 1989; *Financial Times*, 17, 19, January 1989.
59. *International Herald Tribune*, 16 February 1989; *Financial Times*, 16 February 1989.
60. See, for example, *Financial Times*, 8 September 1989.

9 The politics of technology transfer

Harald Müller

Conceptual issues

Technology transfer: a definition

For the purpose of this study, technology transfer means all activities involved in transferring, from one country to another, the knowledge and skills to enable the receiving country to make things; that is the know-how of production processes. This may include: the delivery of machinery essential for further production, the construction of turnkey plants, engineering services for erecting plants and factories, the supply of laboratories and other research and development facilities, the sale of blueprints and software containing information on production techniques, cooperation with other states on research and development and the 'export' of skilled people to other countries.[1]

Contradictory approaches to technology transfer

Technology transfer has become a prominent issue in international relations. Here the areas of foreign economic policy, national security policy and development policy overlap.[2]

In terms of foreign economic policy, there are two conflicting schools of thought: one, of mercantilist origin, maintains that exporting technology is bad in principle, as it supports the emergence of competitors abroad. Exports should be confined to products, not the means to make them. The other school, rooted in liberal economic theory, views technology as a field of comparative advantage like any other, and proposes that those countries that are relatively successful in this field should export technology in return for raw materials and finished goods.

In national security terms, the dispute relates to the broad or narrow interpretation of those technologies relevant to military production. The broad-interpretation school, strongly rooted in the United States, and particularly its defence department, holds that beyond weapons technology proper there are a variety of dual-use technologies which are almost equally relevant to national security. The United States and its main allies must seek the 'comparative security advantage' by maintaining the cutting edge in military technology proficiency. Hence, the transfer of all such equipment presents grave danger. The alternative view has many adherents in Germany. It maintains that expanding the definition of technology which has national security implications creates a practically infinite grey area which may eventually include all civilian technologies. In curbing the transfer of a wide range of technologies a country may hurt its national security interests in two ways: it may limit its own economic growth, which is the basis for a healthy defence industry; and it may lose an important tool for building and maintaining good relations with countries whose benevolence may be essential for achieving national security goals.

In terms of development policy, denying or even controlling technology transfers always causes strong resentment in Third World countries. They see in such policies the attempt to continue imperialism by other means: to relegate developing countries to second-class status forever. In contrast, followers of the 'appropriate technology' school have repeatedly warned against the indiscriminate transfer of all modern, high technologies. They have warned of pernicious consequences if production modes developed in a highly industrialised, administratively efficient, and highly skilled environment are transplanted to an environment of underdevelopment. They propose the selective export of technologies tailor-made for developing countries in close cooperation with people of the countries concerned.

German technology-transfer policy

The basic orientation

The FRG had been supporting the liberal view on exporting technology, seeing it as a matter of comparative advantage; it struggled hard for the narrowest possible interpretation of national-security relevance and it agreed with the development philosophy which counselled the most open attitude possible regarding Third World desires for modern technology.

In principle, there was no discrimination among different regions in the Third World. A volatile region like the Middle East would – except in cases of arms exports – be assessed according to the same criteria as, say, the ASEAN countries. Of course, there were constraints on German export practice under COCOM rules and under other international obligations, but the basic philosophy of liberal transfer applied throughout. Indeed, even in the fifties, when West Germany was among the most 'hawkish' countries in the Western camp, German negotiators in COCOM meetings fought for the narrowest possible list of technologies subject to denial. This policy has brought the FRG time and again into conflict with the United States. The United States, as a global superpower with world-wide security interests and an export and transfer policy which rests on more restrictive principles, was repeatedly annoyed by what it regarded as undue German negligence. In recent years, a series of scandalous stories about German companies helping – illegally or with the knowledge and consent of national authorities – Third World countries with armament programs, including the production of weapons of mass destruction, has damaged the reputation of Germany as a responsible member of the Western family. These events have led to a considerable change in the German attitude and a major effort to reform export law, regulation and implementation; technology transfer policy is greatly affected by these changes.

Economic interests underlying the FRG's approach

This basic orientation of Germany's policy on technology transfer cannot be understood without a close look at its economic structure. Germany is the world's leading exporter, both in absolute terms and in per capita and per GNP standards. On the other hand, the domestic market is not very large and salaries are higher than in most competitor countries. The basic strength of German industry lies in its strong pool of skilled workers, trained via its unique apprenticeship system and in its large number of engineers and graduate engineers. In addition, the backbone of the German industrial system is not the big company, of which only a dozen or so have achieved a world-wide reputation; but rather, the myriad small and medium-sized companies in the machine tools, chemicals and engineering sectors. These companies combine the two main features which make German industry so highly competitive in world markets: specialisation and adaptability. Mass production of uniform goods is not a great competitive strength of German industry; except in a few sectors, the competitive edge lies in the specialisation of industry in tailor-made, high-quality goods and in adaptability to meet the specific needs and desires of customers. Large companies make full use of the strengths of smaller firms, often subcontracting parts of foreign contracts to their smaller partners in the domestic industry.

Specialisation and adaptability provide for an extraordinary dynamic development process in German industry. Inventions are rare that revolutionise production and products. Key developments in the nuclear industry, in electronics and semiconductors have been made in the United States or Japan. Only in the chemical and machine tools industries, does the number of German patents match that of its main competitors.[3] However, German firms have been extraordinarily good at integrating new technologies into their own production methods and products and improving and perfecting them. It is this process of adaptation and integration which characterises the relationship of the German firm to technological development. The technological potential of medium sized and smaller companies in Germany in this process is frequently underrated. A survey in the early eighties revealed that companies with fewer than 1,000 employees account for as much as 20 per cent of R & D expenditure; the comparative figure for the United States was only 6 per cent.[4]

These facts provide the key to understanding German philosophy on technology transfer. As a country with few natural resources, exports are essential to maintain and improve the standard of living and national wealth. Specialised goods are the export niche for Germany, since the markets for cheap mass products are precluded because of high German production costs. Experience has taught the Germans that industry will not stand still and that it is necessary to master and integrate new technologies. As a consequence, there is no fear that export markets could be closed through the export of technology. German industry expects that if it exports a certain production technology today, that technology will be on the market with a new, better, marketable design tomorrow. And since technology as an export product capitalises on the special skills and strengths of German industry, it has been its policy to exploit its comparative advantage in this sector.

The liberal philosophy which underpinned technology-transfer policy in the past was certainly compatible with the basic liberalism guiding domestic-economic policy. It also reflected the economic interests of German industry, and Germany as a whole, as analysed above. This is expressed in Paragraph 3 of the Foreign Economics Law, the basic legal instrument guiding foreign trade and export control policy which says that an export license can be granted if the overall economic interest in realising the transfer more than compensates for the damage done to the interests that were to be protected by the requirement for a licence.

Forty years of such practice have created a vastly differentiated export sector, able to offer foreign customers a panoply of technology: there are large engineering firms such as Lurgi and Lahmeyer which are equivalent to American giants like Bechtel or Brown and Root; the big industrial companies usually possess sizeable engineering departments and are willing not only to sell their products abroad, but also to help recipient countries develop the means to produce them on their own. Last but not least, there is a large number of medium, small and very small specialised firms in virtually every branch of industry engaged in export and technology transfer.

For example, the machinery industry, a sector of primary importance for technology transfer, includes 5,400 companies of which only 169 employ more than 1,000 people. Almost 60 per cent of the sales revenue comes from companies with under 1,000 employees, and small companies – those with less than 200 employees – still produce a quarter of total sales.

One sub-sector of the machinery industry, the machine tool and production systems industry, is practically devoted entirely to selling the technology inherent in its products. The export share of total sales of this industry is regularly about 50 per cent; about 20 per cent of these exports go to developing countries, including about 5–6 per cent to the Middle East. This is fairly standard for industries dealing with technology. The developing world is a minor part of overall business but still sizeable. For small companies, one-off orders from developing countries can well make the difference between a golden year and a desperate struggle for survival. Among the developing countries, the Middle East accounts for a quarter to a third of export sales.[5]

Political interests in technology transfer

The importance of economic interests cannot be underestimated, but it would be a mistake to neglect the political considerations behind German technology transfer policy. First because exports are regarded as a cornerstone of the economic stability of the country, they assume a political meaning *per se*. The traumatic experience of the devastating political consequences of the Great Depression still reverberate through the German political and economic elites some two generations on. It left a particularly deep impression on the people who built the FRG after World War II. Social and political stability, democracy and peace, according to this fundamental faith are all dependent on economic stability which, in turn, depends on continued exports. Technology transfer as a competitive advantage of German industry has thus a political importance easily overlooked by the outside observer.

Political competition with the GDR

In the fifties and sixties, West Germany fought an uphill battle against the increasing recognition of the GDR as the second German state. The claim of the FRG to be the only legitimate representative of the German people has been vindicated recently, but politically it was a losing battle until the eighties. One political instrument of use in delaying the growth of diplomatic relations between developing countries and East Berlin was, naturally, the advantage of close economic relations that Bonn could offer. In this context, the transfer of advanced technology was one of the few incentives where East Germany could not match its Western competitor. Technology transfer, therefore, was one of the instruments of diplomacy in the 'German question' in the first two decades after the division of Germany.

Political competition with other countries

Economic relations and foreign aid were the only instruments West Germany could employ to foster its broader interests in the developing world. After World War II, the country could not compete with other powers in the provision of direct military support or in power projection. Because all military matters had become so tainted and were looked upon with distrust and resentment by a substantial part of the West German public, military aid and arms exports had to be approached with far more caution than in most other developed countries, either East or West. To balance this, the FRG had to cultivate economic relations as a tool to bolster foreign policy in the developing world. Because other industrialised countries were more reluctant to give away the secrets of technology, the more liberal attitude taken by Bonn helped to establish the FRG, in spite of the 'handicap' of not being a military power, as a highly valued partner for developing countries.

The political identity of West Germany

Much of what has been discussed is closely connected to the self-image of the FRG. After the miraculous recovery from the wounds of World War II, West Germany failed to recognise its growing global responsibilities. West Germans, after two failed bids for world power by Germany this century, never developed a healthy and rational relationship to power politics following 1945.[6] While this departure from past practice was certainly welcome in one way, it proved calamitous that an all-too-parochial perspective seduced the Germans into ignoring the massive consequence of their world-wide economic activities. West Germany's global economic presence was its specific form of power, and the same will apply to the united Germany in the future. Where investments, exports and cooperation influence regional security or even endanger world peace, the refusal to accept responsibility was and is unjustifiable. Not negating one's own power but a responsible and measured use of this power is the *sine qua non* of a peace-fostering foreign policy. For this reason, Germany in the future must act in full consciousness of its responsibilities – as the FRG in the past has often failed to do.

In the absence of such a global political perspective, short-term economic interests had gained a monopoly in defining the goals, ways and means of West Germany's foreign economic policy. The consequences of such a policy ran directly counter to the country's own interests. They have done damage to its security and have undermined its international reputation. With the unification of the country, a fundamental change is necessary. By a twist of fate, a cumulation of the worst export scandals in postwar German history have engendered such a change just at the moment when the Germans regained national unity.

Technology-transfer policy decision-making

Designing and implementing German technology-transfer policy is shared by several agencies: the Foreign Office (AA), the Federal Ministry of Economics (BMWi), the Federal Ministry for Research and Technology (BMFT), the Ministry for Economic Cooperation (BMZ) and the Federal Ministry for Finance (BMF). For the export of military technology, the Ministry of Defence is involved. At times, the Office of the Chancellor has also played a major role.

The Ministry of Economics

Within the Ministry of Economics, three divisions participate in technology-transfer issues. The 'sector' divisions are responsible for presenting the interests of the respective industries and companies in inter-agency decision-making. They would also be in contact with the economic attachés in German embassies who are charged with facilitating and supporting contacts between German business and the host countries. The industry desks brief the minister for travels abroad to facilitate talks with colleagues about industrial cooperation, trade and investment. In this endeavour, they are supported by a second branch, the country desks; these will also be involved in the issue of export licenses for 'their' countries.

Under the Office for External Economic Policy and Development Aid, Department VA8 deals with issues of foreign policy and security relating to external economic activities. This is the main department for export controls; it also supervises the Export Licensing Office (BAW), a subsidiary body organised as a separate agency. Until 1989, the BMWi was the agency which oversaw the area of nuclear export licensing.

The main orientation of this ministry is pro-industry and pro-export. It follows the basic principle of export promotion and has grave reservations about an expansion of export controls. As the former minister, Graf Lambsdorff, put it: 'The ministry is called the ministry *for* economics . . . It has a duty to support export activities. A large share of employment depends on the export activities of German business. We have never seen ourselves as an office for impeding exports'.[7]

There is an underlying distrust of foreign interventions and initiatives: such moves, it is suspected, result from competitive motivations rather than from security concerns. Unofficial reports and off-the-record briefings submitted by foreign intelligence services have been disregarded time and again by BMWi officials. As a consequence, the BMWi has frequently resisted requests for

tighter export controls and has almost automatically hurried to defend companies charged with breaches of licensing requirements.[8] Minister of Economics
Haussmann had to admit that 'the awareness of the risks did not increase with
the development of these risks. The granting of licences became too much the
rule: denying licences too much the exception'.[9] This attitude, by virtue of
subordination, was also transferred to the licensing agency, the BAW.

The Foreign Office

Technology transfer has become an issue of eminent political importance. As a
consequence, the Foreign Office, which was only a secondary player in this
political field in the past, has moved to become the main actor in recent years.
The department concerned primarily with the issue is the Office for Foreign
Economic Policy, Development Policy and European Economic Integration.
This is the main department for the design and conduct of export control policy.
It includes the country desks for developing countries in its development policy
branch and the desks for specific industries in its foreign economic branch. One
key office is 431, responsible for foreign nuclear and space policy. This department was largely instrumental in the development of new German nuclear
export policy and has also co-negotiated the missile technology control regimes
[MTCR]. It participates in export licensing in these two areas. Department 424
exercises the same function in the chemical exports field; department 422 has
general authority over cases involving the KriegswaffenKontrollgesetz
(KWKG, War Weapons Control Act).

The attitude of the AA towards sensitive exports has undergone considerable
change in the last thirty years. Initially, the ministry was fighting for the
recovery of German industrial sovereignty in sensitive industries. This included, of course, maximum freedom of action for foreign economic activities.
In the sixties and early seventies, the Foreign Office's foreign-trade policy was
very much devoted to supporting the foreign activities of German business.
During the disputes on nuclear export policy in the early and mid-seventies, the
Foreign Office agreed with other ministries' positions that it was of the utmost
importance to keep the German nuclear industry free from any further impedi-
ments emerging from the new commitment to control the full fuel cycle
domestically and to pursue export opportunities vigorously. This attitude prevailed throughout the seventies; the Foreign Office defended the Brazilian deal
against American criticism and worked in tandem with the BMFT to uphold the
German right to use plutonium. However, the AA opposed the continuation of
nuclear collaboration with South Africa and fought for a strengthening of the
safeguard clauses in the German–Brazilian agreement.

During the eighties, the AA emerged as the major proponent of a more
careful and prudent export policy. It is fair to say that at that time foreign policy
considerations had finally won over foreign economic interest as far as
Department 431 was concerned. On several occasions, the AA challenged
decisions and assessments by the BMFT and the BMWi, argued for more
frequent Foreign Economic Investigations of companies active in nuclear trade
and pleaded for a strengthening of the export-control agencies, although with
little success. It is largely due to the insistence of the AA that no German firm
offered a nuclear reactor to Pakistan, that the Bushire nuclear power plant in

Iran was not completed and that the nuclear cooperation agreement with Pakistan was terminated in 1989.[10]

In the aftermath of the Rabta chemical weapons' plant affair, Foreign Minister Genscher began to devote considerable personal attention to export policy. His vigorous commitment helped to convince the executive to draft comprehensive and far-reaching export control reform legislation and to push it through parliament.

The Federal Ministry of Research and Technology

The BMFT's mandate is confined to those industrial sectors that the government has chosen for special R & D support because it is assumed that private business will not be able to provide the necessary research funds. These are key industrial sectors believed to be essential for the preservation of the FRG as an advanced industrial state and, by implication, a successful exporter. So far, these sectors have been nuclear energy, space, electronics, telecommunication, biogenetics, environmental technology and, to a lesser degree, alternative energy. The industry offices and desks have developed close relations with their client companies. Projects are usually designed cooperatively; during the course of a multi-year project, the cooperation frequently evolves into a symbiotic relationship. As a consequence, in the conflict between promotion and control, the BMFT usually favours promotion.

Beyond its mandate as the main research support agency within the federal government, the BMFT has fostered the growth of these industries and has supported efforts by the BMWi to facilitate foreign business through its own contacts. Particularly in the nuclear sector, the ministry has played a key role in all major German export successes. Often, major export projects start from R & D cooperation agreements in which the BMFT plays a key role. Moreover, the international cooperation bureaux of the central research agencies that are under the aegis of the BMFT are actively involved in such 'precursor projects' for industrial cooperation. As mentioned above, the R & D cooperation projects are in themselves a major vehicle for technology transfer.

The two branches involved in these endeavours are the industrial desks and office 22, responsible for international and – until unification – intra-German cooperation.

The ministry participates in export licensing in a consultative capacity and provides technical expertise. This is often decisive in determining whether a particular item might serve military purposes. In the past, the BMFT has all too often played down the possible military abuse of exports under licensing review. Famous examples include the transfer of beryllium to India, and of a tritium extraction facility to Pakistan.[11]

Other ministries involved in export control

The Ministry of Finance supervises customs. Under its authority is the Customs Criminal Institute, the central body for starting and controlling investigations on breaches of customs law and regulation, including the export law. Alas, this ministry is also the guardian of the budget and has, in the past, favoured a restrictive policy if suggestions for a strengthening of customs and export control were made.

The Ministry of Economic Cooperation supervises development aid. It will usually be involved in major cases of technology transfer and, if such transactions emerge from previous development projects, it will act as a catalyst. While export promotion is not the main mission of the ministry, it has at times put some emphasis on fostering the interests of German business simultaneously with the well-being of the respective client states. In the interest of maintaining a smooth relationship with its partners in the Third World, the advice coming from this ministry has usually favoured transfers.

The Office of the Chancellor is not involved in 'low politics'. As a consequence, it is not involved in routine export projects or in technology-transfer licensing. It is responsible for the coordination of intelligence information that might include evidence for doubtful economic activities. If the matter assumes a highly political character, the office will inevitably be involved. This has been the case, for instance, with the German–Brazilian deal in the seventies and, more recently, with other export scandals. It was the Chancellor's office that reported to parliament on the Rabta case (after its long failure to recognise the significance of incoming intelligence). It then kept track of the efforts of the other ministries to produce convincing remedies for the situation that had caused the scandals.

Governmental–industrial relations

The relations between government and industry in the FRG are close and cooperative. They have been analysed as the prototype of a 'liberal corporatist' system. This description applies well in the R & D sector, domestically as well as for international technology transfer.[12] The task of supporting R & D is divided between the Federal government and the *Länder*. The Federal government supports central research agencies through individual ministries and distributes funds through the Ministry of Research and Technology (BMFT) to companies in well-defined fields of technology. Beyond these limits, science policy falls under the authority of the *Länder*.[13] The executive possesses a variety of tools for influencing the course of industrial development. In Germany's parliamentary system, laws usually originate from government agencies. In the normal course of events, business associations (as well as labour unions) are consulted well in advance before a draft bill is transferred to parliament. Frequently, the initiative for such bills emerges from the associations themselves. In the special committees of the Bundestag, particularly the Economics and the Research Committees, companies and their associations have a second chance to shape the course of legislation.

What is true for legislation applies even more to regulation. Ordnances concerning business are never issued without close advance consultation with the business associations concerned.[14] 'Structural policy' is another policy instrument. It is conducted in collaboration with the EC Commission and the *Länder* governments, and mainly concerns assistance for economically weak regions. Structural policy attempts to improve the infrastructure of regions with below-average economic growth and to give transitional assistance to industries in crisis. In both cases, government funds are mainly employed to give incentives to modern industries to locate in underdeveloped regions and to accelerate innovation in backward industries.

R & D policy, under the auspices of the BMFT, is a crucial tool for fostering technological innovation. The BMFT tries to identify key technological developments far in advance, to discover areas where insufficient funds will be available if R & D is left solely to the private sector and to pump money into these areas. Nuclear technology, space, electronic data processing, biotechnology and environmental techniques are the main support fields of the BMFT.[15]

Besides direct R & D subsidies to private business, there are large governmental or government-sponsored R & D establishments, such as the Nuclear Research Centres in Karlsruhe, Jülich and Garching, the Fraunhofer Gesellschaft, the various institutes of the Max-Planck Gesellschaft and the German Agency for Research and Experiment in Air and Space Technology (DFVLR). Altogether there are thirteen major central research centres (*Grossforschungseinrichtungen*) directly supported by the Federal government in collaboration with the *Länder*. All develop basic and applied technologies up to commercial maturity and engage on a broad basis in international collaboration.[16]

The aerospace sector is a case in point. Here, four ministries foster technology development: the Post and Telecommunication Ministry (Satellites); the Ministry of Defence (military aircraft and rockets); the BMWi (subsidies for the Airbus Company) and the BMFT (Space Research Programme). The various activities of these four ministries have been coordinated, since 1974, by a coordinator for German Aerospace. They encompass governmental purchase orders, R & D and production subsidies, export finance support and insurance of currency exchange-rate risks.[17]

Government–industry collaboration in foreign economic activities

Last, but most important for the area under discussion, is the assistance provided by both the BMWi and the BMFT to foreign economic activities. Scientific and economic attachés in German embassies are expected to look for openings for German companies. In many cases – such as the German–Brazilian nuclear deal discussed below – the government was instrumental in helping companies to get large contracts, and has created the necessary stable politico–economic environment by concluding framework agreements with the host country within which private cooperation can thrive with the necessary degree of confidence.

Of particular importance are the three instruments used to insure private business against risk emerging from different forms of technology transfer. For the most frequent form of such transfer, direct capital investment, the government provides some of the overall investment in developing countries; according to the Ministry of Economics, the share is higher than in most other industrial countries with a different warrant system. A second instrument is the conclusion of agreements with the host country by the government on 'support and mutual protection of capital investment'. Such agreements have been concluded with more than fifty developing countries. Apart from direct investment, capital assets, shares and credits, the agreements also lend protection to patents, brands, technical processes and know-how. Governmental export insurance, the so-called '*Hermes-Bürgschaft*', is available not only for hardware exports but also for income from licences, in so far as they arise from transfer actions equivalent to exports. Thus, industry is protected by a network of governmental instruments against various risks emerging from technology transfer. This has contributed to the willingness of German companies to engage in such transfer activities.[18]

Dangerous proliferation: the dark side of German policy

The overwhelming majority of cases of technology transferred by German companies are in line with the benevolent philosophy described above. However, export liberalism, lack of global perspective and neglect by the top political leadership have caused a considerable number of transfers which have contributed to the spread of weapons of mass destruction and the means of their delivery. The Middle East has been affected strongly by these activities. The following analysis is meant to be illustrative, but is unfortunately by no means exhaustive.[19]

Case 1: the government takes charge: the German–Brazilian deal and its consequences

One of the notorious cases in the 1970s was the 'elephant deal' between the FRG and Brazil in the nuclear sector. Apart from eight light-water reactors, the contract included the complete fuel cycle, from uranium exploration through enrichment to reprocessing. The Federal government was instrumental in bringing the deal about, starting with a basic cooperation contract in science and technology that included the nuclear sector. This agreement was coordinated, on the German side, by the International Bureau of the Nuclear Research Centre, Jülich. The cooperation led to a basic understanding on nuclear collaboration on an industrial scale. At this point, the BMFT, together with the KWU nuclear company, took over the negotiations. The BMFT and the BMWi then supported industry – mainly the nuclear-reactor builder KWU – in getting the contract. The BMFT in particular developed the idea of a complete fuel-cycle technology transfer, persuaded the Brazilian partner not to call for offers publicly and kept KWU in line when the company wanted to split the contract and to compete for the reactor deal only. The German government was instrumental in not concluding the 'London Guidelines' that called for 'restraint' in the export of 'sensitive' or critical technologies in the nuclear sector before the agreement with Brazil was signed. The government believed that the cooperative endeavour would help to dissuade Brazil from engaging in military nuclear projects and to draw it closer to the non-proliferation regime. This was a serious error. In the early eighties it became clear that Brazil was working on a 'parallel' nuclear programme, controlled by the military, and which included enrichment as well as reprocessing technology. Individuals trained under the German–Brazilian cooperation agreement were diverted into this 'parallel' programme. According to an authoritative estimate this concerned some 20 per cent of the 350 or so people trained under the agreement. The centrepiece of the parallel programme was a centrifuge enrichment project, based on technology that was sold to Brazil by a German scientist in the early fifties. It must be assumed that although the technology was different from the jet-nozzle enrichment process transferred under the German–Brazilian agreement, Brazilian personnel acquired considerable basic know-how which they could then apply in the parallel programme. Moreover, machine tools for centrifuge production were exported to Brazil in the 1980s.[20] The story took a dramatic turn in the fall 1990: Brazilian president Collor de Melo announced with great sincerity that the Brazilian military had been working since 1975 – the date the German–Brazilian deal was concluded – on a military nuclear programme and that Brazil had helped Iraq, through a secret nuclear cooperation agreement, to develop its nuclear sector. This included the transfer of know-how about centrifuge enrichment.[21]

Case 2: warnings not heeded: chemical weapons for Libya

One of the most sensational cases of German technology transfer, and one which eventually triggered a fundamental change in policy involved the chemical weapons plant in Rabta, Libya. Current information is that the German company, Imhausen, a medium-sized, family owned, specialized chemical firm that had had R & D support to the tune of DM62 million since 1972 from the BMFT, was approached by a middleman. That person was the director of IBI, a London-based Arab-owned firm with a subsidiary in Frankfurt. According to the 1984 contract concluded with representatives of the Libyan government, Imhausen acted as main contractor, provided basic engineering, supplied relevant parts and, through a subsidiary, GFA, the process steering system and equipment. The contract was worth DM256 million. Imhausen subcontracted parts to the large German firms Siemens (central computer) and Salzgitter Industriebau, a subsidiary of the vast government-owned Salzgitter steel conglomerate (engineering services for pipelaying and electronics). At present, an investigation is under way since there is suspicion that the Salzgitter Industriebau management was aware of the true destination of its contributions.[22] Altogether, some thirty West German companies participated, without being aware of the true nature of the deal, in the construction of the plant. The whole business was conducted under the cover of a fake project, 'Pharma 150', in Hong Kong, in collaboration with still another Frankfurt-based firm, Pen Tsao, actually a subsidiary of Imhausen especially created for the deal. Pen Tsao started a construction side in Hong Kong, in order to be able to answer questions, but equipment officially destined for Hong Kong was diverted to Tripoli. The factory constructed at Rabta also contained a 'metallurgical' department in which shells for the poisonous gas were to be produced. Jürgen Imhausen-Hippenstiel, meanwhile, admitted the offence and was sentenced to five years' imprisonment.[23]

The story offers a particular insight into the many inhibitions which German investigators suffered, owing to the in-built bias in favour of exports and the blind trust in the sincerity of German business people. As early as July 1985, the German embassy in Moscow informed the government about Imhausen's involvement in Libya, including the front company in Hong Kong and the participation of a government-owned company (Salzgitter). The German Federal Intelligence Service denied this information within two weeks. Increasing intelligence on the construction of the Rabta plant and repeated hints at German participation led neither to closer observation of Imhausen nor to a Foreign Economics Investigation (FEI). During an FEI, customs agents are given access to the papers and accounts of a company and can request all necessary information on foreign-trade activities; there is no need for any initial proof; suspicion is enough. When evidence was forced upon the German bureaucracy by American intelligence, and underlined by high-level political intervention, German intelligence, customs and prosecuting agencies uncovered within a few months all the necessary information to indict Imhausen-Hippenstiel. Even then they proceeded with utmost caution and hesitancy to avoid infringing on a possibly innocent company. Once the connections between Imhausen, Pen Tsao and IBI were discovered the investigation was easy. The sad side of the story is that it would have been as easy in 1985 – after the initial information from Moscow – and the Rabta plant would never have been built.

In this case, the company did not request any export licences and acted in a blatant breach of the law. The story highlights vividly the timidity of the bureaucracy when it comes to cracking down on business; the incredulity that such horrible things could be done by honest German business people and the reluctance to approach top policy-makers with such 'trivial' issues as illegal foreign trade actions. The underlying argument was notoriously circular: bureaucracy did not wish to employ more far-reaching measures of investigation because the information at hand did not give reasons for suspicion; but without more rigorous investigation, it was hard to uncover such information.[24] Chancellor Kohl and Foreign Minister Genscher learned of the matter in the summer and autumn of 1988, and once their attention was focused, their subordinates started the successful crackdown.

The case confirms another point mentioned earlier: the enormous time-lag between the identification of a problem and the initiative to find a solution. The first indications of German mercenaries working on chemical weapons in Libya came in 1981. This was not illegal at the time – German law stopped at the border. The Rabta case was necessary to convince German politicians that the participation of German citizens in the production of weapons of mass destruction abroad was so demonstrably against the national interest that legislation was required. There had been a delay of nine years between the identification of the problem and the proposed solution. Again, a prompt reaction could have been an effective deterrent – and Imhausen-Hippenstiel could well have met greater difficulties in persuading his collaborators to work in Libya.[25]

Case 3: Saddam Hussein's pandora's box: German companies arm Iraq

Most notorious was West German support for the large armament programme that bolstered the regional ambitions of Iraq's ruthless dictator Saddam Hussein. German firms were involved in all aspects of his broad armament industry.

The main agent for the construction of Iraq's chemical weapons complex was a small chemical engineering company, Karl Kolb, of Neu Isenburg near Frankfurt, and its subsidiary, Pilot Plant. From 1981, this enterprise worked consistently for the erection of a chemical weapons capacity in Iraq, and in 1984, it got a master contract for the facility. As early as 1982, a source hinted at the nature of the firm's business to governmental agencies. Two years later, the CIA learned about its activities and informed the German authorities. Then economics minister Martin Bangemann (presently European Commissioner for Industrial Policy and the Single Market) suspected that the Americans were motivated by 'competitive envy' and dismissed the information. A second company, WET, founded by ex-employees of the large, government-owned Preussag company, was involved from 1984 and was mainly responsible for acquiring and shipping precursor material from which poison gases could be produced. Later on, it constructed a production facility for precursor materials. Ironically, one of the managers of this company worked as a source for German intelligence. This shielded him and his associates from close scrutiny. Both Kolb and WET staff have since been indicted and now face trial.[26]

Another small company, SIGMA Chemie, supplied small quantities of myco-toxins for Iraq's biological weapons research. Rhema constructed an inhalation chamber that can be used for live experiments to test biological as well as chemical weapons substances.[27]

In the case of the construction of a nuclear-capable, intermediate-range 'supergun', a German company specializing in high-quality steel processing, Ferrostaal, a subsidiary of the large machine tool conglomerate MAN, accepted an order in 1988 or 1989 from the Iraqi-led Italian firm Euromac. The order involved a master contract for a large 'universal forgery' at Tadschi in Iraq. Design and requirements for the facility left little doubt that this was a factory for the production of a variety of artillery pieces. Particular features of the facility, such as the foundations which were designed to withstand very high pressures, and the weight of the pieces for which the forging–lathing system was designed, led to the conclusion that it was here that the 'supergun' would be put together. This was a device that could fire rockets more than a thousand kilometres. Ferrostaal hired for the project, apart from other subsidiaries of MAN, a dozen of the most renowned German construction, machine tools and steel companies. In each case, the transfer of know-how was part of the job. While these firms may not have been aware of the true meaning of the order, this was not true for Ferrostaal, as far as present evidence shows.[28]

Iraqi missile projects, the backbone of its regional power and a threat to strategic stability in the region, profited largely from the good economic relationship with the Federal Republic. MBB, the leading German aerospace concern, worked with Argentina and Egypt on the Condor II, an intermediate-range missile. Egypt, in turn, began to collaborate with Iraq. When the project was officially terminated on German governmental request (initially in 1985, with actual termination as late as 1988), several employees of MBB had already founded a couple of small companies, the CONSEN group, that continued the cooperation with Iraq. MBB continued collaboration with CONSEN and supplied equipment and know-how for a project in which it allegedly no longer participated. The Condor II, also called Badr 2000, a formidable missile with a maximum range of 1200km, was the result of these efforts.[29] Meanwhile, Baghdad pursued a second route, based on the Scud-B missile of which it already had several hundred supplied by the Russians. The Iraqi military hired another small German firm, INWAKO, to help with enhancing the range and accuracy of the missile – the so-called 'project 1728'. INWAKO involved a large number of small German firms in the project. It was terminated due to incipient investigations of INWAKO's dealings.[30] Another small engineering company,

ABC Engineering, provided advanced fuel and additional fuel tanks for the missile.[31]

The most striking development was Iraq's apparent ambition to come closer to possessing nuclear weapons. In this field again, German firms have been instrumental in providing essential technology to the Iraqis. M&M Metalform, a company whose managers were involved in the Gronau enrichment facility construction, acted as a front company for the Iraqi effort. Though evidence which would satisfy a court is not available, the company has been suspected of supplying essential technological information to Iraq for the construction of a centrifuge-enrichment facility. Specialised machine tools for enrichment were delivered. Arbed Saarstahl, one of the most sophisticated steelmakers in Western Europe, was approached to supply specially hardened steel slightly below the level that would have triggered the request for safeguards. The steel was later shipped through Iraq to two Swiss companies for the production of centrifuge end-caps. The equipment was then intercepted at Frankfurt Airport, a rare success for German customs agents. INWAKO was also active in the nuclear sector: it supplied circular magnets for the rotation bearings carrying the centrifuges, one of the most crucial parts of the facility.[32]

Last but not least, Gildemeister Project, a subsidiary of one of the better-known members of the sophisticated machine tool establishment, Gildemeister, was the main designer and constructor of the cornerstone of Iraq's military–industrial complex, the military research and development centre SAAD 19. MBB, again, worked as an important subcontractor.[33]

German export law and regulation: from insufficiency to reform

The legal instruments for the control of technology transfer have been the *Aussenwirtschaftsgesetz* (Foreign Economic Act, AWG) and, derived from it, the *Aussenwirtschaftsverordnung* (Foreign Economic Regulation, AWVO) and, for special military items, the *Kriegswaffenkontrollgesetz* (War Weapons Control Act, KWKG). The latter applies mainly to arms exports and is, thus, of less interest for the subject under discussion. Yet, its definition of arms includes the technology specifically designed to produce arms. Military relevant technology transfer, accordingly, falls under the purview of the KWKG. This is important since, before and after the recent reforms, punishment under the KWKG is significantly higher than under the AWG.

All exports of military technology need two separate licences. One licence is needed under the KWKG and needs the consent of the Ministry of Defence. The other licence is required by the AWG as described below. Licences will usually be given for exports to NATO countries. With regard to extra-NATO destinations, the licensing decision will be subject to an examination of whether German security interests are concerned. As a matter of principle, military technology is not to be licensed in areas of war or 'tension'. Since the latter term is certainly ambiguous, military technology transfers have been hotly debated throughout the history of the FRG.

A particular problem is presented by the establishment of joint ventures in NATO countries, particularly in Europe. Defence-industry collaboration is a declared goal of all Western European countries; within NATO, the IEPG has been established with the special mission of fostering such collaboration, and the WEU also devotes considerable attention to the area. Yet, joint ventures located in partner countries will, in theory, be subject to the export policies of the participating countries. The attempt to question this practice could lead to unwelcome political conflict, impede the construction of a competitive and efficient Western European defence industry and put German companies at a disadvantage. Joint ventures have therefore been a convenient route for West German firms to circumvent the more restrictive policies of their home state.

The KWKG has been considerably changed and amended in 1990 in order to prevent, as far as possible, the continuation of the endless stream of export scandals which have been revealed since 1987. The transfer of technology for atomic, biological or chemical weapons will now be punished by at least one year in prison and, in serious cases, up to life imprisonment (previously the maximum was ten years). For the first time, aid and *support* for such activities is punishable as well as direct participation. Moreover, participation and assistance *by neglect* are now also defined as criminal acts; a perpetrator may face imprisonment for up to three years (if German security and foreign interests, or international peace, are jeopardised as a consequence of the transfer); if such a danger is absent, the maximum penalty for neglect or acts of omission is two years' imprisonment. This clause is important for two reasons: the lawyers of indicted businessmen can no longer hope o rescue their clients unscathed if they argue that the transfer was not *meant* to help another state produce weapons of mass destruction. While this strategy may suffice to prevent maximum imprisonment, the clients may still go to prison. Second, companies and laboratories will be obliged to think through, far more carefully than in the past, their trade and cooperation with third parties; courts will require, on the basis of the new law, proof that all advisable precautions were taken before a contract was concluded or cooperation initiated.

Another major innovation was the extraterritorial extension of the applicability of law. Participation in ABC-weapons projects abroad is now subject to the same punishment as such activities on German soil. This was a difficult decision to take; the last time this sort of extra-territoriality had been applied was in 1941, and the purpose then was to deter exiled Germans from political activities against the Third Reich. Because of this precedent, lawmakers were very reluctant to change the basic territorial philosophy of German criminal law.

The AWG is the instrument for controlling all other exports and technology transfers. This includes those not specifically designed for military purposes but with potential military applications – that is dual-use technology. In an essential difference to the legal attitude prevailing in the United States, the AWG principally frees foreign trade from state control and establishes a right to trade. Restrictions on this right require a special authorisation on the basis of the AWG. Such constraints are legitimate only under international agreements ratified by parliament (Para 5) or to protect German security and foreign-policy interests and international peace (Para 7). The 1990 amendment now permits government to enact transfer constraints for the implementation of 'international cooperation', that is non-ratified executive agreements or informal understandings. In parallel to the KWKG amendment, legislation enacted in July makes exemptions from the 'rule of free trade' applicable to the economic activities of German citizens abroad. This includes, for example, brokerage or transit trade transactions as well as the development and sale of technology by foreign subsidiaries or even foreign companies owned by German citizens abroad (Para 7.3, new). It would also concern the participation of German citizens in industrial projects with possible military applications subject to license – an important new opportunity to control intangible technology transfer. The clause was inserted with the intention of curbing the assistance lent by 'technology mercenaries' to missile projects abroad.[34]

For other technology transfer, Paras 7.3 and 7.5 are important. Paras 7.3 (b) and (c) authorize constraints on the transfer of items 'useful for the development, production or employment of weapons, munitions and other gear for war', and of 'construction plans and other information for the production of such items'. Para 7.5. gives authorization to constrain the 'transfer of patents, inventions, production processes and experiences' with regard to such items.

The maximum punishment for criminal acts against the AWKG in serious cases is now ten years rather than five years. In less serious cases it is five years instead of three years. For misdemeanours, the penalty has been doubled from 500,000 to 1,000,000 DM, still too low a fine given the possible profits from illegal transfers of sensitive items.

In addition, the AWG has been amended to authorize export licensing and control authorities to enhance and exchange their intelligence on the capabilities and activities of German companies. This involves foreign trade activities as well as certain licenses (e.g. permits to handle nuclear material) issued domestically. The authority is confined to the atomic, biological and chemical sector.[35]

Para 28.2. nominates the Federal Office for Economics (*Bundesamt für Wirtschaft*, BAW) as the licensing authority. The BAW works under the authority of the BMWi that acts, as explained below, as the lead agency in the interagency licensing process. A crucial new clause requires companies to nominate an executive officer at board level as 'export executive'. This person will be held responsible for any failure of the company to comply with the export laws. In other words, there is now a substantial personal interest in any board to abide by the rules.

A new amendment in 1992 has further stiffened penalties under the AWG, setting a minimum of two years; this prison term cannot any longer be suspended. The Customs Criminalty Office has been given the authority to open mail, to eavesdrop and to intercept messages of firms and individuals under suspicion. Courts can order the confiscation of the whole sales value of an illegal deal rather than, as previously, the profit only. A new federal office for arms control is being created, liberated from the mission of promoting exports and focusing exclusively on export controls and licensing.[36]

To summarize: recent legislation has extended the territorial scope of the application of German criminal law to deter participation in ABC projects abroad (a most important form of technology transfer – the 'technology mercenary'). It has stiffened the penalties and enhanced the classes of action subject to penalties ('support' and 'neglect'). It has facilitated international cooperation for preventing the unwelcome flow of technology and has created a basis for more effective export-control implementation through an improved information flow to and between export control agencies.

This legislation has been, and is being, implemented under the rules laid down in the Foreign Trade Ordinance (*Aussenwirtschaftsverordnung*, AWVo). The AWVo has been amended in parallel with the process of changing the law. Important changes have been going on since 1984. In its classical form of 1961, Part I of the 'export list', Annex AL to the AWVo, contained three sublists of items: military items, nuclear items and chemical items; Annex L contained several lists of countries for which different rules applied. As for technology transfer, the important aspect was that the 1961 version of the AWVo constrained the transfer of patents, inventions, production processes and experiences (7.5. AWG, then 7.4) only if the destination was a communist country; the same limits and constraints applied to transit trade transactions (AWVo, Paras 40 and 45.2).

One important change to the AWVo occurred as early as 1984. The export of dual-use chemical production plants capable of producing precursor substances for chemical weapons was subjected to licences. This was done by inserting a new items list into Annex AL of the AWVo. In the same year, transfers to Libya were put under the same rules as those to communist countries, as a reaction to growing evidence that Libya was seeking chemical weapons.[37]

In 1988, the government issued a 'guideline for the prevention of illicit technology transfer'; the guideline detailed existing laws and regulations and allowed for more efficient cooperation and information exchange among the agencies concerned. In the same year, the 'nuclear ordinance' was enacted as a classified document. It concerned nuclear and chemical items, which were nuclear related in the AWVo and changed in a considerable way the system of inter-agency decision-making. The Foreign Office, so far a secondary actor, would be given copies of all licences for transfers to EC countries and the United States. For sensitive materials and technology, the BMWi must now ask the Foreign Office's opinion before issuing a licence. Exports to all other countries require the consent of the Foreign Ministry, and in the case of a group of 'sensitive countries' (enumerated on a classified list not published as an AWVo Annex) which included several countries from the Middle East, the prior consent of the Foreign Office is required before the BAW may issue a licence for items assessed as potentially sensitive.[38]

Another landmark change was the AWVo amendment of 27 February, 1989, the first tangible reaction to the Rabta scandal. The amendment made subject to licence all forms of technology transfer included on lists A, B, C and D – hitherto constrained only if the destination was a communist country – to countries not members of the OECD. Likewise, all transit trade transactions involving lists A–D now need licences if the recipient country is not a member of the OECD.[39]

In August 1989, the AWVo was amended again. A new list, E, was added, containing substances that could be used to manufacture biological weapons and equipment for the production of such substances. Moreover, a clearer definition of chemical equipment and factories capable of being used in chemical weapons' production was included.[40]

In October 1989, the definition of 'technology' was expanded to include all transfers of software, including that in non-tangible form. Simultaneously, the transfer of technology (expanded definition) to non-German persons resident in the Federal Republic for less than five years was subjected to licensing as a new kind of technology transfer.[41]

Most recently, the AWVo has been amended to include equipment for the production of parts that could be used for the Iraqi 'supergun'.[42]

Between July and August, the Bonn government took another significant step. It changed its basic policy on nuclear exports. So far, the FRG had been willing to transfer nuclear technologies to countries not parties to the Nuclear

Non-proliferation Treaties under safeguards laid down by the International Atomic Energy Agency. These applied to the items supplied but not necessarily to all nuclear activities in the recipient country. With a cabinet decision of July 1990, the FRG switched to 'full scope safeguards' as a condition for new nuclear supply. Thus, in future, nuclear supplies will be licensed only if in th: recipient country *all* nuclear material is, and will be, under IAEA safeguards. The new policy was announced in Foreign Minister Genscher's speech to the fourth NPT review conference in Geneva in August 1990.[43]

The export-licensing process

Before the reforms of 1989, the following rules applied: for items on the export-control lists, lists A–D in Annex AL of the Foreign Trade Regulation, pursuant to the Foreign Trade Act – a valid licence was needed. The licence was granted by the export-licensing office of the Federal Office for Economics (BAW). Minor licences were granted by BAW on its own. For major exports, an inter-agency decision process under the chairmanship of the BMWi took place. AA, BMFT (for technical expertise) and BMWi participated. Decisions had to be made unanimously (in reality, the AA protested repeatedly but had to retreat before the combined expertise of BMWi and BMFT). On the basis of this decision, BAW would grant or deny the licence.

For non-listed items, BAW would either decide on its own or ask BMWi what to do. BMWi was the absolute arbiter. The Foreign Office could protest – as in the case of the tritium extraction facility – but it had no veto. If BMWi decided no licence was needed, the applying company received a 'negative certificate', stating that the export was not subject to licensing.

Items in transit were subject to licence if German customs had dutifully checked their arrival. The above procedures would then apply. Transit trade transactions (trade by German companies outside of FRG territory) were not subject to licensing.

The 1988–9 reforms have considerably strengthened the role of the Foreign Office. A 1988 decree created a new instrument, a 'sensitive country list'. All major exports, even ostensibly non-nuclear ones, to countries on this list are now subject to inter-agency decision-making, even if the items in question are not explicitly listed. Moreover, all listed nuclear exports to countries outside the EC and the United States must be submitted to the AA.

The implementation of export policy

In the past, the enforcement of export policy was even more deficient than its concepts and legal instruments. The BAW, on paper the main agency for export controls, was notoriously understaffed in the critical nuclear sector. The desk office responsible for nuclear licensing comprised only seven civil servants of whom no more than three were technical experts. It also had to cope with non-ferrous metal exports, a couple of raw materials and advising on chemical arms control and COCOM rules. In the central investigative body, the Customs

Criminal Office, two technical experts could devote only part of their time to nuclear issues. In such a system, controls simply did not work satisfactorily. With more than 100,000 export licence applications in the nuclear field alone, the staff were not able to process them properly. Erroneous filing of documents, the failure to check minor cases of licence abuse and the practice of approaching a suspect firm directly before any on-site investigation (thereby providing a useful warning) all point to a hopelessly overworked and understaffed system.

In addition, the system suffered from an appalling lack of investigative capacity. The Foreign Trade Investigation, the most powerful instrument in the hands of investigators, permits the complete search of documents and questioning of personnel of companies involved in foreign economic exchanges. In practice, this instrument is only applied if a massive initial suspicion already exists. Even the accumulation of briefings and unofficial reports submitted by foreign intelligence services, has in many cases not stimulated a Foreign Trade Investigation since the BMWi feared the disturbance of the orderly operations of the company in question.

The 1989 reforms have led to an unprecedented strengthening of the export-control agencies. In fiscal years 1989 and 1990, more than 200 new positions were set to be created for export-control purposes in the Foreign Office, the Finance Ministry, the Federal Criminal Office and the BMWi. An overwhelming number of those new positions were to be located in the BAW. An extensive system of data collection and exchange between the export control and investigative agencies, based on modern data processing equipment, has been planned. This boost is quite remarkable in a period when government is trying to trim rather than to expand the Federal budget.[44]

In the BAW, what was hitherto a simple desk has become a major department for chemistry, biotechnology and nuclear technology (Dept. VI C) with a total of five desk offices. The offices are responsible for chemicals, biological substances and other materials; chemical and biotechnical plant and equipment; nuclear materials, plant and equipment and the data register for the nuclear, chemical and biological industry. The desks have been better staffed and technically equipped. Within the other sections of main department VI (export controls), the desks VI A3 (information analysis), VI A4 (data systems, data processing and end control), VI D2 (International Import Certificates, important for transit reviews) and VI D3 (data exchange and cooperation with customs and investigative agencies) have also been strengthened. While this is no guarantee of success, the prerequisites for successful export control are now in place.[45]

Conclusion

By sheer coincidence the worst export scandals in West German history, the unification of the country and a sea change in the German attitudes towards technology transfer occurred at exactly the moment when the country assumed new and greater responsibilities. It is obvious from the changes in law, regulation, administration and attitudes at the highest levels of government that by now there is far greater awareness of the potentially dangerous consequences of German economic activities abroad. The considerable concern of its neighbours about what kind of state the new Germany will be has brought home the need to correct attitudes towards export control in order to prevent further and possibly irreversible damage to Germany's reputation. It has been understood that if Germany wishes to keep its self-image of a peaceful and benevolent 'trading state', it must avoid the appearance of a 'merchant of death'. On the narrower plane of economic interest, there is also fear that a continuation of the series of scandals might lead to retaliation from important importers and thereby hurt German export interests.

Whether this new attitude will prevail is not yet entirely clear. The Foreign Office, the Office of the Chancellor, and the top echelons of the Ministry of Economics have all understood and fostered the change. It is particularly remarkable that the minister of economics declared that 'we must today require more control, even when bureaucratisation means a considerable burden for all participants in a country with such a large foreign trade as ours' and requested that in 'sensitive areas' 'a Federal Office *for* Economics must become a Federal Office *against* the Economy'.[46]

Yet in the rank and file of the bureaucracies one wonders whether the new attitude has taken root. Even during the NPT review conference, some in the bureaucracy tried to backtrack on the new policy of full-scope safeguards. Such resistance could be revived when the immediate attention of the top leadership is diverted.

In Parliament, the opposition may keep a more vigilant eye on ongoing export projects and the administration's licensing policies than in the past. It must be noted though, that in the parties of the governing coalition, there was a serious rearguard attempt by members of the Economics and Research Committees to weaken the legislation drafted by the executive.[47] It took the determined commitment of the foreign minister, and the stiff resistance of the Bundesrat, (the second chamber, where the SPD briefly had a majority) to keep the legislation by and large intact.

The coalition deputies were mainly reacting to suggestions from industry and from the major research establishments. Industry is somewhat ambivalent about the changes. On the one hand, it understands the danger to its position at home and abroad posed by an endless series of scandals, and the leading associations must be credited for enhanced efforts to advise their members on avoiding ambiguous deals. On the other hand, the associations opposed important aspects of the new legislation, including the punishment of 'neglect' (or responsibility for acts of omission) and for activities abroad, the broader definition of technology as enacted in February 1989 and the new authority of the export-control agencies to collect a wide variety of industrial data.[48] Given the close relation between the associations and the controlling agencies, much depends on whether industry adapts to the new rules or continues its opposition.

The greatest hope for the stabilisation of the new policy is self-interest. After Germany has enacted legislation that goes beyond what most of its economic partners apply today, there is a keen interest in persuading them to follow suit. With regard to the single European market in 1992, the necessity to agree on common guidelines is most acute. In this process, even those agencies that have been opposed so far to the new policy are forced to defend it vigorously in order to protect the interests of their traditional clients. This coincidence of economic interest and the enhanced role of Germany in foreign affairs, offers the best prospect that future policy on technology transfer will match the responsibility accruing to the new unified state.

Notes

1. The definition applied here is broader than the one used in the United States Export Administration Act that defines technology as 'information of any kind that can be used or adapted for use in the design, production, manufacture, utilization or reconstruction of articles or materials. The data may take a tangible form such as a model, prototype, blueprint or an operating manual . . . or they may take an intangible form such as a technical service' C.F.R., Sec. 379.1(a); cf. also United Nations Centre on Transnational Corporations, *Transnational Corporations in World Development*, Third Survey, New York, 1983, p.163.

2. For the following discussion consult S. Stilwell, *Technology Transfer and National Security: A Bibliography of Journal Articles*, CSIA, Harvard University Working Papers 89–5, 1989; Beate Kohler-Koch (ed.), *Technik und Internationale Politik*, Baden-Baden, Nomos Verlagsgesellschaft, 1986, Part III.

3. Ole Börnsen, Hans H. Glismann and Ernst-Jürgen Horn, *'Der Technologietransfer zwischen den USA und der Bundesrepublik'*, Tübingen, Mohr, 1985, pp.31–2.

4. Ole Börnsen, Hans H. Glismann and Ernst-Jürgen Horn, *Der Technologietransfer zwischen den USA und der Bundesrepublik*, Tübingen, Mohr, 1985, p.20.

5. *Statistisches Handbuch für den Maschinenbau*, Ausgabe, 1990.

6. Hans-Peter Schwarz, *Die gezähmten Deutschen. Von der Machtbesessenheit zur Machtvergessenheit*, Stuttgart, DVA 1985; Reinhard Rode, Handelsstaat oder Republik für Todeskrämer? Frankfurt-am-Main, HSFK, Friedensforschung Aktuell 22, 1989.

7. 110. Session of the 2. Investigative Committee, December 7 1989.

8. Details have been uncovered by the two Investigative Committees: for example Mark Hibbs, 'U.S. Repeatedly Warned Germany on Nuclear Exports to Pakistan', *Nuclear Fuel*, 6 March 1989.

9. Statement before Investigative Committee 2, 22 June 1989.

10. C.f. Harald Müller, *After the Scandals. German Non-proliferation Policy*. Frankfurt, PRIF Report No. 9.

11. Ibid.

12. Häjo Weber, 'Technolkorporatismus – Die Steuerung des technologischen Wandels durch Staat, Wirtschaftsverbände und Gewerkschaften' in Hans-Herman Hartwich (ed.), *Politik und die Macht der Technik*, Opladen, Westdeutscher Verlag, 1986.

13. Wolfgang Krieger, *Technologiepolitik der Bundesrepublik Deutschland*, SWP-AP 2914, Ebenhausen, Stiftung Wissenschaft und Politik 1989, pp.19–30.

14. Cf. Otto Keck, *Der naive Souverän. Über das Verhalten von Staat und Industrie in der Grosstechnik*, Berlin, Dunker and Humblot, 1984; Derek J. Price, *Little Science, Big Science. von der Studierstube zur Grossforschung*, Frankfurt, Campus, 1974.

15. Krieger, pp.21–35.

16. Status und Perspektiven der Grossforschungseinrichtungen, Drucksache des Deutschen Bundestages 10/1327, 16 April 1984.

17. Kurt Hornschild and Gerhard Neckermann, *die deutsche Luft- und Raumfahrtindustrie*. Stand und Perspektiven. Frankfurt and New York, Campus, 1988, pp.100–19.

18. Dieter von Würzen, 'Kapitalanlagegarantien des Bundes zur Förderung des Technologietransfers' in *Gesellschaft zur Förderung des Schutzes von Auslandsinvestitionen* (ed.); *Auslandsinvestitionen und Technologiestransfer. Der Schutz immaterieller Rechte*, 1986 pp.71–81.

19. For the most comprehensive account available, see Egmont R. Koch, *Grenzenlose Geschäfte. Organisierte Wirtschaftskriminalität in Europa*, Munich, Knesebeck und Schüler, 1987 and Holger Koppe and Egmont R. Koch, *Bombengeschäfte. Tödliche Waffen für die Dritte Welt*, Munich, Knesebeck und Schüler, 1990.

20. Based on hearings before the Special Investigative Committee 2, 26 October– 7 December 1989, and its final report; Deutscher Bundestag, 11. Wahlperiode, Beschluss-

empfehlung und Bericht des 2: Untersuchungsausschusses nach Art. 44 des Grundgesetzes, Drucksache 11/7800, Bonn, 1990; Koppe and Koch 1990, pp.356–7.
21. Mark Hibbs, 'Collor Moving to End Influence of Military in Nuclear Program', *Nucleonics Week*, 4 October 1990, pp.6–7.
22. *Spiegel* 27/1990, pp.64–7.
23. *Spiegel*, 25/1990, pp.22–4.
24. Cf. statement of SPD Deputy Gansel, *Das Parlament*, no. 10, March 3 1989, p.9.
25. Deutscher Bundestag, 11. Wahlperiode, Drucksache 11/3995, 15 February 1989. Bericht der Bundesregierung an den Deutschen Bundestag über eine mögliche Beteiligung deutscher Firmen an einer C-Waffen-Produktion in Libyen.
26. *Spiegel* 37/ 1990, pp.112–18; Koppe and Koch 1990, pp.230–42.
27. Koppe and Koch, 1990, pp.223–36; 248–50.
28. *Spiegel* 28/ 1990, pp.54–56.
29. *Spiegel* 39/ 1990, pp.32–3; Koppe and Koch, 1990, pp.293–335.
30. *Spiegel* 37/ 1990, pp.112–18.
31. *Spiegel* 42/ 1990, pp.148–9.
32. *Spiegel* 40/ 1990, p.101; Koppe and Koch, 1990. pp.243–8.
33. *Spiegel* 39/ 1990, pp.32–3; Koppe and Koch, 1990, pp.336–43.
34. Ausschuss für Wirtschaft des Deutschen Bundestages, Drucksache 444/11, 6 September 1989.
35. *Bundesgesetzblatt*, Teil I, 36/27. July 1990, pp.1457–61.
36. *Zeitschrift für Rechtspolitik*, Vol. 25, No. 4, April 1992, p.154.
37. Deutscher Bundestag. 11. Wahlperiode, Drucksache 11/3995, 15 February 1989; *Bericht der Bundesregierung*, p.3.
38. Cf. Harald Müller, *After the Scandals. West German Non-proliferation Policy*, PRIF Report No. 9, Frankfurt, PRIF, 1990, pp.34–45.
39. *Bundesgesetzblatt*, Teil I, No. 9, 7 March 1989, p.341.
40. Deutscher Bundestag Drucksache 11/5045; Bundesrat Drucksache 423/89.
41. Deutscher Bundestag Drucksache 11/5341, 5 October 1989.
42. Deutscher Bundestag Drucksachen 11/7538 and 7539, 4 July 1990.
43. Statement by the Minister of Foreign Affairs of the Federal Republic of Germany to the Fourth Review Conference of the Nuclear Nonproliferation Treaty in Geneva, 20 August–September 14.
44. Deutscher Bundestag Drucksache 11/4350.
45. Information BAW, Press and Public Information Office, January 1990.
46. Statement before Investigative Committee 2, 22 June 1989.
47. Cf. Deutscher Bundestag Drucksachen 11/7219 and 7221.
48. Cf. Deutscher Bundestag, Ausschuss für Wirtschaft Drucksache, 11/4609.

10 Muddling through mined territory: German foreign policy-making and the Middle East

Thomas Risse-Kappen

Introduction[1]

When the coalition forces drove Iraqi troops out of Kuwait under the leadership of the United States and legitimised by UN resolutions, the two largest economic powers in the world after the United States — Japan and the newly united Germany — did not contribute troops. Both pledged to pay billions of dollars to support the coalition effort. But when Japanese Prime Minister Kaifu tried to send some ships on a non-military mission to the Gulf, he ran into fierce domestic opposition. When the Bonn government sent a couple of Alpha jets to Turkey to show solidarity with a NATO ally bordering Iraq, opposition parties criticised the decision as provocative, even though the aircraft were not even able to reach Iraq from where they were based. At the same time, Germany was heavily attacked by some of its neighbours for not living up to its global responsibilities; only half a year earlier, the same allies had expressed fears that the united Germany might assume a hegemonic role in the new Europe.

Bonn's reluctance to play a more active political and military role in the Middle East, comparable to that of Great Britain and France, should have come as no surprise to anybody who has followed German policy toward the region in the past. For the last forty years, the Federal Republic of Germany has generally kept a low profile. Whenever the Bonn government tried to change this and sought to take an active stance in one of the region's numerous conflicts, it experienced trouble domestically and internationally. Examples include Chancellor Erhard's decision in 1965 to assume diplomatic relations with Israel, thereby hampering Bonn's relations with the Arab world for quite some time, and Chancellor Schmidt's attempt in 1980–2 to sell tanks to Saudi-Arabia which was prevented by a domestic coalition of pro-Israeli and anti-arms export groups.

Conventional wisdom holds that the German attitude is to be explained by the specific dilemmas of Bonn's Middle East policy: the legacy of the Nazi past requiring a 'special relationship' with Israel but economic interests in the Arab world as a main supplier of oil as well as a primary export market.[2] While these contradictory goals and interests prevent the Federal Republic from taking a one-sided stance in the Middle East, the dilemmas as such cannot account for the low profile.

To understand why Bonn's conflicting goals towards the Middle East have resulted in a pattern of rather reactive and low-key policies, one has to look beyond the particular issue-area and examine the German foreign policy-making process and its domestic environment. The Federal Republic's foreign policy is driven by dual needs: pursuing goals through cooperation in international institutions and domestic consensus-building when it comes to issue-areas of high public salience. I will argue that the general features of the German foreign policy-making process, combined with the specific dilemmas which the country faces in the Middle East, can explain the rather passive policy pursued by the FRG.

The first part of this chapter deals with the West German foreign-policy-making process in general. I will then look at the political institutions, societal forces and consensus-building processes pertaining specifically to Bonn's Middle Eastern policy and discuss three examples. I will conclude with suggestions concerning future developments.

Germany as a post-nation state: foreign policy-making in the Federal Republic[3]

The legacies of the past

The foreign policy of the Federal Republic cannot be explained without taking the legacy of the past – from Prussian militarism to the Nazi crimes – into account. This is obvious for the country's Middle Eastern policy, but it also applies to the management of foreign affairs in general. Hypernationalism and power-hungry aggression have driven Germany and the rest of the world into catastrophe twice during this century. The lessons of Auschwitz have neither been lost on the country's neighbours in Europe nor on the Germans themselves. As a result, the Federal Republic's foreign policy can be described as the search for compatibility with the international environment while, at the same time, maintaining a sufficient degree of domestic consensus in support of these policies.[4]

First, there is an 'international alert squad' closely watching every move of Bonn's (and future Berlin's) foreign policy for signs that the country is once again returning to an assertive and aggressive foreign policy. The victims and the children of victims of the German Reich constantly remind the country that it should not forget its past and never again return to a policy which threatens the peace in Europe and in the world. This international alertness became obvious again during the process of German unification, but it has accompanied the Federal Republic throughout its history. West German rearmament in the 1950s, for example, only became acceptable to its European neighbours (in particular France) when Bonn agreed to constraints on its defence policy. Chancellor Brandt's *Ostpolitik* in the late 1960s and 1970s raised the suspicion among many Europeans that another axis between Germany and Russia was in the making. Again, Bonn had to give reassurances, particularly in terms of strengthening and enlarging the European Community (EC). In sum and for good reasons, the international community does not allow the Federal Republic to conduct its foreign policy like any other medium-sized power, but expects it instead to live up to higher standards of international cooperation.

Second but no less important, the norms of a 'post-national' foreign policy – an orientation toward international policy-coordination and cooperation – have been internalized by the West Germans themselves. While they are still a long way from living up to the responsibilities resulting from their past, nationalism does not seem to be held in high esteem. National consciousness is low compared with most other European nations, while international cooperation is among the highest-ranking foreign policy goals shared by public opinion as well as social and political groups. Most West Germans support a foreign policy which pursues its goals through cooperation with other nations, either bilaterally or via international institutions such as NATO, the EC and the Conference for Security and Cooperation in Europe (CSCE).[5] In 1990, for example, nationalist feelings were not so much provoked by the prospect of German unification, but by victory in the soccer World Cup. When Chancellor Kohl returned from Moscow in July 1990 having won Soviet acceptance of a united Germany's membership in NATO, he reported to the press in Bonn as if he was just coming back from a business trip to Brussels to negotiate the EC's agricultural policy. In sum, there is not much domestic support for a reassertive foreign policy.[6]

Finally, the German domestic structure reinforces these trends. After World War II, political institutions were created with built-in checks and balances to prevent a re-emergence of hypernationalism.

International cooperation and domestic consensus: the foreign-policy-making structure

Several constitutional provisions influenced by the legacy of the past support a foreign policy orientated toward international cooperation. Article 26 of the Basic Law (*Grundgesetz*), for example, explicitly forbids activities which might disturb international peace, in particular military aggression. It is paralleled by Article 87a which stipulates that the German armed forces may only be used for defensive purposes. According to Article 24.1, the parliament is free to transfer jurisdictional powers to international institutions, while international law is part of the national law and supercedes it in case of tension between the two (Article 25).

West German foreign policy over the last forty years has mirrored the internationalist orientation of the constitution.[7] The conduct of external affairs can be described as 'post-national' in the sense that traditional notions of sovereignty no longer apply. For example, the army became firmly integrated into NATO; as a result, the FRG's defence policy is being decided through policy coordination in Brussels, not in Bonn. The Western Alliance contains German military power even in the post-cold war era. A similar pattern applies to economic policy; the European Community makes sure that the country's economic power does not get out of control.

The orientation toward international cooperation and a 'low-key' attitude in traditional power terms is brought about by a policy-making structure which requires a fair amount of domestic consensus, at least the support of the major players. Furthermore, a secular trend towards the democratisation of foreign policy can be observed over the last ten to fifteen years which further increased the needs for coalition-building regarding major decisions. A closer look at the institutions and processes involved in foreign-policy decision-making reveals a structure of *democratic corporatism*, that is the informal coordination of conflicting objectives through continuous bargaining among state bureaucracies, political parties and interest groups.[8]

The most important institution responsible for the daily conduct of external affairs is, of course, the Foreign Office. Hans-Dietrich Genscher, Foreign Minister 1974–1992, managed to streamline the institution behind the foreign policy he represents – integration into the West and cooperation with the East during the cold war; the creation of a new European security order in the new era. He represented, thus, a conceptual framework for the professionalism of diplomats trained in the tradition of the German civil service.

The second most important institution in German foreign policy is the Chancellerie, since, according to the constitution, the Chancellor determines the general guidelines of policy (*Richtlinienkompetenz*). However, owing to a lack of resources, the Chancellor's foreign policy adviser has never been in a position similar to the National Security Advisor in the United States. On the other hand, West German chancellors from Konrad Adenauer to Willy Brandt, Helmut Schmidt and Helmut Kohl have generally expressed great interest in foreign affairs. While Adenauer and Brandt used to get involved in details of foreign policy and sometimes reduced the Foreign Office to an agency executing the Chancellor's decisions, Helmut Schmidt and Helmut Kohl have at least taken care of the important issues.[9] Other agencies of the Federal Government involved in the conduct of external affairs are the Ministry of Defence (MOD) in charge of national security issues, the Ministry of Economics regarding foreign economic policy and the Ministry of Economic Cooperation concerning relations to the Third World.

However, a mere description of the governmental institutions involved in the execution of foreign policy only gives half of the picture. It is as important to look at the mechanisms of coalition governments. With the exception of the 1957–61 period, no single party has enjoyed an absolute majority in parliament (Bundestag). As a result, coalition governments with their inherent tendency of continuous bargaining to work out policy compromises are the rule in Bonn and will continue to be in Berlin. Furthermore, Germany is a federal state in which elections take place several times a year at the national, state or local level. Thus, a permanent election campaign is underway, since national issues sometimes dominate even local elections. This adds further to the dominance of party politics.

Party politics seems to supercede the bureaucratic politics of government agencies fighting against each other, at least when the issues become subject to public scrutiny. Since the mid-1960s, for example, the chancellor and the defence minister have belonged to the same party, while the foreign minister has been a member of the junior coalition partner, since 1969 the Free Democratic Party (FDP). As a result, the positions of these ministries have been less determined by their respective bureaucratic role in the decision-making process; more important has been the party affiliation of the respective minister. For example, during the Social–Liberal government (1969–82), the FDP-led Foreign Office used to be more conservative than the Ministry of Defence led by a Social Democrat. With the change in government from Helmut Schmidt to Helmut Kohl in 1982, a role reversal took place. Since then, the MOD, now in the hands of the Christian Democrats, has been playing the conservative role, while Genscher's Foreign Office moved in a more liberal direction. A striking example was the West German policy regarding Intermediate-Range

Nuclear Forces (INF). When, in 1978–9, NATO's famous dual-track decision was in the making, it was the MOD and Chancellor Schmidt who pushed for a credible arms control offer against a hesitating Foreign Office. From 1983 on, however, Hans-Dietrich Genscher, now in a coalition with the Christian Democratic Party (CDU–CSU), became the leading arms control advocate and made 'Genscherism' the catch-word for an increasingly pro-*détente* attitude.[10]

Thus, the description of the Federal Republic of Germany as a 'party democracy' extends into foreign affairs, particularly since their salience as an issue has increased over the years.[11] The notion of 'democratic corporatism' applies, since the parties are the most important institutions in the policy network linking the German state to society. As mass integration parties, they are crucial to the selection and channelling of societal demands into the political system. Once the issue in question has become politicised, decision-making can essentially be described as bargaining and coalition-building among party elites. While the parliamentary institutions only play a minor role in foreign policy owing to the stable majority usually enjoyed by the governing coalition,[12] major governmental decisions in foreign and national security affairs generally require the consensus of the coalition parties.

Public opinion, interest groups and societal organisations such as the business community, trade unions and churches usually work through the party system to raise their demands and objections concerning specific policies. The system has proved to be comparatively open to societal demands and has even adapted to the concerns of non-established public interest groups such as environmental initiatives and peace movements.[13] Direct bargaining between special interest groups and government bureaucracies mostly takes place in cases of low public salience. Once issues become politicised and subject to public scrutiny by the media, however, the primacy of the party system takes over. The most recent arms export scandals have been cases in point.

As a general trend, public interest in and scrutiny of foreign affairs have increased over time. Konrad Adenauer was able to push through his policy of integration into Western economic and military institutions without caring much about domestic and societal consensus. Willy Brandt's *Ostpolitik* almost collapsed in 1972 because of a lack of domestic support. On the other hand, Helmut Schmidt and even more so Helmut Kohl had to make sure that their foreign policies were supported by key players in their respective parties, as well as by important societal organisations such as business, trade unions and the churches. As a result, German foreign policy has been democratised over the years.

In sum, the German state institutions, the political culture, and public attitudes alike emphasise consensus-building. Societal polarisation is generally regarded with dismay, in particular, as compared with countries such as France and Great Britain. The consensus-orientated domestic structure corresponds with orientations toward international cooperation as described above. It is not just coincidence that the catchword for the West German domestic political model is '*Sozialpartnerschaft*' (social partnership as a class compromise between business and labour), while many Germans describe their preferred state of international affairs as *Sicherheitspartnerschaft* (security partnership). However, this peculiar domestic structure seems to be less suited to deal with situations and regions in the world which are inherently conflictual. The Middle Eastern policy of the Federal Republic is a case in point.

Dealing with incompatibilities: foreign-policy decision-making and the Middle East

Political institutions, societal factors and the policy network

A huge bureaucracy takes care of the daily conduct of German policy towards the Middle East. Apart from the Chancellerie about fifteen working units of the Foreign Office are directly or indirectly involved.[14] First, there is the commissioner for Near and Middle Eastern policy, with two working units in one of the political departments. Second, working units in the economic department take care of international energy policy, arms exports, and nuclear non-proliferation issues. Third, the European Community (EC) desk coordinates the German input into the European Political Cooperation (EPC) in charge of the EC's Middle Eastern policy. Last but not least, the department for foreign cultural policy is involved in the organisation of the many transnational and transsocietal relations between Germany and the Middle East, in particular Israel.

Several authors have suggested that the Foreign Office usually takes a more pro-Arab stance than other federal agencies, in particular the Chancellerie, and that its diplomats have always been concerned that Bonn's special relations with Israel might jeopardise the country's larger (economic) interests in the Middle East.[15] During the 1950s, for example, the ambassadors in Arab countries helped to prevent Bonn assuming diplomatic relations with Israel. When Chancellor Erhard decided in favour of formal relations with Israel in 1965, Foreign Minister Schröder was adamantly opposed. During the 1970s, Foreign Ministers Scheel and Genscher orchestrated Bonn's policy of 'even-handedness' (*Ausgewogenheit*) and neutrality in the Arab-Israeli conflict, while Chancellor Brandt especially did not hide his feelings in favour of his friends in Tel Aviv.

However, as argued above, Bonn's foreign-policy-making process is not just determined by the bureaucratic roles of the various agencies involved. Party politics is at least as important, especially when it comes to issues of greater public salience. Indeed, during the 1967 June war, when SPD Chairman Willy Brandt was in charge of the Foreign Office, Bonn came out as sympathetic toward Israel, despite official neutrality.[16] The subsequent foreign ministers, Scheel and Genscher, have both been members of the FDP which is closer to business interests and, thus, usually takes a slightly more pro-Arab stance than CDU-CSU and SPD.

While the Foreign Office coordinates the political aspects of German relations with the region, the Ministry of Economics is responsible for the foreign economic policy, in particular the export licensing process as it relates to arms sales. The Ministry of Defence is involved in all decisions concerning national security, in particular, 'out-of-area' issues. Finally, the Ministry for Economic Cooperation has to be mentioned as responsible for developmental aid.

A survey of the political institutions with decision-making power regarding German Middle Eastern policy has to include the EPC. At least the general guidelines of the Federal Republic's approach to the region and to the Arab-Israeli conflict in particular, are no longer decided solely in Bonn but through policy coordination within the European Community. The EPC was set up in the early 1970s with the specific objective of coordinating the policies of the EC member states in two issue-areas, the Middle East and the Conference for

Security and Cooperation in Europe (CSCE, widely known as the 'Helsinki Process').[17]

However, the frequently quoted weakness and slowness of common European responses toward crises in the Middle East have a lot to do with the poor institutionalisation of the EPC. Since the EC members have not been prepared, so far, to give up sovereignty in foreign-policy matters other than those directly involving economic issues, the EPC has been less organised than, for example, the European Commission. The daily business is coordinated by EPC 'desks' in the various foreign ministries, while the directors of political affairs in the twelve foreign offices meet regularly to prepare policy statements to be issued by their ministers or the European Council of the Heads of State and Governments. Since 1981, however, at least a 'crisis procedure' has been set up to permit the EPC to convene within forty-eight hours. One of the consequences of the poor performance of the EPC during the coalition war against Iraq has been to strengthen its institutions to coordinate foreign policies. The first effects became visible when the EC tried to mediate in Yugoslavia and when it quickly reacted to the failed coup attempt in Moscow in August 1991. The political process underway as a result of the Single European Act will further institutionalise the coordination of the EC members' foreign policies.

From the perspective of the German government, the EPC serves two purposes, one concerning its overall foreign policy, the other directly related to the Middle East. First, the establishment of the EPC was actively promoted by the Federal Republic as part of its general support for international cooperation, supranational institution-building and European integration. Thus, the EPC was considered as a first, albeit limited, step toward a common European foreign policy. Second, the EPC declarations on the Middle East served as a convenient cover for German efforts to square the circle between its special relationship with Israel and its economic interests in the region. Policy coordination within the EPC allowed West Germany to continue its low-key approach to the Arab–Israeli conflict and to maintain its policy of neutrality and 'even-handedness' towards both sides, particularly since the 1973 October war.[18] At the same time, however, the Federal government tried to keep EPC declarations as much as possible in line with American policy toward the Middle East in order to avoid the impression that Western Europe and the United States pursued two different approaches. When Israel invaded Lebanon in June 1982, for example, the Federal Republic prevented the EPC from issuing a call for far-reaching sanctions against Israel as recommended by France.[19]

The political institutions carrying out German policy toward the Middle East do not act in a societal vacuum, though. The low-key attitude toward the Arab–Israeli conflict, the Palestinian issue, inner-Arab tensions and NATO's 'out-of-area' crises is, at least partly, due to the fact that the government is constantly exposed to diverging societal demands. The Middle East conundrum is probably the third most salient foreign affairs issue in the political debate, next to East–West and West–West relations.

First, there is a considerable pro-Israeli constituency in west German society mainly motivated by the conviction that, given the legacy of Auschwitz, the Germans are the last people in the world to tell the Jewish state how to behave. Far from unanimously supporting Israel's policy, these groups nevertheless maintain that Germany should restrain itself when commenting on Middle Eastern problems. There is a network of transnational relations with Israel.[20]

Two of the most important societal organisations, the Christian churches and the trade unions, can basically be counted in this camp. The Protestant churches in particular have been active in promoting an honest analysis of the German past and in pursuing a Christian–Jewish dialogue in this context. The Federation of German Trade Unions (Deutscher Gewerkschaftsbund) maintains close relations to Israel's Histradut with an unusually high degree of institutionalisation. More than sixty West German towns and cities are twinned with communities in Israel. Youth exchanges between Israel and the Federal Republic rank second to German–French contacts, both in numbers and in subsidies by the Federal government. These trans-societal alliances do not simply support any policy move of the Israeli government. In fact, while the German–Israeli Society is basically endorsing Israel's policy in the Middle East conflict, the Working Group for Peace in the Near East (Arbeitskreis für Frieden im Nahen Osten) takes a more balanced view. In general, however, the transnational German–Israeli groups exert some veto power over the Federal government's Middle East policy.

Second, compared to the extensive transnational relations between the German and Israeli societies, contacts with the Arab world are rather limited. The German–Arab Association headed by the FDP politician Möllemann cannot match the German–Israeli Society in terms of members or political influence. However, the weak trans-societal relations with Arab countries are more than balanced by considerable German business interests in the region, particularly in the oil-producing countries.[21] The 'Near and Middle East Association' (Nah- und Mittel-ost-Verein) serves as a clearing house between the West German business community and Arab countries, while the Federation of German Industry (Bundesverband der deutschen Industrie), as business's main lobbying organisation, promotes trade with the Middle East based on a favourable political climate. Given the country's dependence on foreign energy resources and the considerable investment of German companies in the Arab world, the economic relations with the Middle East weigh heavily on policy decisions, even when no explicit demands are raised by the business community. Indeed, German industry usually keeps a low profile in policy debates. It normally prefers to lobby the relevant government agencies directly and expresses its views publicly only when German policy seems to threaten vital business interests. Speaking out is no guarantee, though, that the demands of the business community are successful in shaping German policies.

In sum, the societal basis of German Middle East policy reflects the country's dilemma between the special responsibility toward Israel and vital economic interests in the Arab countries. There is no societal consensus on Middle Eastern policy other than a general preference for a low-key attitude as far as the Israeli–Arab conflict is concerned and for friendly relations to as many countries in the region as possible. It comes as no surprise, therefore, that the main policy network linking society to the political system in Germany, the party system, is equally split on the issue.

Interestingly enough, the traditional division in German politics between left and right does not matter very much when it comes to Middle Eastern affairs.[22] This again became apparent during the war in the Gulf. Attitudes cut not only across party affiliation, but also across the usual divisions *within* the parties. As a result, the SPD's left wing is typically as divided on the Arab-Israeli conflict as the CDU/CSU's right wing and strange coalitions regularly occur across party lines. This means, of course, that consensus-building in favour of an active policy in the region in one way or the other, is rather difficult.

To begin with, support for Israel can be found in all parties represented in the Bundestag. The German-Israeli Parliamentary Association has more members than any of the other parliamentary friendship groups with foreign countries. In June 1982, for example, a cross-party coalition stopped the Bundestag from adopting a resolution which was considered to be too critical of the Israeli invasion of Lebanon.[23] The parties on the left have traditionally advocated that the lessons of the German past should not be forgotten and that, therefore, the Federal Republic should be very sensitive in its dealings with the Middle East. In the 1950s, for example, the Social Democratic Party was the only party that unanimously endorsed the reparation treaty with Israel. The SPD – through the Socialist International – is also the only German party with special ties to a political grouping in Israel, the Labour party, a relationship long backed by the personal friendship between former chairman Brandt and Shimon Peres. These transnational ties were one of the reasons why the Social Democrats became increasingly critical of Israel's policy after Labour lost power in the late 1970s.

However, no German party simply endorses Israeli policy come what may. The CDU–CSU has been basically divided between pro-Israeli politicians who are conscious of the German past and those representing economic constituencies. Finally, there used to be a minority of conservative politicians who identified with the Palestinian cause for reasons to do with *Deutschlandpolitik* and the right of self-determination. The FDP's comparatively more pro-Arab stance has nothing to do with special feelings toward these countries but results from the close relationship between the party and business interests. On the left, the issue is particularly painful for the SPD and the Greens. On the one hand, there is a group motivated by special links with Israel or a consciousness regarding the legacy of Auschwitz or both. On the other hand, left anti-militarism and support for the peaceful resolution of international conflicts has put most Social Democrats at odds with the policies of Prime Ministers Begin and Shamir. Moreover, many left-wing intellectuals of the so-called 1968 generation who are now prominent SPD politicians, used to sympathise with the Palestinian cause. However, their anti-militarist beliefs prevent them from joining the business community in support of arms exports to Arab countries or from promoting active German military involvement in the Gulf.

To conclude, the German policy network channelling societal demands into the political system is as divided as the society itself between conflicting goals regarding Middle Eastern policy. Since the divisions cut across party lines, the same conflicts repeat themselves frequently no matter which party is in power. The mechanisms of democratic corporatism and of coalition governments further complicate consensus-building. Given the conundrum of conflicting interests and demands permeating both society and the parties, 'veto coalitions' preventing certain policies are far more common than 'support coalitions' able to push through certain actions. The result has been the well-known German low-key approach toward the Middle East. Three examples underline this analysis.

Example 1: Germany and crises in the Middle East

The Federal Republic's policy of neutrality in the Israeli–Arab conflict came under severe stress during the 1973 October war when Israel, at first, seemed to lose militarily and, at the same time, Arab countries threatened an oil embargo against those supporting the Jewish state.[24] At first, the division of labour between SPD Chancellor Brandt who publicly supported Israel, and the FDP Foreign Minister Scheel who promoted the policy of 'even-handedness' and a common approach within the EPC, seemed to work. On the one hand, Bonn which had not been consulted tried to ignore American arms shipments to Israel via a Northern German port during the first two weeks of the war. On the other hand, and under increasing Arab pressure, the Federal Republic supported the EPC efforts to prevent an oil embargo which culminated in the declaration of 6 November 1973. This called, among other things, for the Israeli withdrawal from the occupied territories and the recognition of the legitimate rights of the Palestinians.[25] This double-edged policy collapsed when the press disclosed the American use of the port at Bremerhaven to resupply Israel which was particularly embarrassing since no other European state was allowing the United States to use its airspace at the time. Now the Foreign Office took over and prohibited any further delivery of weapons to Israel from West German territory. Brandt disclosed later that the shipments would probably not have been halted, had the United States used one of the smaller German ports and had the ships not flown the Israeli flag.[26] Bonn's decision caused a major conflict with the United States as well as a crisis in West German–Israeli relations. The EPC declaration was used to cover the factual policy shift from implicitly supporting Israel to endorsing the Arab viewpoint.

While Bonn's policy during the October war was basically thrashed out between the Chancellerie and the Foreign Office without much public involvement, the next Middle East crisis in which the Federal Republic had to take a stance occurred in the middle of the 1980 election campaign. This time, the German constitution served as the excuse to continue the low-profile attitude. The superpower relationship had deteriorated in the aftermath of the Soviet intervention in Afghanistan and, in addition to that, President Carter was locked in the Iran hostage crisis. As a result, the European allies came under increasing pressure to contribute military forces to the Gulf in order to secure the Western oil supply against either Soviet or Iranian intrusion.[27] In Bonn, the problem immediately became an issue in the election campaign with the CDU–CSU originally favouring the deployment of West German forces in the Middle East and the SPD vehemently opposing it. The military, however, were reluctant to commit Bundeswehr troops to the Gulf. The Foreign Office as well as the Defence Ministry questioned the constitutionality of such an employment.

The above-mentioned Article 87a of the Basic Law stipulating the defensive purpose of the German armed forces was interpreted as preventing any military involvement in conflicts outside the territory covered by the North Atlantic Treaty. Interestingly enough, Article 87a does not say anything about the territorial scope of the defence. Thus, the constitutional interpretation was not just about legal issues; it was also motivated by political interests. The restrictive interpretation of Article 87a united a broad coalition of societal groups and political parties supporting it for a variety of (sometimes conflicting) reasons: anti-militarism on the German left, in the peace movement and in some of the churches and trade unions; widespread disagreement with American politics in the aftermath of the Afghanistan crisis; and fear that German military involvement in the Gulf region would hurt the relations with the Arab world as well as with Israel, a view supported in all political parties. In sum, opposition to West German military involvement in the Middle East brought together a formidable coalition of those concerned about becoming entrapped in an American policy of global containment and those with a specifically Middle Eastern agenda. As a result, both Chancellor Schmidt and his successor Kohl resisted American pressures. They only conceded that the West German navy would take over some tasks of American ships in the North Atlantic and the Mediterranean which had been sent to the Gulf. Throughout the 1980s, reference to Article 87a of the Basic Law was used by the German government to disguise disagreements with Washington's handling of 'out-of-area' crises.

Example 2: arms exports to the Middle East

The 'out-of-area' issue and the restrictive interpretation of Article 87a provide an example of how, in a domestic coalition, conflicting goals reinforce each other to prevent a certain policy. The question of arms exports to the Middle East, however, has been more divisive, since two broadly supported principles of German foreign policy clash in this case. As mentioned, international cooperation is a primary goal of the country's foreign policy. Thus, security policy is orientated toward the peaceful resolution of conflicts. Foreign economic policy, on the other hand, is to be guided by the principles of free trade, especially given the Federal Republic's dependence on exports. The goals of international peace and free trade inevitably clash when it comes to arms exports. Moreover, different domestic constituencies such as the business community on the one hand, and, for example, the churches and large factions in all political parties, on the other, favour different policies none of which is able to gather sufficient domestic support in a climate of 'democratic corporatism'. As a result, the legal provisions to regulate arms exports are one more case of muddling through incompatibilities.[28] Article 26.2 of the Basic Law stipulates that trading arms has to be authorised by the Federal government. Two laws tried to implement this provision, the Arms Control Law (*Kriegswaffenkontrollgesetz*) and the Foreign Trade Law (*Aussenwirtschaftsgesetz*). While these laws adopted rather restrictive criteria for the authorisation of arms sales, the guidelines implementing them became less restraining over the years, a tendency which only changed after the most recent scandals which involved the delivery of dual-use technologies to Libya and Iraq.[29] The guidelines were formulated directly as a result of Bonn's Middle Eastern policy; they were first issued as a consequence of the domestic turmoil in the early 1960s when secret arms deliveries to Israel became public and led to serious drawbacks in German–Arab relations. The 1971 guidelines, for example, tried to prohibit any arms exports to 'areas of international tension', including the Middle East. These restrictions, however, did not prevent the Federal Republic from becoming a major arms supplier with almost half of its weapons exports outside the NATO area going to the Middle East.[30] In 1982, the guidelines were changed again and arms transfers outside the NATO area are forbidden except in cases in which 'vital foreign and security interests' are at stake. These legal provisions tried to square the circle between export-orientated business interests and efforts to promote a foreign policy orientated toward the peaceful resolution of international conflicts.

Moreover, it quickly turned out, as every new arms scandal proved, that the bureaucracies which were supposed to control and authorise arms transfers served in fact as promoters of business interests rather than executioners of the laws to restrict these exports.[31] The federal agency in charge is the Ministry of Economics, while the Foreign Office and the MOD have consulting roles. By law and by its own bureaucratic tradition, the Ministry of Economics is orientated toward export promotion rather than export control. In the past its officials were, therefore, less inclined to implement restrictive arms export rules which ran counter to their beliefs. Foreign Office officials were reluctant for other reasons to put brakes on arms exports. They feared this might hurt West German relations with foreign countries, particularly the Arab world. To put it differently, the domestic supporters of a more restrained West German arms export policy were usually not represented in the policy-making routine with regard to specific export decisions.

However, the picture of a policy-making process characterised by an intimate relationship between the arms industry and the Federal bureaucracy changed once a specific export decision became politicised and the mechanisms of democratic corporatism and party politics took over. The futile efforts by both Schmidt and Kohl to sell West German heavy-armoured tanks to Saudi Arabia during the early 1980s were a case in point.[32] In 1980–1, when the Schmidt–Genscher government was inclined to respond favourably to Saudi Arabian requests, it met with stiff opposition. All parties – above all the governing SPD – were divided but not along the usual lines between right and left. A powerful coalition against the arms deal was formed. This was composed of Israel's supporters on the conservative side and principal opponents of arms exports on the left. Advocates of the arms deal with Saudi Arabia, on the other hand, included pro-Arab left-wingers and pro-business conservatives in all three parties. They were backed by the business community which – in a reversal of its usual policy – spoke out publicly in favour of the deal.

The coalition against the sale of West German tanks to Saudi Arabia ultimately prevailed, mainly because the issue became part of the larger peace debate dominating politics in the Federal Republic at the time. In 1980–1, the peace movement protested against the deployment of Intermediate-Range Nuclear Forces (INFs) following NATO's 1979 'dual-track decision'.[33] The peace debate heavily affected the SPD, and the arms deal issue became intermingled with it. In order to ensure continuing party support for his pro-NATO policy, Chancellor Schmidt had to give in on another issue to appease the SPD left. The Saudi Arabian arms deal turned out to be a perfect candidate, since it was not very popular anyway.

Two years later, the new CDU–CSU–FDP government tried it again. As in 1980–1, the most outspoken supporters of selling German Leopard tanks to Saudi Arabia were to be found in the business community and in the Bavarian CSU, while the SPD – now in opposition – were unanimously opposed. Moreover, Foreign Minister Genscher sided with the FDP's left wing and was opposed, too. As a result, the anti-arms exports coalition of parts of the CDU–CSU, the FDP and the SPD – not to mention the Greens – carried the day again, although it was considerably weakened because of the change in government. While the Kohl government was prepared to sell all kinds of weapons to the Saudis, heavy-armoured tanks were excluded from the list. Finally, Saudi Arabia gave up on the political bickering in Bonn and decided in favour of a British tank.

The example reveals a pattern in the German arms exports policy-making process: in the absence of public scrutiny, the free-trade orientation of the federal bureaucracies and the business community prevails over broader considerations of foreign and security policy. The arms industry has, therefore, found numerous ways to circumvent export restrictions in the past. Every once in a while, the free-trade attitude leads to scandals: for example, the revelations that German industry helped to build plants to produce chemical weapons in Libya or Iraq. It remains to be seen whether this pattern will change as a result of the most recent tightening up of export regulations following the latest round of scandals.[34]

However, once an arms export issue becomes public, the mechanisms of democratic corporatism work. Foreign- and security-policy interests enter the decision-making process and, so far, domestic coalition-building has worked against the weakening of export restrictions, especially where the Middle East is concerned. In most cases, domestic alliances between supporters of Israel and advocates of foreign policy geared toward the peaceful resolution of conflicts emerged. So far these have been stronger than economic interests.

Example 3: Germany and the Gulf War

When Iraq invaded Kuwait in August 1990, the Federal Republic was in the midst of the most profound transformation since it was founded in 1949. The revolutions in Central Eastern Europe had resulted in the request of the East Germans for immediate unification with West Germany. Throughout the autumn of 1990, unification dominated the country's political agenda including the federal election campaign which resulted in a landslide victory for the Kohl–Genscher government. Compared to the problems of unification, the escalating crisis in the Gulf moved to the back-burner of public debate. When asked to join the multinational force in the Gulf, the German government again invoked Article 87a of the constitution. While Bonn supported the international efforts to counter Saddam Hussein, the domestic coalition against a military 'out-of-area' involvement was still in place. However, the three major parties agreed at the end of August to work out a constitutional amendment which would allow German troops to serve in future UN peacekeeping missions.[35]

Around Christmas, as the deadline set by the UN ultimatum gradually approached, and Iraq made no move to pull out of Kuwait, it suddenly occurred to the German public and most politicians that war was no longer a remote possibility. The first reactions were of anxiety – *Kriegsangst* – expressed by politicians, church leaders and the public at large. An anti-war mood and the demand to give economic sanctions more time to work dominated when the coalition forces started the air campaign on 17 January 1991. Germany quickly became the country with by far the largest peace rallies in the Western world.[36]

However, the atmosphere in Germany changed immediately when Iraqi Scud missiles hit Israel, raising the possibility of a chemical attack employing weaponry developed with German assistance. Of course, the psychological image invoked consisted of the gas chambers in Auschwitz. Peace protesters were accused of siding with Iraq and of ignoring the military aggression of Saddam Hussein. Politicians raced to Israel to pledge Germany's unwavering support for the country, including the promise of military aid to balance the dual-use technologies delivered by German companies to Iraq. In other words, the newly unified Germany went on an emotional rollercoaster ride. Again, two highly valued goals clashed in the minds of most people. On the one hand, there was a deep-seated aversion to war. On the other hand, people realised that the German Nazi past serves not only as a warning against war, but also as an exhortation to resist aggression and that there was a 'special responsibility' for Israel. As always in Germany's relations with the Middle East, the political cleavage cut across party lines, with some of the most vicious debates occurring among those on the left. The conflicting goals were visible even in public opinion polls.[37]

The political results of these contradictory feelings, attitudes and goals were mixed. On the one hand, the war in the Gulf caused a further tightening of German arms export controls.[38] On the other hand, efforts by leading Christian Democrats to seize the opportunity and to prepare the country for a future role as a traditional 'great power' through a constitutional amendment permitting the use of German troops outside the NATO area failed for the time being. Since such an amendment requires a two-thirds majority in parliament, the opposition parties will have to consent for this to be passed. However, the SPD was deeply split on the issue. While former Chairman Willy Brandt argued that Germany should not continue to stay out of international crises,[39] the SPD left remained adamantly opposed to a constitutional amendment. As a result, German troops might well be permitted to serve in a UN peacekeeping force as 'blue helmets' in the future. But it is not even clear that the Bundeswehr would be allowed to fight as part of a UN force, not to mention having a military role in a coalition force such as the one which fought Iraq. There is not and never has been the consensus on these questions which would be required for a constitutional amendment.

Conclusions: Plus ça change plus c'est la même chose

I have tried to show in this chapter that the low-key and rather passive German policy toward the Middle East is not only to be explained by conflicting international and domestic pressures leading to incompatible goals. It also results from a peculiar decision-making process orientated toward consensus-building in a country in which both the political culture and the policy-making institutions favour a structure of 'democratic corporatism'. Since the policies toward Israel and the Arab countries invoke conflicting societal demands which cut across the divisions of the political parties, the Federal government's leeway to conduct an active foreign policy in the area is rather limited. To a certain degree, Germany's low-key policy in the region seems to be over-determined.

Will German unification change this, and is the economically more powerful united Germany likely to pursue a more active policy toward Israel and the Arab countries? I doubt it. First, the policy-making structure did not change with unification. Since East Germany chose Article 23 of the (West German) constitution as the path to unification, it has simply become another part of the Federal Republic. As a result, the West German political institutions and its domestic structures now extend into the East. United Germany is not a new entity, but a somewhat larger Federal Republic.

This general remark also relates to the Middle East. With regard to domestic coalition-building processes, one could even argue that the east Germans, who have avoided facing German history for the last forty years as a result of state-proclaimed 'anti-fascism', are likely to make up for this. Current waves of neo-Nazism among angry and frustrated young people notwithstanding, the politically active groups in the former East Germany are likely to join those in the West who support the traditional low-key approach and resist policies which might be perceived as anti-Israel. In any case, however, the former West German social coalitions and the political parties will dominate the debate about the Middle Eastern policy of a united Germany.

Secondly, the process of unification is not finished with the formal accession of East Germany to the Federal Republic. To work out the social, economic, cultural and psychological consequences of unification will take into the next century. As a result, united Germany will continue to be preoccupied with itself for the forseeable future, and its foreign policy will continue to concentrate on Europe, the United States, and the successor states of the Soviet Union. There will simply not be much energy left to reconsider German Middle Eastern policy fundamentally.

Third, the continuation of a German low profile in the region might also be the result of the international repercussions of unification. The 'international alert squad', already mentioned, is still concerned about the united Germany's political, economic and military power, despite all reassurances. Note that Israel was the only country whose government publicly announced its opposition to unification. As a result, any sign of change in German Middle Eastern policy will be watched closely. Once again, Germany has to prove that it has definitely broken with its past. A re-assertive German policy in the Middle East would do nothing but increase concerns. The Federal Government, the political parties and the societal organisations are well aware of this and will probably act accordingly.

As argued above, the war in the Gulf, as the first test of how the united Germany will deal with Middle Eastern issues in the future, basically confirms the analysis. Once again, the Federal Republic found itself torn between incompatible goals. Thus, the Gulf War is likely to have only two consequences for German foreign policy. First, export controls over the arms trade have already been tightened and will become the subject of much closer public scrutiny in the future. Second, Germany will strongly support a joint-European approach toward the region, particularly if the peace process actually takes off. Apart from this, German domestic structures, external pressures and the process of unification itself will most likely ensure that the cautious approach of the Federal Republic toward the Middle East will not undergo dramatic changes in the foreseeable future. United Germany will not become a major player in the region.

Notes

1. I thank Helmut Hubel for critical comments on the draft of this chapter.
2. For a discussion of these dilemmas see, for example, Friedmann Büttner and Peter

Hünseler, 'Die politischen Beziehungen zwischen der Bundesrepublik Deutschland und den arabischen Staaten' in K. Kaiser and U. Steinbach (eds), *Deutsch-arabische Beziehungen*, Munich–Vienna, 1981, pp.111–52; Susan Hattis Rolef, *The Middle East Policy of the Federal Republic of Germany*, Jerusalem Papers on Peace Problems, No.39, Jerusalem, The Magnes Press, the Hebrew University, 1985.

3. The notion of 'Germany' is used in the following whenever my remarks apply to both the former West Germany and the unified German state. Such a use of the term seems to be justified, since 'German unification' basically meant the extension of the Federal Republic's political, economic and social system into former East Germany.

4. The 'compatibility-consensus' theme to explain West German foreign policy was introduced by Wolfram Hanrieder, *West German Foreign Policy 1949–63*, Stanford, Stanford University Press, 1967.

5. For empirical evidence see Gebhard Schweigler, *Grundlagen der aussenpolitischen Orientierung der Bundesrepublik Deutschland*, Baden-Baden, Nomos, 1985; Thomas Risse-Kappen, *Die Krise der Sicherheitspolitik. Neuorientierungen und Entscheidungsprozesse im politischen System der Bundesrepublik Deutschland*, Mainz–Munich, Grünewald-Kaiser, 1988, Chapter B.4. See also the – albeit polemical – analysis by Hans-Peter Schwarz, *Die gezähmten Deutschen. Von der Machtbesessenheit zur Machtvergessenheit*, Stuttgart, Deutsche Verlags-Anstalt, 1985.

6. While former East Germans appear to be slightly more nationalist than former West Germans and a lot more xenophobic, they are even less inclined to accept a German 'great power' role in Europe than others in the West. See *Das Profil der Deutschen*, *Spiegel-Spezial*, No.1, Hamburg Spiegel-Verlag, 1991, p.48.

7. On West German foreign policy in general see, for example, Helga Haftendorn, *Security and Détente. West German Foreign Policy 1955–1982*, New York, Praeger, 1984; Wolfgang Hanrieder, *Germany, America, Europe. Forty Years of German Foreign Policy*, New Haven, Yale University Press, 1989; Ekkehart Krippendorf and Volker Rittberger (eds), *The Foreign Policy of West Germany*, London, Sage, 1980.

8. On the notion of 'democratic corporatism' see Peter Katzenstein, *Small States in World Markets. Industrial Policy in Europe*, Ithaca, Cornell University Press, 1985, pp.30–6; idem, *Policy and Politics in West Germany*, Philadelphia, Temple University Press, 1989. On the West German foreign-policy-making process in general see Helga Haftendorn et al. (ed), *Verwaltete Aussenpolitik* Cologne, Wissenschaft & Politik, 1978; Haftendorn, 'West Germany and the Management of Security Relations: Security Policy under the Conditions of International Interdependence' in Krippendorff and Rittberger, *Foreign Policy*, pp.7–31; Frank R. Pfetsch, *West Germany: Internal Structure and External Relations*, New York, Praeger, 1988.

9. On Adenauer's foreign policy see Arnulf Baring, *Im Anfang war Adenauer* Munich, Deutscher Taschenbuch-Verlag, 1971. On Brandt see Günther Schmid, *Entscheidung in Bonn*, Cologne, Wissenschaft & Politik, 1979. On Schmidt cf. Helga Haftendorn, *Sicherheit und Stabilität. Aussenbeziehungen der Bundesrepublik zwischen Ölkrise und Doppelbeschluss*, Munich: Deutscher Taschenbuch-Verlag, 1986.

10. For details see Thomas Risse-Kappen, *The Zero Option. INF, West Germany, and Arms Control*, Boulder, Westview, 1988.

11. See, for example, Kurt Sontheimer, *Grundzüge des politischen Systems der Bundesrepublik Deutschland*, 5th ed. Munich, Piper, 1976; Reinhold Roth, *Parteiensystem und Aussenpolitik*, Meisenheim, A. Hain, 1973.

12. The one exception was 1972 when Chancellor Brandt lost his majority in the Bundestag over the controversies concerning *Ostpolitik*.

13. For evidence see Risse-Kappen, *Krise der Sicherheitspolitik*.

14. See 'Organisationsplan des Auswärtigen Amtes', January 1990.

15. See, for example, Lily Gardner Feldman, *The Special Relationship between West Germany and Israel*, Boston, Allen & Unwin, 1984, pp.158, 166–71; Rolef, *Middle East Policy*, p.56; Michael Wolffsohn, *Ewige Schuld? 40 Jahre Deutsch–Jüdisch–Israelische Beziehungen*, 2nd ed. Munich, Piper 1988, pp.30–31, 34–35, 37, 39.

16. See Büttner and Hünseler, 'Die politischen Beziehungen', pp.125–6.

17. For details see Udo Steinbach, 'Die europäische Gemeinschaft und die arabischen Staaten' in Kaiser and Steinbach, *Deutsch–arabische Beziehungen*, pp.185–204; Joseph H.H. Weiler, 'The Evolution of A European Foreign Policy: Mechanisms and Institutions' in I. Greilsammer and J.H.H. Weiler (eds), *Europe and Israel: Troubled Neighbors*, Berlin, De Gruyter, 1988, pp.233–54; Alain Dieckhoff, 'Europe and the Arab World: The Difficult Dialogue', *ibid.*, pp.255–82.

18. See Amnon Neustadt, *Die deutsch–israelischen Beziehungen im Schatten der EG-Nahostpolitik*, Frankfurt-am-Main, Haag & Herchen, 1983.

19. See Ilan Greilsammer, 'Reflections on the Capability of the European Community to Play an Active Role in an International Crisis: The Case of the Israeli Action in Lebanon' in Greilsammer and Weiler, *Europe and Israel*, pp.283–302; Rolef, *Middle East Policy*, p.15.

20. For details see Niels Hansen, 'Verbindungen in die Zukunft. 25 Jahre diplomatische Beziehungen zwischen Deutschland und Israel', *Aus Politik und Zeitgeschichte*, No.15, April 6 1990, pp.8–18; Feldman, *Special Relationship*, pp.142–56, 215–43; Karlheinz Schneider (ed.), *20 Jahre Deutsch-Israelische Beziehungen*, Berlin, Deutsch–Israelischer Arbeitskreis für Frieden im Nahen Osten e.V., 1985; Wolffsohn, *Ewige Schuld?*, pp.126–37.

21. For the following see Aziz Alkaza, 'Die deutsch–arabischen Wirtschaftsbeziehungen. Entwicklung und Zukunftsperspektiven' in Kaiser and Steinbach, *Deutsch–arabische Beziehungen*; Ernst Eberhard Hotz, 'Die Bedeutung des arabischen Öls für die Bundesrepublik', ibid.; Rolef, *Middle East Policy*, pp.31, 39; Wolffsohn, *Ewige Schuld?*, pp.127–30.

22. See Feldman, *Special Relationship*, pp.215–16, 220–1, 223; Wolffsohn, *Ewige Schuld?*, pp.121–4.

23. Feldman, *Special Relationship*, p.XII.

24. See Willy Brandt, *Begegnungen und Einsichten. 1960–1975* Munich, Knaur, 1978, pp.597–601; Feldman, *Special Relationship*, pp.170–1; Rolef, *Middle East Policy*, p.14–15; Wolffsohn, *Ewige Schuld?*, p.39.

25. Willy Brandt indicates in his memoirs that he was not pleased with certain wordings in the EPC declaration. See *Begegnungen und Einsichten*, p.598.

26. According to Rolef, *Middle East Policy*, pp.55–6.

27. See Michael Wolffsohn, *German-Saudi Arabian Arms Deals. 1936–1939 and 1981–1985*, New York, Peter Lang, 1985, pp.66–8. For a general discussion of this issue see Maurizio Cremasco, 'Do-It-Yourself: The National Approach to the Out-of-Area Question' in J.I. Coffey and G. Bonvicini (eds), *The Atlantic Alliance and the Middle East*, Pittsburgh, University of Pittsburgh Press, 1989, pp.147–92, 165–7; Rolef, *Middle East Policy*, pp.12–13.

28. See, for example, Ekkehart Ehrenberg, *Der deutsche Rüstungsexport*, Koblenz, Bernard & Graefe, 1981; Christian Loeck, 'Die Politik des Transfer konventioneller Rüstung – Strukturen und Einflussfaktoren im Entscheidungsprozess' in Haftendorn, *Verwaltete Aussenpolitik*, pp.209–24; Wolffsohn, *German-Saudi Arabian Arms Deals*.

29. See Harald Müller's chapter in this volume.

30. See Rolef, *Middle East Policy*, pp.57–8; Wolffsohn, *German–Saudi Arabian Arms Deal*, p.73.

31. The same problems occurred with regard to West German nuclear exports. See Harald Müller, *After the Scandals. West German Nonproliferation Policy*, Frankfurt-am-Main: Peace Research Institute, Report No.9, 1990.

32. See, in particular, Wolffsohn, *German–Saudi Arabian Arms Deals*, pp.69–103. See also Rolef, *Middle East Policy*, pp.40–1; Wolffsohn, *Ewige Schuld?*, pp.40–4.

33. For details see Risse-Kappen, *Zero Option*.

34. See Harald Müller's contribution to this volume.

35. See *New York Times*, 21 August 1990.

36. See 'Die Kinder des Friedens', *Die Zeit*, 1 February 1991.

37. On the one hand, overwhelming majorities of public opinion endorsed the effort by the coalition forces to drive Iraq out of Kuwait. On the other hand, similar majorities continued to resist the idea of sending German troops to fight outside the NATO area. See 'Polls Show Support for War, Even in Germany', *New York Times*, 29 January 1991; 'Der Rest ist Schadensbegrenzung', *Die Zeit*, 8 February 1991. The debate on the Gulf war among German intellectuals is largely documented in various editions of the weekly *Die Zeit*, January–March 1991. See also 'Den Ernstfall nicht gewagt', *Der Spiegel*, 11 February 1991.

38. See Harald Müller's chapter in this volume.

39. See, for example, his interview with *Der Spiegel*, 'Warum sollen wir nicht dabeisein?', 11 February 1991. See also 'Gulf War Sets Off Crisis for Germans', *New York Times*, 17 February 1991; 'Attacken auf eine Institution', *Die Zeit*, 1 March 1991; 'Kohl wünscht eine Grundgesetzänderung', *Frankfurter Allgemeine Zeitung*, 2 March 1991; 'Genscher at Eye of Policy Debate', *New York Times*, 22 March 1991.

11 Reflections on German policy in the Middle East

Josef Joffe

The determinants of diplomacy

German policy in the Middle East is complicated, but not difficult to understand. Essentially, three variables account for most of the policy. One factor is the claim of *realpolitik*, which pulls the FRG toward the Arab world with its command over a strategic resource (oil), its demographic strength and its vast potential market. The second – opposing – force derives from Germany's Nazi past; so the moral burden bequeathed by the Third Reich tends to tilt German diplomacy toward Israel. Finally, there was the exogenous variable of the cold war which, though acting indirectly on Bonn's Middle East diplomacy, was perhaps the weightiest of them all. Since all three factors have usually pulled in different directions, German diplomacy in the Middle East has been an endless complicated balancing act.

History versus realpolitik

The main complicating factor is history and, more specifically, that of Israel. Without Israel and Germany's horrifying historical legacy, German diplomacy in the region could have been quite straightforward. The Federal Republic might have established intimate, indeed far better relations with the Arab world than have the United States, Britain or France because Germany suffers from none of their historical handicaps. Britain and France are the two ex-colonial powers which carved a motley bunch of ahistorical Arab states out of the carcass of the Ottoman Empire. Between them, they first ruled and then dominated the region from the Levant to the Gulf and from Egypt to Morocco. Thereafter, they left behind not only political artifices (with the exception of Egypt, perhaps) but also the enduring suspicions of those whom they had once colonised.

In the process of decolonisation, both Britain and France were trapped in a succession of rearguard battles, culminating, but not ending, in the abortive Suez intervention of 1956. France fought one of its most brutal wars against an Arab nation (Algeria), and after 1962, it took Paris years to establish normal and then semi-privileged relations with the Arab world. The United States, though not plagued by a colonial past, was soon seen as the ugly heir to the expelled French and Britons – as an outside power trying to acquire precisely the dominant position in the area its Western predecessors had been forced to abandon.

Germany, on the other hand, theoretically might have been ideally positioned to resume the role to which Kaiser Wilhelm II had vainly aspired. Seeking a 'place in the sun' for his country, Wilhelm clumsily tried to stake out a German claim in the Middle East by personally venturing forth to Damascus and Jerusalem at the turn of the century and by driving his famous *Bagdad-Bahn* ('Baghdad Railroad')[1] straight into the heart of Britain's possessions. Raising France's resentments[2] as well as Russian and British suspicions, the Baghdad Railroad as symbol and tool of German expansionism additionally helped to push all three powers toward the anti-German alliance that proved the Reich's undoing in World War I.

In the end, the German foray into the Middle East ground to a halt in Versailles in 1919 when Germany was forced to cede all of its colonial possessions. Yet the loss of empire almost half a century before Britain and France had to yield theirs turned out to be a tidy gain in the decades to come. Germany's post-World War I conflict with the classic colonial powers helped to nurture the seed of that notorious 'German–Arab friendship' the Wilhelmine Empire had planted in the 1890s.[3] In World War II, Hitler would try to manipulate that tradition by seeking to enlist the Great Mufti of Jerusalem and the Egyptians against the Western allies. Even today, that recollection – tainted as it is by the holocaust – still strikes fond memories in Arab hearts.

In the aftermath of World War II, the absence of a colonial past, the flawed tradition of 'German–Arab friendship' and Germany's vaunted economic prowess might have been promising assets on the books of German Middle East diplomacy. But even if Bonn's postwar leaders had returned to Wilhelm's *Grosspolitik* dreams, which they did not, they could not have translated these assets into a flourishing Middle East enterprise. They had been devalued drastically by Germany's murderous Nazi past.

To begin with, Germany was an outcast among outcasts, occupied by the United States, the Soviet Union, France and Britain who held their wards (West and East Germany) on a tight leash. Before Bonn could begin to conduct a foreign policy, it had to acquire the right to have one. Above all, the three Western zones (to become the Federal Republic in 1949) had to regain sovereignty. Sovereignty could only be devolved, and that meant subordination to the victors, whence would flow the trust that Hitler's heirs could only regain by doing voluntarily what otherwise would have been imposed. Early West German foreign policy was thus strictly a function of Allied, and above all, American policy.

To regain sovereignty also required the moral rehabilitation of a nation which, in its Nazi incarnation, had perpetrated the most unspeakable crimes against humanity. In the case of the Middle East, *realpolitik* initially – but only initially – buttressed what morality demanded, that is at least financial amends to the survivors of the holocaust and to Israel as legal heir of the slaughtered victims. *Realpolitik* required that the new Germany, still a ward of the United States, make a gesture that would impress both the government and the electorate of the United States. Without such amends, Chancellor Konrad Adenauer stated: 'Germany could not have achieved respect and equality in the community of nations.'[4] The result was the *Wiedergutmachungsabkommen* (Restitution Agreement) of 1952 by which the FRG pledged, among other payments, DM3 billion to Israel.[5]

But, given the state of war between Israel and the Arabs, one command of *realpolitik* collided immediately with another. And so a second key component of German Middle East policy fell into place: compensation to the Arabs. Just before the Luxembourg Agreement (1952) was signed by the FRG and Israel, the Arab League had launched a ferocious pressure campaign against Bonn. Chancellor Adenauer recalled in his memoirs: 'I was not willing to be turned aside by the threats of the Arab League.' This agreement, he wrote, 'rested on a compelling moral obligation' and was therefore not business as usual.[6] Nonetheless, Bonn worked hard not to alienate the Arab world. The FRG made sure, the Chancellor noted, that the restitution agreement could not used for the 'delivery of arms, ammunition or other military equipment to Israel'. Nor would Israel be allowed to re-export German goods for the purpose of hard-currency earnings which might pay for arms imports. Finally, Bonn stood ready to balance the economic scales by 'contributing to the economic development of the Arab states'.[7]

It is this balance, established in the early years of the Federal Republic, that would determine West German Middle East policy in the decades to come. Obligation to Israel and what Adenauer and his successors would call the 'tradition of good and amicable relations with the Arab nations' were the opposite poles of West German diplomacy as it was played out before the backdrop of the cold war. Since the FRG remained chained to the centre of that conflict, the cold war would regularly come to haunt the country's Middle East policy – regardless of how much Bonn tried to avoid choice and commitment.

National interest versus bipolarity

Though intruding from the outside, the cold war has left a heavy imprint on Bonn's Middle East diplomacy, adding to the complications already engendered by the clash between *realpolitik* and *moralpolitik*. The impact of bipolarity was twofold. First, the cold war shaped – indeed, dictated – Bonn's central interests, and within that grand strategy, the Middle East was destined to remain, literally, a remote concern. In fact, West Germany virtually had *no* Middle East policy in the 1950s, trying to avoid *any* autonomous policy outside the Euro–Atlantic realm. Until the late 1960s, West German foreign policy was practically *Westpolitik*. Its universe was occupied by NATO and the European Community (EC), and the twin focus of diplomacy was on the United States, West Germany's transatlantic protector, and on France, its key European ally. From the late 1960s onward, *Westpolitik* came to be flanked by *Ostpolitik*, the attempt to reach a *modus vivendi* with the Soviet Union and its East European satrapies, which would eventually mature into a stable *détente* relationship. In the Middle East, on the other hand, the FRG would have been perfectly happy to have no policy above and beyond the steady penetration of markets. Or as Konrad Adenauer put it quite truthfully, the FRG had 'no political aspirations whatso-ever' in the Middle East.[8]

But, second, the Federal Republic was also the most dependent client of the United States – which did and does have 'political aspirations' in the Middle East. Though Bonn instinctively tried to tend its own European garden and to stay out of extra-European quarrels, it did owe allegiance to the United States, its great patron and protector in the cold war. So if Bonn did pursue a regional diplomacy, it was derivative – a function of the FRG's foremost preoccupation, the East–West conflict in Europe where Bonn was both the key stake and a central actor. This derivative policy, in turn, broke down into two strands.

On the one hand, the FRG as a classic client state habitually followed the cues of the United States (this will be considered below). On the other hand, Bonn's peculiar role on the cold war stage also dictated a specifically *West* German interest in the Middle East: to block the international legitimation of the FRG's 'counter-state', the German Democratic Republic (GDR), in the Third World. To purchase Arab goodwill in its rivalry with the GDR, Bonn extended economic aid to the Arabs and withheld diplomatic recognition from Israel, while otherwise busying itself with building profitable trading relationships with all sides. Yet in the end, as we shall see, political abstentionism *cum* economic penetration proved impossible – which is why Bonn's Middle East policy became so complicated without being so difficult to fathom.

Arms and the Arabs: a case study in constraints

In 1965, Bonn suddenly established diplomatic relations with the state of Israel – something it had resisted for a decade. Conversely, its hostile brother, the German Democratic Republic, suddenly broke through the wall of isolation Bonn had thrown up around it to block any advances into the Middle East and the rest of the Third World. Suddenly, a nightmare materialised that Bonn had strenuously sought to dispel during the very same decade. This double failure elucidates emblematically the interplay of the three factors underlying German Middle East diplomacy: national interest, the burden of history and bipolarity.

In 1952, just after the conclusion of the Restitution Agreement with Israel, Bonn was still the *demandeur* – pushing for diplomatic ties which Jerusalem, pointing at the Hitler past, rejected. A mere three years later, the tables were turned. Now, Israel began to press for official relations while the Federal Republic began to play for time. To understand this surprising switch we must go outside the Middle East and turn to the main arena of German foreign policy: the cold war.

Cold war dilemmas and Mideast fiascoes

The year 1955 marks a twin watershed in postwar German history. Both German states were handed (limited) sovereignty by their respective patron powers, and hard on the heels of West Germany's admission to NATO in the same year, Bonn established diplomatic relations with the Soviet Union. Though something of a diplomatic coup, the Soviet connection had a nasty price. By exchanging ambassadors with Moscow, Bonn for the first time had opened an embassy in a capital that also had official relations with the German Democratic Republic – a state that in Bonn's eyes had no right to exist and had only one legitimate function: to liquidate itself for the sake of reunification. Hence, the international recognition of the GDR had to be blocked at all costs – all the more so after 1955 when *two* German ambassadors in Moscow had established a powerful precedent for the recognition of both states by one and the same country. To build a dam against further recognition of the GDR, Bonn swiftly proclaimed the 'Hallstein Doctrine' which labelled the GDR's recognition as an 'unfriendly act tending to deepen the partition of Germany'.

The 'Hallstein Doctrine' was intended to deter Third World waywardness in the rivalry between the two successors to the Third Reich. In fact, it set a trap for Bonn that would be sprung in Cairo ten years later – with the unwitting help of Israel and the United States. To keep the Arabs from recognising the GDR, the Federal Republic was paying not only direct bribes in the form of economic assistance (at one time, Bonn even offered to finance Egypt's Aswan Dam project) but also in the coinage of diplomatic good behaviour. Accordingly, Bonn would not recognise Jerusalem because that was expected to bring down swift Arab retaliation in the guise of the GDR's recognition by the Arab world.

Enter the two other factors of Bonn's Middle East diplomacy: the moral obligation toward Israel and the political obligation toward the United States. By 1957, a clandestine arms relationship between the FRG and Israel had begun to flourish. At first it was one-sided, with Israel delivering small arms and ammunition to the young Bundeswehr. Three years later, in March 1960, a secret meeting between Israeli Prime Minister David Ben Gurion and Chancellor Konrad Adenauer gave birth to a much larger relationship. In the course of the conversation, Adenauer apparently pledged DM200 million worth of arms plus DM2 billion in credit.[9]

Though at home Adenauer ran into the opposition of his cabinet, the balance was tilted in favour of Israel by an exogenous weight, the United States. Willing to extend military aid to Israel but unwilling to reap Arab hostility (this was the era of the great Soviet–American contest for the allegiance of the Third World), the Kennedy Administration (1961–3) encouraged, if not pressed, Bonn to act as the go-between. The triangular relationship was continued under Chancellor Ludwig Erhard and President Lyndon B. Johnson, who also urged the Germans to act as a heavy-arms supplier for Israel. The centerpiece of the package was reportedly 200 M-48 tanks which travelled from Germany via Italy to Israel.[10]

It was a request neither Adenauer nor Erhard could reject. To turn down the United States in the midst of the Berlin Crisis (1958–62) would have been suicidal for a country that needed every ounce of Western support in the struggle against Soviet pressures. Nor did Erhard have much choice after he acceded to the chancellorship in 1963. As Adenauer had to buy American loyalty against Khrushchev during the Berlin Crisis, Erhard had to work hard to keep it after the resolution of the Cuban Missile Crisis (1962) which set the stage for the first postwar *détente*. In the process, the United States was no longer willing to identify the FRG's separate conflict with the Soviet Union (over postwar borders and the GDR) as its own, pushing instead for limited agreements with Moscow that ignored Bonn's hitherto sacrosanct claim according to which any *détente* was conditional on progress toward German reunification.

By the autumn of 1964 the arms deal had become public. Under heavy Arab pressure, Bonn tried to wriggle out of its predicament by offering a diplomatic deal to Egypt and to Israel: the FRG would terminate the arms relationship and increase its economic aid to Egypt while extending formal recognition to Israel. But in the meantime, another actor had appeared on stage, the GDR, which saw a perfect opening in its search for international legitimation. While the Arab world threatened the FRG with economic boycott and brandished the stick of diplomatic ties with East Berlin, East German leader Walter Ulbricht began angling for an invitation to Egypt. Escalating the pressure game, Egypt's President Nasser finally extended that invitation which led to the first official visit of an East German leader outside the Soviet bloc (February 1965). In retaliation, Bonn offered diplomatic relations to Jerusalem, and in counter-retaliation, most Arab countries broke with Bonn.[11]

The trap had been sprung, and the why and wherefore was neatly summed up by a remarkably prescient editorial in the left-of-centre *Frankfurter Rundschau* written seven months earlier: 'The Federal Government, facing Israel and the Arabs, has been inspired by the happy hope of landing all the fish with a net of semi-formal and semi-secret relationships. The strategy was to be good friends with the Arabs, the arch-enemies of Israel, to fashion closer ties with the Jewish state than met the eye and, finally, to please the United States.'[12]

Arms, Israel and oil

In the 1960s, the dilemma of *realpolitik* versus obligation versus alliance loyalty ended in a disaster for German Middle East diplomacy that could only be explained by the peculiar exigencies of the cold war. To lighten its moral burden *vis-à-vis* Israel, Bonn had slipped into a clandestine arms relationship with Israel. To please the United States, its indispensable ally against the Soviet Union in a peculiarly 'hot' phase of the cold war, Bonn had extended and deepened that relationship. To win the battle of legitimacy against the GDR, the Federal Republic had at first sought to buy off the Arabs and then, with its anti-GDR campaign in tatters, proceeded to punish them by executing precisely what it had sought to avoid: the formal recognition of Israel in 1965.

A mere eight years later – during the Yom Kippur War of 1973 – the same drama unfolded once more. In the meantime, however, the main cold war stage of German diplomacy had been rearranged. As a result, the outcome would change, too – offering an object lesson in the shifting relative weights of the three factors shaping Bonn's Middle East policy.

On 6 October 1973, Egypt and Syria attacked Israel in a two-front war, scoring some impressive advances in the first week of the war. On 24 October a report of the *Nordsee-Zeitung*, a paper published in the port city of Bremerhaven, made public what Bonn had been content to ignore: that Israel was being resupplied with American material based in West Germany. What apparently broke the tacit agreement (the United States would resupply, Bonn would not interfere) was the fact that, at this point, Israeli ships had begun to dock in the American-controlled part of the port. In reaction, the Federal Republic lodged a strong protest with the United States about what it termed a 'breach of German neutrality' in the Arab–Israeli war.

This episode can be read in two ways. First, since German protests came only at the very end of the war, when Israel had moved from existential danger to a victorious offensive, they can be interpreted as face-saving gestures (necessitated by journalistic indiscretion) which in no way threatened the security of Israel. Second, the very fact that this formal protest was launched in the first place, thus ranging the Federal Republic against both Israel and the United States, betrayed an altered setting – which was a far cry from the 1960s when Bonn brought down the ire of the Arab world on itself by arming Israel and deferring to the United States.

The critical new variable, rearranging the cold war stage of German foreign policy, was the new *Ostpolitik*. By 1973, the Federal Republic had completed a grand bargain with the Soviet Union and its Eastern European allies. *Vis-à-vis*

Moscow, Poland and Prague, Bonn had all but renounced its claims to the formerly German-controlled territories absorbed by these three countries after World War II.[13] Also by 1973, Bonn had all but recognised the GDR, abandoning its long-standing policy of isolation. The new *Ostpolitik* virtually amounted to a peace settlement with the Soviet Union, and as such, it severed a good many dependencies on the West. Having shelved its separate conflict with Moscow, the Federal Republic was no longer so thoroughly compelled to trade German deference for Western loyalty. *Détente* with the East, in short, spelled less dependence on the West, and particularly on the United States. No longer in the business of isolating the GDR, Bonn also no longer needed to bribe or blackmail Third World countries which used to brandish the recognition club for financial or political gain.

The new setting of West German diplomacy explains one part of the 1973 watershed, when Bonn, instead of arming Israel as go-between for the United States, tried – or at least pretended – to stay America's hand in the final phase of the Yom Kippur war. The other part of the explanation consists of a three-letter word: oil. Two days into the War (on 8 October 1973), the six Arab members of OPEC met in Vienna. Using the war as a pretext, they decided (with Iranian cues from backstage) to raise oil prices. On 17 October they met again, this time announcing a monthly production cut of 5 per cent – to be repeated month by month until Palestine was at last liberated. Though it is unclear whether production actually was cut, the strategy was doubly rewarded. The price of oil rose fivefold, and the Middle East policy of the European Community immediately went into a sharp pro-Arab tilt. Thus it was no surprise that Bonn felt both free (because of *Ostpolitik*) and compelled (because of the embargo) to execute a gesture of public defiance against the United States and Israel.

Although bipolarity had lost some of its hold and though the oil crisis had added urgency to the shift against Israel, Bonn could not completely escape the hold of history. In a poignant formulation, Chancellor Willy Brandt put it thus: while Bonn refused to choose sides in the Middle East conflict, there could be no 'neutrality of the heart and the conscience'. The relationship with Israel was of a 'special nature', and there could be no 'wriggling out' of the lessons of history.[14]

These were powerful sentiments, but by 1974, the key codeword of Middle East diplomacy had become *Ausgewogenheit* – 'evenhandedness' between Israel's right to exist within 'secure and recognised boundaries' and the 'universal recognition of the Palestinians' right to self-determination'.[15] It was enough to prompt the Arabs to reclassify the Federal Republic from 'hostile' to 'friendly' for the purpose of oil deliveries.

Realpolitik and *Moralpolitik*: a changing balance

Together with the completion of *Ostpolitik*, the Yom Kippur War and the oil embargo mark the second great watershed in German Middle East diplomacy – but by no means the end of the ancient clash between *realpolitik* and *moralpolitik*. And so, the Federal Republic continued to manoeuvre between two extremes defined by Anglo–French and American policy. Roughly speaking, France and Britain have pursued an Arab-leaning[16] policy while the United States has acted as armourer and 'ally of last resort' for Israel.

That cleavage between the three major Western powers sharpened the Federal Republic's ancient quandary. For the sake of European integration, Bonn could not distance itself too much from its two key European allies in London and Paris. On the other hand, the Federal Republic shared one structural characteristic with Israel as long as the main threat to German security emanated from the Soviet Union. The United States underwrote the security of both countries which made for tight bonds of dependence. So the original dilemma between coldly calculated interest and the enduring hold of the Hitler past came to be wrapped up in a larger one: how to build a Western European entity (implying a common Middle East policy) that might complement, if not ultimately replace, the Atlantic connection and how to preserve precisely that tie as ultimate reinsurance against the Soviet Union.

This quandary-within-a-quandary would shape German diplomacy in the 1970s and 1980s, keeping in place an enduring structural constant: the derivative nature of German Middle East diplomacy. Put differently, until the end of the cold war *circa* 1990, there could be no such thing as an *autonomous* German policy in the Middle East. In one way or another, it responded to the cues delivered by a much larger setting.

One example is the vaunted 'Euro–Arab dialogue' launched by the European Community in the wake of the 1973 oil crisis. The purpose was twofold: to create a European Middle East policy distinct from that of the United States and hence to reap the benefits flowing from a more pro-Arab diplomacy. The European initiative required Bonn to pursue a tougher line toward Jerusalem – which it did. Yet cognisant of its obligations to Israel and the United States, Bonn at the same time applied the brakes to the EC's foray. Though all the West Europeans, heeding the call of oil and numbers (eighteen Arab League members versus one – Israel) – dashed off to embrace the Arabs after 1973 (some of them, like France, in search of separate arms-for-oil deals), the Federal Republic quietly but persistently blunted the sharper anti-Israeli blade wielded by France.

When the EC, in its famous declaration of 6 November 1973, granted the Arabs two major points by stressing the 'legitimate rights of the Palestinians' and enjoining Israel to terminate its 'territorial occupation',[17] Bonn made sure that the pronounced pro-Arab emphasis demanded by the French would not prevail. Similarly, the 1980 'Declaration of Venice' by the EC, another landmark in the annals of the Community, is generally seen as compromise between more extreme French language and West Germany's dilution strategy.[18]

What motivated Bonn to act as advocate of Israeli interests in European councils? According to Chancellor Helmut Schmidt, perhaps a greater friend of Israel than his visceral dislike for Israeli Prime Minister Menachem Begin suggested, it was *not* memory and moral obligation: 'I agree with Mr Begin that the Germans should have a bad conscience about Hitler and the Nazi past. Contrary to Mr Begin, though, I think that a bad conscience should not be the reason for West Germany's support of Israel.' [19] This is an interesting explanation of German Middle East diplomacy. Even a cursory glance at the FRG's interests suggests that there are very few intrinsic reasons for the backing of Israel, and hence Schmidt's dictum raises more questions than it answers. From Adenauer onward, 'West Germany's support for Israel' has routinely hamstrung a policy that otherwise might have reaped great profits in the Arab world. Neither an ex-colonial power like France or Britain nor a world power like the

United States, the FRG was ideally positioned to convert technological prowess and economic excellence into political clout.

Since Bonn did not pursue this 'natural' strategy, one must ask: what else if not the morally admirable obeisance to past sins could explain a policy that so often proved self-defeating?[20] It certainly is not the 'Jewish factor'; compared to the United States, Britain and France, the Jewish community in the Federal Republic (30,000 out of a population of 60 million) is definitely on the small side.[21] Nor is it strategic interest, centred, as in the American case, on Israel as the foremost regional power – as a kind of 'continental sword' for the West. A medium power at heart, the FRG does not have any strategic interests in the Middle East – at least not of the kind that motivates American policy. To be sure, there are strong cultural affinities between Germany and Israel, but these are hardly stronger than Israel's ties to France and Britain which have not stood in the way of a generally pro-Arab policy.

In fact, even Helmut Schmidt, the chancellor (1974–82) most critical of Israel, would speak of the 'special moral and historical quality of German–Israeli relations'.[22] Yet morality that is not grounded in interest appears to be a fickle guide to policy, especially as the historical memories recede that originally gave rise to the 'special relationship'. As one looks to the future, two factors might progressively weaken the hold of history on Germany's Middle East diplomacy.

One is a simple insight from human psychology. Guilt, if not relieved, will eventually turn into the opposite of submission, namely resentment against the source of these troubling feelings. Second, inherited guilt will inevitably wane as the perpetrators of the holocaust succumb to biology and as their children – the leadership generation in Germany today – yield power to those who acquired their political consciousness in the 1970s and 1980s, that is under the aegis of a solidly democratic and respected German polity.

Though inchoate and virtually subconscious, the revolt against inherited guilt first broke out on the threshold of the 1980s, flowering into an ugly bloom during the Lebanon War in 1982. One illustrative episode is the aborted German–Saudi arms deal whose origins reach back to 1975, when the Saudi government first tabled a request for 600 Marder armoured personnel carriers (APCs). At that point, the Schmidt government still refused. By 1981, however, a deal was in the making – for a package that was variously described as entailing 150 Leopard II main battle tanks (MBTs) plus 1,500 APCs or even 300 Leopard IIs plus 2,700 APCs and tracked air-defence vehicles. That deal-in-the-making followed one side of the logic of post-1973 policy: to fashion preferred ties to key oil suppliers and to staunch with German exports the balance-of-payments' drain engendered by dearer oil.

In the end, the panzers did not roll to Araby, even though Helmut Schmidt apparently pushed the deal. By the time he traveled to Riyadh in the spring of 1981, it had become clear to him that his Social Democratic Party, still generally pro-Israel and anti-arms exports, would not let him arm a foe of the Jewish state with classic weapons of the offensive. His frustration occasioned a famous outburst on the flight back to Bonn when Schmidt opined that 'German foreign policy in the 1980s must not be [forever] overshadowed by Auschwitz.'[23]

Within the larger society, pent-up resentment and the unconscious search for moral relief broke through the dams for the first time during Israel's war in Lebanon in the summer of 1982. The wave of anti-Israeli passions reached a high watermark after the Sabra and Shatila massacre of Palestinians by Falange troops – for which Germans blamed the Israelis rather than Lebanese killers. Young Germans on the left in particular, but also their elders in the respectable segments of the German press, were inordinately fond of drawing a comparison between the Nazi siege (and annihilation) of the Warsaw ghetto and the Israeli blockade of Beirut that was designed to drive the armed forces of the PLO out of the Lebanese capital.

The psychological roots of that ugly comparison were not difficult to fathom. If the Israelis were like the Nazis, then the heirs of the victims no longer had a special moral claim against the children of the perpetrators. Suddenly, the moral score had been evened: if the Jews, behaving like Nazis, were just as bad as the Germans, Israel no longer deserved a special moral dispensation. Or even better: by raging against the evils inflicted on Palestinians by Jews, young Germans presumably could prove to themselves and the rest of the world that *they* had scaled new heights of moral excellence while the Jews had sunk to the moral depths once occupied by their fathers. In either case, the guilt the parents had passed on to their children would vanish by projection – whereby the burden was transferred on to the shoulders of the Jewish accusers now unmasked as hypocritical sinners.

Also at the time of the Lebanon War, a new genealogy of guilt was introduced in the debate – which had a similar rehabilitative function. Accordingly, the *Germans* – though at one step removed – were responsible for the plight of the Palestinians, and therefore the Palestinians, rather than the Jews, deserved the benefit of German moral support. The logic of the argument went as follows: only because of what Hitler had done to the Jews was the state of Israel born,[24] entailing the disenfranchisement and dispersal of Palestinians. Therefore, the Nazis ultimately had wronged the Palestinians, and therefore Germans had a special obligation to help restore Palestinian rights. And so moral and political pressures on Israel were not only legitimate but a veritable historical duty.

Such arguments, rising from leftwing 'anti-Zionists' in the streets into the upper reaches of the political and journalistic establishment, had the evident, though unconscious function of dispatching a moral burden the postwar generation had willingly assumed and carried forward into the 1960s and 1970s. (This stands in sharp contrast to the East Germans and Austrians who, portraying themselves as victims of Nazism, on the whole refused to accept any responsibility.) By the mid-1980s, however, the old consensus began to yield to the conviction that forty years of penance (a magical number in Judaeo–Christian culture) were enough. That sentiment acquired its most dramatic expression in the misbegotten Bitburg ceremony on 8 May 1985, the fortieth anniversary of Germany's surrender) when Chancellor Kohl inveigled President Reagan to extend the hand of forgiveness over the graves of Germany's fallen of World War II – which turned out to contain the remains of Waffen-SS members.

The next test was the Gulf War (1990–1) which began with the invasion of Kuwait in August 1990 and ended with the Allied victory and Iraq's expulsion in February 1991. At first, it looked like a replay of the reaction to Israel's Lebanon invasion in 1982. While the government hesitated to take a stand, the peace movement took to the streets not to protest against the arsonist – Iraq – but against the fire brigade, especially against the United States which was depicted as manipulating moral cant for profit (blood for oil) and power political ends. According to a key slogan, the remedy of war was worse than the original aggression. Not even a life-threatening attack on Israel, as some voices had it, could warrant war, which was the greatest of all evils. And after all, was Iraq so different from Israel, a country that had occupied Arab lands since 1967? Whence it followed that Israel was at least partially responsible for the Iraqi invasion as well as for the Scud attacks on itself.[25]

These were echoes of 1982, a new act in the drama of guilt relief. But then came the twist. When Iraqi Scud missiles began to rain down on Israel, when Israelis began to don gas masks to protect themselves against Iraqi poison gas produced with lavish, though illegal assistance by German firms, the mood changed. In January of 1991, Foreign Minister Hans-Dietrich Genscher rushed to Israel with a cheque for DM250 million in hand, followed later by German Hawk anti-aircraft and Patriot anti-missile missiles. And Chancellor Kohl proclaimed: 'Israel should know that it can count on our solidarity in these dark days.' By delivering defensive material, 'we act according to the special responsibility [the Federal Republic] has always demonstrated toward Israel'.[26]

Though at first hesitantly shown, that 'special responsibility' was continuity *par excellence*, regardless of the quest for 'normalisation' enacted in the 1980s. Though Germany was by now reunified and liberated from the shackles of the cold war, German policy in the Middle East would not emulate the hardheaded *realpolitik* pursued by France and Britain. Almost half a century after the holocaust, German diplomacy still paid tribute to a special obligation to Israel. The holocaust, as President Richard von Weizsäcker emphatically put it on 3 October 1990, the day of national rebirth, had been the 'most horrible of crimes'. And he vowed that 'we shall forever remember the victims'.[27]

Conclusion: enduring patterns of German policy

Ideally, the Federal Republic would have preferred to have *no* policy in the Middle East. The reasons are quite obvious. A client state in the 1950s, the Federal Republic's interests were riveted on the battle lines of the cold war in Europe, and in that arena, the Middle East at best played a tertiary role. The bulk of German energies were focused on matters close to home: the American connection, the European integration venture and the enduring tensions with the Soviet Union.

As West Germany passed from its vaunted economic miracle to moral rehabilitation, the scope of its diplomacy did not expand *pari passu*. In the meantime, the 'economic giant' had learned to appreciate the low costs associated with acting the 'political dwarf'. Why tread into the minefield of the Middle East where Germany's former great power interests had long ago disappeared in the shifting sands of time? Why get involved in a game dominated by the two superpowers which, while acting out their global rivalry in the Middle East, also brought a modicum of order to the region? (Presumably, not even the pre-Gorbachev Soviet Union would have permitted the destruction of Israel.)

As elsewhere in the crisis regions of the Third World, the FRG preferred to behave more like Switzerland – or more apropos, like Japan – than like France or Britain. Building profitable trading relationships with all sides, while leaving the onerous task of order and stability to others, the FRG instinctively tried to act like a quintessential small power – in the manner of the 'freerider' who enjoys the collective goods provided by others.

Except that these reflexes – the natural response of a nation that had over-reached, failed badly and then learned to enjoy the pleasures of abstentionism – collided head-on with other key interests of the Federal Republic. For the sake of moral rehabilitation, the young German state was early on drawn into a 'special relationship' with Israel which led to an endless balancing act between Israel and the Arabs and between commercial interest and moral obligation. The second factor that pushed the Federal Republic into the minefields of the Middle East was its strategic dependence on the United States. Hence, Bonn at first obediently followed American cues (for example on arms deliveries to Israel in the 1960s). Later, the Federal Republic commenced a second balancing act – this time within the Western community where Bonn sought to mediate between the United States (favouring Israel) and France (favouring the Arabs).

Even after West Germany had acquired the badge of 'economic giant', it basically pursued the classic strategy of a small state. Such states normally eschew global responsibilities, leave the task of world order to others and seek to manoeuvre quietly in the interstices of great power and regional conflicts. That instinct found its emblematic expression in the one segment of the Middle East where Israel (and the historical burden associated with that relationship) was at least not initially at stake: in the Gulf during the Iran–Iraq war (1980–8) and the far larger confrontation engendered by the Iraqi invasion of Kuwait in 1990.

While the major Western states successively arrayed themselves on the Iraqi side in order to contain the greater evil that was revolutionary Iran, the Federal Republic quietly assumed the role of Iran's preferred interlocutor and most important trading partner. When the issue of force projection arose, Bonn went exactly halfway, sending navy units into the Eastern Mediterranean for the 'relief' of other NATO countries so that they might dispatch their ships to the Gulf. That manoeuvre went some way towards muting the resentments of those NATO members (the United States, France and Britain) who had sailed directly into harm's way to uphold the balance against Iran. Yet at no time did this dues-paying strategy run the risk of appearing to take sides against the Khomeini regime.

When the war again broke out in the Gulf in August 1990, Bonn executed virtually the same strategy. Again, it refused to send forces to the Gulf, instead dispatching eight minesweepers to the vicinity of Crete, where Iraqi mines were presumably few and far between. After much browbeating, Bonn then consented to contribute material aid to the American effort by pledging initially $2 billion in support, which was later raised to $5.5 billion.[28] (A significant portion of the aid was surplus material from the East German army which went into liquidation after reunification in October of 1990.) The militarily most significant contribution was, characteristically, an act not of commission but of tacit consent whereby the United States was allowed to use its bases and supplies in Germany for reinforcement in the Gulf.

As during the Iran–Iraq war, a predictable debate arose in the wake of the Iraqi invasion — and again with a predictable outcome. To begin with, the government tried to stay out of the conflict; its condemnation of Iraq was as hedged as its support for the *ad hoc* alliance harnessed by the United States. After the air war had broken out, Chancellor Kohl's first official sentence was: the news has made us *'tief betroffen'* – 'we are filled with consternation.' The allies deserve 'our solidarity' but 'German soldiers will not be deployed to the Gulf'.[29] In other words, Germany could not get involved in the business of force projection 'out of area'. The reason was the same as previously given during the war in the 1980s: a constitution that allegedly enjoined the government to commit troops for defensive purposes only, these being narrowly restricted to the protection of the national space. In fact, the West German – and since 1990, the all-German – Basic Law' is far more permissive than the abstentionists claim. Expressly, Article 24 of the Basic Law allows for participation in 'collective security' ventures, hence, at a minimum, in military arrangements sponsored and legitimised by the UN under Article 43 of its Charter. That article in fact *requires* all members to participate in sanctions, including military ones. By accepting the UN Charter without reservation, the FRG *ipso facto* had actually accepted a *duty* to join collective security arrangements.

Moreover, the very same Article 24 provided the constitutional foundation for the FRG's membership in collective defence systems such as NATO and the WEU. A disinterested constitutional lawyer therefore would have a hard time arguing that the Basic Law legitimates membership in a military coalition like NATO, on the one hand, but proscribes German participation in a multilateral Gulf force, on the other. Moreover, even the Basic Law lends wide latitude to the concept of 'defence', sanctioning force, for instance, in defence of ships at high sea or other assets far removed from the country's borders. (There was no constitutional debate when German border forces liberated a hijacked Lufthansa jet in Mogadishu in 1976.)

In short, it is not the constitutional debate that lies at the heart of the matter but the deeply rooted political reflexes that seek shelter in legal argument. The real purpose of that debate, now ten years old, is not to pay homage to the constitution but to buttress an abstentionist posture that, given Germany's past, was initially both understandable and appropriate. Some forty-five years after massive and global German 'force projection' had brought unprecedented misery to Germany and the world, the German political establishment and the vast majority of public opinion remain unready to commit force for purposes other than self-defence narrowly construed. That bespeaks the refusal to behave like a 'normal' great power – one that pursues not only narrow national interest but also a vision of world order for the sake of which it might employ the *ultima ratio*.

Such a refusal, of couse, betrays the enduring hold of history on a nation that has internalized two lessons in the twentieth century. First, when Germany did resort to force, as in two World Wars, dismal failure was the ultimate price. Second, when the use of force became a taboo, as after World War II, West Germany prospered beyond imagination. As the traditional great powers paid with blood and treasure for their interventions round the world – in Algeria, Afghanistan or Vietnam – West Germany was free to enjoy the economic benefits of low defence burdens and the political profits of being an enemy to none.

Such powerful lessons are not easily unlearned – even in the 1990s when the constraints of the postwar system have vanished while a united Germany moves, willy-nilly, into the ranks of the great powers (though without the ultimate badge of nuclear weapons). Hence, Germany's basic instincts, born in cataclysmic defeat and nurtured by the profits of abstentionism, are likely to endure beyond the demise of the bipolar order once shaped and maintained by the United States and the Soviet Union. Though not risk-free, that order was inherently stable – thanks to the mutual containment of the two superpowers and the constraint they imposed on their lesser but more adventurous clients in the Third World.

If the Middle East is destined to remain the greatest source of global instability, then Germany's greatest dilemma has just begun. Though the world of the 1990s has become 'unipolar', given the break-up of the Soviet Union, the United States is not capable of imposing order on the Middle East on its own; this, surely, has been the first lesson of the world's confrontation with the Iraq of Saddam Hussein. Without an almost world-wide coalition and the financial contributions of the rich, the United States presumably could not have begun, let alone sustained, the confrontation with Iraq for any length of time.

If this is the enduring lesson, then Germany will be asked to do more rather than less. At a minimum, Germany will have to act far more responsibly in the arena of technology transfers. Iraq's chemical weapons capability and, as it turned out after the war, its all but completed nuclear potential could not be divorced from the reckless machinations of German industry and the toothless export-control regime of the German government. At a maximum, Germany will be called upon to go beyond export controls and financial 'dues' to make unambiguous political commitments in favour of regional order and to back them up with force. Yet all previous experience suggests that Germany will prefer to evade clear-cut choices and commitments in the Middle East, as elsewhere in the troubled regions of the world. In terms of history, an endless balancing act is understandable. In terms of world order, the future will require more. This is Germany's great dilemma in the 1990s and beyond.

Notes

1. In 1888, the Reich and the Ottoman Empire concluded a concessionary treaty which was intended to connect Berlin via Belgrade to Ankara. In 1903, three years after Wilhelm II's accession to the throne, Germany obtained a second concession all the way to Baghdad.

2. The French consortium obtained only a 30 per cent stake in the enterprise.

3. In the 1920s, the Germans built an arms and munitions factory for the first Pahlevi ruler in Tehran that survived all regimes and all wars – all the way into the Islamic Republic.

4. Konrad Adenauer, 'Bilanz einer Reise', *Politische Meinung*, No. 115, 1966, p.15.

5. Until the mid-1980s, payments to individual claimants – to survivors and heirs – came to a total of DM80 billion, according to German government sources.

6. *Erinnerungen,1953–1955*, Stuttgart, Deutsche Verlags–Anstatt, 1984, p.155.

7. *Ibid.*, pp.153 and 154.

8. *Ibid.*, p.155.

9. There are no authoritative German accounts of this episode. For some of the details from an Arab perspective, see Mohammad Abediseid, *Die deutsch-arabischen Beziehungen: Problem und Krisen*, Stuttgart, Seewald, 1976, p.154 ff. For a journalistic version, see *Der Spiegel*, No. 9, 24 February 1965.

10. See also *The New York Times*, 21 January 1965, p.1.

11. On 12 May 1965 formal relations with Israel were announced. Thereafter Syria, Egypt, Jordan, Iraq, Saudi Arabia, North Yemen, Lebanon and Algeria withdrew their ambassadors from Bonn. Egypt recognised the GDR on 10 July 1969. Between 1969 and 1971, all of the Arab states that had broken with Bonn resumed formal relations.

12. Hans-Herbert Gaebel, 'Unangenehme Möglichkeiten', *Frankfurter Rundschau*, 31 October 1964, p.3.

13. The Soviet Union had annexed East Prussia while Poland, as compensation for the annexation of eastern Poland by Moscow, was shifted westward to the Oder-Neisse Line. The Soviet Union had reclaimed the Sudetenland, ceded to Hitler under duress in 1938.

14. *Verhandlungen des Deutschen Bundestages*, 9 November 1973, p.3849.

15. Thus Foreign Minister Hans-Dietrich Genscher in an article for the semi-official journal *Aussenpolitik* ('Dimensionen deutscher Aussenpolitik heute'), No. 4, 1974.

16. Prior to the 1962 Evian Agreement which bestowed independence on Algeria, France had been Israel's closest ally – delivering advanced arms and the early wherewithals of Israel's future nuclear weapons capability. In 1956, Britain and France had colluded with Israel in the Suez War against Egypt. Only after Algerian independence, and especially after the Six-Day War, did France shift toward the Arab side.

17. See the text of the declaration, *Europa-Archiv*, No. 2, 1974, p.D30.

18. Cf. Thomas Oppermann, 'Israel und Palästina: Reifprüfung der Bonner Aussenpolitik', *Europa-Archiv*, No. 14, 1980, p.437. A key phrase of the Declaration stresses the 'renunciation of force or the threat of force by *all* parties' (emphasis added). That formula was discussed with Israeli Foreign Minister Moshe Dayan during his visit to Bonn in September 1979 and was touted by German officials as a specific German contribution to the Venice Declaration. See Susan Hattis Rolef, 'The Middle East Policy of the Federal Republic', *Jerusalem Papers on Peace Problem No. 38*, Jerusalem, The Magnum Press, 1985, p.47.

19. In an interview with a reporter of the *Jerusalem Post*, published on 22 June 1979 which was later denied by the Chancellor's Office. For the background of this episode, see Susan Hattis Rolef, *op. cit.*, p.61, footnote 83.

20. One possible answer is that Bonn's enduring though ever more qualified support for Jerusalem did not come with an economic price tag attached. In the 1970s, that is from 1970 to 1982, West German exports to the Arab world increased *seventeenfold* – from DM2 to DM34 billion.

21. After reunification in 1990, the relative size of the Jewish community shrunk even more, as the absorption of the GDR added but a few hundred Jews among the 17 million East Germans to the Federal Republic writ large.

22. *Verhandlungen des Deutschen Bundestages*, 7 May 1981, p.1711.

23. As quoted in *Der Spiegel*, 11 May 1981, p.28. For the most exhaustive study on the episode, see Michael Wolffsohn, *German–Saudi Arabian Arms Deals, 1936–1939 and 1981–1985*, Berne, Peter Lang, 1985, Part II. In 1980, Helmut Schmidt had reportedly called Menachem Begin a 'threat to world peace'. As quoted *ibid*, p.59.

21. To Israelis who had fought and bled in 1948–9 to secure their independence in the face of overwhelming odds, this logic added historical insult to moral injury.

25. For an analysis and some choice quotes, see Henryk M. Broder, 'Unser Kampf: Henryk M. Broder über die Ressentiments der deutschen Friedensbewegung', *Der Spiegel*, No. 18, 29 April 1991.

26. Declaration before the Bundestag, 30 January 1991. Excerpts in 'Es gibt für uns Deutsche keine Nische in der Weltpolitik', *Süddeutsche*, 31 January 1991, p.10.

27. 'Nun gilt es, in der Freiheit zu bestehen: Die Rede Richard von Weizsäckers beim Staatsakt im Wortlaut', *Der Tagesspiegel* (Berlin), 4 October 1990, p.4.

28. The exact figure is not clear. Most accounts mention \$5.5 billion, others DM11 billion, which, at the exchange rate of early 1991, would come to \$6.5 billion.

29. 'Regierungserklärung', 17 January 1991, Bonn, Presse- und Informationsamt der Bundesregierung, 17 January 1991, No. 17/91.

12 Germany and the Gulf

Udo Steinbach

In the past, the Federal Republic of Germany was not among the European countries noteworthy for the high profile of its policy *vis-à-vis* the Middle East. In fact, its economic performance in the region – and political visibility there – seemed to be so far apart that observers were tempted to make the point by saying that Germany in the Middle East was 'economically a giant but politically a dwarf'.

Even if this is not totally incorrect as an overall assessment, an exception must be made with regard to the Gulf region. With the outbreak of the war between Iraq and Iran in September 1980, German diplomacy appears to have been more consistently directed towards bringing about an end to the war than was the policy of any other major power, European and non-European, and of the European Community as a whole. In this part of the Middle East, the German government acted with much greater farsightedness in comparison to its hand-ling of the Arab–Israeli conflict. At some point it even took the risk of isolating itself from its Western partners after certain political steps and initiatives and to come under pressure at home, as it was reproached for being too lenient about the violations of human rights by both warring regimes, especially Iran. The two visits by Foreign Minister Hans-Dietrich Genscher to Tehran, one in July 1984, approximately in the middle of the war, and the second in November 1988 shortly after its end, highlight this exceptionally daring approach.

Germany's failure to formulate a consistent reaction and policy towards Saddam Hussein's aggression against Kuwait and its hesitation to align itself with the allies by a military commitment was mainly due to the fact that the government was intensely absorbed by the German unification (3 October 1990) and the first all-German national elections (2 December 1990).

What are the parameters of Germany's policy in the Gulf area? Is there anything one can anticipate, in reviewing the past, about how ready a united Germany will be in the future to act in a more self-assertive way in areas where German interests are more at stake than has been the case previously? This chapter seeks to address these questions.

The historical dimension

Historically, Germany has not been among those European countries politically involved in the Middle East and North Africa to the extent that it could have decisively shaped the fate of the region between the end of the eighteenth century and World War II. Politically divided until the 'Reich' was established in 1871, Germans were largely absent while other Europeans were scrambling for influence and domination. It was only with the Berlin Congress (1878), where Chancellor Bismarck assumed the role of an 'honest broker', that

Germany entered the scene as a power, realising that the future of the 'sick man on the Bosphorus' would have repercussions on the European balance of power. Over the following four decades, Germany and the Ottoman Empire increasingly became allies as they worked together in the military and economic fields. When both were defeated in 1918, at the end of World War I, this was not only the end of the Reich's attempt at putting a foot into the Middle East, but also led to a coalition of powers, which precluded Germany from asserting a major influence in the region. It was not until Germany began participating in a European Middle Eastern policy in the early 1970s that the region again became an issue of major political concern for the country's policy-makers.

It is significant that after Turkey it was Persia that continuously attracted some German attention from the middle of the nineteenth century.[1] A number of treaties and accords were concluded after 1857, dealing with trade and business relations as well as with the establishment of a German representation in Tehran (1885). The most significant achievement in the relations between both sides in those early days was the founding of a German school in Tehran as a joint venture in 1907 – in which besides Persian, Arabic and French a number of classes were taught in German – and which soon enjoyed a high reputation throughout the country. Following its closure during World War I, the Iranian government in 1922 decided to reopen it as the German–Iranian Trade School. It soon achieved the reputation of being one of the country's most successful and respected institutions for general and vocational training, to the extent that soon more such schools were opened in Isfahan, Shiraz, Tabriz and Meshed. In addition, in 1934 German professors founded the Tehran Technical Highschool (*honarsara-ye ali*), the most important place for higher technical teaching in Iran after the Technical Faculty of the University of Tehran, from which by 1953, 600 engineers had graduated.

Since the beginning of the sixties, economic relations between the Federal Republic and Iran broadened to the extent that on the eve of the revolution Germany was Iran's most important trading partner with respect to imports.[2] But the significant cultural element in the relationship was never totally obscured: in 1975 Chancellor Helmut Schmidt and Prime Minister Amir Abbas Hoveyda issued a joint declaration expressing the readiness of both governments to cooperate in the founding of the Gilan University in Rasht. While Iran committed itself to financing the project, Germany was to assist in the planning of the university, in assembling the curricula and in outlining the research projects as well as contributing to the staff by sending German professors. The university became operational by 1978 but was closed after the revolution. The German Cultural Institute (Goethe-Institut) managed to survive the revolution and, eventually, was the last foreign cultural institution to be shut down (1987). Although in general cultural interaction between Germany and revolutionary Iran was far from lively, there were a number of cultural events even after the closure of the Goethe-Institut. First and foremost was a series of German–Iranian colloquia held in Hamburg and Tehran, at which both sides discussed the religious, philosophical, political, social and economic foundations of both the states and societies as well as (October 1990) the issue of human rights. The meetings were attended by a number of high-ranking personalities, religious and non-religious, from the Islamic Republic.

On the political level, German-Persian (Iranian) relations hardly ever reached a similar quality in comparison to economic and cultural relations.[3] Strong

Russian and British influences hardly left room for developing stronger political bonds. This was dramatically demonstrated when in 1941 the Soviet Union and Britain interfered in Tehran to depose Reza Shah on the grounds that his policy was too much inclined toward Germany.[4] And after World War II his son Mohammed Reza Shah increasingly brought Iran under the American umbrella mainly as a countervailing force against Soviet pressure. Moreover, German–Iranian political relations were not untroubled, as in the sixties and seventies there was widespread criticism of the autocratic regime of the Shah from German liberals and leftists. They sided with tens of thousands of oppositional Iranian students living in the Federal Republic and mobilised German public opinion against the Shah. This was a matter of concern and resentment for Iran.

Obviously there is no comparable background regarding Germany's relations with the Arabs in the Gulf.[5] The British domination over the region, Iraq as well as the 'Trucial Coast', was an obstacle against developing a German–Arab relationship comparable to that with Iran. For a short while in the thirties (1932–7), the German government showed itself interested in having access to oil production in the region through buying shares of the British Oil Development Company (BOD).[6] This was dropped when the Berlin government eventually decided to forego these efforts in order to minimise the vulnerability of oil supply (in view of the possibility of war) and to rely mainly, therefore, on synthetic production of petrol and other fuel. After that, Berlin did not make strong and decisive political efforts to put a foot into the Gulf area. This became obvious when an attempt by Rashid Ali al-Gailani and other Iraqi nationalists to rid the country of British influence (1941) was only half-heartedly supported.

For Saudi Arabia, it is true that as early as 1929 a Treaty of Friendship had been concluded between Berlin and King Abd al-Aziz. Later on, between 1937 and 1939, negotiations were conducted regarding a considerable German arms delivery to Saudi Arabia, but the deal was never ratified mainly because both parties linked it to political interests and expectations which the other side was not ready to fulfill.[7] When the war broke out, the issue became moot. With the failure of the Gailani uprising, the British military intervention in Iraq and with the British–Russian intervention in Iran alluded to above, Germany remained absent from the region until the sixties.

Bilateral relationship

With hindsight, one can hardly say – with the probable exception of the construction of the Baghdad railway around the turn of the century – that Germany ever had a consistent idea of what the Gulf should look like politically in order best to suit its interests. In fact, these interests were not significantly distinct from those of the other Western powers. Topping the list was political stability, which would ensure that the oil supply from the Gulf region was not in danger and that its exports to the buyer countries, the number of which increased constantly from the sixties, were not impeded. There was particular concern, probably at its peak during the seventies and the first half of the eighties, that Soviet influence in one way or another would penetrate the region, bringing – with the exception of Iraq – its pro-Western orientation to an end.

In fact, the relationship with Iraq[8] until the middle of the seventies was a delicate one mainly owing to the socialist orientation of the Baath regime and its close links with the Soviet Union (a Treaty of Friendship and Cooperation had been concluded in 1972 between Moscow and Baghdad). Iraq, like most of the other states, had severed diplomatic relations with Bonn after the West German government established diplomatic relations with Israel in 1965. In retaliation, Baghdad in 1969 was the first Arab and non-communist government to establish diplomatic relations with the German Democratic Republic, thus recognising the legitimacy of the East German state. Diplomatic relations with Bonn were only restored in 1974, after the Arab League had decided in March 1972 to allow its members to carry out this step. (In fact Iraq – together with Syria and South Yemen – had opposed the decision.) From then on, two German embassies operated in Baghdad (in the same vein, the West German cultural institute, Goethe-Institut, coexisted with its East German counterpart, Herder-Institut). In fact, after South Yemen, where, after the withdrawal of the British, communists took over under the cover of the 'National Liberation Front', Iraq turned out to be the second East German stronghold (in ideological, political, economic as well as security and military terms) among the regimes in the Middle East. This only started to alter when, from 1978 onwards (revolution in Afghanistan, change of alliances in the Horn of Africa), Baghdad started distancing itself from Moscow.

As to Saudi Arabia and the other Gulf states, which were not for the most part independent sovereign states before Britain withdrew from this region where it had been predominant for around one and a half centuries, relations were nearly exclusively economic. With the steep rise in the price of oil, business with the Arab Gulf states expanded considerably by the beginning of the seventies. The setting up of a Saudi–German 'businessmen's dialogue' reflected the new quality of the relationship with Saudi Arabia in particular and with the other Arab Gulf states in general.

Given the dimensions of economic relations, both sides increasingly felt frustration about the virtual absence of a political quality in the relationship. For this reason Bonn and Riyadh started thinking about giving their relationship a deeper basis through cooperation in the field of defence. At the same time, German–Saudi talks over German arms, especially tanks (Leopard) to be delivered to Saudi Arabia, reflected a new concern in Bonn over the stability of a region upon which Germany had become so dependent. It was no longer possible to avoid considering whether or not Germany was to make a contribution on its own to secure overall political stability in the Gulf region. Although the German–Saudi arms deal eventually failed due to domestic and international opposition (mainly Israeli), the deliberations reflected a new thinking about Germany's role in the Gulf.

Security in the Gulf: a challenge to Germany's foreign policy

By the beginning of the eighties, political leaders in Bonn came to recognise that security in the Gulf region could no longer be reduced to the demand for a settlement of the Arab–Israeli conflict.[9] The revolution in Iran, the Soviet invasion of Afghanistan and the outbreak of hostilities between Iraq and Iran had demonstrated how fragile and volatile were the regional and the international dynamics and alliances of conflict. Given the dependence of the West in general and the Federal Republic of Germany in particular on oil supplies from this part of the world (by the beginning of the eighties West Germany still obtained around 40 per cent of its oil supplies from the Gulf), developments of this kind could have alarming repercussions for the industrialised West.

The faster pace of armament by Saudi Arabia and other states in the region, the bid to establish an independent political line through regional non-alignment and steps towards closer economic and political cooperation (in March 1981 Saudi Arabia, Oman, Kuwait, the United Arab Emirates, Qatar and Bahrain set up the Gulf Cooperation Council) had shown that the states in the region were paying greater attention to their security problems.

The Federal Republic of Germany had sought to respond to the changes following the collapse of imperial Iran by upgrading its policy in the Gulf. It had not just been a matter of more diplomatic visits being paid (outstanding among these had been the June 1980 visit to Bonn by King Khaled of Saudi Arabia and the April 1981 visit to Riyadh by Bonn Chancellor Helmut Schmidt); Bonn had also tried to lend diplomatic encouragement to regional cooperation as a factor of stability and a prerequisite for greater independence from the superpowers. In the Islamic Conference Organisation in particular, it felt it had found a starting point for such a policy (special attention being paid to the January 1980 Islamic Foreign Ministers' Conference in Islamabad, their May 1980 conference in Islamabad and the January 1981 Islamic summit conference in Taif). But this illusion was finally shattered by the outbreak of hostilities between Iraq and Iran and the helplessness of all outsiders when it came to settling the conflict.

Worried that they might be dragged against their will into disputes between the superpowers (referred to in the final declaration of the Taif Islamic summit conference), the regional powers turned to Western Europe as both an international focal point in their bid for greater political independence and as a partner who could contribute towards their security. This was particularly important since the United States, as a result of political developments in preceding years, had lost credibility as a guarantor of security and stability, and closer cooperation with the Western superpower would have – in the wake of a revival of Islam as a reaction to Westernisation – subjected most regimes to heightened domestic opposition.

In this connection increasing importance was attached to the Federal Republic of Germany as a neutral or at least disinterested and non-intrusive power. Its major political importance in the European Community could no longer, even by the most strenuous efforts at self-denial, be played down; equally, since the Federal Republic of Germany was free of the taint of colonial tradition, there was no risk of close cooperation leading to renewed dependence. So Bonn was prevailed upon to make a more active contribution towards maintaining security in the region by a number of Gulf states. Recourse to verbalisation and diplomatic nuance would no longer be enough nor in the long run would a limitation of its contribution to boosting economic cooperation. The new quality of relations was envisaged by all partners in the Gulf as genuinely comprehensive. Ruling out political costs (and risks) no longer seemed possible. In the Gulf region, there was a genuine feeling of being threatened, regardless of whether or not this sentiment was shared in Europe or whether the latter felt that regional arms build-ups were a suitable response to the threat.

Whether or not to export tanks to Saudi Arabia was thus a challenge to Bonn to put in a more active and politically higher-profile appearance where the interests of the Federal Republic of Germany were involved. The principle of not exporting arms to crisis areas was not felt to be valid by the governments concerned; the question was surely whether this might not have the opposite effect, leading to greater instability and imbalance, thereby heightening the potential for conflict, especially in connection with the Arab–Israeli conflict. Two considerations seemed relevant in this context:

- The political weight carried by Saudi Arabia both within the Arab context and in connection with the Arab-Israeli conflict had been considerably over-rated in previous years. The history of the kingdom as a whole and in the 1970s in particular – the decade in which Saudi Arabia came to the fore as a factor in Middle East policy – showed that the country had neither played nor sought the role of a hegemonial power. It aimed first to maintain an intra-Arab balance within which the risk of a threat to the kingdom from a dominant Arab power was minimised. Second, the Saudi regime was striving with all the means at its command (almost exclusively financial and monetary) to back or bring to power conservative forces in its part of the world.
- The establishment at that time was primarily interested in the stability of the entire Middle East with a view to maintaining political status quo.

For a variety of reasons, the German–Saudi deal did not materialise: on one hand, domestic opposition insisted that selling arms to Saudi Arabia constituted a violation of German law, which stipulated that no weapons were allowed to be sold to areas of political and military tensions; on the other, Israeli Prime Minister Menachem Begin launched a campaign not only against the deal, but against German Chancellor Helmut Schmidt personally, mobilising even the American government to intervene. Eventually the idea was dropped, leaving among the Saudi leadership a serious doubt regarding Germany's determination to become a major political actor in the region.

The Iran–Iraq war

When the war broke out on 23 September 1980, one hardly could have expected a stronger reaction from the German government than from other Europeans. With American diplomats still being held hostage in Tehran, and after pro-longed tension along the Iranian–Iraqi border for which the Iranian government could have been at least partially held responsible and after a militant propaganda campaign against the West and Israel as well as the neighbouring Arab countries, the aggressor Iraq was not as strongly condemned by any party or international organisation as was the case under different circumstances (for example Saddam's aggression against Kuwait ten years later). This strange reluctance and passivity towards the aggressor, the Iranians believed clearly demonstrated a lack of impartiality by the international community. The Iranians therefore persistently demanded proof of such impartiality by making a strong condemnation of Iraq by the UN a precondition for participating in any negotiations under its auspices.

Beside words, there was no serious action by outsiders to stop the fighting. The German government, over the preceding decade, had tried to coordinate its

Middle Eastern policy in the framework of the European Community, more specifically, of the European Political Cooperation (EPC): German input to the various declarations was quite significant.[10] In the wake of the outbreak of the war in the Gulf, the European Community had issued a number of declarations. But from the beginning it turned out that the political positions among the leading member states of the Community were too far apart to enable them to make a serious contribution to a settlement. The United Kingdom, siding closely with the United States, had adopted an inimical attitude *vis-à-vis* Iran. France was not ready to put her traditionally close economic relationship with Iraq at risk by confronting the Iraqi regime too harshly over its aggression. The German government, which had already played a major role in the negotiations that led to the release of the American hostages (20 January 1980) and was seen from Tehran (against the background of former German–Iranian relations) as the most trustworthy among European governments, soon attempted to win the mullahs' confidence and, thus, to gain a position from which it would be possible to bring the parties to the negotiating table.

Given these differences it is understandable that the reaction of the Community was so weak. Nor did individual European governments have any clear idea about what constellation would best fit European interests. The resolutions issued at the outbreak of the war and periodically reiterated over the years were hardly enough to exert forceful pressure on the belligerents to end the fighting.[11]

Besides references to concern over the conflict, the principle of non-interference and support for peace efforts, other points were the concern over attacks on civilian targets (27 February 1984), and the call on the members of the Western European Union (WEU) to refrain from arms supply to the warring countries (3 September 1984). And, in a resolution on 26 February 1988, the Europeans showed themselves deeply concerned over the use of chemical weapons and condemned the violation of international law.

German–Iranian economic relations, which had suffered a setback in the wake of the revolution, soon recovered reaching an unprecedented peak in 1983 with German exports to Iran amounting up to more than DM7 billion. Bonn's diplomacy, eventually, was given a high profile, when Foreign Minister Genscher visited Tehran in July 1984. Among the subjects discussed, the Gulf war was naturally at the top of the agenda. Clearly, the purpose of Genscher's trip was to make the Islamic leadership confident that the international community was seriously interested in halting the war and in contributing to a fair peace agreement which would take into consideration the interests of both sides. Showing himself convinced that Tehran was ready for a political dialogue and economic cooperation with Western states, Genscher urged his fellow foreign ministers in the European Community not to leave Iran isolated and to make visits to Tehran. 'Nothing would be more wrong than to isolate this great and important country', he stated.[11] And in order to prove his credibility to act as an honest broker, he claimed 'that the great powers should stop supporting the Iraqi regime, if they wanted real peace'.[12]

Although this visit yielded no concrete result whatsoever, consultations between the two sides continued. Between 1984 and 1987 parliamentarians travelled at various times to Tehran and, occasionally, there were contacts on the ministerial level, such as between the German Minister of Economy, Martin Bangemann, and the Iranian Deputy Foreign Minister, Larijani, in April 1986 in Algiers. On the other hand, there was a constant possibility of a setback partly because public opinion exerted pressure upon the government to show more concern about violations of human rights in Iran and partly because of activities launched by the Iranian opposition in Germany which led to clashes with pro-Khomeini groups. Thus, German–Iranian official relations faced a dramatic turn when in October 1986 violent clashes occurred between the two sides at the Frankfurt book fair and, in retaliation, radical Islamic groups by force swept into the garden in front of the German embassy in Tehran and tried to break the doors in order to storm the building.

It was only in 1987 that German efforts to mediate between the parties and bring about a ceasefire obtained fresh momentum. The beginning of the year saw an escalation of warfare against civilian targets ('war of the cities') and against oil tankers to the extent that the Western oil supplies from the Gulf might have become adversely affected. Eventually, the United States decided to protect part of Kuwait's tanker fleet by putting eleven vessels under the American flag and giving each of them protection by a naval escort for as long as they were in range of Iranian military activities. With more nations joining and supporting the American action, at the height of the naval presence in the Gulf by late fall, there were approximately sixty Western vessels in the region (with around thirty from Western European countries).

Obviously, the American decision could hardly have been called balanced and impartial, leaving Iranian tankers exposed to Iraqi attacks while protecting Kuwaiti tankers exporting oil. Indeed, there was an uneasy feeling in Bonn about it and it was feared that it might stiffen Iranian intransigence regarding any outside attempt to bring about a mediated settlement. Active German participation would have run counter to the political line pursued since the early stages of the war. Although this was not official reasoning, it nevertheless has to be seen behind the decision in Bonn not to participate in the build-up. Officially, the German position was that the German constitution did not allow deployment of troops outside of the NATO defence area. The most the German government did was to dispatch a small naval unit to the Mediterranean to replace units of other NATO members which had been dispatched to the Gulf.

Concomitant with the increase of a Western military presence in the Gulf, serious efforts were made at the UN to find a formula on the basis of which fighting would be ended and a peace settlement reached. After more than five months of consultations, UN Security Council Resolution 598 was passed on 20 July. It called upon Iran and Iraq to end the fighting immediately and to withdraw their troops behind internationally recognised borders. Most important with regard to Iran, compared with previous resolutions, the text of 598 reflected the efforts by some of the non-permanent members of the council, among them the Federal Republic of Germany, to shape the resolution in a way which would make it more palatable to Iran than previous ones. This eventually was achieved by inserting a stipulation requesting the UN Secretary General 'to explore, in consultation with Iran and Iraq, the question of entrusting an impartial body with inquiring into responsibility for the conflict'.

As far as German–Iranian bilateral relations were concerned, 1987 had not begun well. Following a German TV programme which ridiculed Ayatollah Khomeini, the Iranian government reacted angrily, expelling two diplomats from the German embassy in Tehran and closing the German Cultural Institute, which had not only survived the revolution but was the only foreign cultural institute still open in Iran. Furthermore, two Germans had been taken hostage by pro-Iranian groups in January in Beirut, apparently in retaliation for trials at German courts against two Lebanese brothers, Mohammed and Ali Abbas Hamadi, charged with terrorist activities.

Relations, however, soon improved again to the extent that in May Bonn tried to mediate in the 'war of the embassies' which pitted France and Iran against each other and eventually led to a break in diplomatic relations on July 17. In addition, Tehran promised to exert its influence in Beirut to have the two German hostages released (which occurred in September 1987 and September 1988, respectively).

German–Iranian cooperation culminated in July in the wake of the passing of UN Resolution 598. Foreign Minister Velayati visited Bonn on 23 July. On this occasion, he was not only received by his German counterpart, Hans-Dietrich Genscher, but as a gesture of particular respect, by President von Weizsäcker and Chancellor Kohl, too. In their conversations, Genscher asked Iran to 'observe restraint which is now necessary in this conflict'. He urged that the UN Secretary General be allowed to fulfil his task. By this he referred to efforts by Mr Peres de Cuellar to get Iran to accept the resolution. In order to demonstrate the balanced German approach, Genscher afterwards talked to the Iraqi ambassador to Bonn, calling on Iraq to show restraint in the war as well.[13]

The most significant gesture, however, was made by Genscher after his Iranian guests had departed. In a radio interview he unequivocally stated that Iraq had started the war and had used chemical weapons at various junctures. With this statement he was the only internationally known politician to echo a claim Iran had always made, and the fulfilment of which was seen in Tehran as a precondition to sitting down and holding negotiations to end the war. It is open to dispute just how effective – in practical terms – the intervention of Germany's foreign minister actually was. While Iraq accepted the resolution as a basis for negotiations, Iran refused. Tehran kept claiming that a clear and unambiguous statement regarding the responsibility for the outbreak of the war was required before it could agree on a ceasefire. But in comparing Tehran's first reaction to Resolution 598 immediately after it had been passed with the official comment of 14 August, one notices that the latter is softer and more forthcoming, in so far as the Iranian government declares its readiness for further cooperation with the Security Council on the matter.

The final twelve months of the war were a painful mixture of bloody warfare and secret diplomacy. As far as information is available, Bonn once again played a crucial part in bringing about a breakthrough. In the autumn of 1987 differences surfaced as to how to deal with Iran. Great Britain, for its part, appeared inclined to follow the American line and joined the call for another UN resolution which would increase pressure upon Tehran. Germany, on the other side, backed away from pressure by arguing to not take the risk of splitting the Security Council and thereby risking a veto. This view was shared by Washington and London when in the spring of 1988 Iraq resumed its bombing raids against Iranian cities and civilians. From March, there were hints from Tehran that Iran would be ready to give in. One of the occasions for conveying this message was provided by the meeting of Genscher and Velayati in Athens on 29 March 1988 (at which agreement was also reached on another trip by Genscher to Tehran later in the year). Subsequently, a chain of direct and indirect contacts and consultations with representatives of the two warring parties ensued, with Bonn at the centre. At the end of June the Iraqi Foreign Minister visited Bonn.

The decisive phase came after the American Frigate *Vincennes* inadvertently shot down an Iran Air civilian plane on 3 July 1988 in an incident which killed 298 people. Coordinating its policy mainly with France and Italy, German diplomacy now aimed at using the discussion about the event in the UN to make Resolution 598 effective with regard to a ceasefire. When the Iranian government finally accepted the ceasefire on 17 July 1988, it had to be attributed largely to German diplomacy. Seen in the perspective of a German Middle Eastern policy at large, Bonn's mediation effort in the Gulf was its most outstanding success so far. Prior to this, Bonn had never acted so consistently and pragmatically in the Middle East. Never before, moreover, had it been ready to run the risk of political differences and even controversy with its Western allies in stubbornly pursuing its own course.

In the wake of the ceasefire, relations with both parties remained good. In the case of Iraq, misgivings were soon overcome, while with Iran relations took on the look of a special relationship. When the second of the German hostages taken earlier in Beirut was released, the way was open for a second trip by Genscher to Tehran at the end of November. The fact that a few days ahead of Genscher's trip the Iraqi vice president, Taha Muhy al-Din Ma'ruf, had come to Bonn for three days demonstrated the interest of Iraq, too, in maintaining good relations with Germany despite previous irritations.

For the following one and a half years (1989–August 1990) until the outbreak of the second Gulf crisis, German relations with the Gulf countries remained mainly economic. But given the debt burden (in the case of Iraq), continuing uncertainties on how to do business with foreign companies (in the case of Iran) and the depletion of financial resources following the war, perspectives were not too bright. In addition, the ideological nature of the regime as well as the volatile situation in Tehran continued to cause trouble for German–Iranian relations. In particular, the 'Rushdie affair', that is Ayatollah Khomeini's death sentence against Salman Rushdie for his *Satanic Verses*, brought about a serious setback. It is true that difficulties had already arisen on the occasion of Genscher's visit to Tehran in November when the Iranian government ignored Genscher's concern about improving human rights. The latent crisis then erupted over Khomeini's order to kill Rushdie. Whereas in the past Genscher had shown himself inclined to play down the negative features of the Islamic regime in order to keep the relationship normal, this time he reacted more rapidly and vehemently than most of his European colleagues. The German–Iranian accord concerning cultural relations, concluded during his visit to Tehran, was not to be put into practice as long as the death sentence was in place, and a meeting of the joint economic commission was cancelled. The German parliament issued an all-party declaration in which Khomeini's call to kill Rushdie was condemned as a declaration of war against the Western legal and value system, international law and the Charter of the UN. Even before the EC formally decided to recall its ambassadors, the German ambassador was ordered to return to Bonn. Although Bonn eventually did not insist on bringing the issue before the UN, relations deteriorated. Tehran retaliated by charging that German engineers and technicians supported Iraq's missile programme and accused Germans of being involved in an espionage affair. Tensions escalated to the point that radical elements in Tehran put pressure upon the government to break diplomatic relations. It was only after Ayatollah Khomeini's demise and Rafsanjani was elected president of the Islamic Republic (July 1989) that tensions subsided.

The second Gulf war

Given the dramatic developments in Germany after the downfall of the Berlin Wall on 9 November 1989, and fully absorbed by the process of unification, it is hardly surprising that Germany did not show a high profile in the Gulf during the period preceding the outbreak of the Kuwait crisis. Economically, business with the Arab Gulf states continued stagnating and – seen over the entire year 1990 – showed a marked decline, most significantly in the case of Iraq (where German exports fell by 44 per cent to DM1.22 billion). This, however, was compensated by an increase of exports to Iran by 65 per cent (over the whole of 1990).

In the middle of the process of German unification, Saddam Hussein's aggression against Kuwait marked a political challenge which was not, at the beginning, given due attention in Bonn. Whereas Washington, London and Paris were able to concentrate fully on the management of the crisis, for the politicians in Bonn, the Gulf was understandably only a sideshow in the political arena. This was not to change even after unification (3 October) given the numerous political and economic problems in the five new states (*Länder*) whose seriousness had not been anticipated.

On the eve of unification, although a lot of fuss had been made in the international press about the future German role in international politics resembling that of a superpower, this had not been appreciated or welcomed by large parts of the German public. To be confronted now with the request to deploy German troops outside the NATO defence area, a request which the West German government for a variety of reasons had constantly tried to evade, generated irritation on the political scene in Bonn – all the more so, as the first all-German elections were to be held on 2 December and the military build-up in the Gulf was causing increasingly hostile reactions and emotional uproar all over the country. In addition, revelations that German enterprises had a considerable share in developing the Iraqi weapon arsenal in sensitive fields placed additional pressure on Bonn's policy in the crisis. For even though the government did not bear direct responsibility, the official bodies responsible for controlling Germany's foreign trade could be blamed for not having functioned in a proper way.

Germany officially confirmed right at the outset of the crisis that it found itself bound by all Security Council resolutions. In particular, the arms embargo was immediately put into effect. (In 1989 Germany had delivered goods worth DM2.2 billion to Iraq and DM860 million to Kuwait.) When President Bush announced on 8 August that he would send troops to Saudi Arabia, the question whether or not Germany would add her share to the operation was implied. On 10 August, the German government decided to send a unit of mine sweepers to the Eastern Mediterranean which were to operate depending on the developments in the region. This set in motion a debate on whether or not such a measure was in accordance with the constitution, and the government felt itself compelled to make clear that prior to changing the constitution the boats would not be ordered to enter the Gulf.

While the debate about a German contribution to the military build-up in the Gulf was going on, efforts were undertaken to liberate around 400 Germans held hostage in Baghdad together with other nationals (according to the official Iraqi version they were 'guests' of the government), many of whom had been taken as 'live shields' to militarily sensitive areas. Incoherence which appeared after a trip by former Chancellor Willy Brandt to Baghdad through which he – as well as other elder statesmen – made an effort to liberate German hostages, were symptomatic of the lack of principle and orientation of the German government in the crisis. While at first categorically opposed to Brandt's undertaking, the government changed its mind and, eventually, gave Brandt its backing when it turned out that a large part of the population favoured the trip, and the leader of the Social Democratic Party tried to score political points with that during the election campaign.

The allied military build-up was watched apprehensively and expectantly by large parts of the German population. In fact, never before – with the exception of the June 1967 war – had a crisis in the Middle East stirred up such public interest. And since the days of the controversy about re-arming, the peace movement in Germany had not succeeded to such an extent in mobilising public concern. When the Turkish government in December 1990 asked for the Allied Mobile Force – to which Germany contributes troops and fighterplanes – to be sent to Turkey, even this contribution under a 'normal' Nato commitment became an issue of controversial debate within the political parties, in the media and among the public at large.

After the decision was taken not to send the mine sweepers to the Gulf, German activities concerning the Gulf crisis went into two directions; for one, humanitarian assistance was given to the refugees, mainly to those streaming into Jordan before their evacuation to their home countries; second, Bonn committed itself to giving financial assistance to the countries affected by the embargo (mainly Turkey, Jordan) and taking part in the allied forces (mainly Egypt).

As far as the second direction is concerned, it only became known when Operation Desert Storm was over, to what extent Germany – while not being a member in the military alliance – had supported the allied military machine. Following the end of the Iran–Iraq war, it is true, the American Central Command under General Schwarzkopf had prepared plans for a variety of contingencies in the Gulf region, but, nevertheless, in August 1990 it turned out that there was a lack of strategic sea transport for American troops in Germany and German supplies. In retrospect it is obvious that the war could not have been waged as it was had it not been for Germany acting as a logistical turntable for the United States and Great Britain and lending effective aid to solve the difficult supply problems. Among others, Germany provided sixty ABC tracker tanks ('Fuchs') at a per unit price of DM3.3 million, hundreds of trucks, tank wagons, 600 shower vehicles, 2,000 radio units, 120 lowloaders for tank transportation, fork-lift trucks, containers for drinking water, 200 tents, 1,000 beds in Bundeswehr hospital units, more than 50,000 tank and artillery grenades, 40,000 water canisters, 150,000 atropin ampoules (worth DM800,000) and nearly half a million sandbags. To complete the equipment of the British, French and the Italian expedition corps, the Bundeswehr basically helped out with munition and spare parts. Turkey received 80 fighting tanks (Leopard I), tank munition, artillery munition, ABC protective masks, tank defence weapons and much more.[14]

In addition to this material aid, Bonn contributed a large amount of first-class equipment from the National People's Army of former East Germany. There were also substantial transport services carried out for expedition troops or for the allies who remained in Germany (especially the British). And finally there was aid given to Israel (especially Patriot air-defence equipment, submarines, transport services) and financial aid given to Arab states in the region as well as to the International Committee of the Red Cross. All together this added up to DM17.2 billion. Why was Bonn so secretive? Why was the German response to Turkey's request for assistance according to Paragraph 5 of the NATO contract so weak? And why did the German soldiers in Turkey behave so childishly? Was it because they did not have the support of the Federal government? Why was this support so hard to detect?

Political courage had been lacking to affirm what was seen as necessary and to lend leadership to a consistently divided public opinion, which is a common enough feature in democracies. There are several reasons for this. One is the present government's increasing habit of anxiously scrutinising the signals from the streets or from the latest opinion polls; furthermore, the government's revered ideology of keeping the peace has degenerated into nothing more than a practical political task. And finally, there is the reduction and exclusive focus of debate on security policy, in so far as such a debate was even carried out in the Federal Republic, on nuclear weapons and the relative strength of conventional troops in East–West relations.

However, although after the Iran–Iraq war competing security problems were out in the open, German politicians either ignored them or put off tackling them. Thus, there was an interaction between a domestic political issue in which the government was not leading boldly and the international repercussions which saw the consequent loss of credibility of Bonn with the allies. In the end Kohl and Genscher's political pusillanimity cost the taxpayers much while weakening their faith in their leaders.

The lack of leadership on the part of the German government was not the only reason that public debate and reactions to the events at some stages were almost out of control. The ambivalent strategy of being massively involved, on one hand, but shamefully hiding this involvement out of domestic political considerations led to massive criticism abroad and even accusations that German attempts at looking for a 'deal' with Saddam Hussein would undermine the credibility of the alliance's threat to resort to military measures if Saddam were not to comply with UN resolutions by 15 January 1991. Unrealistic expectations about Germany's real power and influence (as contrasted to her economic power and potential) gave way in the West to bitter recriminations about German inconstancy and cowardice, her commercial instincts and self-centred reflexes all being the antitheses of what alliances were supposed to represent.

Moreover, the government's non-policy literally backfired when at the end of January, the first Iraqi Scud missiles exploded in Israel. In the course of the ongoing discussions about who had contributed what to the build-up of the Iraqi armament, it had been revealed that German firms and experts had a considerable share in refining Iraq's missile technology and in the production of chemical weapons. Although this had been done on a private basis (officially Germany had stopped military exports to Iraq by 1982), the government could be blamed for having failed to impose strict control over all exports directed to the Middle East, especially those of 'dual use'.

With the missiles hitting Israeli cities and in a state of uncertainty whether or not they would carry chemical warheads, the Israeli population sat in their rooms insulated against gas and with their gasmasks ready to hand. All of a sudden, many Israelis – but many Germans as well, cutting across the political spectrum – came to associate the ongoing events with the holocaust, the annihilation of millions of Jews in gas chambers. As the government had failed to 'sell' clearly the significant German contribution towards the anti-Saddam alliance, Germany's only 'contribution' now appeared to have been that it had assisted Saddam in improving his military capacity in sensitive domains such as missiles and chemical technology. Once more Germans could be blamed for lending their hand to the annihilation of Jews.

While this argument in substance obviously was exaggerated and probably exploited to mobilise Germans to increase their contribution to the alliance in general and Israel in particular, the German government reacted in a frantic way trying to appease everyone. Highest-ranking delegations from all political parties and members of the government rushed to Israel, demonstrating their concern and lending support in various ways. The fact that eventually the government agreed to supply Israel with two submarines showed to what extent Germany's Middle Eastern policy was unhinged. For clearly this step sharply contradicted the basic principle not to deliver armaments to areas of tension on the basis of which the government had in the past refused arms to Arab countries.

It was only when perennial Foreign Minister Genscher travelled to Amman, Cairo and Damascus (in the middle of February) that German Middle Eastern policy showed signs of recovering and gave reason to hope that it may find its way back to the principle to which it had adhered for the last two decades, that is the 'balance' between the two sides, Israel and the Arabs. For a brief while the two foci of German Middle Eastern policy – the Gulf conflict and the Arab–Israeli conflict – were interrelated mainly due to the government's inappropriate handling of the former. Once again Germans had been caught up in their own history, which had prevented them over past decades from having a Middle Eastern policy of their own.

Nevertheless, in the aftermath of Desert Storm, when the sand had settled, Germany against all odds found itself in a stronger position than before. The allies, especially the United States, eventually came to realise and appreciate the German contribution as essential for the success of the alliance. Israel had to realise that united Germany, despite initial uncertainties eventually committed herself to its survival to a tremendous extent. And for the Arabs, the outstanding feature in the picture of a new Germany is unification. Germany's becoming one nation again sharply contrasts with the Arabs' own recent performance, which has proved once more how far away they still are from unity which they have been dreaming of and articulating for so many years.

And for the majority of Arab people who either openly or silently in their hearts resented the alliance of Arab states with the United States against another Arab country, Germany remains unsullied. It appears not to have participated in an act of demonstration of Western superiority over the Arab world. (This has to be seen against the historical fact that in the perception of the Arabs, Germany did not take part in the post-World-War I colonisation of the Middle East, either.)

In the Gulf, in particular, German policy has returned to its pre-1980 dimensions. Then Germany's presence in the Gulf was not based on a political concept, but mainly was the result of its economic relations with individual Gulf states. Opportunities were seized as they presented themselves. It was only after 1980 that the Federal Republic tried to make use of its relations (mainly with Iran) for political purposes. As in the past, Iran continues to be the most important economic partner in the region.

Iraq has lost its relevancy as a political and economic agent in the region. The Gulf states, mainly Saudi Arabia and Kuwait, reward the Western members of the alliance (mostly the United States and Great Britain) for having defended them against Saddam Hussein through allotting lucrative business opportunities to them. And as to their external security, instead of seriously further pursuing schemes to establish a regional security system, they prefer to rely on bilateral military cooperation with the United States.

Directly after the war, Bundeswehr sanitary and transportation units were deployed to help the Kurdish refugees in Iran, German minesweepers and a Transall transporter and three helicopters of the Luftwaffe were deployed to bring UN inspectors to Baghdad and for other surveillance missions by that world organisation in Iraq. All this went practically unnoticed and hardly stirred up any public debate. It seems that the second Gulf crisis, which had stirred up so many irritations as far as Germany's role is concerned in the country itself as well as abroad, eventually may turn out to have been a healthy experience. It is true that the discussion about united Germany's future role in 'out-of-area' missions still has to be conducted in the country, and the constitution will probably be changed in accordance with its results. But whatever the results are, there is a feeling cutting through all political groups and public opinion that in principle after unification the new Germany has to shoulder a greater share of the burden for maintaining peace and stability in the world. From that point of view the two successive Gulf crises should be considered catalytic events of major importance for the evolution of Germany's foreign policy and its stature in the future.

Notes

1. Friedrich Kochwasser, *Iran und wir. Geschichte der deutsch-iranischen Handels- und Wirtschaftsbeziehungen*, Herrenalb Erdmann, 1961.

2. Horst Poller (ed.), *Wirtschaftspartner Iran*, Stuttgart, 1978.

3. Yair P. Hirschfeld, *Deutschland und Iran im Spielfeld der Mächte. Internationale Beziehungen unter Reza Schah (1921–1941)*, Düsseldorf, Droste, 1980; Ahmed Mahrad, *Die deutsch–persischen Beziehungen von 1918–1933*, Berlin, H. Lang, 1974 and *Dokumentation über die persisch-deutschen Beziehungen von 1918–1933*, Bern, H. Lang, 1975.

4. Ramin Alexander Sepasgosarian, 'Inter Arma Silent Leges. Zum 50. Jahrestag der alliierten Invasion in Iran' in *ORIENT 32* 2, 1991, pp.265–84.

5. Ghazi Shanneik (ed.), *Die Beziehungen zwischen der Bundesrepublik Deutschland und den Arabischen Golfstaaten (GCC)*, Bonn, 1990.

6. Helmut Mejcher, *Die Politik und das Öl im Nahen Osten. Vol. 2: Die Teilung der Welt, 1935–1950*, Stuttgart, Klett-Cotta, 1991.

7. Helmut Mejcher, 'Saudi-Arabiens Beziehungen zu Deutschland in der Regierungszeit von König Abd al-Aziz Ibn Saud' in Linda Schatkowski-Schilcher and Claus Scharf (eds), *Der Nahe Osten in der Zwischenkriegszeit 1919–1939*, Stuttgart, Franz Steiner, 1989, pp.109–27.

8. Rüdiger Robert, 'Die Bundesrepublik Deutschland und der Irak – Eine Bilanz', in *ORIENT 22*, 2, 1981, pp.195–218.

9. Udo Steinbach, 'German Policy in the Middle East and the Gulf', in *Aussenpolitik* (German Foreign Affairs Review) 32 No. 4, 1981, pp.315–31; Karl Kaiser and Udo Steinbach (eds), *Deutsch–arabische Beziehungen. Beziehungsfaktoren und Probleme einer Neuorientierung*, Munich and Vienna, Oldenbourg, 1981.

10. Udo Steinbach, 'Germany' in David Allen and Alfred Pijpers (eds), *European Foreign Policy-Making and the Arab–Israeli Conflict (Part I: National Approaches to the Arab–Israeli Conflict)*, The Hague, Martinus Nijhoff, 1984, pp.91–106; Othman Othman, *Die Nahostpolitik der Europäischen Gemeinschaft im Hinblick auf die Palästinafrage aus arabischer Sicht*, Münster, Lit, 1991; Amnon Neustadt: *Die deutsch–israelischen Beziehungen im Schatten der EG-Nahostpolitik*, Frankfurt, Haag und Herchen, 1983.

11. *Le Monde*, 25 July 1984.

12. *Le Monde*, 24 July 1984.

13. *Frankfurter Allgemeine Zeitung*, 24 July 1987.

14. Michael J. Inacker, *Unter Ausschluss der Öffentlichkeit? Die Deutschen in der Golf-Allianz*, Bonn and Berlin, Bouvier, 1991; Karl Kaiser/Klaus Becker, *Deutschland und der Irak-Konflikt. Internationale Sicherheitsverantwortung Deutschlands und Europas nach der deutschen Vereinigung*, Forschungsinstitut der DGAP (Arbeitspapiere zur Internationalen Politik, Bd. 68), Bonn, Europa Union Verlag, 1992.

Index